T0329895

HARVARD STUDIES IN BUSINESS HISTORY · 54

Published with the support of the
Harvard Business School

Edited by

Walter A. Friedman

Lecturer of Business Administration
Director, Business History Initiative

and

Geoffrey Jones

Isidor Straus Professor of Business History
Faculty Chair, Business History Initiative

HARVARD BUSINESS SCHOOL

Paris *to* New York

The Transatlantic Fashion Industry *in the* Twentieth Century

Véronique Pouillard

HARVARD UNIVERSITY PRESS

Cambridge, Massachusetts & London, England 2021

Library of Congress Cataloging-in-Publication Data

Names: Pouillard, Véronique, author.
Title: Paris to New York : the transatlantic fashion industry in the
    twentieth century / Véronique Pouillard.
Other titles: Harvard studies in business history.
Description: Cambridge, Massachusetts : Harvard University Press, 2021. |
    Series: Harvard studies in business history | Includes index.
Identifiers: LCCN 2020044117 | ISBN 9780674237407 (cloth)
Subjects: LCSH: Clothing trade—France—Paris—History—20th century. |
    Clothing trade—New York (State)—New York—History—20th century. |
    Fashion design—France—Paris—History—20th century. | Fashion design—
    New York (State)—New York—History—20th century. | Globalization.
Classification: LCC HD9940.F8 P369 2021 | DDC 338.4/774692094436—dc23
LC record available at https://lccn.loc.gov/2020044117

Contents

Paris *to* New York

Introduction

ashion is one of the world's most dynamic industries, with a global retail value of around $3 trillion and a 2 percent share of the global gross domestic product. Over the past decade, the fashion industry has enjoyed annual average growth of 5 percent globally. The largest subindustry of fashion is women's wear, with a global retail value of $621 billion; men's wear is valued at just over $400 billion. While China is currently the largest exporter of apparel, Europe is second, and most of the industry's design and value creation still takes place in Europe and the United States. The American fashion industry currently employs more than 1.8 million workers, and in New York it accounts for three out of ten manufacturing jobs. Among the world's fifty-largest fortunes, several are from the fashion industry, including those of Bernard Arnault, owner of Moët Hennessy Louis Vuitton (LVMH); Amancio Ortega, founder of Industria de Diseño Textil SA (Inditex, home to Zara and other brands); and Stefan Persson, successor to his father, Erling, founder of Hennes and Mauritz (H&M). Their global groups are headquartered in Europe.[1]

Fashion is not only one of the most dynamic industries; it is also a cultural phenomenon in its own right. The work of major designers such as Christian Dior, Paul Poiret, Yves Saint Laurent, and Madeleine Vionnet, among many others, is displayed in retrospective exhibitions in the world's most prestigious museums. These designers' names are recognized around the world, and many are the subject of multiple biopics distributed in theaters globally. They created exclusive products for the elite but also managed to become part of the general consumer's imaginaries. These examples are indicators of the economic and symbolic capital that the fashion industry created over the twentieth century. In order to understand how it was possible for the fashion industry to generate such capital, it is necessary to uncover its history. The fashion industry is a composite of firms that create, make, and retail the widest array of personal goods, clothes, and accessories ranging from the ordinary to the exclusive. The creation of innovative clothing design is the common denominator of all the cases studied in this book. Production chains in the fashion industry are complex. This book does not attempt to cover the production of raw material, notably thread and textile; nor does it seek to provide an overview of retail, which has been the topic of important studies previously.[2] The history that unfolds in this book focuses on creativity in fashion design. It is the history of a negotiation between innovation and commercialization, which developed within the business and institutional cultures of France and the United States, with a focus on Paris and New York. Various cases of bilateral or multilateral relations between fashion centers are important and have been the topic of other studies. This book focuses on the relation between Paris and New York as paradigmatic, but not unique, to the industry.[3] Firms based in Paris set the tone for a global fashion culture, especially in terms of women's fashion, the segment of the market in which cyclical changes were particularly pronounced and important. New York was the main center for the mass production of fashions, often but not always made in the style of designs created in Paris. Interlocked in cooperation and competition, the symbiotic relation of the two cities helped create a fast-growing fashion economy.[4]

The history of transatlantic relations in the twentieth century approaches the different legal, cultural, and political contexts that distinguish European nations, France among them, from the United States. A goal of this book is to further contribute to reconnecting the historiographical threads of the socioeconomic history of the transatlantic relations and the world of fashion.[5] During the final years of the nineteenth century and until the postwar period, New York was the world's largest center of garment manufacturing, and yet its industries relied heavily on Paris for design inspiration. This dynamic casts a different light on the idea of a hegemonic Americanization of Europe. In the fashion industry, Europe—and Paris in particular—occupied a central position and was the global style leader until the 1960s. How did a handful of local Paris entrepreneurs establish and sustain global hegemony over style? And what were the strategies of the French firms after the stylistic hegemony of Paris haute couture was over?[6]

In order to answer these questions, this book explores the ways in which the French couture entrepreneurs strategically sought connections across the Atlantic. Whether these entrepreneurs and their transatlantic colleagues were developing their domestic markets, trading with their international clients, or expanding their own initiatives globally, fashion firms on both sides of the Atlantic strategized to respond to a fickle and often unpredictable demand for fashion.[7] American fashion buyers, trend scouts, and designers crossed the Atlantic to attend the twice-yearly couture openings. In Europe, they bought merchandise and found out what they would be selling in the United States one or two years hence. Most Paris fashion entrepreneurs traveled to New York as well, to meet with clients and to understand what the American consumers wanted. From there, Paris couturiers toured America, lecturing and signing contracts with local manufacturers for whom they designed exclusive garments and accessories. The travels, networks, and circuits of dissemination between the two continents played a central role in the rise of the fashion industry.

In the United States, fashionable manufactured clothing reached the masses earlier than in France. Paris couturiers admired the force of production of the New York garment district and complained that the American entrepreneurs copied their creations and sometimes counterfeited their brands as an essential part of their work. Such narratives of opposition between two very different national industries and two fashion cities are buttressed by the nature of the firms: an enduring couture trade based on craftsmanship in France and mass production in the United States. Therefore, this book does not aim to provide a strict comparison, as the two cities may at times be too different to allow a properly comparative study. Rather, it aims to trace the changing transfers and power relations between the Paris and New York fashion firms. The history of the competition between the two cities should not obscure their interdependence and complementarity.[8] The transatlantic history of fashion reveals a powerful combination of competitive advantages that produced a dynamic industry.[9]

In order to examine the history of the fashion firms, this book explores the roles of entrepreneurs, institutions, and innovation. Fashion entrepreneurs have risen to prominence for their design and brand identities, which have also partly overshadowed the history of their firms' management. In smaller or earlier firms, capital was most often provided by self-financing and familial networks that remained involved in a firm's management. The firm was generally named after the head designer, such as Madeleine Vionnet and Christian Dior in Paris and Hattie Carnegie and Nettie Rosenstein in New York. Designers' names evolved into brand names through a process that went faster for Paris firms than for New York firms. Head designers worked with managing directors who remained in their shadows, though their contributions to strategy were essential.[10] Therefore, these pages seek to underline the roles played by Louis Dangel, Armand Trouyet, Sylvan Gotshal, Ellen Engel, Monique de Nervo, and Jacques Rouët, to cite but a few of the managers who, as much as the star designers, were significant figures in this transatlantic history.

The interplay between Paris and New York over the course of the twentieth century helps us understand why the fashion industry is structured as it is today. For most of the century, fashion was fragmented into many small shops, and part of its oversight took place beyond the firms themselves, in employers' syndicates and professional organizations that lobbied governments to obtain better conditions for the business. Professional networks that developed the relations between industrial clusters played a central role. In addition, governmental actors at the city and state levels influenced the development of the fashion industries and interacted with firms and with professional syndicates, notably the Chambre Syndicale de la Couture Parisienne and the New York Fashion Group.[11]

The history of fashion is a history of creativity in capitalism.[12] Innovation is at the core of all economic history, and in the fashion industry, innovation covers business creativity, design novelty, industrial design, and symbolic capital. In some areas of the fashion trade, intellectual property rights—from design copyright to logo and trademark protection—generated authenticity and revenue.[13] Over the course of the twentieth century, fashion increasingly catered to the masses, yet batch production remained dominant, even for large fashion groups. The swift renewal of innovation drove fashion firms to adopt models of flexible specialization. Fashion was in many respects pioneering in the development of post-Fordist economies.[14]

The chapters follow a chronological structure, tracing successive waves of internationalization in the fashion industry. Fashion has been challenging to business historians because, for most of its history, it was formed of small firms that often left few traces besides their designs and advertisements. The chapters aim to offer group portraits as well as to focus on one or a handful of main characters and firms. These characters are not just designers but also managers. All of them are essential in that they changed the industry in which they worked. Innovation in the fashion industry has an unusually high record of women and lesbian, gay, and bisexual innovators, and a high number of fashion entrepreneurs may also be viewed as textbook cases of rags-to-riches stories. This should not obliterate the extremely competitive aspects of the industry, however, or the low wages paid to a large majority of those it employs.[15]

The Paris couture cluster went through an initial episode of internationalization just before World War I. A handful of early Paris-based fashion multinationals, including the firms Beer, Boué Sœurs, Drecoll, Paquin, and Worth, branched out mostly in London and then, for some of them, in New York.[16] The activity of these firms was slowed down and in some cases halted by the war. As the industry regained its prosperity during the 1920s, a few Paris couturiers tried to set up shop in the United States, including the renowned Madeleine Vionnet.[17] In a corresponding movement, US designer Mainbocher ventured across the Atlantic to become part of Paris couture. The entrepreneurs who tried to settle on the opposite side of the Atlantic confronted challenges ranging from direct local competition and trade barriers to the limited capitalization of their enterprises. In some cases, changing legal regimes, tax regimes, buying habits, and languages created competitive advantages; most often, however, they presented insurmountable obstacles. Periods of crisis and war further acted to erode the prosperity of the transatlantic fashion business.

It took several decades of trial and error for transatlantic fashion to flourish. The first success came with the foundation of the Paris house of Christian Dior in 1946 and the opening of its first overseas branch, in New York, in 1948. Dior and his teams shifted the business model of haute couture from a reliance on craftsmanship to an emphasis on brand licensing. Other couturiers soon followed in his footsteps. The financial structure of the Dior conglomerate changed the organization of Paris couture and brought it to the international markets. Backed by French textile industrialists, Dior became a global luxury brand. During the postwar period, higher salaries and taxes aggravated the economic difficulties of the traditional model of haute couture, which drove these houses to undertake financing arrangements with larger corporations or groups. Often described as the financialization of the luxury industries, this process resulted in an acceleration of the global development of fashion brands and the globalization of luxury, the products of which became available to wider groups of consumers.

The last phase of the transformation of the industry started in the 1960s, when the complementary relationship between Paris and New York evolved into a multipolar system of fashion capitals, including London and Milan and, gradually, a number of Asian fashion centers, notably Tokyo, Shanghai, and Mumbai. Fashions in the second half of the twentieth century were no longer dictated by wealthy elites but also came from the street—from commercial mainstream production as well as from critical countercultures and subcultures. The fashion industry developed global supply chains at a time when important parts of its manufacturing were relocated to areas distant from the fashion capitals, including parts of Asia, North Africa, and, after the fall of the Iron Curtain, eastern European countries. The structure of the industry was reshuffled. Luxury groups, global ready-to-wear retailers, and vertically integrated affordable fashion firms became the new actors that offered fashionable goods at every price point. The transatlantic fashion routes occupy a crucial place in this history, as they were a transformative step toward a global system.[18]

Chapter 1 examines the history of the early fashion multinationals. During the couple of decades that preceded World War I, a dozen Paris couture entrepreneurs, including Paquin, Beer, and Martial and Armand, branched out to London, Vienna, and New York, where they catered to cosmopolitan elites avid for luxurious fashions. In the United States, the New York garment district was a much more fragmented landscape of producers that mass-manufactured garments to be sold at various price points. Many New York manufacturers did not directly retail the garments they manufactured but instead acted as wholesalers to American department stores, which retailed the products under their own brands. These early international fashion networks were caught up in the turmoil of World War I. American buyers and journalists continued traveling to Paris despite submarine warfare in Atlantic waters. The attraction of Paris fashion was powerful, and its reproduction was a guarantee of commercial success for New York–based firms. The overall economy of Paris couture suffered from the war. In 1917, the year the United States officially entered the conflict, Paris saw the biggest strike ever among its couture workers, who were exhausted by the war effort. That same year, Jeanne Paquin became the first woman to preside over a French employers' syndicate, the Chambre Syndicale de la Couture Parisienne.

Chapter 2 traces the history of the Paris couturiers' early attempts to brand their creations as authentic and to branch out in New York. Nearly all early fashion multinationals, most of which had survived the war, closed their overseas branches and limited their activity to Paris and to commercial branches in the French coastal resorts, and enjoyed a period of relative prosperity during the 1920s. In addition, a young crop of Paris haute couture entrepreneurs catered to the "new woman" of the era. They were ready to develop a modern aesthetic to suit freer bodies. At the forefront of this new couture were two women, Gabrielle Chanel and Madeleine Vionnet, who had each risen from great poverty to reach a place among the most successful businesswomen of their times. Vionnet, the most celebrated Paris couturiere in the United States, is studied as the central case in this chapter in order to show the processes that shaped the authenticity of Paris fashions on the domestic and international markets. The early interwar period was marked by dense commercial exchanges between Paris and New York fashion entrepreneurs. Fashions were modernized, but made-to-measure still dominated garment consumption in France, where only one-third of fashion goods were produced by manufacturers or in the workshops of department stores. During the interwar period, entering the Paris haute couture shows became a privilege reserved for authorized private clients and foreign manufacturers. The best clients of haute couture were from the United States, but whereas fashion design was included in the French law protecting authors' rights, it was not protected in the United States. Vionnet led the way for Paris entrepreneurs to build up intellectual property rights portfolios and, in so doing, to market the authenticity of their production.

Chapter 3 explores the impact of the economic downturn on the fashion industry. During the Great Depression, haute couture remained centered in Paris, resting nearly entirely on French financial capital. Paris couturiers kept traveling to the United States for commercial purposes. Customs authorities ignored the fact that haute couture was a vehicle for the transmission of design and taxed it as a luxury product. The raising of trade barriers, and the contraction of international commerce and foreign direct investments, had dramatic consequences for the international fashion business. To survive the crisis, couturiers used strategies such as compressing overhead costs and diversifying into branded products. Paris couturiers managed to keep a foothold in the United States during the Great Depression mainly by opening branches there that specialized in perfumes and cosmetics produced in the United States under French brand names. American production was characterized by more mechanization and by wages that were higher than in France. Eighty percent of the garments sold in the United States were manufactured in New York. But the New York fashion industry also counted among its leaders a crop of high-end, creative entrepreneurs such as Hattie Carnegie and Maurice Rentner, who thought that American fashion could innovate in its own right and who worked to promote and protect original US fashion design. The National Recovery Administration, launched by the first Franklin D. Roosevelt administration, imposed codes of good practice on the fashion and garment business, among other industries. Both in France and in the United States, economic upturn finally followed, in the years 1937–1939.

The recovery of the fashion industry was cut short by the war, and Chapter 4 examines how the occupation of most of France, including Paris starting on June 14, 1940, upset the structure of the fashion industry. While France was cut off from most importing markets, including the United States, New York positioned itself as the new creative center. Mayor Fiorello La Guardia publicly supported New York's ambition to replace Paris as the world's fashion capital. In Paris, the industry had to keep employees at work and justify the existence of haute couture during wartime, as well as avoid the Nazi authorities' interest in relocating all couture workshops to Berlin. Couturiers emphasized the notions of craftsmanship as a way to legitimize their creative output in the wartime context. The Chambre Syndicale de la Couture Parisienne became a professional group within the corporatist structure set up by the German occupation authority. Paris couture, despite being cut off from major foreign markets, remained profitable during the occupation by selling to clients in the neutral countries and to the occupier. The city of New York, despite the wartime restrictions, strengthened its position as the world's fashion capital and gained momentum during World War II. Paris was liberated from August 19 to 25, 1944, and its status as a fashion capital seemed uncertain at that moment.

Chapter 5 addresses the deep transformations that characterized the postwar period, during which Paris came back as a major laboratory of design and again attracted international buyers and journalists, thanks to the consolidation of talented designers who had emerged in the late interwar years, such as Cristóbal Balenciaga, and the rise of newcomers like Christian Dior, who opened his own enterprise in 1946. The next year, he created a sensation with a new line of women's fashions that seemed to present a radical aesthetic break from the restrained lines of wartime rationed clothing. Dior set about creating licensing agreements for numerous lines of tie-in products carrying his brand, in this way bringing Paris original designs to the international markets. This innovative strategy was made possible by substantial investments by Marcel Boussac, France's "king of cotton." Dior branched out, starting with New York in 1948. Boussac's management rested on a complex international structure of assets based not only in France but also in Latin America and in the United States. So far, the Paris fashion industry had remained a local cluster fostered by a rich hinterland supplying high-quality materials and by international commerce. This changed during the postwar period, as couturiers explored new strategies for expansion.

Chapter 6 examines the shifts that took place in the 1960s: the causes of the decline of haute couture, the rise of ready-to-wear designers (*stylistes*), and the development of global luxury branding. The new dynamism of French ready-to-wear was influenced by travel to the United States under the auspices of the European Recovery Program, also known as the Marshall Plan, which came about in 1948. The French government invested resources in both haute couture and ready-to-wear, despite the apparent contradiction there. Haute couture was acknowledged to be a conceit of the past, but the government was not ready to abandon either the symbolic capital of the industry or its value as a style laboratory. In 1950, a group of haute couture houses federated to create their own ready-to-wear collections. At the end of the decade, the Chambre Syndicale de la Couture Parisienne opened an office in New York, thanks to a subvention from the French government. New York was still the nerve center for fashion in the United States. While the United States declined to include fashion in its copyright law, trademark law was buttressed by the 1946 Lanham Act, allowing for a better protection of fashion origination through branding. During those years, French couturiers won their first cases against counterfeiters in the United States, but the client base of haute couture was disappearing quickly. Confronted by the challenges of adapting to rising labor costs and compensating for the diminishing discretionary revenue of its private clients, haute couture survived supported by brand licenses. Larger groups of consumers who had never been able to afford haute couture could now acquire Christian Dior lipstick, Yves Saint Laurent scarves, and Pierre Cardin ashtrays. Branding was the luxury firms' answer to mass production.

Chapter 7 examines how, over the last decades of the twentieth century, fashion production moved from the West and its hubs, such as the New York garment district, to regions where wages were cheaper, in southern Europe and elsewhere in the United States, and then to altogether low-cost countries, especially in Asia. In the West, areas that had traditionally specialized in fabric and garment manufacturing converted part of their activity into creation, design, and media, often supported by governmental programs aiming to compensate for the loss of manufacturing jobs. Paris and New York remained gatekeepers of the fashion business and were joined in this role by London and Milan. Alongside these important players, fashion capitals and holdings developed around the world from the 1980s. Yet close observers remain unsure about the creative potential of these groups as far as design is concerned. Today, it is yet uncertain that the Global South will play a leading role in the future of the fashion industries.

Chapter 1

The Early Internationalization
of Haute Couture

A t the turn of the century, Paris reigned over the empire of fashion. At the top
of the Paris fashion business was a woman, Jeanne Paquin, who directed the
haute couture house of Paquin. Born Jeanne Marie Charlotte Beckers on l'Ile-
Saint-Denis, a commune north of Paris, on June 23, 1869, Jeanne was the illegiti-
mate child of medical doctor Frédéric Beckers, aged forty-eight at the time of the
birth, and Marguerite Bourgeois, twenty-two, registered without profession.
Dr. Beckers legally recognized Jeanne as his daughter. At sixteen, Jeanne Beckers
started working as a model—one of the less prestigious positions in the trade—at
the couture house of Rouff. The hours were long and the pay lower than that of the
other jobs in couture, save for apprenticeship. Jeanne worked there for three years,
leaving in 1889 for a similar post at the house of Paquin, Lalanne and Co., where
she made a strong impression on Isidore Jacob, a partner in the firm. Jacob had
started calling himself "Paquin" as his business name. Jeanne gradually took over
design responsibilities, and in 1890 Isidore and Jeanne reopened the haute couture
house under the sole name of Paquin at a more prestigious address: 3 rue de la Paix.
They married the next year. In 1899, Isidore Jacob received from the French government the right to change his name legally to Isidore Paquin.[1] Isidore and Jeanne
rose to prominence in the Paris fashion industry, but in 1907, Isidore died of kidney
failure. Jeanne, who had previously assumed the post of head designer, was now on

her own. She took over her late husband's responsibilities, combining design and business management with skill and confidence. In just a few years Jeanne Paquin became a key figure in the fashion trade not only at home but also overseas.[2]

The sociologist Thorstein Veblen, a contemporary of Jeanne Paquin's, observed that fashions were a mark of the leisure class, of people who not only were prosperous but could afford to participate in leisurely pursuits. The fashionable dress of women in the West bore the imprint of masculine domination, as the impracticality of women's clothes—which involved corsets and long, voluminous skirts—prevented them from living a very active life. Through plates and newspapers, high-class fashions were made known to all, turning fashion into one of the most visible signifiers of class and gender inequality. Paris was a fashion design center for the rest of the world. Consumers in the rest of France, in foreign countries, and in the colonies adopted Paris fashions for many reasons, including aesthetic appeal, acceptance of social rules, aspiration, and modernization. The publicizing of fashion in the printed media, at the world's fairs, and in big-city department stores contributed to a common imagination and aspiration among various consumer strata, including those who could not afford such purchases. Fashion, as a marker of class, could provide the wearer a passport to enter into a world to which she initially did not belong.[3]

The Beginnings of Haute Couture

Before the French Revolution, fifteen hundred couturieres were registered in the Corporation des couturiers, the trade association for that profession located in Paris. They worked only to cut, assemble, and finish the garments, which was called work *à façon*—the term from which the English word *fashion* originated. When clients went to a couturiere in Paris, they had to bring their own fabric. Madame Roger, an early nineteenth-century entrepreneur who established her firm at 25 rue Louis-le-Grand, changed the business model of the couturiere into haute couture. Clients no longer needed to bring their own fabric to Roger. Instead, she offered complete dressmaking services, including a choice of fabrics and the garnishing of the outfit with matching trims and ribbons, all of which was done on the premises of her firm (see Figure 1.1). Roger had a more extensive role in the design of fashions than the previous members of the corporation.

FIGURE 1.1 Advertisement card for the English-speaking clients of couturiere Madame Roger, 47 Boulevard Haussmann, in 1888.
Reproduction courtesy of Librarie Diktats.

In so doing, she doubled her profits, as she added the cost of fabric to the price of dressmaking work.[4]

Essential to the new haute couture was the presence in Paris of the largest numbers of small shops and craftspeople who created notions and accessories. Makers specialized in one type of product: buttons, feathers, flowers, ribbons, laces, and so on. The nearly infinite variety of their specializations supported the creativity of haute couture. Equally important were the group of textile middlemen who presented seasonally updated collections of fabrics to the couture industry. The firm J. Claude Frères, founded by brothers François and Victor Jean-Claude in the 1830s, was one of the most prominent of these brokers; it specialized in selecting fabrics, cutting samples, organizing them in albums, and selling them, as a service to fashion manufacturers and retailers. Such sample firms thus offered information that circulated between the fabric makers in the provinces and the dressmakers in Paris and abroad.[5]

The trade of Paris haute couture started in the mid-nineteenth century with Roger at the forefront of innovation; however, fashion histories most often cite Charles Frederick Worth, an English immigrant in Paris, as the founding father of haute couture. Having worked for several years in prominent Paris novelty firms—first Aurelly, then Gagelin & Opigez—Worth started to show his original designs midcentury. He made a name for himself when displaying his work at the Great Exhibition of 1851, held at London's Crystal Palace. In 1858 Worth opened his firm, the house of Worth, in Paris with capital provided by a Swedish partner and manager, Otto Bobergh, who retained his share in the firm until 1871, when Worth bought it back from him. Worth cultivated the image of an artist and entertained friendships with numerous clients, including European royals. His wife, Marie Vernet, was his model and saleswoman. She visited illustrious clients and courts, showing her husband's drawing albums and fitting high-profile patrons. With Worth, the image of the couturier as an artist contributed to a relegation of business partners to the designer's shadow. Worth also masculinized the profession of fashion designer in the public eye.[6]

The beginning of Worth's business was contemporary to the invention of the sewing machine, which made the development of the fashion industry possible by allowing faster reproduction of designs for wider markets. Several innovators who had developed their ideas and improvements, including Isaac Merritt Singer and Elias Howe, simultaneously claimed the invention of the sewing machine. They solved the dispute by setting up together one of the first patent pools in history, the Sewing Machine Combination, in order to reward half a dozen innovators at the same time. The patent pool lasted from 1856 to 1877 and had the effect of slowing down the innovation of sewing machines, making them a long-term investment subject to relatively few changes. Most importantly, the Singer Manufacturing Company provided its customers with excellent service that included repair, making its machines a reliable product.[7]

Paris couture found its pride in aesthetic innovation and in handcrafted work. And yet, the early haute couture firms did not shy away from using the sewing machine in their workshops. Labor was organized according to technical innovation: long and linear seams were machine made, and intricate finishing and ornamentation were done by hand. Worth's workshops were able, when a client demanded it, to turn in a perfectly fitted dress in twenty-four hours. Worth dresses had the allure of exclusivity, yet the firm offered several seasonally fixed types of skirts and bodices that could be mixed and matched, therefore standardizing production. Dresses by Worth often featured one skirt that could be matched with two different bodices. Each of these bodices was made in the fabric that matched the skirt, but each one's cut was different. Typically, one bodice had longer sleeves and covered the chest, which made it suitable for daytime, while the other bodice had shorter sleeves and an open neckline, transforming the two-piece dress into evening wear. As expensive as they were, such couture garments could serve for various occasions. The history of Worth garments shows that haute couture was made to last much longer than one season. For example, the Countess Greffulhe, a muse of Marcel Proust's who inspired a character in *In Search of Lost Time,* owned a Worth dress made of black silk velvet decorated with appliquéd lilies in ivory satin. The Worth workshops delivered the spectacular dress in 1896, and Greffulhe wore it for four years before having it altered to suit the more sober fashions of the 1900s.[8]

Quality of fabric and of ornaments gave an exclusive cachet to each haute couture outfit and could increase its price. A high sense of drama in shape, color, and ornament that characterized Worth fashions put wealth and beauty on display. Worth came to be known as an arbiter and even, metaphorically, as a dictator of fashion, as he was convinced that he knew exactly which variation of his designs and which colors fit each client best. Both Roger and Worth counted European royalty and courtiers among their clients. Worth sent his gowns to the foreign courts and, whenever needed, sent along seamstresses to help with fittings and adjustments. Couture had its roots in Paris but went to meet its wealthiest patrons in Europe, in Russia, and in America.

The new haute couture that was born in the mid-nineteenth century catered to a wider clientele than today. The price of couture varied considerably, sometimes tenfold from the cheapest to the most expensive designs at the house of Worth, according to the price of raw materials and time spent on embellishments. The middle class also consumed haute couture at the turn of the century. Famously, in 1902 the house of Worth hired a young employee, Paul Poiret, who was creatively driven and had an extraordinary sense of color, to design cheaper lines for Worth. In direct line from the commerce of novelty, houses like Worth contained several departments, intended to serve any type of couture. This diversification in models and prices contributed to make haute couture a profitable business.

Entry prices attracted middle-class clients, who started by buying one or two simple pieces, like a *paletot*, a type of long fitted jacket that, worn over simple dresses made at home or bought ready-made, could elevate an entire series of outfits. Then, as their fortunes grew, these clients increasingly bought more couture, which they had learned to appreciate early on.[9]

In 1868, Worth, along with the clothing manufacturer Salé, founded the Chambre Syndicale de la Couture, des Confectionneurs et des Tailleurs pour Dames, an employers' syndicate that aimed to represent the collective professional interests of French entrepreneurs specializing in haute couture, dress manufacturing, and women's tailoring. The use of the sewing machine and experimentation with the serialization of designs created a common ground between haute couture and manufacturing, at a time when craftsmanship was not yet celebrated as a way to create class distinctions between different types of garments. The Chambre Syndicale came to fill the void left after the guilds and corporations—and more precisely the Corporation des couturiers, which had represented couturieres from 1675 to the Revolution—were abolished by law, as stated in the Law of Allarde of March 2 and 17, 1791. The foundation of an employers' syndicate was aimed at establishing common prices for the workforce, thereby avoiding social unrest and cutthroat competition between firms. In 1899 the director of a workshop, called the *première*, could earn 5,000 to 30,000 francs per year, while her workers earned between 640 and 1,120 francs per year, or five to forty times less than her. The seasonal workforce that came only to complete orders earned even less and did not find work to do every day, which left an important part of the workforce in precarity. This situation alarmed social workers, who pointed to the insecurity of the lives of the seamstresses who depended on private charity should they lose their job, get sick, or have family members to care for.[10]

Paris Couture, British Firms

Dressmaking was an international trade for a cluster of firms that included Aine, Béchoff-David, Chéruit, Diemer, Jenny, Laferrière, Margaine-Lacroix, Montaillé, Perdroux, Premet, and Raudnitz & Cie, none of which is still in existence. Numerous haute couture houses opened retail branches in the French holiday resorts of Biarritz, Cannes, Deauville, and Nice. In the first two decades of the twentieth century, haute couture branched out beyond France, with shops opening in

Bucharest, Buenos Aires, Cairo, London, Madrid, Monte Carlo, New York, and Saint Petersburg. Most of these branches were short-lived initiatives, except for a small group of French couturiers who first set up shop in London, and between 1896 and 1908, established private companies limited by shares (Ltds.) following the British Companies Act of 1867. These firms included Paquin in 1896, G. Beer in 1903, Martial and Armand & Co. in 1905, Boué Sœurs in 1906, Dœuillet in 1907, and Ch. Drecoll in 1908. The goal of these couturiers was to better reach their British and American clientele and to grow the volume of overseas business. Two London-based firms made the opposite movement and opened a Paris branch: Lucile Ltd., which opened a branch in Paris in 1919, following its expansion to New York in 1911, and the tailor Redfern, which opened in both London and Paris in 1881, then in New York in 1884.[11]

The house of Paquin was the first Paris couturier to branch out to London, where it incorporated a limited liability company on November 11, 1896, and a branch at 39 Dover Street, Mayfair, on March 30, 1897. Paquin's design studio remained in the Paris mother ship on rue de la Paix, now technically a branch of a British firm. The capital of Paquin Ltd. was half a million British pounds in 1896, the largest in the haute couture trade. Isidore Paquin had borrowed £40,000 (then 1 million French francs) to constitute his capital, of which a first installment of £10,000 was reimbursed in 1900.[12] Isidore and Jeanne Paquin lived in Paris year-round.[13] Of the most prominent haute couture firms that started limited liability companies in London, the second largest was the house of G. Beer, founded in 1886. Gustave Beer, who was the founder and head designer, managed the firm along with his partner, administrative director Ludovic Badin. In 1903, Beer and Badin founded a new branch, G. Beer Ltd., in London. They mentioned the house of Paquin as the example they followed. Like Paquin, the house of G. Beer kept its design and most sales operations in Paris, where it employed two hundred people in sales and administration alone in 1909. Beer eventually had commercial branches in London, Nice, and Monte Carlo. The capital of Beer's British Ltd. was £480,000 in 1903, nearly as large as Paquin's.[14] Other Paris firms with much smaller capital and volume of business branched out to London as well. Martial and Armand opened a limited liability in London on February 2, 1905, under the direction of design and business partners Armand Cahen and Jules Henri Renou. This firm had a capital of £55,000. In this case too, the firm's design studio and workshops were in Paris, with retail shops in Paris, London, and Monte Carlo.[15]

The shareholders of the first haute couture multinationals were of two kinds. In the first, one or two dozen capitalists owned the majority of the shares of each firm, and among them were the directors of these firms. The other, bigger group was made up of large numbers of individuals who each owned a very small number of shares, often just one or two ordinary shares. Most of these small investors are listed as seamstresses and dressmakers, at least half of them being women. The managers of the London-based haute couture limited liability firms interested their workers in their capitalist ventures.[16] Directors of haute couture houses could be the main owners of the business, like Lady Duff-Gordon at Lucile Ltd.; others were contractually hired, as was initially the case with Jeanne Paquin. All managers and chief designers in the industry were paid a fixed annual sum in addition to a percentage of the profits. The direction of a fashion firm usually involved one artistic director and one managing director. The Paquins, Isidore and Jeanne, were employees of the Paquin Ltd. firm. The couple received a fixed annual salary plus a variable interest in the firm's profits, which they received as a yearly lump sum.[17] In the case of G. Beer, the designers' salaries were the subject of critiques. The accumulation of such high revenue from dresses was met with skepticism by contemporary French financial journalists, who wrote that the salaries of artistic director Beer (62,500 French francs per year in 1903) and his associate, Badin (50,000 French francs per year in 1903)—in addition to which each received an annual 5 percent of the firm's profits—were too high.[18]

The expenses required to run an haute couture house were considerable. In 1907, the house of Paquin made a yearly profit of 12 million francs. Paquin had a leadership position in haute couture, and its profits totaled more than those of its two largest competitors combined. Of this, each year the firm spent 4 million francs on fabrics. Another 4 million went to pay the 1,350 people employed at Paquin: 1,000 manual workers and 350 salespeople, administrative employees, and models. The firm employed fifteen cooks, who served over seven hundred meals daily to the employees. The highest salaries went to the saleswomen, who earned up to 50,000 francs per year, and heads of workshops, who earned between 10,000 and 30,000 per year. The lowest salaries went to entry-level workers and models. The remainder of the firm's expenses went to overhead costs. Each year, 250,000 francs was paid in rent for the location on the rue de la Paix. The same amount was spent on the employees' meals served in-house. Energy costs amounted to 50,000 francs annually; the fresh hydrangeas that adorned the balconies of the rue de la Paix facade cost 25,000 a year. The firm paid 20,000 annually in delivery costs and 80,000 in taxes and patents, both in France and in Great Britain.[19]

Haute couture houses advertised their business through various channels. They participated in the world's fairs and international exhibitions, where fashion was marketed as a sign of civilization. At the 1900 Paris World's Fair, Paquin showed dresses along with fellow couturiers in the halls; in addition, the firm dressed a monumental statue representing the archetypal Parisian woman that signposted the entrance of the exhibition grounds. Paquin's board of directors believed the fair played a role in the firm's high profits in 1900 and 1901.[20]

The archives of these early haute couture multinationals give precious indications of the networks formed by their boards of directors, which were composed of London- and Paris-based businessmen. Three of the early haute couture multinationals had women designers at the helm: Boué Sœurs, Lucile, and Paquin. Yet no women sat on the boards, with the exception of Lucile Ltd.: Lucy Christiana (née Sutherland), Lady Duff-Gordon—best known as a survivor of the *Titanic*, and based in Riverdale-on-Hudson, New York—was chairwoman of both Lucile (New York) Ltd., founded in 1911, and Lucile (Paris) Ltd., founded in 1919. The London branch of Boué Sœurs was a private firm founded in London on May 21, 1906, with a capital of £40,000. Its shares were concentrated among a more limited number of shareholders than in the other early international couture firms. Although Jeanne and Sylvie Boué gave their name to the firm Boué Sœurs, designed the clothes, and managed the firm, including at the international level, its board of directors was composed exclusively of men, most notably Philippe Montégut, who had married Sylvie Boué, and Achille d'Etreillis, husband of Jeanne Boué.[21]

At Paquin Ltd. in 1896, the year the London branch was founded, the board of directors was made up of chairman John Barker, managing director Isidore Paquin, and four other businessmen; two of these men were members of the British Parliament. James Bailey, a Conservative member of Parliament from 1895 to 1906, was in the hotel business in London and was also a board member of two department stores, Harrods and D. H. Evans (which changed its name to House of Fraser in 2001). Barker, the other MP on the board of Paquin Ltd., was a politician elected twice to the House of Commons.[22] Other haute couture limited liabilities had prestigious administrators on their boards. For example, the chairman of the house of Ch. Drecoll Ltd. was the British press magnate and Conservative politician Davison Dalziel, who was also the longest-serving member on the board of that firm. The British department stores were important shareholders and supplied numerous board members to the haute couture firms. The connection between business and politics observed here among board members of haute couture firms would be less common after World War I, especially in France. The communications expert Edward Bernays notes that, apart from the Worths, French couturiers were excluded from the high society of the interwar period.[23]

During the ancien régime, couture was primarily a female profession, but this changed when Worth rose to prominence. Worth and his sons, who took over the firm, claimed that men had the best eye to see and to design what would make women elegant and attractive. Still, numerous women entrepreneurs participated in Paris haute couture.[24] Once widowed, Jeanne Paquin took up extra tasks and became the general managing director of her enterprise. The board was still directed by British MP John Barker. Jeanne Paquin's interventions in front of the board of directors of Paquin Ltd. show that she had authority in her analyses of the firm's financial situation and economic context. She was a poised speaker, and her audience respected the quality of her argumentation. As a managing director she developed the overseas expansion of her firm and assumed leadership in professional associations. Moreover, her strategy of keeping a large cash reserve was deemed conservative by the board but proved useful at the outbreak of World War I.[25] Paquin's creativity favored wearability, and her designs were considered less spectacular than those of Worth or Poiret. Couture changed drastically during Paquin's career, with innovations such as the removal of the corset and the inclusion of Middle Eastern and Asian influences. Paquin adopted these elements in a form that was often more subdued than in the works of her fellow couturiers, which may be one of the reasons for the profitability of her firm. Paquin also carried her creative interests much further, particularly by actively promoting her firm's activities abroad. The firms Lucile Ltd. and Boué Sœurs Ltd., with their Paris, London, and New York branches, were also led by women, but compared with Paquin they were smaller.[26]

Georges Aubert and the Early Financialization of Haute Couture

Against this backdrop, a banker, Georges Aubert, started playing with the idea of financialization of haute couture. Born in 1869, Aubert traveled to South Africa and to the United States during his youth, later writing a series of essays in which he narrated his experiences abroad, including *La finance américaine* published in 1910.[27] Back in France, Aubert devised the project to build a more ambitious business model for haute couture, based on what he presented as American methods. Aubert thought that the Paris couture firms lacked international ambitions because of their limited financial means. But this did not happen in the United States. Instead, Aubert's first attempts focused on Paris and London, where in 1907 he founded the first company aimed at financing haute couture, the Vendôme Syndicate Ltd., with the modest capital of £6,000. Aubert planned to use the syndicate as the financial arm of his portfolio of fashion firms. He chose the name for place Vendôme, the heart of the luxury district in Paris, where he had his residence at number 22. One of the first couturiers that Aubert included in his portfolio was the firm of his friend Georges Dœuillet, in existence since 1899 at 18 place Vendôme. In July 1907, Dœuillet opened a British limited liability with a capital of £200,000, while the Paris division of the firm remained active throughout the existence of Dœuillet Ltd., from 1907 to 1924.[28] On April 29, 1907, Dœuillet and Aubert made an agreement stating that Aubert, through his firm Vendôme Syndicate Ltd., could buy several thousand shares of Dœuillet and that the Central Industrial Trust Ltd., which had contributed to the formation of the Vendôme Syndicate, would be able to buy a similar amount of shares in Dœuillet. This did not mean a majority or even a controlling stake in Dœuillet, though, as together these investments amounted to less than 10 percent of Dœuillet's capital.[29]

After just over a year of existence, however, Aubert proceeded to the voluntary liquidation of the Vendôme Syndicate in 1908. He reinvested the modest capital of the syndicate in haute couture houses in which he already owned shares: Dœuillet, Beer, and the Paris-based house of Agnès, a firm founded on May 28, 1907, on the basis of an older Maison Agnès bought for 225,000 francs. Aubert reorganized the latter firm to form the French société anonyme Agnès, with a capital of 800,000 French francs in 1907, raised to 2 million in 1913.[30] At that point the capital had been entirely reimbursed to the subscribers.[31] The board of administrators of Agnès included Georges Aubert, president, and Count Jean Récopé, Paul Benazet, Henri Lippens, and André Taillade; as with the other firms in which Aubert was involved, its financial service was the French bank Oustric. The artistic director of the Agnès concern was Jeanne Havet, who became known in the industry as Madame Agnès although she was not the founder of the house.[32]

In 1907, Aubert moved the house of Agnès from rue Louis-le-Grand to rue Auber. The Oustric bank, which then became involved in the capital of Agnès, was across the street, at 8 rue Auber. Aubert planned the merger of Agnès with another haute couture house. But members of the general assembly questioned this move, and negotiations ceased in 1913. That same year, Count Balbiani replaced Aubert as the head of the Agnès board of administrators. In 1914, Havet voiced new disagreements with the board over management of the firm. The main point of contention was the growth of the haute couture house, which Havet wanted to keep expanding. As the artistic director of the house of Agnès, Havet managed to assemble a group of shareholders who together owned a majority of ten thousand shares of the haute couture house; voting out the current board of administrators, she became president of the board in 1914. The financial press commented that this was a quite exceptional demonstration of power from a woman in the couture business. Aubert remained financially invested in the capital of Agnès. In subsequent years, Aubert invested in the capital of other fashion firms and launched multiple mergers and acquisitions. His project was to offer these firms more capital in order to help them branch out to the United States.[33]

Prosperous Paquin

Little documentation exists of the financial history of haute couture; thus, the industry is something of a black box. The couturiers themselves voiced various reasons for this state of affairs; keeping the numbers a mystery made their trade seem more prestigious, for example, and they wanted to protect their clients' accounts from the public eye. Another explanation is that most haute couture firms then kept day-to-day accounting that was functional but also rather rudimentary. At the turn of the century, Paris haute couture firms did not publish their balance sheets.

The history of Paris couture firms in London shows the development of a management model that brought haute couture closer to the department stores by way of the boards of directors and major investors. In contrast to those in Paris, some of the British-based haute couture limited liability firms published their balance sheets. The archives available for these firms show partial series of net profits during the years 1897 to 1912 for Paquin Ltd., 1902 to 1924 for Dœuillet Ltd., and 1908 to 1925 for Martial and Armand & Co.[34] In the case of Paquin Ltd.,

**FIGURE 1.2 The house of Paquin dressed this monumental statue of the
Parisienne that graced the entrance to the grounds of the 1900 Paris World's Fair.**
Author's collection.

the most important haute couture firm during the years documented here, profits were very important. The financial journalists of the era called the firm "prosperous Paquin." Its net profits reached a first all-time high of 82,613 pounds, 7 shillings, and 9 pence in 1900, the year of the Paris World's Fair in which Paquin held a prominent place, as shown in Figure 1.2. In 1908, a comparison of net profits for the three firms for which series exist shows that Paquin made the highest profit, of 88,820 pounds. The house of G. Beer, whose capital was nearly as high as Paquin's, made a net profit of 39,729 pounds.[35]

Paquin was a British firm that opened a Paris branch in 1896 and henceforth had to pay taxes in both countries. For the year 1900, the firm's London branch increased its profits by 800 pounds over 1899, but the firm had to pay an extra 2,338 pounds in income tax. The board of directors accepted this situation and did not, in those years, discuss a possible modification to the statutes of the firm, because such an international setup in couture was perceived as having more advantages than drawbacks.[36]

Seasonal variations further affected the profits of haute couture. It was crucial to make good sales in the high season, when a collection was presented to both private clients and corporate buyers. The archives of the house of Agnès show that in the years from 1907 to 1910, sales regularly reached rock bottom in July and in December, sometimes down to 20,000 francs per month, just before the showings of the big collections. But in August 1910, sales rose to 330,000 francs at their highest point, when Agnès presented her winter collection. Seasonal irregularity is one of the markers of creativity-induced risk for the haute couture houses. This fragility could be mitigated by the fidelity of private clients.[37]

Haute couture was sensitive to exogenous factors, notably to crises in politics and finance. Paquin's sales peaked in 1900–1901. The board members thought that this was caused by the optimism created in the wake of the 1900 World's Fair. Paquin then experienced a crisis in 1907 because of the effect that the financial crash in the United States had on its American private and corporate buyers. Wartime would be another source of difficulties for haute couture.[38] Other firms, like Dœuillet, and Martial and Armand, made more modest profits but remained in decent financial health until World War I. As a comparison, in 1911 Martial and Armand made a net profit of 10,226 pounds, while Paquin reached its highest prewar net profit, which amounted to 134,716 pounds. Haute couture profits diminished sharply during the war and were further impacted by the considerable loss of value of the French franc, which had abandoned the gold standard at the outbreak of the war. Martial and Armand was in the red in 1915, in 1917, and again in the early 1920s.[39]

Even in times of peace, haute couture firms faced significant challenges. Alfred Chandler has shown that unsold stocks of clothes created a risk that grew with time as the clothes in stock became increasingly unfashionable. His observation applied to large-scale retailing firms, especially department stores. In the case of haute couture, most of the garments were bespoke, and what remained in the firms' stocks was mainly fabrics and precious materials like fur. Provided that the conditions of conservation were good, most raw-materials stocks did not depreciate. The value of Paquin's stocks was rather stable: in 1897, they amounted to 15,152 pounds, and in 1902, to 20,605 pounds. But Paquin shares were exchanged at a rather modest price compared with the prosperity of the firm, brand value, and stable stock value. The question, then, is what held Paquin from being valued higher if not its stocks.[40]

To find an answer, we can examine Paquin's accounting, which shows very high sums in a post called "sundry debtors." This phrase was used to designate unpaid clients' accounts. Sums owed by clients of Paquin reached amounts that could be ten times the value of the firm's stocks and more than twice the firm's profit. Paquin's accounts show a continuous rise in sundry debts: in 1897, the sundry debts amounted to 106,755 pounds, and in 1902, to 196,627 pounds. The sundry debts were also, for each year, roughly double the very high net profits of Paquin. Clients of high-end shops were slow to pay for reasons of prestige. It was tactless to ask clients to pay their bills and inconceivable to switch to a system of cash payments, reflected board member Sir Alfred Newton. The more prestigious the client, the longer she waited to settle her bills. According to Newton, who aimed to reassure the firm's shareholders, these sums were usually paid back in due course. The sundry debtors' accounts were closed on December 31 of each year, at the time that debts reached their highest level. The clients continually replaced their debts with new ones. Despite shareholders' warnings about possible losses both of orders and in dividends, Paquin did not refuse credit to clients.[41] Sundry debts were so high that they were considered the reason why haute couture firms could not make better use of their capital. They were also considered an obstacle to investments in modernizing equipment. The issue of sundry debtors shows that it was difficult to change the notion of service attached to haute

PAQUIN & JOIRE

PAQUIN FUR
CREATIONS
are now directly
available to American
women at a saving of
the import duty
through the founding
of this establishment
where a staff of Paquin
experts will reproduce
models in the distinc-
tive fashions charac-
teristic of their Paris
Salon.

*A wonderful sable
coat executed by the
French House, Paquin
& Joire, 398 Fifth
Ave., New York*

398 Fifth Avenue, 36th and 37th Streets, **New York**

FIGURE 1.3 In 1912, Jeanne Paquin opened a branch in New York,
directed by her half brother Henri Joire.
Vogue.

couture, even after it had become incompatible with the thirst of the firms for
cash flow. This was especially problematic when haute couture houses tried to
branch out into foreign markets (see Figure 1.3).[42]

Jeanne Paquin developed the international advertising of her company as a part
of globalizing couture. She toured the United States in 1910, showing 150 designs on a dozen mannequins. Paquin spent half a million French francs on this

initiative, but she refused to sell anything on the American market during her tour, which she presented instead as an artistic exhibition.[43] In turn, other couturiers started to explore the US market. Poiret, who had established his own firm in 1903, went on an American tour the year after Paquin.[44] In 1912, Paquin opened a shop selling furs under the name Paquin-Joire at 398 Fifth Avenue in New York. Paquin had hired Henri Joire, her younger half brother, as a joint manager for the Paris shop in 1909. In 1912, she put him, along with his wife, in charge of the management of the New York shop. Paquin's efforts in the dissemination of one of the key French industries abroad was acknowledged when in 1913 she was the first French woman fashion entrepreneur to be named Chevalier of the Légion d'Honneur. She pursued her international career by opening two additional branches of Paquin Ltd., in Buenos Aires in 1912 and in Madrid in 1914. Paquin was the most profitable of all Paris haute couture firms and was directed by a woman. The gender shift toward women couturiers was confirmed by the new generation of younger entrepreneurs who started their activity during those years and who all, like Paquin, were from modest backgrounds: Jeanne Lanvin started her business in 1909, Madeleine Vionnet in 1912, and Gabrielle Chanel in 1913.[45]

Sewing in New York

Seen from the United States, haute couture was a high-class industry that had no equivalent in the largest American centers, while New York had developed as the world's major center for garment manufacturing. *Godey's Lady's Book,* America's most read women's magazine, published from 1830 to 1898, brought fashion into many homes. New periodicals—like *Harper's Bazaar,* published since 1867, and *Vogue,* founded in the United States in 1892—extended fashion's reach. American women living in prairie cabins wore calico dresses for everyday life and work. They made their best clothes, worn on Sundays and special occasions, sometimes with the help of local seamstresses who worked from designs brought to them by the fashion pages and rendered accessible through the wide dissemination of paper patterns. New York was the bridgehead for fashion dissemination, where all buyers and journalists converged to keep abreast of the new trends. Publications and buyers working for large retail centers all over America circulated trends to the largest consumer market in the world.[46]

The French couturiers who, like Boué, Paquin, and Poiret, crossed the Atlantic with the project of exploring new markets visited several American cities, notably two important centers of retail on the East Coast: Boston, home to the department store Filene's, and Philadelphia, home to Wanamaker's. But Paris couturiers were first and foremost attracted by New York, the heart of the American garment industry, where the majority of the clothes worn in the United States were designed, cut, sewn, and sold to retailers. Immigrants—among them many Jews from Germany, from other countries of central Europe, and from Russia—provided a constantly renewed flow of men, women, and children to work in the city's garment industries. There was no need to master English, the language of the new country, to operate a sewing machine or to finish garments by hand. Workshops specialized by garment type—for example, coats, suits, or dresses—as well as by price, which determined the quality of the textile and manufacture. The American garment industries were divided into two groups: the tailored, or cloak and suit, industry and the draped, or dress, industry. Men, women, and children working at home in tenement buildings were responsible for a significant segment of clothing production in New York, especially in the lower grades of manufacturing. Work was divided between jobbers and contractors. Jobbers decided on styles and bought the primary materials. Some had their own employees to cut the fabrics, and others subcontracted cutting as well. Then the jobbers distributed the work to contractors, who assembled the garments. Contractors were small units of production: on average, their workshops counted twenty-five employees, and there was much turnover in this part of the industry. Subcontracting, a way by which an industrialist delegated all or part of his production to workshops owned by a third party, was at the core of problems in labor conditions. The jobbers tended to play out the competition among contractors in order to bring down their costs. The lack of direct control over the workshops and the pressure for cheaper production resulted in both reduced wages and increased demands on the workers (see Figure 1.4). In the lower echelons, work was distributed at home to women, who often reverted to redistributing some of their orders among their family to complete a sufficient number of pieces in the required time. Historians have shown how the conditions of production fluctuated over time and how positive developments in labor were never guaranteed stability.[47]

The production of a dress from the idea to the retail floor started with the choice of a design. The sample maker created one dress from that design. That proto-

FIGURE 1.4 Photograph of a New York garment manufacturing workshop, ca. 1910.
Reproduction courtesy of Kheel Center for Labor-Management Documentation & Archives, Cornell University.

type was used by the pattern maker to draw and cut patterns for each part of the garment, in all of the sizes that were expected to be manufactured. Then, the manufacturer chose the fabric, which was placed on tables in several layers—the more layers, the cheaper the price of the garment. This was called the *lay*. A cutter would then cut all the pieces of the pattern through the lay. Cutters, who were usually men and were the best-paid workers in the trade, used a vertical blade for the bulk of the work and a circular machine for finer work and smaller pieces. All the cut parts corresponding to one garment were then assembled in *bundles*. Errand boys took the bundles to the operators, mostly women, who assembled the dresses on sewing machines. Assembled dresses then went to the finishing department. Then clothes were finally sent to pressing. The price of a dress was a function of the quality of fabric, the attention to design, and the care spent in manufacturing operations. The price of the garments organized the New York workshops along categories of production.[48]

Starting a firm at the turn of the century required very little capital; a few hundred dollars could be enough to start a workshop. American fashion firms were usually very small and not listed on the stock exchange, resulting in a greater freedom in the conduct of business for the entrepreneurs, who did not have to comply with a board of shareholders. Within the different specializations of the New York garment industry, the dress business registered the fastest growth because it required the least expensive material and the fewest technical skills. Dresses were considered the chief product of the American garment industry.[49] One of the entrepreneurs who started modestly was Maurice Rentner. Born in Poland in 1889, he immigrated as a child to the United States with his half brother Harry. At seventeen, Rentner started working for a shirtwaist manufacturer as a salesman. Three years later, in 1909, he started on his own, manufacturing shirtwaists and dresses under the name Gill & Rentner on 24th Street. A bit later, the two brothers moved to West 33rd Street. In 1923, Maurice and Harry split. Maurice then briefly partnered in Louis Lustig & Maurice Rentner Inc. In 1928, the two brothers were back in business together, as Maurice and Harry Rentner Inc., but would split again after a few months.[50]

A good designer was known to be essential to the success of any dress business in New York, which is why designers were paid better than head seamstresses and tailors. Yet the New York designers were anonymous. Unlike the Paris couturiers, they were most often paid by the hour, did not enjoy long-term positions, and remained in the shadows of the industry. While Paquin, Beer, and Dœuillet had become brand names, Maurice Rentner and his fellow manufacturers working in New York did not enjoy a similar celebrity. Rentner considered himself to be of more modest origins than the German Jews who were often more settled and occupied more patrician positions in the city's garment industry. But he had the advantage of impeccable taste, and his flair for aesthetics allowed him to make the right choices regarding what would sell well during the coming seasons. In his first years in the business, Rentner made the choice to produce decent-quality clothes while cutting costs, pushing the quality higher and the workforce prices down, and he kept his workshops outside of the unions until 1932. Nonunionized workshops paid their workers less than the unionized firms and could expect that the workers would not follow strike orders emitted by the unions.[51]

The transfer of the making of clothes from home to the factory brought important changes to the lives of workers, who were increasingly employed away from home and commuted to the production centers. This change was especially visible in the shirtwaist industry—the segment of the garment industry that made women's shirts. Larger workshops and more organized spaces developed into medium or large units of several dozen or even a hundred workers. Machines in workshops were similar to those used at home yet more specialized and faster; gradually, foot power was replaced by electrification. While 64.8 percent of sewing machines in the garment industry were treadle-powered in 1900, this was the case for just 20 percent of the machines in 1911. The ranges of quality and prices in the garment industry were diverse, yet the work relied on human agency and manual work, whether in cheaper manufacturing or in haute couture.[52]

During those years, the bulk of the American mass manufacturing of wholesale garments and apparel shifted from its original production site on Manhattan's Lower East Side, where Rentner had started his career, toward the part of the city known as the garment district, a portion of Manhattan delineated by 20th and 40th Streets and by Broadway and Eighth Avenue. In this crowded area, workshops made a substantial part of the clothing sold in the US domestic markets. Pennsylvania Station (whose construction was finished in 1910) became the commuting node for both workers and fashion buyers. Upon arriving in the city, buyers found everything they needed, including entertainment, within a few blocks' radius.[53]

The most ambitious of the New York garment manufacturers invested in the real estate of this part of town, contributing to a change in the appearance of the city by financing the building of skyscrapers that hosted their workshops and showrooms. In 1919, Rentner was among the investors in a milestone of the New York garment district, the Garment Center Capitol Building at 498 Seventh Avenue, shown in Figure 1.5, and he kept investing in real estate as his career grew, at 500 Seventh Avenue and elsewhere, in the garment district.[54]

Cutting across style and quality, a major dividing line ran through the garment district between unionized and nonunionized workshops. The latter could pay cheaper wages and further pushed competition in the fashion industry. In unionized shops, however, tensions arose along gendered lines, as men tended to be given the most skilled jobs (for example, cutters), and the rules of the American Federation of Labor, the main union, did not serve the needs of the unskilled women workers. Over time, tensions grew on both the production line and the gender line, resulting in increased strikes. The most important of these erupted in 1909 and 1910 among women garment workers, demanding better conditions for factory work. Their movement became known as the Uprising of the Twenty

FIGURE 1.5 Advertisement for the Garment Center Capitol, a real estate landmark in which numerous fashion entrepreneurs invested, including Maurice Rentner.
Women's Wear Daily, *March 11, 1927, p. 9. © Fairchild Publishing LLC.*

Thousand. The biggest labor revolt of women in America at that point in history, it contributed to wider unionization, especially of women workers through the International Ladies Garment Workers Union (ILGWU).[55]

The next year, a labor accident of major proportions further pushed demands for change in labor conditions in New York. The Triangle Shirtwaist Factory fire of March 25, 1911, resulted in the deaths of 146 workers, most of them women, some of them teenagers. The fire started in the factory, located on the eighth, ninth, and tenth floors of the Asch Building at the north corner of Washington Place and Greene Street. Despite regulations, the factory's exits were locked to prevent workers from taking unplanned time off or sneaking out merchandise for unauthorized resale. The fire started from a cigarette—forbidden by the workshop rules—that had fallen into a bin of fabric scraps and spread rapidly on the factory floor, too quickly for all the employees to escape. The 146 workers who died were caught in the fire or jumped from the building's windows. The Triangle Shirtwaist Factory fire was the fourth-deadliest work accident in the history of the United States. It played a political, social, and symbolic role in the development of conscientious workers, government, and the public. The accident provoked strong reactions among the population, the trade unions, and the legislature of the State of New York, which voted in new regulations, including new safety rules and systematic inspections to verify their enforcement. Other improvements made in the following years included revisions to wages and to the length of the workday. New York's garment workers became the best paid in the world during the interwar period, but the securing of decent labor conditions remained a constant subject of tensions, especially in the lower-grade manufacturing trades.[56]

Fashion in World War I

On August 3, 1914, France entered into World War I, but the United States would only declare war on Germany on April 6, 1917. Numerous fashion professionals continued traveling to France during the four years that the war lasted, navigating the Atlantic despite warfare to see the new designs that Paris kept producing.[57] Among them was *Vogue* director Edna Woolman Chase, who—much later, at the outbreak of another war in 1939—shared her memories of World War I with a group of professionals, the New York Fashion Group: "I was in Paris this summer also. . . . In 1914 as in 1939, August was the month the French dressmakers held their Openings, but in those days they were not quite so early. Then, the important houses did not show until about August 10th. . . . While France mobilized the eager American buyers snatched at every garment they could get—taking the original model, finished or unfinished, because, of course, it was impossible at that moment for couturiers to take any orders for duplication."[58]

An entire generation of couturiers experienced the war as soldiers. The young crop of male couturiers that included Paul Poiret, Jean Patou, Lucien Lelong, and Edward Molyneux was mobilized at the onset of the conflict in 1914. Some of these absentee couturiers closed shop, while others delegated the pursuit of their business to assistants. Soon after the mobilization, the Paris couture industry went back to business.[59] Despite the initial moment of panic, Paris couture remained in operation throughout the war nearly untouched, in Chase's memory: "Looking back at the records of the last war I find that except for that first season of 1914 when there was great disorganization owing to the mobilization of the troops, France never really missed holding her regular Spring and Autumn Openings. In fact, the couture industry was so well organized again by the Autumn of 1915 that a group of French houses sent a large and beautiful collection of winter models to New York, and again under the auspices of *Vogue* there was a great Fashion Fête at the Ritz. Society and trade flocked to see the new French clothes and most of the models were bought by the New York shops."[60]

Chase was correct in her recollection that the haute couture openings kept their regular seasonal schedules. In November 1914 the French couturiers associated with *Vogue* magazine organized a "Fashion Fête" in New York, showing haute couture dresses and aiming to raise funds for the Paris couture workers on the home front and for the war orphans. The couturiers repeated the Fashion Fête in 1915, and during that same year, an important group of Paris couturiers exhibited their designs at the Panama–Pacific International Exposition in San Francisco. At the Chambre Syndicale de la Couture Parisienne, committee members had decided by twelve votes to fifteen that they would not participate as a collective; instead, they sent works as individual participants.[61]

Some American fashion-business insiders were skeptical as to the independence of the New York garment industry from Paris, while others—notably Edward Bok, the editor of the *Ladies' Home Journal*—believed that American design could lead. A new US tour that Paquin carried out in 1914 was met with opposition by groups of American buyers who resented French competition in their own country.[62] American manufacturers liked to advertise their products as typically Parisian, which was not forbidden under US law but was viewed by the French entrepreneurs as unauthorized taking—even when the garments had been designed in the workshops of the Lower East Side. The interest that Paquin and Poiret developed in the conquest of foreign markets went hand in hand with their desire to capitalize on the dissemination of their designs. Authentic Paquin could only be bought in the firm's branches, insisted chairman John Barker at a board meeting in March 1914. Counterfeits were met with disapproval because, as Barker added, Paquin designs were the fruit of great "thought and labour."[63] Soon an antipiracy campaign ensued on both sides of the Atlantic, led by Poiret. With a modest capital of 50,000 French francs and a staff of eight people, Poiret opened a small boutique in the rue Auber in 1903. In the years that followed, Poiret renewed the feminine silhouette, moved the waistline and shortened the skirts, or even replaced them with harem pants. Poiret, along with Chanel, Paquin, and Vionnet, was among the couturiers who gave women's bodies a new freedom. All this earned him fame and financial success. He earned 6,500 francs with his July 1906 collection, 500,000 francs in July 1913, and over 12 million in the following five months. Poiret did not stop there. In 1911 he was the first couturier to venture into perfume. He named his perfume business Les Parfums de Rosine, after his first daughter; but by doing so, he missed the opportunity to capitalize on his name. That same year, Poiret also opened a school in decorative arts for young girls, named after his second daughter, Martine. Ateliers Martine soon expanded to include an interior design business. In so doing, Poiret was a pioneer in the art deco movement, which would reach a peak with the 1925 Paris Exposition des Arts Décoratifs.[64]

Poiret was also one of the first couturiers to try to capitalize on the American copies of his designs.[65] In 1913, he traveled to the United States and spent three weeks lecturing in Baltimore, Boston, Buffalo, Chicago, New York, and Philadelphia. He spoke at Carnegie Hall and took the stage in department stores Gimbel Brothers, Macy's, and Wanamaker's. During this tour, Poiret launched his costumes of Asian and Middle Eastern inspiration on the American market. He secured a commercial contract with the New York firm Larrymade Waists, for which he provided original designs of blouses for US retailing.[66]

Back in France, Poiret united his peers and, on June 14, 1914, founded the Syndicat de défense de la grande couture française et des industries qui s'y rattachent (Syndicate of Defense of French Dressmakers), an association smaller than the Chambre Syndicale. Poiret was president of the new syndicate, and Jacques Worth was its vice president. The Defense Syndicate opened a New York office in 1914, represented by Philippe Ortiz of *Vogue* magazine. In 1916, Poiret spoke to his peers in the Chambre Syndicale to denounce the copying of Paris creations, first and foremost by German and Austrian firms, but also by American manufacturers. The *New York Times* published the complete version of Poiret's discourse, in which he wished to "wage war against the intrusion of foreign firms in France"; to "fight against imitation and counterfeiting"; and to "fight against the invasion of foreign workers." With this new Defense Syndicate, Poiret aimed to increase the protection of haute couture designs on international markets and to regulate design dissemination through the *Vogue* pattern service that sold official Paris couture patterns. But the association was short-lived, because its uncompromising policies deterred the average international clients, who bought a few designs in Paris and sought inspiration to design their collections for overseas markets. Poiret kept nurturing ambitions on the US market. In 1916 he introduced a line of ready-to-wear described as genuine reproductions, licensed to New York manufacturer Max Grab and bearing a special label. Poiret had expected the American market to pay royalties to Paris couturiers, but this did not happen.[67]

The discourses on the appropriation of Paris fashion by American firms appear to be considerably nuanced. Most of the so-called French garments sold in America were retailed with fake origins. The majority of designs were created in America, as well as the fashion plates published in the American press. Numerous shops closed in the summer and advertised that they were going to see the collections in Paris but never went any farther than New England to observe what the American socialites wore. Paris fashions sold in America, observes historian Marlis Schweitzer, were heavily mediated by the US industry. It thus hardly comes as a surprise that, during World War I, Paris couturiers distanced themselves from Poiret's view and sought a more moderate stance toward both American markets and design copying. In 1915, couturiers Callot Sœurs, Jenny, Premet, and Martial and Armand left the Defense Syndicate. The houses of Lelong and Paquin voiced their disagreement with Poiret's views. Soon after, the Chambre Syndicale took over the syndicate's antipiracy activities on a more moderate line. Among this group of moderates was Paquin, who in 1913 had become the vice president of the Chambre Syndicale. Her peers then elected her president of the Chambre Syndicale from 1917 to 1919, making her the first woman to preside over an employers' syndicate in France.[68]

Anti-German Couture?

Anti-Germanic sentiments, fueled by the idea that the Berlin and Vienna fashion industries were competitors that threatened to supplant and destroy French fashion, were present among Paris fashion entrepreneurs before World War I. Berlin and Vienna were important centers for the printing of fashion magazines and fashion plates, which the French couturiers tended to despise as being counterfeited from their own publications. During the war, the French fashion business was marked by an unprecedented surge of patriotic spirit and exacerbated anti-Germanism. This altered the existing connections between the French fashion business and the entrepreneurs who had bases, or even merely connections, in Germany and Austria-Hungary.[69]

This general spirit of fashion chauvinism threated to have severe consequences on one Paris couture firm, the Société Ch. Drecoll, which was exposed for its connections with the enemy during the war. The firm had been founded by Christoph von Drecoll in Vienna on the basis of a previous fashion business. In 1895, Drecoll was purchased by a group of investors: Sylvain Kahn, who had obtained French citizenship; Albert Sally Berg, a German couturier; a Swiss, Pierre Besançon de Wagner; and Wagner's Belgian wife, Marguerite van Speybrouck.[70] Kahn and Berg, who brought 300,000 French francs to the capital of Drecoll, opened a Paris branch in 1903, managed by Wagner. In 1908, the Paris firm Ch. Drecoll was replaced by a British firm, Ch. Drecoll Ltd., founded by Kahn, Berg, and Wagner on the model of Paquin Ltd. The society Ch. Drecoll Ltd. managed two haute couture houses, one in Vienna and the other in Paris. The capital of Ch. Drecoll Ltd. was then £296,000. Advertisements of the Paris branch highlighted the firm's Viennese origins.[71]

At the outbreak of the war, the firm's connections to Austria and Germany turned against its owners. Eugène Aine, president of the Chambre Syndicale, voiced critiques directed at the Drecoll firm's enemy origins. These critiques were in turn echoed in the French National Assembly by representative Adrien Gaudin de Villaine during a discussion of the statuses of enemy business in France.

Wagner, managing director of Drecoll, resented these critiques and attacked Aine in the civil court on the grounds of defamation, demanding 200,000 francs in damages. Maitre de Monzie argued in court on behalf of Wagner that the firm Drecoll Ltd. was British and that its board's president was the British press magnate Davison Dalziel. Aside from Wagner and Berg, all the board members were British. Drecoll's capital, now amounting to 500,000 francs, was in Dutch and British hands. Aine hired lawyer Auguste Champetier de Ribes for his defense and rallied the support of his fellow members of the Chambre Syndicale to his anti-Germanic position. The Chambre paid the costs of Aine's lawsuit. Wagner got out of the lawsuit without the damages he had asked for, but the outcome still contributed to a toning down of anti-Germanic discourses within Paris couture.[72]

Couture and Confection

In 1910, Paris couturiers sought to better establish their profession by distancing themselves from the *confection*, then the French name for garment manufacturing. Several Paris department stores, the best known of which was La Belle Jardinière, produced ready-made clothes and workwear for men and women. The production of ready-made clothes in France was divided among the workshops at the department store, workshops independent from the retailers, and individuals working at home. The customers tended to consider the stores' offerings to be functional but also rather drab garments that, in the absence of effective standardization of sizes, were often ill fitting. Two larger, more modern manufacturing firms were founded during the 1910s. Marcel Boussac, a young textile entrepreneur, created his Comptoir de l'Industrie Cotonnière in 1911. After selling supplies to the French army during World War I, Boussac started reorganizing the Comptoir and various small firms; in 1917 he transformed the Comptoir de l'Industrie Cotonnière into a société anonyme, organizing the industrial production of textiles and manufactured clothing, notably through his branch firm La Toile d'Avion. The second of these new, innovative manufactures was the Société Parisienne de Confection (SPC), founded in 1916 by Théophile Bader, owner of the department store Les Galeries Lafayette, to address the growing interest in French ready-made clothes. Bader and Boussac rationalized production and, in the years to come, built modern factory workshops that offered an industrial model of mass production that marked a break with both earlier cottage industries and couture.

In 1910 couture and confection decided to split their employers' syndicates, which had been united since 1868. Indeed, early haute couture firms like Worth mentioned in all their communications that they produced *confections*, or ready-made garments, as well as haute couture. While French confection massively industrialized in the 1910s, the haute couture firms sought to establish their independence from the new form of production. From then on, the couturiers gathered on their own in the Chambre Syndicale de la Couture Parisienne.[73]

The war had a profound impact on living conditions on the home front. The workers, their unions, and the employers' syndicates regularly discussed, or fought about, questions of salaries. One of the most pressing issues was to establish whether payment should be made in relation to piecework—that is, according to results—or as an hourly wage, based on the occupation time of the workers. Another issue was the length of the workday and the workweek. In December 1913, at the high-pressure time of year preceding the Christmas holidays, representatives of the haute couture workers asked the Chambre Syndicale to have their workweeks scheduled in the same way as the "English week," which at that time meant closing the workshops at noon on Saturdays and having Sundays free. But the employers in the Chambre Syndicale replied that switching schedules to adopt the English week would be detrimental to their profession, as Saturdays were days for shopping, parties, and balls.[74] Then, at the onset of the war, the haute couture firms, including those that were members of the Chambre Syndicale, decided to diminish hourly wages. Workers in couture faced mounting difficulties in making ends meet. In 1917, their working conditions, characterized by long hours and wages as low as fifty centimes per day for beginning apprentices, had become untenable, and the patriotic drive behind the war effort was wearing out as it seemed that the conflict would never end. Massive strikes took place in the haute couture industry between May 11 and 23, beginning at the house of Jenny. Despite the ideal of preserving a united home front, the French strike movements peaked in 1917. The highest number of strikes took place in the textile and garment industries: a total of 360 strikes involving 125,272 strikers.[75]

Members of the Chambre Syndicale had uneven views on the dialogue that they should have with the workers. Several members, notably Eugène Aine, who was the head of Aine-Montaillé and specialized in mourning dress, were known to be aware of the social problems in their trade. Mourning clothes were characterized by the high speed of work required to finish the garments on time, as they were ordered for funerals; this added considerable pressure on the workers. Aine was also known in the profession for his political leaning toward social Catholicism. Both Aine and Paquin agreed to sit down with the Christian trade unions, notably the Confédération Française des Travailleurs Chrétiens, of which numerous couture workers were members, but they remained unresponsive to the demands of the communist workers, whether unionized or not.[76]

During the 1917 strikes, fears of political instability added to economic pressure, which made it unusually difficult for Aine and Paquin, the leading figures of the Chambre Syndicale, to rally all members behind an agreement on workers' wages. Nonetheless, the Chambre Syndicale membership and another employers' syndicate, the Chambre des Tailleurs-Couturiers, set up a commission to address the strikes and asked Paquin to be its president. Paquin and the commission members opened the dialogue with the workers and accepted two demands: a raise in the hourly wage, and the adoption of the English workweek. The workers' representatives accepted the settlement, but contestation arose from within the ranks of the employers' syndicates; some members thought that Paquin had ceded too easily to the workers' demands. The hourly wages were readjusted before the adoption of the new rules. In the wake of these discussions, Aine offered his resignation from the presidency of the Chambre Syndicale, and Paquin then took over, with the aim of finalizing the labor reform. At the end of World War I, Paquin was at the end of her career. She stepped down from the presidency of the Chambre Syndicale in 1919 and retired from the direction of her firm the next year, handing over the design of the Paquin collections to her assistant, Madeleine Wallis.[77]

At the turn of the century, Americans had become the most important buyers of haute couture, based on large and new fortunes. A growing middle class in the United States was eager to access fashionable goods. They replaced the nineteenth-century clientele composed of the French high bourgeoisie and aristocrats from various European countries and from Russia.[78] The Revolution of 1917 had turned the world of most haute couture clients upside down, and some White Russian noblewomen who had fled the regime shifted from being the most discerning clients of haute couture to the industry's best entrepreneurs and its sought-after workers. In the small world of Paris couture, ruined Russian and central European aristocrats found a profession to support themselves in exile. A handful opened their own haute couture houses in Paris: the houses of Irfe, Kitmir, and Myrbor were established by Russian exiles and helped bring new skills and aesthetics to Paris fashion. The house of Kitmir, for example, specialized in embroidery and worked in partnership with a new, innovative couturiere, Gabrielle Chanel. Another group of émigrés that increasingly entered the Paris fashion world from the 1910s onward were the numerous Armenian immigrants who had fled violence and genocide in the Ottoman Empire. Many opened small businesses in tailoring, shoemaking, and manufacturing in wholesale couture. On both sides of the Atlantic the dress trade was quick to absorb waves of immigrants and integrate them in the culture of the fashion industry.[79]

Exiting Britain

The house of Paquin's sales picked up in 1913, but this was followed by losses in 1914. For the first time since its foundation in 1896, Paquin Ltd. did not pay any dividends to shareholders.[80] Unrecovered debts led to more difficulties. Eventually, the risk carried by sundry debts hit home: many of Paquin's clients who bought their clothes on a line of credit did not settle their bills when war broke out. The house of Paquin had to tap into its reserves to survive. Paquin's conservative strategies, through which the firm had accumulated the maximum amount of cash reserves planned in its statutes—then £150,000—and refused to distribute them to shareholders, were paying off. Although documentation of the firm's finances remains fragmentary for the period of World War I, Paquin remained active during the conflict. The years 1915 and 1916 were marked by losses as well, albeit minor ones in comparison with 1914. Profits came back in 1917, and from then on Paquin worked to regain prosperity.[81]

The 1920s were marked by drastic changes in haute couture. Consumer culture changed as well. To this should be added the important loss of value of the French currency during the decade. Paquin still paid taxes on revenues in France and in Great Britain, and in such a context the firm's board of directors, in 1923, again examined the possibility of dividing the business into two separate firm units, one based in Paris and the other in London. Yet, the benefits of internationalization still seemed significant enough to maintain the status quo for a few more years. Jeanne Paquin died in 1936. The house of Paquin remained active until 1956.[82]

Variations in the exchange rate between French francs and the British pound made taxes a heavier burden for the British couture limited liabilities with most of their operations located in France. The first haute couture firm to react to this situation was Ch. Drecoll Ltd., in 1922. That year, the administrators of Drecoll started winding down the London-based firm and replacing it with a French firm.[83] In the early 1920s, maintaining a British limited liability firm was no longer a sound financial decision for a Paris haute couture house. Apart from Paquin, all the haute couture limited liabilities organized the liquidation of their British firms and opened new French companies. London was no longer the most profitable place to open an haute couture firm, even in the case of Edward Molyneux, a British veteran who had opened an haute couture house after the war. Molyneux had British ties and a nearly all-British board of directors, yet he chose to open his firm in Paris in 1919.

With the foundation of a series of limited liabilities headquartered in Great Britain but doing most creation and retail in Paris, haute couture had engaged in a first period of internationalization before World War I. Haute couture designs created style leadership for a global fashion culture that flowed from the center to the periphery and from elites to mass consumers. These entrepreneurs had contributed to the creation of an international culture, but most of them closed their British firms in the early 1920s. The main reason that fashion businesses reverted to a local model was the steep change in currency values that took place at this time. During the transition from the nineteenth to the twentieth century, Paris haute couture fostered imitation all over the world, and New York, the world's largest garment manufacturing center, capitalized on more or less faithful renditions of fashions imagined in Paris. The next step for the Paris couturiers was to try to gain new markets in the United States, since their designs were in favor there. World War I put a halt to this first internationalization of haute couture, and in the ensuing years, the tense economic situation presented obstacles to a renewal of internationalization for haute couture.[84]

Chapter 2

Branding Haute Couture

O n April 13, 1921, Monsieur Hallard, court bailiff, accompanied by a police officer, rang the bell of the couture house of Henriette Boudreaux in
the rue Vignon, a narrow street in the Opéra neighborhood, between the
Madeleine church and the Galeries Lafayette department store. Henriette Boudreaux
would have preferred to send away the unannounced visitors, but they reminded her
that, according to the law, she had no choice but to admit them. On the premises,
Hallard operated methodically, putting aside eight dresses and one cape of precious
silks. The men swiftly folded, piled, and boxed the materials, then left with the stacks
in their arms. After their departure, the seamstress tried to restore some order to her
shop. Boudreaux owned the enterprise, which catered to a solid middle-class clientele. Her wedding dresses had been photographed in glossy magazines featuring socialites and nobility.[1] Boudreaux had received warning signs that Hallard would
visit. Six weeks earlier, on February 24, one of her clients, Madame de Bigault, had
been required by the same bailiff to hand over a new dress that Boudreaux had just
delivered to her, because it was a counterfeit of an haute couture design. Now a dozen
beautiful pieces, nearly ready to be delivered, had just been swept from her work
table. She had to reimburse her suppliers, and the clients for whom she had been
making these dresses would not come back.[2]

Months later, on December 30, 1921, Boudreaux was standing in the dock in
the Twelfth Chamber of the small-crimes court (*correctionelle*) of the Seine.
Though it was the very end of the year, the small-crimes court was bustling with

activity. Judgments proceeded throughout the day on cases involving theft, fraud and swindling, vagrancy and drunkenness in public, child molesting, and violence. Boudreaux had arrived to the court as a free woman. Most counterfeiting lawsuits were about the wine trade; offenders included dealers being sued for wine adulteration, having added water, sugar, or sometimes more dangerous substances like plaster or chemicals to their wines sold at retail. Some of them faked popular drinks like Byrrh or Quinquina Dubonnet. Wine producers took the matter seriously, and their syndicates were quick to sue the counterfeiters.[3] The French winemakers lobbied the government for more legal protection of the *terroir* and of public health, and the increasing number of court cases was an indication that they were pressing toward their goal. It would still be fourteen years before they achieved, in 1935, the institution of the controlled denomination of origins, or Appellations d'Origine Contrôlée.[4]

Seamstress Boudreaux had been summoned to the court by Madeleine Vionnet, one of the most celebrated designers of the interwar period. Vionnet's house, though already famous, was still small, and Boudreaux probably did not anticipate the outcome of the audience that took place that day. The court carefully compared the dresses taken from her premises, as well as the dress seized from Madame de Bigault, with designs signed by Vionnet, who had registered all of them with the industrial board known as the Conseil des Prud'hommes de la Seine prior to the seizures, depositing photographs of the front, back, and sides of each garment. The board had registered them in sealed envelopes bearing the dates of the deposits: October 5 and 14 and December 22, 1920, and March 9, 1921. Now these envelopes were opened and brought to the court, where officers, in the presence of the prosecutor (Procureur de la République), compared every feature of the Boudreaux garments with the Vionnet designs.[5] In five cases, the court judged the "servile copy" (*copie servile*) of Vionnet by Boudreaux.[6] In four others, said the court, Boudreaux had copied the essential features with some modifications to dissimulate imitation.[7] The judgment also indicated that, in certain situations, Boudreaux had made two or more copies of a Vionnet original, with only small modifications. This was true of a design characterized by several rows of horizontal fringe that was a particular success with Boudreaux's clients at the time.[8] Important witnesses testified for Vionnet. Her fellow couturier Jacques Worth talked about the need to reinforce the laws protecting designs. Sem, a caricaturist who drew portraits of Vionnet and her clients for the newspapers, spoke up to say that his friend was a great artist. Cécile Sorel, an actress and client of Vionnet's, made an appearance in the court and praised Vionnet's work as a form of art.[9] Boudreaux acknowledged the copying but argued that she had only taken inspiration from drawings published in fashion newspapers. Although Bailiff Hallard had found no Vionnet originals in Boudreaux's workshop, the court concluded that Boudreaux was not being honest in her attribution of her inspiration, deciding that her copies could only have been made by a person with an intimate knowledge of Vionnet's originals.

Boudreaux was condemned on the grounds of the author's rights law of July 1793, as revised in March 1902. In its judgment regarding Boudreaux, the court also evoked the law of 1909 protecting applied and industrial arts, noting that Vionnet's designs were "the result of personal experience and work, and adding most often to their elegance, their very certain taste, a cachet of undeniable aesthetic originality that individualizes them."[10] The same paragraph of the judgment mentions that fashion creations were generally included in salons and exhibitions along with other arts and crafts. Boudreaux had to pay 1,000 francs in fines, plus 12,000 francs to Madeleine Vionnet for the damages incurred. The counterfeited garments were confiscated and handed over to Vionnet. Boudreaux had to pay for the publicity of the judgment rendered against her as well, totaling six articles in newspapers chosen by Vionnet, not to exceed 500 francs apiece. In total, Boudreaux owed 16,000 francs, in addition to the loss of the nine garments.[11]

After Boudreaux left the court that day, her case was followed by that of two sisters; Mesdames Miler, the younger and the elder, were called next into the Twelfth Chamber. The Miler sisters had their room and workshop at 77 rue des Petits-Champs, between the Opéra and the Sentier, in the garment manufacturing district of Paris and not far from Boudreaux's workshop.[12] The two sisters had received a similar visit by Bailiff Hallard, who had seized seventeen dresses in their workshop, of which eight were considered, following a thorough comparison with the actual Vionnet registered models, to be slavish copies of Vionnet's work.[13] The counterargument presented by Bâtonnier Raoul Rousset, the Milers' defense lawyer, was that the sisters created their own designs and did not need Vionnet's productions, particularly because it was evident that fashion, Rousset insisted, followed the taste of the times. This line of reasoning was to no avail: the Miler sisters were condemned according to the same terms as Boudreaux. Nor was this the end of the good news for Vionnet. The next day, the last in the year 1921, Vionnet's victory was reported on the front page of *Women's Wear Daily*, the most important trade journal of fashion professionals, which was published in New York. The columns of the trade paper mentioned that the interest shown by American buyers in purchasing Vionnet designs through copy houses had been a major reason for her to press charges.[14]

From Rags to Riches

Madeleine Vionnet was born in 1876 in a modest milieu. Some sources say that her mother may have been a demimondaine in Monte Carlo; she later opened a successful cabaret in Paris and left Madeleine's father, who then raised the child himself. The young Madeleine was a good pupil, but her father could hardly afford a long-term education for her, so she began working as the apprentice of a *petite couturière* at age eleven. Vionnet enjoyed her work and quickly discovered that she had talent for couture. At eighteen, she married a patrolman, and soon they had a child. After a couple of years, Vionnet left her husband and child in Paris and went to work in London, primarily to learn English. She worked first in an asylum for the mentally ill, then for several small fashion businesses, and eventually she found a position at Kate Reilly's, a London shop making copies of Paris dresses. During Vionnet's absence, her child died in an accident. Little is to be found in the archival sources on the impact that her departure, then the loss of her child, had on Vionnet. But later in her career, she developed charities for her workers—including nurseries and donations of funds for infant care—which indicates that this loss may have left a deep scar on her.[15]

Back in Paris after five years in London, Vionnet found work with several fashion firms.[16] In the early 1920s only a few haute couture houses were incorporated as anonymous societies (*sociétés anonymes*), and in nearly all such cases, a majority of the shares remained in the hands of the couturier, or head designer.[17] Couture firms tended not to reveal their sales, and French law did not require enterprises that were not capitalized on the stock exchange to publish their accounts, even when they were *sociétés anonymes*.[18] The finances of most firms relied on textile manufacturers for credit and foreign corporate buyers for cash. Until the early 1930s, an average of only 25 percent of the business was done with corporate buyers, who paid cash. Textile manufacturers like Rodier or

Bianchini-Férier, the most important suppliers to couture during the interwar period, eased the burden borne by these houses by providing small quantities of fabrics in advance and then waiting to see what would sell in a collection before offering more of the relevant materials. Such loans were justified by the fact that couturiers represented "star salesmen" for these textiles.[19]

The young Vionnet apprenticed in the haute couture house of Callot Sœurs, which had been founded in 1895 and was then directed by four sisters, Marie Gerber-Callot, Marthe Bertrand, Regina Tennyson-Chantrell, and Joséphine Crimont. Vionnet was soon promoted to the rank of *première*, the director of a workshop. She became a close collaborator of Marie Gerber-Callot's, who draped her creations directly on a mannequin without preliminary sketching—a method that Vionnet adopted in her own creative process. Gerber-Callot emphasized the sleeves and started building dresses on the pattern of kimonos, a method that represented a rupture with traditional dressmaking habits, according to which the bodice and sleeves would be cut as separate pieces and then assembled to fit the three-dimensional body. Gerber-Callot's cutting methods were influential on Vionnet, who praised the quality of her apprenticeship at the house.[20]

Gerber-Callot was a pioneer in the fight against counterfeiters, alongside Paquin and Poiret. Actions by these couturiers pushed forward the French case law protecting the fashion industries.[21] In January 1920 the Callot sisters sued a counterfeiter named Giordano for the illegal reproduction of designs that they had created.[22] That same year, Gerber-Callot was made a chevalier of the Légion d'Honneur. She asked to be welcomed by the couturiere who had received the distinction before her, Paquin.[23] The judgment against Giordano strengthened the case of the couturiers against copyists. Counterfeiters were not allowed to reproduce haute couture designers in drawings, in print, or in the form of a new item of clothing. The judgment also called out the *character of novelty* that had been discerned in Callot's realizations, but this was already a thorny issue. How does one qualify novelty in an industry that produces clothes? Clothes have certain necessarily recurring elements: a body, sleeves, a skirt. Is it even possible to create *new* designs?[24] The Callot judgment mentioned that a design need not necessarily show novelty in each of its parts in order to merit protection. Succeeding judges of such things should therefore rely on a comparison of the model and the copy in a synthetic rather than analytical manner.[25] A designer, like an artist, could legitimately find inspiration in former works, but this should not provide a loophole to the counterfeiter, because "it is not possible that two persons absolutely foreign to one another and that do not work together could arrive, without the help of a document, to combine a design whose likenesses are so striking."[26] Such milestone cases made French law the most protective legal system for fashion design.

Fashion played a central role in the accession of women to entrepreneurial careers. In France, a law of July 13, 1907, gave women access to professions apart from their husbands' careers, provided that said husband would not go to court to prevent his wife from working. The law also stipulated that women had administrative powers over the production of their work, which included the freedom to dispose of their authors' rights without spousal authorization. This, in turn, allowed women to register their own creations and to fulfill all of the administrative duties attached to the registration process. Studies of women innovators and registered patents in both France and the United States demonstrate that women in the nineteenth century were represented only marginally among the innovators. The domestic economy in general and the textiles and garments industries in particular were, however, domains where women's innovation was prominent. The notion of an author's rights dated back to the French Revolution, but when Callot won her first lawsuit in 1920, her access to full rights as the author of designs had been in place barely a dozen years.[27]

In 1907, Madeleine Vionnet left her post as a *première* at Callot and accepted a post as a *modéliste* at the house of Jacques Doucet. This was a step up for Vionnet, because she was now fully acknowledged as a designer. Her collaboration with the house of Doucet lasted for five years, after which she founded her own haute couture house, in 1912, although the deed for the partnership "Madeleine Vionnet & Cie" dates from 1919. She settled at 222 rue de Rivoli with a total capital of 700,000 French francs. Vionnet brought 100,000 French francs in business assets. Henri Lillaz, the owner of the Paris department store Bazar de l'Hôtel de Ville, carmaker Emile Akar, and Bader, owner of the Galeries Lafayette, each contributed 200,000 French francs. In 1923, Akar stepped down as an investor and was replaced by Eduardo Martinez de Hoz, an Argentinian businessman famous for his passion for racehorses. Martinez de Hoz had married Dulce Liberal, a Brazilian woman who was a loyal client of Vionnet's and one of the most elegant haute couture patrons of her time. The details of Vionnet's capitalization reflect the tendency of couturiers to rely on a close-knit model of capitalization.[28] Vionnet achieved rapid renown as a creative designer and a consummate technician.[29] She was particularly at ease with the delicate techniques of the *flou* (blur): lightweight dresses for which she often used fabric on the bias, turning it at an angle of forty-five degrees from the straight grain.[30]

The Sword and the Shield

Vionnet was the designer and the public figure of her namesake firm. She worked with a managing director, Louis Dangel, who was educated as a lawyer. Vionnet hired Dangel in January 1919 to be her director under a five-year contract. Vionnet, Lillaz, and Akar signed Dangel's contract, which gave him responsibility for the management of the firm, including the hiring of employees, accounting, and managing supplies and stocks. He received a fixed salary of 60,000 francs per year, which was half of Vionnet's own salary. In addition, Dangel received the same share of the firm's profits as Vionnet: 10 percent of net before taxes.[31]

Vionnet and Dangel used intellectual property as both a shield and a sword, to protect haute couture creation and to attack copyists. It was Dangel who took the initiative to sue Boudreaux and the Miler sisters.[32] In September 1920, the house of Vionnet started campaigning in the press, with an announcement in the daily *Le Temps:* "It is reminded that the law of 1909 protects the couture designs. Any reproductions, any copies, even more or less hastily camouflaged, are forbidden."[33] In the same press insert, Vionnet added details that outlined the thinking process behind the protection of her designs. A fear of being copied on the French markets, but maybe even more so abroad, comes through clearly.[34] The judgments rendered against Boudreaux, the Miler sisters, and other counterfeiters were widely published in the French press; Paquin had similarly involved the press in her campaigns for design protection in the years 1900–1910. Dangel, in his position as manager of the firm, used a paid advertising channel but asked that reports of the fashion piracy lawsuits be published along with the crime news, called in the French dailies the *faits divers*. We cannot know whether this strategy was conscious or serendipitous, but in so doing, he signaled fashion piracy as a criminal activity. Fees owed by copyists paid for Vionnet's advertising, which appeared across the full spectrum of the French press, from the communist *L'Humanité* to the conservative *Le Figaro*.[35]

In January 1921, Vionnet published a new series of advertisements (see Figure 2.1) featuring her label, comprising three elements: her autograph, a

We again inform our
NEW YORK
customers that

Madeleine Vionnet

does not sell to Agents or Dressmakers; that her models are
registered according to the Law,
that nobody has the right to
copy them or to have them
copied and that no one has the
right to sell them without special
license from

MADELEINE VIONNET

No firm whatever holds such a
license and those who state they
are selling

MADELEINE VIONNET

models are merely imitators and
are deceiving the Public

MADELEINE VIONNET

kindly requests American Ladies
to inform their friends of these
facts and to spread the truth
abroad that:

MADELEINE VIONNET

creations are only to be obtained in Paris, 222, rue de
Rivoli.

FIGURE 2.1 Madeleine Vionnet advertises
her sales policies to her New York customers.
Women's Wear Daily, *August 2, 1921, p. 47.*

special series of numbers, and her fingerprint. To be sure of owning an original Vionnet dress, customers were invited to unpick the dress label and send it to Vionnet's firm along with their name and address, the name and address of the retailer, and the date of purchase. Another insert, titled "Headhunting," prompted the denunciation of copyists, offering a reward of at least 1,000 French francs to anyone who would bring the name of a copyist to Vionnet.[36]

During the same years, Vionnet developed her branded logo and image. She registered her brand and had a trademark logo made by the Italian futurist artist Thayaht. The logo represented a woman draping one of Vionnet's dresses on herself; it also evoked her initials, "M.V.," and was emulated by Boudreaux (see Figure 2.2). Vionnet used it on everything from her letterhead to her wrapping paper, on which she had it placed in a repeated geometric pattern.[37]

In 1921, Vionnet launched a separate brand for ready-made reproductions of some of her designs under the name Eva Boex, who was presented as a London-based French entrepreneur with the exclusive right to reproduce Vionnet's garments. These reproductions were expected to sell for 800 to 1,000 French francs, rather than the usual 4,000 to 5,000 French francs for the originals. It was a pioneering move. Couturiers had started to experiment with perfume lines, and Poiret had even experimented with home decor. But none were yet producing their own ready-to-wear or wholesale lines in the early 1920s, and Vionnet became an innovator in wholesale couture. Designs were protected by Boex's autograph signature, a special series number, the tagline "license Madeleine Vionnet," and Vionnet's fingerprint. Authentication was promised to clients under the same conditions as for haute couture garments. For quite a while, international buyers thought that Eva Boex was an actual young industrialist, before they realized the name was a fictional character invented by Vionnet to promote her own copies, which were produced at a rate of at least three copies per original design. The name covered a branch of Vionnet's activity carried out in workshops situated at 14 rue de Castiglione, one block away from her first couture house on the rue de Rivoli.[38]

Vionnet's new venture under the Boex name met with various obstacles. On the one hand, commissionaires pointed out that until Boex was able to manufacture her wholesale garments in the United States, her exports there would be subjected to a 60 percent duty that would hinder her ability to compete with other wholesalers. On the other hand, the trade press anticipated that private clients would object and even stop buying if the Vionnet collections were copied for the Boex wholesale market at a much lower price and an inferior quality. Boex undermined the typology of Paris garments and the distinction between original and copy. Even with all of this in mind, however, *Women's Wear Daily* concluded, "There is no doubt, however, of even the objectors' interest in the venture; and in contrast to those who scoff at those who praise it as the first step in the development of a very real movement to protect fashion ideas and commercialize them properly to the benefit of France."[39] The invention of wholesale couture realized by the Boex line was ahead of its time, but Vionnet failed to capitalize on her own brand name for her wholesale line.

Professional Syndicates against Piracy

In 1921, Dangel founded the Association pour la Défense des Arts Plastiques et Appliqués, whose goal was to form an alliance of haute couture and other creative professions in the name of the repression of copyists. Most Paris haute couture entrepreneurs were members of the Chambre Syndicale.[40] The late nineteenth-century movement for industrial self-government developed in France into two categories of associations. The first was the commercial *comptoir*, or cartel, which "classified products, fixed prices, set production quotas, arranged transport, and operated a common selling office."[41] The second was the employers' syndicate, of which the Chambre Syndicale is a good example, although at times, some of its actions exceeded this category and ventured into the sphere of activity of cartels, notably when fixing the prices of the workforce and establishing filtering systems for clients and media. As an employers' syndicate, the Chambre Syndicale was a group of capitalists who engaged in collective action by organizing locally and internationally, studying legislation, tariffs, and tax regimes, and developing programs for the workforce.[42] This employers' syndicate gathered together the directors of creative couture houses in Paris—that is, firms that designed their own original fashions. In interwar France, the Chambre Syndicale was the only organization of fashion professionals acknowledged by the government, the National Economic Advisory Board (Conseil national économique), the textile manufacturers syndicate (Union syndicale des tissus), and the workers' unions as having a mandate to sign collective labor agreements. The members of the Chambre Syndicale elected its president every year on the principle of one firm, one vote. The president was helped by a yearly elected board composed of two vice presidents, a secretary, a treasurer, and an auditor, who were all managing directors of haute couture firms. The members also elected a committee that prepared decisions and managed the main routine tasks of the association.[43] Nationally, the umbrella organization for fashion professionals was the Association Générale du commerce et de l'industrie des tissus et matières textiles, which listed over sixty local employers' syndicates as members and actively promoted its social work.[44] The Chambre Syndicale devoted much effort to the management of the workforce. Another aspect of the association's activity might be characterized as gatekeeping, including the arrangement of the calendar of haute couture shows.[45]

Dangel's Association pour la Défense des Arts Plastiques et Appliqués aimed to supplement the work of the Chambre Syndicale by battling copyists and counterfeiters.[46] The association pooled financial resources to advertise members' activities in press campaigns and to document their cases. It was dedicated to helping all of its members register their designs and, when needed, to taking counterfeiters to court. The association sued counterfeiters in the small-crimes court rather than in the consular jurisdiction or labor court (*juridiction consulaire*, especially the Prud'hommes). Such a procedure was in itself a signal that copying was obviously theft. In the beginning, the association was hosted by Madeleine Vionnet's firm, next door at 220 rue de Rivoli, before it moved with the firm to 50 avenue Montaigne, and later secured an independent location at 10 boulevard Malesherbes. The association broadcast via a large sign the statement "Copier c'est voler" (Copying is robbery), which became the slogan of couturiers against piracy. The slogan was also carved in a luxurious fresco in Vionnet's salons. In 1925, the same slogan appeared on the walls of the exhibition of couture at the Exposition des Arts Décoratifs in Paris.[47]

Dangel's association decided to expose counterfeiting by seizing designs and garments[48], and in the United States it soon became "famous for its warlike anti-copyist activities."[49] Its membership in 1923 included Vionnet, Poiret, Chéruit, Worth, Lanvin, and Drecoll.[50] The firms that remained outside the association were considered to be more "in favor of American methods of production."[51] In 1923, Dangel lobbied the French government to demand a unification of the international copyright law and to grant international protection to haute couture design. In the American press, Dangel unequivocally deplored the exploitation of French couture by international buyers, who reproduced Paris fashion without paying royalties on design: "American wholesalers have founded a complete spy system in Paris, through which, in return for big bribes, they procure exact designs of the new styles before they are offered to the public. A few weeks later, department stores from New York to San Francisco are flooded with cheap duplicates, some even having the effrontery to forge the original labels of the Paris houses. We regard this as a species of gigantic international thievery, bringing gravest injury to France's most important export business."[52]

Over the following years, the actions of Dangel's association contributed to building case law that conferred the status of art to haute couture productions in France. The association lobbied for the drafting of international fashion-related copyright laws throughout the 1920s and opened negotiations with Germany in 1929. Germany had one of the most complete systems of copyright law outside of France, as well as an extremely active garment manufacturing industry. A Franco-German agreement in this area did not materialize.[53]

In 1922, Vionnet moved from the rue de Rivoli into the Hôtel de Lariboisière, at 50–52 avenue Montaigne, an address that is still prestigious in Paris haute couture. The move had been made possible by a renewed partnership between Vionnet and Bader. The building was sumptuously decorated, and Vionnet increased the number of her workshops to seven.[54] Vionnet sued everyone she suspected of counterfeiting, but she persisted in opening her doors to all visitors. She advertised sales, and between sales she hosted thematic events like an exhibition of artistic lingerie (*lingerie d'art*), for which she listed public open hours in the dailies.[55]

A Legal System Rooted in the French Revolution

The judgments of December 30, 1921, against Boudreaux and the Miler sisters were based on two texts of law. The law of 1793, revised in 1902, was the French law on authors' rights, passed during the French Revolution. The principle of the right of the author to her work replaced the ancient monopolies on publication and other artistic domains. Two years earlier, in 1791, the laws of Allarde and of Le Chapelier had abolished the guilds and the corporations, replacing the ancien régime's commercial privileges with the freedom of trade.

The authors' rights law was rooted in the project of the Enlightenment to recognize the property of the author regarding creations of the mind. This point had been the subject of intense debates on the nature of work, in the sense of *œuvre*, and on the nature of authorship. It was not obvious to an eighteenth-century individual that an author could be owner of the expression of his thinking in the books he wrote, or in other creations of his mind. One strand of interpretation that relied on the works of the marquis de Condorcet is the utilitarian view, which finds that there is no inherent property in intellectual or artistic ideas. Granting exclusive legal rights regarding ideas to a private person is only justified if it encourages the production and transmission of new ideas, so public interest should therefore guide the legislator in a proper utilitarian understanding of intellectual property. Another strand of interpretation on copyright is the subjectivist view put forth by numerous Enlightenment intellectuals, including Diderot, Locke, and Fichte, all of whom agreed that there is a natural right to property in the expression of ideas. The recognition of this by the law therefore simply echoed a natural fact, and it was not solely the public good but also the rights of the author that should guide the legislator. Legal battles ensued over these concepts all over Europe and in the British colonies of America prior to independence, with various outcomes.[56]

The French law of 1793 derived from the subjectivist interpretation of copyright, but subsequent case law was not very protective of the decorative arts.

The consequences of the industrial revolution on the reproduction of human works, including works of art, were slow to arrive to the law, or to culture in general. In 1902, a reworking of the 1793 text offered the decorative arts better protection by extending the field of application of originality and thus the possibility of proving the theft of original models. The new version was called the *loi Soleau*, after the law's main author, Eugène Soleau.[57] It specifically protected all visual arts, including the design and sculpture of ornament, whatever the merits, importance, use, and destination—even if individual—of the original work. It did not specifically cover fashion design, but the mention of ornament enabled a body of case law that conferred authorship rights to haute couture design.[58] Soleau contributed to the protection of such works through a system of registration that allowed one to easily prove anteriority. A copy or photograph of the work was registered by a specialized court in a sealed envelope called the *enveloppe Soleau*.[59] This procedure was fast, effective, and cheap. In a case of counterfeiting, the designer asked the police to establish the theft. A police officer or bailiff was sent to investigate the counterfeiter and seize the objects—dresses, prototypes, sketches—of litigation, as in the case of Vionnet's pursuits against Boudreaux. The objects were then sealed and transmitted to the clerk's office of the court. Copyists tried to avoid seizures by keeping the originals with them for as brief a time as possible, and by varying the hours of their communication with their clients. Couturier criticism of the French law of 1902 centered on the fact that procedures for recording an infraction were too slow and that penalties were insufficient to act as a deterrent to further infractions.[60]

The second text of law used in the Boudreaux and Miler sisters' judgments was the law on industrial property. On July 14, 1909, the law on the protection of industrial design (*Protection des dessins et modèles*) was amended to acknowledge industrial property, replacing an obsolete text from 1806. The new text granted full protection to any industrial design characterized by its novelty, as long as the design had been registered by the Institut national de la Propriété industrielle or the Greffe du tribunal de commerce. The challenge here was to prove the novelty of the design, especially in industries where certain traditional shapes and forms were common. Case law was therefore important to help define the precise application of this law. The law of 1909 was soon used by the fashion trade as a companion to the 1793 law on authors' rights that had been amended in 1902. French fashion case law came to be distinguished by its joint reliance on these two laws during the interwar period.[61]

The lawsuits waged by Vionnet against Boudreaux and the Miler sisters thus rested on the combination of authors' rights and industrial property law. Another option would have been to use the patent law to protect fashion creativity. Laws on patents had been passed for the first time in 1790 in the United States, and in 1791 in France, to protect technical and scientific innovations. Patent registration involved the payment of administrative costs and an investment of time to complete the procedure. For these reasons, patents were not the most convenient way to protect a fashion design. Couturiers tended to work very fast to prepare their collections. By the time they could successfully register a patent for an innovation, the design would have been out too long and already lost some of its value.[62]

In the United States in the 1920s, however, fashion firms had little choice but to try to use the patent law if they wanted to protect their designs. Fashions were not included in American copyright law, which made protection more difficult in the United States than in France. Entrepreneurs and lawyers sought to use patent law to protect the activity of the fashion industry in America.[63] In France, it was mostly used to protect technical innovation in the fashion industries. Vionnet, however, sought to add patent law to her legal arsenal. In September 1923, she took out her first patent, for fabrics that she used in her designs.[64]

Copying Started at Home

Boudreaux, in response to the lawsuit brought against her by the Société Madeleine Vionnet et Cie, argued that she had obtained the inspiration for her copies in the fashion press, but the judge did not endorse that argument. Instead, he thought that Boudreaux had found inspiration by directly observing the Vionnet models and becoming familiar with every detail of Vionnet's intricate cuts.[65] So how would a copyist have obtained such access to haute couture originals? The American designer Elizabeth Hawes later recalled a "general atmosphere of bootlegging" in the Paris couture of the 1920s.[66] A former sketcher and copyist, Hawes insisted that copyists were simply doing a *degraded business*. Hawes's moral stance resonated with an emerging discourse, especially prominent in the French fashion magazine *Fémina*, that promoted the purchasing of originals by all who could afford them.[67] The traffic in counterfeited fashion objects is today notorious for its direct link to the activity of wider criminal organizations, but I have found no trace of this link during the interwar period.[68]

By the late 1930s, the revenue lost to copying by the French couture industries was an estimated 500 million French francs yearly, according to journalist George Le Fèvre, who realized a long inquiry on fashion copying during the 1920s.[69] Another contemporary expert on fashion, Philippe Simon, published higher estimates.[70] Armand Trouyet, the second lawyer to become administrative director at Madeleine Vionnet & Cie after Dangel, thought that haute couture houses should obtain damages calculated by multiplying the number of counterfeiting labels by the average price of a garment produced under that label, but no concrete proposition was ever voiced to that effect. Who was responsible for such losses? Illegal copying was an international trade, but Paris couturiers lamented the fact that it started at home, because the copyists had to be as close to their sources as possible and because copying required a capable workforce—one that was also most easily found in Paris.[71] In 1929, Lucien Klotz, secretary general of the Société des Droits des Auteurs et des Artistes, estimated the number of Paris copy houses at over one hundred and deplored the inefficiency of French laws.[72] Three years later, journalist André Beucler wrote that there were five hundred copy houses in Paris.[73] Copying was evidently a thriving black and gray market. All transactions were made in cash, giving copy houses an advantage over haute couture houses, which had to extend credit to their clients, often for months. Copy houses were paying the 1.1 percent tax on turnover, but not the 10 percent luxury tax on goods. According to his inquiry, the average copy house employed between sixty and seventy workers and declared only 12,000 French francs annually. The government was losing 8.9 percent in tax revenue on the copyists' sales. Copy houses generally maintained a double set of books as well. It was also the case that the repression of copying was difficult in the early 1920s. The system of *consignation* demanded that couturiers who requested the seizure of models in a copy house give a deposit proportional to the number of designs seized, which meant having on hand a sum that could amount to a thousand French francs per design.[74]

In 1923, the magazine of the Chambre Syndicale, *L'Officiel de la Couture et de la Mode*, described the copy houses located in Paris and noted that some survived entirely off the reproduction of designs copied from the dozen most prominent *grands couturiers*.[75] The French media of the time show little opposition to the lawsuits against copyists. An allusion to this question can be found in a news story from the socialist paper *Le Populaire de Paris:* "Madeleine Vionnet, seamstress, filed a lawsuit against two of her peers, *de petite race*,[76] whom she reproached to have copied her designs." The article goes on: "Hadn't it been a scandal that any *petit bourgeois* woman could exhibit, in the Café du Commerce, the super chic peel that covers, at Larue or at Maxim's, the well-feathered carcass of a luxury chick? The court understood. It condemned Mrs. Miler to pay to the irascible Madeleine Vionnet 16,000 francs in damages: Mrs. Boudreaux will only pay 12,000 francs. Each will, additionally, pay to the state treasury a 1,000 francs fine."[77] Haute couture was not immune to the problem of class, although the topic was generally treated with discretion. The tone of the press clipping from *Le Populaire de Paris,* in this respect, represents a rare demonstration of a revulsion against the aesthetic and moral supremacy of the couturier.[78] Haute couture in the interwar period was affordable to a wider stratum of consumers than it is today. But the price of haute couture compared with the salaries meant that, apart from maybe a few saleswomen issued from high society who had their own sources of income aside from their labors, the couture workers could not afford to consume the products they made.

Inside the Workroom: Trade Secrets in Intellectual Property Rights Strategy

The workers at haute couture houses were sometimes accused of using their proximity to design creativity to earn additional money through illegal copyist networks. In 1931, a worker could receive an average of fifty to one hundred French francs for sneaking out a new design. Haute couture workers were also hired for after-hours work in copy houses, where they would be asked to replicate what they had seen and done during the day.[79]

Along with the three previously discussed classical categories of intellectual property rights—trademark, copyright, and patent—was another one, perhaps more difficult to define, that might be subsumed under the concept of the trade secret. The emphasis of the couturiers' intellectual property strategies might rest to varying degrees on some of these rights, according to place and time and to entrepreneurial preferences. During the 1920s, the haute couture houses increased their surveillance of their workers and developed a policy of professional secrecy that produced strict rules for the trade. The statutes of the Chambre Syndicale outlined that it was perfectly legal for a couturier to insist upon rules regarding the employment conditions of haute couture workers. Leaving one couture house for another could be considered a breach of contract, and litigation between haute couture houses and employees on these grounds was quite common in the industry. Most of these conflicts played out at the employment tribunals (Conseil des Prud'hommes). The section in charge of the fabric industries for the Seine Department met on Fridays. Cases were exclusively work-related litigation, and most questions were about the payment of wages. Counterfeiting was not part of the realm of law covered by the trading court, but, at times, litigation between workers and employers touched on the question of intellectual property rights. In the second half of the 1920s, the case of Martiale Constantini, *modéliste-décoratrice*, and Muguette Buhler, *dessinatrice*, both of whom worked for Madeleine Vionnet & Cie, sheds some light on the relationship between the employees and the ownership of their contribution to their workplace.[80]

Buhler entered the house of Vionnet in May 1925, earning 1,000 francs per month and a hot lunch on workdays, which would start at 9:00 a.m. and last until 7:00 p.m. (4:00 p.m. on Saturdays). Only Sunday was work-free. Upon starting her job in 1925, Buhler had, like all employees in the firm, been asked to sign a clause of design confidentiality that had been prepared by Armand Trouyet, the house's managing director at the time. It read as follows: "The creations of Madeleine Vionnet, being registered and published according to the law, it is forbidden to reproduce them, or to draw inspiration from them. You declare accepting to work to the benefit of the Société Madeleine Vionnet, and you also declare knowing that every copy, every reproduction, even modified, of the designs, results for its author in the penalties issued by the law."[81]

Over the next five years, Buhler's salary was raised to 1,250 francs per month, and eventually, in 1929, 2,200 francs per month. Buhler had high hopes of being promoted to *modéliste* and felt that she was a participant in creating designs.[82] On November 13, 1929, Buhler arrived at work and saw that the closet where she kept her personal objects and drawings had been unlocked and that everything had been taken without notice. Buhler had one key to the closet, and the management of the firm had another key. Upon discovering that the closet was empty, Buhler called the police and filed a complaint of theft.

But the next day, Trouyet gave Buhler notice to leave her position without a clear reason. Another employee, *décoratrice-modéliste* Constantini, expressed her solidarity with Buhler.[83] Subsequently, Constantini was also given notice without a stated reason. Both Buhler and Constantini then sued Vionnet at the trading court, seeking reparations for having been laid off so abruptly and, in the case of Buhler, for having lost her personal belongings and drawings. Each employee asked for 1,100 francs in salary, 13,200 francs for breach of contract, and 50,000 francs in damages. The trading court granted them each 1,100 francs for salary due.[84] The correspondence between Vionnet and Trouyet and the two employees shows that the atmosphere in the workplace had deteriorated. Vionnet, who had at first been very happy with the two women, had in recent months noticed that they were arriving late and cultivating "a spirit of revolt and anarchy."[85] Trade secrets in this case seemed to have rendered the atmosphere of the workshops quite oppressive, and Buhler felt cheated when she discovered that her drawings had been taken. According to the statement by the firm's direction, the change happened suddenly, when Vionnet ordered that all drawings within the workshops be stamped with the firm's mark; this was done overnight and was the reason why the closet in which Buhler kept her drawings had been raided. Vionnet, in return, declared that she was furious that Buhler had "introduced a police officer in her House," and Constantini was fired because she showed solidarity with Buhler.[86]

The case of Buhler and Constantini shows that being a *modéliste* was a coveted position that came with responsibility in a context of trade secrecy.[87] Although work litigation and counterfeiting litigation took place at different courts, Vionnet was represented by the same defense lawyer, Maître Flach, in either type of case. In the late 1920s, the monthly salary for a *modéliste* in a Paris haute couture or haute mode firm could be as high as 4,000 French francs—which was also the price of one Vionnet dress. For comparison purposes, we know that during the 1920s, aside from her financial interest in the firm, the fixed salary of Vionnet herself was 10,000 French francs per month. *Modélistes* had the right to three months' notice prior to dismissal, as opposed to one month's notice for seamstresses. Several cases show that houses could be reluctant to assign workers the title of *modéliste*. It was also a contentious position thanks to the ambiguity surrounding who actually represented a work's creator—was it the *modéliste* or the entrepreneur? Who owned a design, if the *modéliste* had created it? The trading court cases underline "the secrecy that is attached to the designs" and conclude that ownership of such designs went to the entrepreneur.[88] A way to reinforce trust between the leadership and employees was to offer them some perks, and in haute couture firms that include Vionnet, the development of welfare benefits for employees occupied an important place in the management. Besides philanthropy, the link between welfare and the preservation of knowledge within the industry was a coherent part of the management culture in haute couture.[89]

American Capital?

The first wave of globalization that took place during the nineteenth century receded after World War I due to abrupt changes in currencies and increased protectionist measures taken by Western governments. Restrictions in citizenship and law made travel more difficult, and branching out abroad with one's business became more difficult as well. Yet the cosmopolitan networks of the Paris fashion milieu were bristling with rumors of the interference of foreigners in the capital of haute couture houses: "Almost every Saturday Madame Blank, who owns an exclusive couture establishment, lunches leisurely and quite exquisitely at a smart Parisian restaurant with Monsieur Done, who controls a big chain of French department stores. Almost every Monday a report spreads through Paris that the department store chain has bought the couture enterprise; that it is to be the nucleus of a chain of couture businesses to be operated under an American centralized control system."[90]

Even as the haute couture industry engaged in large part in international commerce, haute couture houses remained firmly anchored in Paris. This may have something to do with the French textile industrialists who were catering to haute couture. Their work was rooted in local tradition, and production was tied to specific areas of France: Lyons, especially for silks; the North, for woolens and linens; and other specialized regional clusters. Many textile manufacturers set up retail outlets in Lyons and Paris, as well as abroad. The manufacturer Coudurier, Fructus, Descher, for example, had shops in Paris and Lyons, but also in London and on Madison Avenue in New York in 1921. Others were represented only in Europe, such as Diederichs Soieries, which had factories in Bourgoin-Jaillieu and shops in Paris, Lyons, London, and Brussels. Likewise, Olré had shops in Paris, Nice, London, and Brussels.[91]

In the early 1920s, most haute couture houses kept their retailing in Paris and in fashionable seaside resorts such as Biarritz, Cannes, Deauville, and Nice. By 1923, Jeanne Lanvin had outlets in Paris, Cannes, Deauville, Biarritz, Madrid, Barcelona, Rio de Janeiro, and Sao Paulo. Yet the Paris houses tended toward self-financing, and their capital remained largely in local hands. American business and Paris couture had shown interest in a potential partnership between textile and fashion firms, but they faced two principal challenges: individual couturiers asked for selling prices for their enterprises that prospective American buyers considered to be too high, and the couturiers insisted on retaining control of their businesses. American silk manufacturers knew they would benefit from the proximity of a strong creative driving force, and in 1923 they offered to host the Paris couturiers in New York, should they be willing to work exclusively for the Americans. The French textile manufacturers urged the Paris couturiers to refuse, arguing that they were helping Paris haute couture enough not to be abandoned by it. The initiative from the Americans raised fears that, should the French couturiers accept it, all of Paris haute couture would soon be relocated to New York. In some instances, the Chambre Syndicale objected to having members relocate to the United States. Examples of foreign participation in Paris haute couture remain limited.[92]

Branching Out

Boudreaux and the Miler sisters were required to pay heavy fines to Madeleine Vionnet. Despite these lawsuits, copying remained rampant. Couturiers stated that since the existing legal system did not allow sufficient protection across borders, the best strategy against copying was to branch out to foreign markets and sell their own copies across the Atlantic.[93]

Paquin had tried this with her fur branch in New York, but that did not last more than a few years. Another Paris firm that branched out early to the United States was the house of Boué Sœurs, founded in 1897 as a *société en nom collectif* with capital of 500,000 French francs.[94] Boué Sœurs became famous for its lingerie, for its use of embroideries and lace. It made a house signature out of ornate dresses adorned with motifs of polychrome bouquets of roses on white or pastel backgrounds. Soon, it started exporting and branched out to St. Petersburg, Bucharest, and Cairo. Its success with American clients encouraged it to open a New York branch in 1915, at 13 West 56th Street, hiring American employees for its workshop and sales floor.[95] The prospects were excellent: American clients had been reluctant to travel to France since the onset of the war, and they were delighted to see fine Paris couture being retailed in New York. The Chambre Syndicale "strongly objected" to Boué Sœurs branching out to New York, on the grounds that the outsourcing of labor was a concern for the profession of haute couture.[96] To manage their branch, the sisters took an average of six to eight transatlantic trips per year. In New York, however, the house of Boué met with difficulties. In the fall of 1915, the two sisters were called into court, along with their employees Eva Strauss and Georges Guédal, on the grounds that they had imported costumes and other merchandise in violation of the Contract Labor Law, which meant that they had not paid the expected tariff duties on importing wares into the United States. The judge concluded that the sisters were probably not fully aware of the American law and ordered them to pay a fine of $5,000. The sisters were then free to pursue their New York trade, which they did. Boué Sœurs was also subjected to the trials of copying, and in at least one case, the house sued a New York department store on counterfeiting grounds.[97]

In 1926, the house was subjected to an in-depth inquiry by American tax administrators. In Paris, Montégut, the husband of one of the sisters and the director of the house, was asked to show the complete accounting of his enterprise to American tax agents under the threat of a full embargo of all goods arriving in New York. Montégut refused to open his books and shared his concerns with the American consul, who then gave him eight more days to disclose the required information. The garments sent by Boué from Paris to New York were, upon arrival, subjected to heavy fines and seized. M. Kamp, director of customs in Washington, DC, decided to have Boué's wares investigated further.[98] To this end, he opened the packages and sent their contents to half a dozen New York fashion firms for their expert opinions. Montégut complained that these garments were immediately copied by the same New York firms. He also argued that fraud on his part was impossible: all merchandise sent from France to the United States was subjected to a 100 percent tariff upon entry—10 percent for the delivery service and 90 percent for the American tax administration. Every package was accompanied by a precise tax form (*feuille consulaire*) that registered all prices and benefits. From this, concluded Montégut, the American tax administration was making a significant profit. He concluded that "the aim pursued can only be the copy of our models and the knowledge of the secrets of our trade, in order to create, in the United States, an industry competing with ours."[99] In Paris, the house of Boué Sœurs stopped advertising in 1933 and maintained a reduced level of activity, while the firm remained in activity in New York during the rest of the 1930s.[100]

The dresses created by Vionnet often launched trends that were widely followed on the international markets, and especially in the United States.[101] Vionnet was well aware of the importance of the American market and the power of American buyers. The Paris correspondent for *Women's Wear Daily* pointed out that Boudreaux had been condemned on the grounds of her acquaintance with American piracy networks.[102] But the minutes of the lawsuit show that the connection between Boudreaux and potential American copyists could not be proved in court.[103] Vionnet was nevertheless eager to make it to the American market, and in the fall of 1923, she signed an agreement with New York manufacturer Charles Grutman, who owned the high-end firm Charles and Ray, at 785 Fifth Avenue, a ladies' tailor and importer. Charles and Ray obtained the right to show twenty-nine designs created exclusively by Vionnet. She authorized the firm to make signed reproductions, also called "true originals," of a selection of her designs to sell to American private customers. The New York firm would pay Vionnet a royalty of 10 percent of the sales price of all Vionnet garments sold in 1924. Charles and Ray was charged with reproducing the Vionnet models without variation in materials, trimmings, or style. Garments bore Vionnet's tag and fingerprint in addition to a Charles and Ray tag. Over the course of this particular venture, Charles and Ray would pay Vionnet a total of $90,383.[104]

Barely a few months after this agreement was signed with Charles and Ray, Vionnet embarked for New York, on January 26, 1924. Her recently appointed lawyer and director, Trouyet, had arrived a couple of weeks ahead of her. She planned a two-month trip to the United States and settled at the Plaza Hotel in New York.[105] Vionnet announced that she planned to "produce her garments in American materials and, at the same time, use American labor. Her plan is to develop and train the Americans employed by herself and her aides who are sailing with her on this trip."[106] Vionnet showed a full collection on the premises of luxury specialty shop Hickson's, at 661 Fifth Avenue, which was directed by Saul Singer, and she subsequently developed her own line for Hickson's.[107] The complete list of what Vionnet took with her to the United States appears in one of the three sales books from her Paris firm that escaped the later destruction of parts of Vionnet's archives and are now kept at the Union Centrale des Arts Décoratifs.[108]

According to dress historian Betty Kirke, the couturiere realized as soon as she arrived in New York that most of her designs had already leaked through copyist networks, so she created new designs on the spot. Vionnet's garments and workrooms occupied a whole floor at Hickson's, and society magazine *Harper's Bazaar* published a feature announcing the opening of Vionnet's New York branch and describing the work of the Association pour la Défense des Arts Plastiques et Appliqués. The relationship between retailing in the United States and trying to eradicate counterfeiting in the industry was obvious to the public.[109] Vionnet immediately started training American workers in the techniques of reproduction of her famously difficult patterns: "Mlle Vionnet says that she will be willing to teach her ideas of workmanship to the individual houses who purchase her models."[110] The bias-cut technique perfected by the couturiere allowed her to sell her original garments with very little fitting, but working the fabric on the bias was a delicate process, because the side seams were curved. To obtain a smooth line, seamstresses had to develop elaborate techniques for finishing the inside of the seams.[111] Despite such technical difficulties, the technique encapsulated its own means of standardizing sizes, as Kirke noted, and the use of the bias cut allowed the fabric to slightly stretch and therefore adapt to a small range of sizes.[112]

For the further production of her designs in the United States, Vionnet registered a company under the name Vionnet, Inc., incorporated in the State of New York for a limited duration of six months.[113] One hundred shares of no-par stock were issued under the supervision of attorneys Rose and Paskus, a renowned downtown Manhattan law firm founded in 1875 that still exists today under the name Proskauer Rose LLP.[114] Vionnet's incorporators were C. G. Hoffmann, A. B. Kilkenny, and C. A. Springstead. Vionnet kept her New York headquarters in the Hickson building.[115] At this point, it was decided that Hickson would act as an exclusive agent for the retailing of Vionnet's American-produced dresses in the best department stores in the country. In order to make the purchase of Vionnet's originals attractive to American retailers, Vionnet, Trouyet, and Hickson's director Saul Singer carefully timed the release of the collections simultaneously in Paris and New York.[116]

But while Vionnet was showing at Hickson's, *Women's Wear Daily* went to interview Charles Grutman, the owner of the firm Charles and Ray, with whom

Vionnet had settled on an agreement regarding the exclusive sale of her models
to New York private clients the year before. The journalist asked Grutman what
he thought of Vionnet's venture with Hickson's. Grutman answered that he had not
been informed of Vionnet's new plans for American development, but that this
would not interfere with his own business of selling exclusive Vionnet dresses.[117]
One month after Vionnet had sealed the deal with Hickson's, however, Charles
and Ray filed a lawsuit against Vionnet at the supreme court of Westchester
County, an affluent suburb north of Manhattan, demanding $100,000 for breach
of contract. Charles and Ray argued that it had an agreement to handle Vionnet's models on a royalty basis in the local market, and that Vionnet had violated
the conditions of this agreement.[118] Vionnet's lawsuit echoed the problems that
had bedeviled Boué Sœurs on the American market.

Despite her resounding popularity in the United States, however, Madeleine
Vionnet did not pursue the venture of Vionnet, Inc., after the six-month trial period outlined in the American incorporation act. Hickson's kept showing Vionnet's originals and offering high-quality, acknowledged reproductions for several
years. Although owner Saul Singer had a reputation as a skilled businessman,
Hickson's suffered at the start of the Depression and eventually filed for bankruptcy in 1931. Other high-end New York retailers featured Vionnet imports in
their collections after the end of the Vionnet, Inc. venture.[119] Assessing the success of Vionnet's American venture is challenging in the absence of complete
financial records, although the interrupted series of sales records kept at the
Union Centrale des Arts Décoratifs reveals a diminishing of Vionnet's sales over
the years of the Great Depression.[120]

One thing is clear: Vionnet's American experience had an impact on her business methods. In the fall of 1926, she entered into the wholesale reproduction of
her models in Paris upon the opening of her workrooms in a new industrial
building behind Hôtel de Lariboisière that had been built for the production of
her designs. Her staff was increased to twelve hundred in high season. Vionnet
allegedly developed her own wholesale reproduction because "buyers have found
the intricacy of her dresses difficult to copy," according to the press.[121] Furthermore, historians have shown that, starting in the nineteenth century, the structure of companies—especially when founded on the principle of limited liability—
could be more flexible in France than in America. Aside from her initial capital
of 100,000 francs in business assets, Vionnet had received support from several

investors. With that capital of 700,000 francs, she had chosen to retain a private liability structure that gave her flexibility, yet this capital was insufficient to buffer the risks inherent in any incursion into the American market.[122] Reliance on local investors and self-financing mechanisms may have cost firms further development and, in the case of couture, potential transnational growth.[123] Both Boué and Vionnet were sued in the United States not for counterfeiting but for other business matters. The French intellectual property rights system was the most powerful of all. Law was also a weapon that was available to American entrepreneurs, albeit with a different scope, to protect themselves from the competition of their French counterparts.

Chapter 3

Dressing *for* Crisis

You are going to Paris! Dozens of books have been written telling you *what to see*—from the precious Sainte-Chapelle to the Ritz bar at noon. Now, we are writing to tell you *where* to *buy.*" In the 1920s, tourism brought nearly two million people to Paris each year, of whom nearly three hundred thousand were Americans. In their shopping guide to Paris, American sisters Louise and Thérèse Bonney showed them the way to the luxury district of place Vendôme, the department stores, and the small couture workshops. A journalist and photographer based in Paris, Thérèse Bonney was also a lifelong intimate friend of Madeleine Vionnet's, and took several portraits of the couturiere, including the one in Figure 3.1. Bonney's admiration for Vionnet did not prevent her from advising American tourists to buy knockoffs in her no-nonsense guide to Paris. Haute couture customers were of two kinds: a wealthy elite of private customers bought 70 to 80 percent of the production of haute couture; a few hundred corporate buyers, who visited Paris twice a year, bought the rest. Corporate buyers paid 20 to 50 percent more than the private clients. The difference counted as a one-time fee for the reproduction of authentic couture on their domestic markets. Foreign corporate buyers applied to the Chambre Syndicale to obtain buyers' cards, and journalists for press cards, which were their passports to enter the haute couture houses. Corporate purchases came with an attached sheet of directions and fabric samples.[1]

FIGURE 3.1 Thérèse Bonney took several pictures of Madeleine Vionnet, who in this image from 1925 is adding her thumbprint to tags for the garments she created.
Reproduction courtesy of Librairie Diktats.

Buyers visited Paris at the time of the openings—in late January or early February for the summer presentations, and at the beginning of August for the winter ones. In the late 1920s, an estimated two hundred New York manufacturers systematically visited the two major yearly collections. Americans made up the largest number of foreign buyers, followed by English, Belgian, German, Italian, and South American buyers. The average cost of a buying trip from New York to Paris was estimated at $2,000, which is $28,000 in 2019 currency. In the evenings they enjoyed the nightlife of the Paris bars and clubs, including watching onstage performers like Joséphine Baker, who was also a favorite haute couture muse who enjoyed wearing high-end design off the stage. Paris was the place for Americans to experience a society without prohibition, and where racial tensions seemed less prominent than at home.[2]

In New York

Fashion-conscious New Yorkers could buy couture-inspired garments at a wide range of prices in their hometown. Andrew Goodman, manager at the luxury department store Bergdorf Goodman, described the aspirational hierarchy of New York retail: "Maybe if she buys it at Bergdorf Goodman today, and her daughter buys it at Russeks tomorrow [. . .] their cook is going to get it at Macy's or Gimbel's the day after that." All these shops sold reproductions of Paris couture. Macy's had one of the most extensive in-store French couture departments, with its Little Shop. In March 1929, it featured a Lelong reproduction at $89.75, and a Vionnet "hostess gown" in replica at $74.75.[3] Producing fashion was more expensive in New York than in Paris. The American workforce earned better wages, which was due to the strength of the dollar against the franc. In 1920, the price of a dress that required fifty hours of work was twenty-four dollars in Paris and sixty-two dollars in New York. By 1926, the price was down to fourteen dollars in Paris for what sold for sixty-two in New York. But sweatshops remained endemic in a system that allowed the jobbers to play the competition between contractors.[4] Besides a thriving garment business, New York had its own couturiers. In the mid-1920s, the luxury businesses on Park Avenue between 34th and 96th Streets made over $280 million—or, in today's currency, nearly $4 billion—a year in sales, with couture ranked first among them. Hattie Carnegie was the best-known New York high-end fashion designer of the interwar period. Born Henrietta Kanengeiser in Vienna in 1889, she set up her first shop in New York with business partner Rose Roth in 1909 under the name Carnegie Ladies' Hatter. Carnegie bought out her partner in the 1910s. In 1923 she opened a boutique on 49th Street, where she sold collections of Vionnet, Chanel, and self-designed clothes. Carnegie understood the necessity of both capitalizing on her brand name and diversifying into other price ranges. Individual items in her Spectator Sports lines retailed at $16.50 in the late 1920s, today around $200.[5]

Other women in the New York fashion industry developed their own professional networks with the idea of using them as an asset in their careers. They founded the Fashion Group in New York in 1928, initially as a division of the National Retail Dry Goods Association (NRDGA). The Fashion Group aimed to gather women fashion professionals over monthly lunch meetings and started with seventeen women at a New York tearoom. Among them were journalist Virginia Pope of the *New York Times;* fashion editors Edna Wolman Chase of US *Vogue,* Carmel Snow of *Harper's Bazaar,* and Julia Coburn of the *Ladies' Home Journal;* and consultant Tobé Coller Davis. Designers included sportswear pioneer Claire McCardell, milliner Lilly Daché, and Hollywood costume designer Edith Head. Dorothy Shaver, who was yet to become the first woman president of a department store, at Lord & Taylor, represented the retail branch. Elizabeth Arden and Helena Rubinstein were members in their roles of beauty entrepreneurs. In 1931, Eleanor Roosevelt, then First Lady of the State of New York, joined the group. Membership grew fast, to 375 in 1931, and 886 in 1938. The group founded its first regional chapter in Cleveland in 1932, followed by others in Chicago in 1934, Los Angeles and San Francisco in 1935, St. Louis, Boston, and Minneapolis in 1936, Pittsburgh in 1937, Philadelphia in 1938, and Washington, DC, in 1940.[6] The New York Fashion Group's monthly meetings featured guests such as Paul Mazur of Lehman Brothers, editor Condé Nast, and photographer Edward Steichen. During the meetings, members read cables highlighting the last trends from Paris, Biarritz, Monte Carlo, and Palm Beach. Members were asked "to cast aside [their] Modest Violet Complex," speak in public, and share information on business strategies. Every month the Fashion Group announced all members' travels: who was going where, on which ship, and for how long. The group announced experts and couturiers visiting New York from abroad if they could not be present and invited any visiting Paris couturier to speak at the meetings. The Fashion Group gave visibility to the careers of women.[7]

The Great Depression

The US fashion industries were hit very hard by the Great Depression, which followed the stock market crash of October 24 to 29, 1929. The Depression really came into effect in France in 1931, but French clothing and haute couture exports had begun to diminish before the crash of Wall Street. The export of French apparel to the United States declined by 100 million francs in 1928. Clothes ranked fourth among French exports in 1913, second in 1925, eighth in 1929, and then sank to twenty-seventh place in 1935.[8] To make matters worse, in the spring of 1929, the passing of the Hawley-Smoot Act had the effect of raising the tariffs on goods entering the United States. Tariffs were ad valorem, calculated on the sale price of the goods. Couture was characterized by high added value, which reinforced its vulnerability to any fluctuation in tariffs. The Revenue Act of 1913, also called the Underwood Tariff, signed under a Democrat administration, had lowered the tariffs. It had been followed by the Fordney-McCumber Tariff (1921–1922), which was based on a significant increase for most incoming products.[9]

The Hawley-Smoot Tariff Act was on the agenda of the Republican Party for several years. It raised tariffs in most categories of goods by 5 percent, but the most spectacular increase was on haute couture products: embroidery, tulles, spangles, and lace were subject to a 90 percent ad valorem tax upon entrance to the United States. Successful nineteenth-century liberal economies were built not on an absence of barriers but on a planned implementation and release of protectionist barriers that aimed to protect specific segments of the economy. Timing played a major role in the success of such policies. Recent historical research supports the interpretation that the Republican protectionist policies increased the instability leading to the crash, and indeed, as a consequence of Hawley-Smoot and the Depression, a tariff war began. European countries retaliated by raising their own barriers, which increased the slump in the international garment trade. Some countries extended their protectionist measures into prohibition schemes. In the spring of 1932, French champagne was forbidden in Denmark for a few weeks, before a policy of quotas was introduced. In Romania, imports of French haute couture were temporarily forbidden in 1929. Facing international protectionism, the French government lowered the luxury tax on haute couture from 12 percent to 3 percent in 1929.[10]

The impact of the Great Depression was particularly visible on the fashion buying offices and the commissionaires. American firms called their resident buyers back home. The Allied Purchasing Corporation in 1929 catered to retail stores such as Lord & Taylor, James McCreery & Co., and Jordan Marsh & Co. By December 1929, the Allied Purchasing Corporation had rescaled all of its European operations, laying off staff members and downsizing from the seven floors it had occupied at 9 Cité Paradis, which cost 800,000 francs a year to rent, to modest premises. After supporting their foreign clients for a few seasons, the commissionaires started to resent them for attending the presentations without buying anything. As the Depression deepened, the commissionaires went for mergers and liquidations. But the major problem during the crisis was the sensitivity of luxury businesses to monetary fluctuations. In 1933, the devaluation of the dollar hit France. The French franc remained in the gold standard until 1936, becoming for the time much more expensive for American buyers. Most fashion businesses in Paris cut prices in order to retain at least a portion of their American customers.[11]

The French government was aware of the symbiotic relationship between haute couture and the tourism industry, which experts labeled as invisible exports. As a consequence of the Depression, Paris hotel activity receded. While 296,174 Americans had visited Paris in 1929, only 74,322 traveled to the city in 1934. For fashion buyers, the usual cost evaluated at $2,000 for a round trip between the American East Coast and Paris could be cut down to $1,200 by traveling second class, sticking to 100 franc hotel rooms, and considering $12 a day enough for living expenses. Deluxe traveling services were discontinued in 1931.[12]

In Paris, hundreds of firms disappeared as a consequence of the economic crisis. The house of Boué Sœurs stopped advertising in 1933 and closed the doors of its Paris establishment in 1935, though it remained open in New York, where couture shows were still going on in 1939. In 1934, the Paris haute couture house of Augustabernard closed its doors, as did the couturier specialized in mourning Aine-Montaillé. In 1929, 187 couture firms failed; the number of failures rose to 331 in 1932. There were still 297 new failures in 1933. These figures were even steeper in the other clothing industries, including mass production, with 299 failures in 1929, a record high of 717 in 1932, and then 628 in 1933. But the number of one-person couture businesses skyrocketed, going from 657 in 1926 to 1,537 in 1931. Starting a one-person operation was often chosen by employees laid off by failing firms. Qualified seamstresses who did not strike out on their own often went to work for undeclared artisans for low wages.[13]

In 1942, the French Ministry of Commerce analyzed the impact of the crisis on Paris couture. The resulting report showed that French exports diminished drastically. The report also underlined that while most big fashion houses managed to last, the *moyenne* and *petite couture* were most severely hit.[14] Haute couture thus proved comparatively the most resilient of the fashion industries. Despite the high number of failures, a smaller group of new designers set up shop during the crisis. Nina Ricci opened a French limited liability (SARL) in 1932. Robert Piguet, former designer at the houses of Poiret and Redfern, opened in the fall of 1933, at the height of the Depression. Véra Boréa opened a *société anonyme* (SA) in 1934.[15]

Among these rising talents was Mainbocher, the only American couturier to have a long-lasting career in Paris. Born Main Rousseau Bocher in Chicago, he trained as a painter and a singer before finding a job as a fashion editor at the Paris office of *Vogue,* where he eventually became editor in chief. He left the magazine to open his own couture house in Paris in 1929. This was a rare case of a house backed by three American-born investors. In 1934, Mainbocher bought back all of its stakeholders for a total capital of $40,000. American customers prized its designs, which were widely advertised in the US edition of *Vogue* and gained a reputation for being discreet, rather conservative, and standing the test of time. Prices started at $350 for a dress. Mainbocher capitalized on its American success to open a second shop in New York in the late 1930s. His most iconic client was the Duchess of Windsor, American-born Wallis Simpson, known as one of the most elegant women of her time. Mainbocher designed her 1937 pale blue wedding dress, which became a hit: thousands of copies could be found in all price ranges, from $10.75 and up.[16]

Tie-In Products to Get Out of the Crisis

The financial capital of couture firms remained largely in French hands. American businesses had previously shown interest in partnerships with Paris couture, but individual couturiers set the prices for selling their enterprises too high for American buyers, while insisting on retaining control of their businesses. Paris couture firms adopted multiple strategies to reach American clients. Jean Patou opened an American bar in his haute couture house and hired American models for his Paris shows. Patou also welcomed Andrew Goodman, heir of New York department store Bergdorf Goodman, as an intern at the haute couture house. In his memoirs, Goodman wrote that Patou had asked him to play an undercover role to help the Paris police dismantle a counterfeiting business. Goodman was very amused by the adventure.[17] Most importantly, couturiers soon understood that perfume was a lucrative source of revenue. Poiret had been the first to launch his own perfume line, Les Parfums de Rosine, in 1911. He did not consider capitalizing on his own name—a mistake that subsequent couturiers did not repeat. Chanel started her perfume branch in 1921, Patou in 1925, and Lelong in 1926. In May 1930, Patou created an American company for his perfumes, Jean Patou Inc., with a capital of $2 million; Laurence A. Steinhardt and bankers Marcel Ullman and Robert C. Adams directed the American firm. French couturiers used the department stores to retail their perfumes and cosmetics in America. In 1938, the Americans were the first buyers of French perfumes, absorbing one-thirteenth of the production. French exports of cosmetics to the United States amounted to 486,608,000 French francs, among which 291,265,000 francs were spent on perfumes, the rest on oils and soaps.[18]

In France, most couturiers launched cheaper clothing lines and opened boutiques, shops selling sports lines and accessories, aiming to cash in on couture brand names. In 1932, Chanel made cotton evening dresses and sold them for half the price of her silk ones. In 1937, the house of Heim started its line Heim Jeunes Filles, tailored to the young. The most remarkable of these initiatives was that of Lucien Lelong, who successfully launched designer ready-to-wear at the height of the Depression. Lelong was born in Paris in 1889. He trained at the Hautes Etudes Commerciales, and when World War I broke out, he was sent to the front. Lelong came back a war hero, decorated with the Croix de Guerre and the Legion of Honor. Upon his return, he opened his own couture house in Paris, the private society (*commandite simple*) Lucien Lelong et Cie on September 13, 1918, with the financial support of his father, Arthur Lelong, who was a couture industrialist before him. In 1925, the term of Lucien Lelong's first society expired, and he founded the SA Lucien Lelong, again with the financial support of his father. Together, both men owned the majority of the capital of the firm, which had grown to 1,400,000 francs. The statuses of the firm allowed for a single administrator, who was Lucien Lelong himself. The American buyers felt at ease with Lelong. During the interwar period, his firm became one of the largest in Paris couture. Lelong acted as art director, managing the work of a team and selecting the best of their creations to build the general line of his collections (see Figure 3.2). Lelong used the adjective *kinetic*, meaning "in movement," to describe silhouettes created "with the purpose of giving the wearer a pleasing appearance while in motion."[19] In 1927, Lelong married one of his in-house models, émigré Russian princess Natalie Paley, granddaughter of Czar Alexander II. The

"I AM MOST HAPPY TO DEDICATE TO YOU THIS EVENING GOWN ENTITLED 'MADRIENE'.."

says LUCIEN LELONG

Inspired by the charm and sophistication of American women, Lelong has created this new evening gown for the smart patrons of Loeser's. And with infinite skill this great artist has moulded lustrous satin into a striking version of the rippling tiered silhouette with the smart trailing line in back. Original, $325. Copies at . . $89.50

THE transformed Loeser's that bids you welcome is more than a great store in a new dress. For the openings of its individual shops are occasions of unusual interest. From centers of fashion all over the world come new and lovely things to grace the charm of the woman who dresses in smartness.

Paris, through her distinguished couturiers, sends the freshest fashions for the delectation of Loeser's patrons. Lelong has done for you this charming evening gown . . . the inspiration of a new fashion era that glorifies youth and demands the loveliest expressions of your personality. And who could do it more exquisitely? Who could create so deftly—in shimmering satin— the new clinging silhouette that dips and flutters, moulding itself into gracious, flowing lines? Only a very great artist, you will agree!

Lelong writes us: "I have been informed of the important transformation which your great shop is undergoing. I want to congratulate you and say that I am most happy to dedicate to the New Shop of Loeser's my evening gown entitled, 'Madriene'—which I consider to be one of my very best. Again, my sincere best wishes for your continued happiness. Lucien Lelong."

The translations of Lucien Lelong's choicest models are presented in the Gown Shop. A ravishing collection which shows what grace a supreme designer can command when the heart as well as the hand is in his work.

FULTON AT BOND
TRIANGLE . . . 8100

LOESER'S

. . HOW DIFFERENT
HOW UNCHANGED

FIGURE 3.2 Paris couturier Lucien Lelong, who had excellent relations with American firms, created dresses for authorized reproduction by American manufacturers.
New York Times, *September 22, 1929, p. 25.*

couple was surrounded by a brilliant network of socialites and artists that included poet Jean Cocteau and dancer Serge Lifar.[20]

In 1925, the French Ministries of Fine Arts, Public Instruction, and Labor offered Lelong the chance to visit the United States for a study trip. Lelong talked to the Chambre Syndicale prior to his departure, disclosing some figures: "Last year, the Haute Couture, that is the leading houses, produced model coats and gowns valued at $25,000,000. Four-fifths of our production gets now exported; the United States have absorbed half of our exports. Last August, more than one thousand American buyers visited me [at the house of Lelong], representing 600 American houses that now import Paris designs."[21]

Lelong visited American factories and met labor experts in Washington, DC. He wanted to observe American women in order to understand how to meet their needs.[22] Other couturiers went to the United States and wrote travelogues. Marguerite Besançon de Wagner, a Belgian working under the name of Maggy Rouff, was one of them. She opened her house in January 1929 on the avenue des Champs-Elysées. Her in-laws before her had, in the same building, directed the house of Drecoll. In February 1931, Rouff boarded at Le Havre on the Ile-de-France and sailed to New York. In her role as president of the PAIS, an association against copying and counterfeiting founded by Madeleine Vionnet and her lawyer Trouyet, Rouff had her 1931 conference tour sponsored by the French government. She lectured for the press and business audiences in major cities and at Northwestern University. Upon her return, she wrote an account of her American experience in a book, *L'Amérique au microscope,* which mixed admiration with criticism.[23]

French writers seemed captivated by the modernity of America during those years. Medical doctor Georges Duhamel published an early critique of the United States in *Scènes de la vie future* (1930) and was followed by the diatribes of Robert Aron and Arnaud Dandieu in *Le Cancer américain* (1931). The most famous of these French visions of America is to be found in Louis-Ferdinand Céline's novel *Journey to the End of the Night* (1932). Paris couturiers, by contrast, showed little interest in the rationalization of production that could be found at Ford in Detroit or in the Chicago slaughterhouses that had so impressed Duhamel. Their interest focused on the American woman—a new icon, bolder, freer than the stereotypical Frenchwoman. American ready-made fashions blurred the differences between classes and between morals, wrote Rouff, whose opinion of American women was close to that of Céline. Paris couturiers were also curious about the differences between their profession's organization in France and the haute couture house in America. In Paris, the haute couture house was a complete entity, from creation to retail. The designer and the brand were merged in a single name. In America, noted Rouff, the haute couture house had little visibility; instead, fashion happened at the department store. The American market remained elusive to Rouff, who kept traveling to New York on faster lines. But she chose London to open Maggy Rouff Ltd., in the fall of 1937. Her London shop catered to private clientele, and she asked corporate buyers to address all their orders to her Paris salons.[24]

Lelong was introduced as a new committee member of the Chambre Syndicale in June 1928. That same year, he founded Lucien Lelong Inc., an Illinois corporation, for making and selling perfumes and cosmetics. In July 1929, Lelong started leasing a New York office, at 657 Fifth Avenue, to serve as East Coast headquarters for his perfume and cosmetics venture and from which to manage his sales to the department stores. These offices also hosted the New York headquarters of his brother Pierre Lelong, who ran a French textile firm under the name Soieries Péhel and specialized in the production of haute couture fabrics. The brothers traveled together to New York on various occasions.[25]

Lelong and his wife, Natalie Paley, split in 1931. Paley went on to pursue an acting career in Hollywood. That same year, Lelong was invited again to New York, and his visit made headlines. In the late 1920s, Lelong had hired an advertising agency in the United States. When launching his perfume business in America, he commissioned the work to Chicago-based advertising agency Earle Ludgin. Ludgin subcontracted the task of organizing and publicizing Lelong's visit of 1931 to a specialist, Edward Bernays, who immediately accepted the job. Bernays was on his way to becoming the most important expert in public relations of the twentieth century. He arranged Lelong's appearances in the American media and his social agenda. CBS invited Lelong to a radio show, where the couturier talked about perfume and about design. Lelong's overall goal was to obtain a slender line, which he thought to be much more important than the flattery that color could offer. Further on his tour, star journalist Edna Woolman Chase of *Vogue* invited Lelong to a meeting of the Fashion Group. Chase probed him about his attitude toward American copyists. Lelong answered with manifest discomfort, torn between his loyalty to couture and the demand of American markets.

That spring, Lelong sold his gowns at Harry Bendel's; then, starting in 1934, he sold a line of furs at I. Magnin. From 1934–1935 onward, Lelong designs appeared in the fashion sketches used by the house of Davidow, a New York–based business that manufactured and retailed reproductions of Paris and London fashions.[26]

Most Frenchwomen owned a smaller wardrobe than American women. Simone de Beauvoir remembered that during the interwar period, the American working girl spent much more on clothes and beauty than her French counterpart. Lelong was then the couturier who had the deepest knowledge of the American market, and it is therefore not surprising that he became a pioneer in launching his own line of designer ready-to-wear. In 1934, Lelong launched a line of ready-made clothes that he called Robes d'Edition. Other couturiers had previously attempted ready-made dresses—first Vionnet, then Patou, whose initiatives lasted only a few months—but Lelong managed to make it work. Lelong opened a new wing in his couture house to show the Editions collection. American buyers expected his initiative to fill a gap between manufacturing and bespoke couture. The difference between Robes d'Edition and ready-to-wear was, according to the couturier, the constant renewal of designs in a limited number of reproductions. In 1934, Robes d'Edition clothes were made in five sizes, and alterations (costing about fifty francs each) could be added to the price of the dress. Prices ranged from 300 francs for a wool dress up to 2,200 for an evening ensemble with a coat trimmed in ermine. Fabrics were available in twenty different colors, of good quality—for example, a pure silk crepe marocain. Lelong guaranteed a minimum weight for the fabrics he used. The next year, alterations were included in the price of the dresses, which ranged from 350 francs up to 900 francs.[27] In an interview for the US edition of *Vogue,* Lelong stressed that if ready-to-wear was nothing new to the American market, high fashion still had to be bespoke couture from Paris. For his collection, he preferred to use the analogy of a limited edition of a book, and he emphasized the precision of the techniques used in his workshop, as opposed to mechanized *confection.* In the Robes d'Edition catalog, Lelong printed a warning that counterfeiters were exposing themselves to lawsuits, but no personal invitation or press card was required to attend the Editions shows. In the fall of 1934, Edition had created year-round employment for six hundred workers.[28]

Can the innovation in production by Lelong be considered ready-to-wear, and was "ready-to-wear" used at the time to describe manufactured dresses in France? Historian Guillaume Garnier mentions that the word *confection,* inherited from the nineteenth century, was in use during the 1930s to describe "the industry of non-bespoke clothing," or garments machine-made in series, and had a reputation of poor quality, as a distinction from couture, which was supposedly of high quality and gave direction in trends.[29] The term *ready-to-wear,* or *prêt-à-porter,* was not yet in wide use in France. During the interwar period, the Chambre Syndicale decided that only foreign manufacturers would be invited to shows and allowed to reproduce haute couture garments. French manufacturers could not buy haute couture for reproduction. Instead, they gathered information "through the keyhole," from the fashion press, and by watching the elegant public at events like horse and car races. Information circulated through the designers and workers. In addition, the status of manufacturers often made connections with couture unavoidable. The wives of industrialists were often clients of haute couture. For example, Anna Weill was a regular client of Lanvin's and Vionnet's, but also the wife of Albert Weill, who ran a prominent French ready-to-wear firm, and through his wife's wardrobe was informed of the last developments of haute couture. There were also exceptions. Théophile Bader, the owner of the Galeries Lafayette, was a shareholder in the houses of Chanel Parfums, Patou, and Vionnet. He managed to purchase haute couture designs but was periodically attacked for counterfeiting by couturiers who were not part of his portfolio of brands. Nevertheless, the prevalence given to foreign manufacturers created a peculiar dynamic of increased discrepancy between center and periphery.[30]

French manufacturers were varied in size. Some firms specialized in one type of garment, like L. Morel, with workshops at 32 rue du Sentier, who made coats and created "models all year long." Others firms offered full lines of clothing, like the Etablissements Cain & Rheims (abbreviated as Carha), an SA founded in 1923 that produced eight hundred high-quality garments a day. In 1927 the enterprise invested in five thousand square meters of new workshops, modernist buildings, and luxurious décor for presentation to buyers, on avenue de la Soeur Rosalie, near the unfashionable neighborhood of the Place d'Italie. Its full collection amounted to five hundred designs of coats, tailored suits, dresses, and a full sports line. The company had its own retail shop at 62 rue du Louvre, equipped with a bar and grill room, so as to offer the best services to the American clientele.[31]

Some of the *confectionneurs* worked first and foremost for the department stores, like the Société Parisienne de Confection (SPC), dedicated to producing the garments sold by the department store Galeries Lafayette. The SPC produced between five hundred thousand and six hundred thousand dresses annually, plus large quantities of underwear, blouses, skirts, and men's garments.[32] Wholesale business, or *couture en gros* (wholesale couture), was a distinct category specializing in crafting and selling for foreign or domestic retailing. Embroidered and beaded dresses were an important part of this production in the 1920s. Some enterprises capitalized on a narrow offer, like the beaded shift dress in the case of the Paris registered trademark La tunique Radiah, embroidered with flowers, leaves, and arabesques in beads of gold, silver, steel, and crystal. It was intended for the foreign markets, by way of commissionaires and international buyers. In the late 1920s, the range sold by the wholesale houses expanded. The fashion for beaded dresses faded, and the wholesale business had also learned to better integrate "the spirit of haute couture," producing more varied up-to-date designs.[33]

In the mid-1920s, France nurtured the ambition to impose itself as the premier country not only in high fashion but also in the dress-manufacturing industry. Firms developed intermediary categories of ready-made dresses, under such categories as "lingerie dress" and "French little hand-made dress." These were made in large series in France and in Belgium for the local retailers and for the US market, where they were known as "stock dresses." They were good-quality products, presented in a cycle of perpetual renewal rather than at fixed opening dates like haute couture. Some firms specialized in such series, like the brand Toutmain, owned by Isidore Berthe and valued by both local and international clients. Toutmain registered its own designs for intellectual property. In the late interwar years, Toutmain sold up to a thousand dresses daily.[34]

French manufacturing firms were a place for transfers of skills between France and the United States. For example, the French enterprise Marobe (my dress) was taken over by American management in 1929. The firm produced a complete line of clothing for women at popular prices. Some pieces were proposed in good-quality fabrics from Rodier. Besides the ubiquitous borrowing of Paris designs, transfers of management and techniques—including in the ready-to-wear lines—

were multidirectional. During the 1930s the American manufacturer Lazarus & Co. adopted French methods in stock management. American companies thus far had stocked dresses by line or by design. Lazarus decided to stock dresses by size instead and, in so doing, imitated the stocking methods of the French garment manufacturing firms.[35]

Competition in the domestic dress-manufacturing industry, which attracted a growing segment of foreign buyers from the United States and from South America, pressured the haute couture firms to meet the demand for more affordable lines. Lelong traveled again to America in October 1935. The French minister of foreign affairs, Pierre Laval, commissioned him to study the working conditions in the American clothing industry. That same year, Lelong designed the wedding dress of Laval's daughter, Josée, who was to wed René de Chambrun, a French American lawyer at the Cour d'appel in Paris and member of the New York bar. Among Chambrun's early clients was Gabrielle Chanel. She used his services when trying to solve her business difficulties with the Wertheimer brothers, to whom she regretted having sold 90 percent of her perfume business. Pierre Laval would become the head of the Vichy government of Maréchal Pétain from April 1942 to August 1944.[36]

Mergers and the End of the Aubert Syndicate

The haute couture business model was fragile because it lacked liquidities, was exposed to seasonal variations, and offered too much credit to private clients. A possibility for overcoming such weaknesses was to finance several couturiers under the umbrella of a larger group. During the interwar period, financier Georges Aubert pursued in Paris the enterprise he had launched before World War I in the Paris-London couture trade. He organized mergers and acquisitions between an increasing number of haute couture houses. In 1927 Aubert merged the house of Dœuillet with the house of Doucet; he then replaced the Dœuillet-Doucet entity he had created with one firm called the Société de Haute Couture Parisienne. Aubert's project was to offer the merged entity more capital in order to make it competitive internationally and branch out in the United States. In September 1929, Aubert's portfolio included the haute couture houses of Agnès, Beer, Drecoll, Poiret, and the Société de Haute Couture Parisienne, and two wholesale dress manufacturers, Ernest Levy and Germaine Patat. Aubert (see Figure 3.3),

EUROPEANS FAR BELOW AMERICANS, SAYS FRENCH BANKER

Georges Aubert Writes Book Which Sounds a Note of Warning to Financiers Abroad.

Time Not Far Off, He Says, When the United States Will Have Distanced Older Nations.

Georges Aubert.

FIGURE 3.3 Financier Georges Aubert embarked upon mergers and acquisitions in Paris haute couture, aiming to create enough liquidities for them to branch out in the United States. Aubert was caught in Ponzi schemes during the Great Depression and had a tragic ending.
New York Times, *March 5, 1911.*

had also helped a former employee of Poiret's, Alfred Lenief, open the house of Lenief in 1922.[37]

Aubert cut overhead costs. In December 1929 he used the store of Agnès in the rue Auber to host another business, the novelty house of Kirby Beard & Co., while Agnès continued her business upstairs in the workshops. Haute couture professionals could see the advantage of suppressing one lease, and some personnel, but they were divided about such effects on their industry, because the profitability of Aubert's management was not immediately visible in all the firms that he bought. The couture house Dœuillet-Doucet reported a loss of 1,442,000 francs in 1929, compared with a profit of 4,436 francs in 1928. The house was showing general expenses of 8,978,161 francs in 1928 and "bad debts" of 232,577 francs. To address the financial problems of the enterprise, Aubert reduced its capital from 11,000,000 to 8,300,300 francs in 1930. Still unable to completely redress the finances of Dœuillet-Doucet, Aubert closed it to re-create, from its stock in trade, a new firm called Mirande.[38]

Aubert also merged the houses of Drecoll and Beer, and then, in 1931, he merged Agnès and Drecoll-Beer. Drecoll, founded in 1904 with a capital of 500,000 French francs, was transformed in 1925 into an SA, with a capital of 7.5 million French francs and 850 employees. Aubert's project of merging Agnès with Drecoll was initially postponed because the shareholders could not reach a quorum. Just after the merger, in the spring of 1931, the house of Agnès-Drecoll showed a net profit of 556,686 French francs. Agnès-Drecoll was resilient and lasted until 1963. Still, the Paris couture milieu was reluctant to embrace Aubert's strategies. He was not included in the two most important employers' syndicates, the Chambre Syndicale and the Protection Artistique. The couturiers did not perceive Aubert's management as a rescue measure in times of crisis, but rather as speculative maneuvering that was detrimental to the profession. Couturieres who were laid off in Aubert's firms, notably at the house of Mirande, protested that they had been unduly fired and, in some cases, replaced by younger and lesser-paid employees.[39]

Aubert's takeover of Poiret's business shows similar tensions. Artistic minded and very present on the American fashion scene, Poiret was, however, plagued with financial difficulties and unable to face his mounting debts. In 1925, Poiret sold the exclusive use of his name for France and abroad on luxury articles, clothing, and fur to the financiers Aubert and Count Jean Récopé, both of whom were part of the French Oustric bank group. Then Aubert and Récopé hired Poiret as the artistic and technical director of Maison Paul Poiret for a ten-year term. Poiret received a monthly allowance and a percentage of the profits of the couture house.[40] In 1928 Poiret went to the United States for three months, undertaking two transcontinental trips and giving conferences along the way. Before his departure, he had set up contracts with a dozen American manufacturers for the production of exclusive Poiret designs of fabrics, underwear, gloves, and furniture. The United Textile Print Works would handle the textile printing. Dresses, hats, and shoes would be reserved for the branches that Poiret, on his way from France, had announced he would launch in New York and Hollywood. Upon returning to Paris, he soon abandoned his American prospects. The French managers of Maison Paul Poiret communicated their intention to cancel their contract with Poiret. Pushed again by financial difficulties, Poiret tried to interest the American firm Contempora in his interior design business, Ateliers Martine. Contempora was a New York–based studio founded in 1928 by designers Lucian Bernhard, Rockwell Kent, Erich Mendelsohn, Bruno Paul, and Poiret himself, who was a vice president of Contempora at the end of May 1929. But at that point, the relation between Aubert and Poiret was strained. Poiret broke off and then lost the rights to use his name for an haute couture firm to Aubert.[41]

In the spring of 1931, Poiret decided to start a new couture house. He settled at 12b rue de Pressbourg and chose as his brand name Passy 10–17, the number of his phone line. The couturier sent off invitations printed not with his name but with his face, commenting, "I sold the rights to my name but my face is still my own." The firm Société Anonyme Art et Couture, formed with a capital of 1 million francs, stood behind Poiret's brand Passy 10–17. The main investors in the firm were textile companies headquartered in Lyons, Roubaix, and Troyes. But the creation of the SA Art et Couture took place right as the economic crisis hit France with full force. Numerous old clients who had followed Poiret to his new establishment disappeared. It soon became clear that the new enterprise was about to fail. The board then fired Poiret as head designer and hired two modelists to replace him in drawing the current collections while the board sought a new head designer. Then, on January 1, 1933, the board hired Louis Dangel, who had previously been Madeleine Vionnet's lawyer and managing director, as the new managing director for SA Art et Couture. Dangel set to the task of redressing the finances of the firm. He reduced the capital to 500,000 francs, paid off the debts, and obtained a reduction in the rent and the trading license of the shop. He appointed the head of the textile firm Chatillon Mouly & Roussel to preside over the board of directors of SA Art et Couture. Dangel had his sister, sculptor and couturiere Yvonne Dangel, hired as the new head of design for the firm. He again reduced the capital of the firm to 100,000 francs and used his connections to finance this capital. In 1934 Dangel managed to obtain the support of Marcel Boussac, president of the textile group Boussac of the manufacturing firm La Toile d'Avion, who brought 50,000 francs to SA Art et Couture, to be converted into one hundred shares. But after a few months it became clear that the firm's financial health was not improving and that the new shares would not be issued anytime soon. The SA Art et Couture closed its doors in 1935. When the failure was declared in March, the firm had 291,957 francs left in assets and a whopping 1,845,867 in liabilities. Boussac set out to recuperate the capital he had given to Dangel, which he recovered after making obstinate demands. The SA Art et Couture was the ephemeral missing link between Poiret, Vionnet, and the new haute couture that would develop after World War II, in which Boussac would play a central role.[42]

As for Poiret, his attempts at financial recovery failed. Despite the monetary support extended to him by his colleagues in the Chambre Syndicale de la Couture Parisienne, Poiret spent the rest of his life in poverty, until his death in 1944.[43] During the crisis, the French media revealed that the consortium of the Banque Oustric, of which Aubert and Récopé were members, had engaged in Ponzi schemes and was now exposed to failure. According to historian Guillaume Garnier, Aubert subsequently committed suicide in 1932.[44]

Maurice Rentner and American Fashion Origination

During the interwar period, the most important entrepreneur of the New York garment district was Maurice Rentner, called by his peers the dean of the trade. In 1927, the volume of Rentner's garment business reached an annual $5 million: "tops in the firm's record as a leading style setter." The US garment industry used the word *style* to describe a new design. Although the terms *fashion* and *style* were often used interchangeably in everyday language, in the garment industry "a new style" was the expression used to designate a new garment design in a current fashion. Seventh Avenue manufacturers said they "gambled" on the

87

new fashions. Designs had to be accepted by the American consumers, and in this interchange, the experts who were able to pinpoint what would sell from the Paris shows had a crucial role to play (see Figure 3.4).[45]

A new group of experts, mostly Americans this time, gained prominence in translating trends for the growing mass markets for fashion during the interwar period. Tobé was the most famous of them. She was born Taube Coller Davis in Milwaukee, Wisconsin, where her father had a men's wear shop. She studied domestic economy in her hometown before leaving to pursue her ambitions in Manhattan, where she was hired by the firm of Franklin Simon and assigned a mission: "find ideas." In June 1927, Tobé started a similar business on her own, with four clients, to whom she was selling weekly fashion reports. A year later, she had twelve clients and hired two assistants. Tobé cabled news from the Paris openings and published weekly reports addressed to fashion professionals in which she delivered trend forecasting, fabric samples, and the latest fashion news from Paris. She also gave the addresses of places where one could buy up-to-date designs in New York. The Chambre Syndicale attacked some of these shops as copyists—like, for example, model renter Elsie Cobin, who in New York showed collections of imported Paris designs and rented them for a fee to American manufacturers, a practice that Paris couturiers considered unfair.[46]

In 1929, Tobé started her Fashion Forum, in which she presented the latest ideas seen at Paris fashion openings to the American manufacturers and retailers. Tobé incorporated her firm Tobé Fashion Director on May 20, 1930, with a capital of $5,000 and settled her offices at 1540 Broadway. The firm became simply "Tobé" the next year. Tobé completed her reporting activities with frequent conferences. She talked about fashion buying at events like the New York Convention of the NRDGA. She wrote seasonal fashion reports for the *New York Times*.[47] In 1934 Tobé opened new offices at 500 Fifth Avenue, doubling her floor space. An annual subscription to her weekly report of some fifty pages cost between $500 and $3,000, depending on the sales volume of the client. In the midst of the Depression, her business made $100,000 a year, and according to *Fortune* magazine, she was the "best known women's wear merchandise adviser in the US." Her clients now numbered over a hundred and included Macy's, Bamberger's, Hall Brothers, Eaton's in Canada, and Harrods in London. Tobé then had over a hundred employees. She sent her assistants to hunt trends in the Colony Bar in Manhattan, Palm Beach, Newport, and Paris. That same year, Tobé also

48 · Women's Wear, Wednesday, November 21, 1923

FIGURE 3.4 Maurice Rentner, the dean of the New York garment district, imported Paris designs for legal reproduction. Several prominent couture brands feature here, notably Poiret, but also Miler Soeurs, who was sued for piracy by Madeleine Vionnet.

Women's Wear Daily, *November 21, 1923, p. 48.*

started using a different medium, working on a movie—featuring beachwear—produced by Pathé News.[48] Tobé was a more Parisian and upper-class fashion consultant, but she would also advise for budget lines that retailed between $7.95 and $15. Tobé's firm sold trends rather than clothes. She showed what from the Paris creations was adaptable for American tastes.[49]

From 1929 onward, several other fashion consultants started offering fashion forecast programs. The publisher Fairchild, home of the main trade newspaper *Women's Wear Daily*, offered a seminar on the analysis of the economic situation, textiles, and styles in women's garments. New York fashion consultant Amos Parrish, of Amos Parrish Inc., an enterprise specialized in retail consulting, organized the Amos Parrish Clinic, a biannual program held for fashion buyers from all over the United States that ran on five consecutive days in New York. In the late 1920s, Parrish hired Paul Nystrom, a professor of marketing at Columbia University, for collaboration. At the height of the Depression, the consulting activities of Tobé, Fairchild, and Parrish increasingly advertised themselves as predictors of trends. Parrish claimed that scientific methods had replaced guesswork, resulting in a much more efficient use of budgets and stocks.[50]

But the use of the word *forecasting* in fashion was controversial because the nature of the forecasters' methods was neither clear nor scientific. Manufacturer Maurice Rentner published an opinion piece in the trade press titled "In Simplest Words—Fashion Forecasts Are *Bunk!*" Rentner preferred lobbying in favor of higher-quality dress. Changes in fashion, he added, were to be found in subtle details rather than in cheap fads.[51] His peers credited him with developing the American Look, especially in suits and evening wear, often cut from imported fabrics. Rentner hired a team of sketchers, patternmakers, and designers to develop his own ideas of clothing. Many of these collaborators would later establish their own businesses. Rentner was one of the longest-lasting manufacturers in the garment district. He diversified his activities, as a bank director and a board member of several hospitals. He joined the advisory boards of several schools, charities, and organizations, including the Park Avenue Synagogue, the Garment Center Congregation, the National Jewish Hospital in Denver, the Affiliated Dress Manufacturers, and the Park Avenue Association.[52]

Rentner thought that designers interpreted and created variations on fashions, and that true fashion creators or innovators were very rare. He had exceptionally good taste and a strong sense of color—to such an extent that his friends and family felt pressure to always look impeccable—but did not claim to be a creator. During the 1930s, once he had established himself in the business, he went to Paris to see the collections for his own inspiration and purchased haute couture with the legal right to reproduce it. Rentner made seasonal investments, taking a risk in his creative view on the industry and in the unpredictability of the public's response. The buyers selected what they considered to be the appropriate designs for the American market, and if these designs were foreign, they imported them at high costs. Lower-priced manufacturers that illegally copied designs brought back from Paris hurt the supply chain. Although Rentner had once been one of them when he was a young manufacturer, he was now eager to protect his well-established business from the copyists who put lower-priced copies on the market and thus cut off follow-up orders to the higher-end manufacturers.[53]

In Washington, DC, the first register of copyrights, Thorvald Solberg, had voiced the necessity to adopt in the United States a protection similar to the French law, just before World War I. From then on, congressmen proposed successive revisions of the copyright law in order to include the protection of fashion design, but they faced lasting resistance. The arguments against inclusion of fashion in the copyright law rested on the principle that the practicality of garments set the fashion industry in a different category from art. Subsequent American debates never left the grounds of this dichotomy between practicality and aesthetics, underlining that if an object had to be utilitarian (*utilitaire*), it could not be high art.[54]

During the mid-1920s, this debate developed into the Vestal Bill, aimed at fast and inexpensive registration of industrial designs, including fashions. US secretary of commerce Herbert Hoover gave his approval to the Vestal Bill. Hoover had sent a commission to the Paris Exposition des Arts Décoratifs of 1925 that reported on the thriving French craftsmanship seen there. Charles R. Richards, chairman of this commission, was also a member of the American Association of Art Museums. When appearing at a hearing for the Vestal Bill in 1926, Richards expressed that American firms were reluctant to employ designers because of piracy. The idea behind the bill was that increased protection would foster original American design and, in turn, its independence from the European arts.[55]

But not everyone was of this opinion. For many fashion entrepreneurs, fashion copying, a symptom of a fast-growing economy, responded to the booming demand of the masses. Owners of department stores, gathered under the banner of the NRDGA, composed the major group of opponents to the Vestal Bill. Passing the Vestal Bill meant, for them, the prospect of fake claims, of an inability to reorder, and of the loss of a season's business if copyists were discovered after ordering. The NRDGA members feared that copyright owners would be able to exert pressure on their retail prices, and that this would concentrate the power in the hands of a small number of high-end manufacturers. The rounds of discussion on the Vestal Bill that followed weighed the retailers' fear of control against the potential benefits of protecting original design.[56] The opponents to the Vestal Bill contended that America was the world's first democracy of fashion. They made three points to support their argument: individual freedom, importance of mass distribution to the US economy, and the world's widest price range in clothing. During this discussion, some congressmen wondered what impact the Vestal Bill would have on the working girl's lifestyle. The bill, they argued, would build the monopoly of a few—the Paris couturiers and their higher-end American importers—against Main Street consumers. To sum up, the bill was "designed to take away from the poor working girl the right to wear the same pattern of goods that the wealthy people do." And yet, the same congressmen also stated that aspirational trends were welcome as long as the average consumers pursued them without excess. That is, copying designs into cheaper lines was welcome; however, as a consequence, an American woman dressing beyond her means would be questioned about the source of her income—and therefore about her morality.[57]

The other camp, which along with manufacturer Maurice Rentner and lawyer Sylvan Gotshal aimed to curb copying, argued that copying was stealing and that copyists engaged in unfair competition. They made further arguments in favor of the Vestal Bill: copyright protection would create employment for American designers, and it would improve the conditions of competition in manufacturing without harming the choice between competitive lines at competitive prices. These arguments rallied a majority, and the Vestal Bill was passed by the House in 1930. It then had to be passed by the Senate, but on that date, the Congress was adjourned.[58] The discussion over the Vestal Bill was therefore reopened in the Senate Judiciary Subcommittee on Patents, Trademarks and Copyrights the next year. A new argument developed in the Senate about the wide range of products that the bill had to cover. This led to further delay, and the debate came to focus not on whether the bill could be passed but on which parts of it could reasonably be passed. By 1940, thirty-nine bills for patent and copyright law revisions in relation to fashion had been proposed to the Congress, but all failed to receive approval.[59]

During the interwar period, the French law provided the strongest protection available to fashion design. The law enhanced the thesis of no difference between visual arts and applied art. French copyright law made no distinction between a fashion design and a painting: a fashion garment and a painting were both art. One can therefore argue, from the definition of fashions as variations on a fixed number of shapes, that there was no difference between commercial art and a "pure" art form in the French law. In the United States, the text of the copyright law was amended to cover a growing array of artistic forms, including popular music and advertising design. It is therefore not the distinction between high or pure art, on the one hand, and commercial art, on the other, that mattered, but the normative construction of high art and utilitarian object and the delimitation between them in the letter of copyright laws on both sides of the Atlantic. The difference in the laws in the two countries was aligned to the interest of protecting each one's stronger industry: couture in France, and mass manufacturing in America.[60]

A New Deal for Fashion Manufacturing

To the question of whether America was able to establish its own haute couture industry, *Fortune* magazine answered that the United States already had one and all it lacked was self-confidence. There was enough money to nurture the growth of haute couture in New York. Top American designers earned as much as, if not more than, their Paris counterparts, and prices of high-end US designs were sensibly in the same bracket as those in Paris, then between $90 and $300, considering that the cost of producing a couture dress in New York at that time was almost double what it cost in Paris. The argument made in *Fortune* was twofold. First, it was paradoxical that in the country of P. T. Barnum, high fashion had not been better able to advertise itself. Second, Paris was to haute couture what Hollywood was to the film industry. Fashionable American women were dreaming of Paris, not of New York. The lesser visibility was in most cases because American designs went directly from an anonymous Seventh Avenue workshop to the department store—however prestigious, like Bergdorf Goodman or Jay Thorpe—but without being showcased along the way by a couture house.[61]

In 1932, Maurice Rentner founded a new professional association with the direct purpose of fostering original design: the Fashion Originators Guild of America. The guild originally comprised the higher end of New York's fashion business. Soon after its incorporation, it counted 130 members, most of them New Yorkers. Member firms employed at least one in-house designer and produced between 200 and 450 new designs per year—Paris reproductions, adaptations, and "totally US designs" created in New York. New members of the guild promised to refrain from buying or selling illegal copies of designs. The guild sent undercover investigators to retailers and kept a list of the ones selling unauthorized copies (in the industry's jargon, this was known as red-carding). There had been other initiatives by American retailers aimed at curbing copying before. As early as 1912, a group of entrepreneurs founded the Society of American Fashions with the purpose of opposing false labels. A bit later, in 1925, the American Association of Dress Manufacturers launched a campaign against the piracy of Paris haute couture, in connection with the Better Design in America movement.[62]

Rentner's guild began to find its members in the highest end of the market, including the prominent New York fashion firms Nettie Rosenstein, Elizabeth Hawes, and Muriel King. The list of guild members in the years 1932 and 1933 included Hattie Carnegie, Jo Copeland, Joseph Halpert, Omar Kiam, Anna McCormick, Bergdorf Goodman, Saks Fifth Avenue, the Filene Brothers, Jay Thorpe, and Bonwit Teller & Co. All were upper-grade dressmakers, manufacturers, or retailers.[63] The list of the textile associates of the guild included French high-end textile manufacturers Bianchini-Férier, Coudurier, Fructus, Descher, and Ducharne, which sold their fabrics to the high-end guild couturiers and department stores. The guild members scheduled their own fashion shows in New York over one week. This idea of a week of fashion openings, fostered by the guild, predated the establishment of New York Fashion Week by Mayor Robert Wagner in 1956.[64]

In 1933, Franklin D. Roosevelt launched the National Recovery Administration (NRA), created by the National Industrial Recovery Act (NIRA), as the major platform for the implementation of New Deal measures to defeat the economic crisis. The NRA implemented codes of fair competition to regulate American industries. The fact that the NIRA was conferring the force of law on the codes brought a new dimension to the guild's activity. On July 5, 1933, Earl Dean Howard, deputy administrator of the NRA, and five representatives of the New York apparel industries met at the Hotel New Yorker. Rentner, in his position as chairman of the guild, was one of them. The purpose of their meeting was to prepare a brief, called in professional jargon the "code," for the US apparel industries: cloaks and suits, dresses, millinery, furs, hosiery, and other garments. They had a week to prepare the code before hearings started in Washington, DC. The meeting addressed three key issues: the minimum wage in apparel industries, workers' maximum hours, and the required number of codes for the apparel group. Less than two months later, the guild was the first association in the trade to establish the five-day workweek, with an average of thirty-five hours for guild member firms, compared with forty-four in the rest of the industry. The adoption of these measures stood in contrast to Rentner's practices as an immigrant entrepreneur who had run nonunionized shops a couple of decades earlier.[65]

Guild members saw the NIRA as an opportunity to curb copying. Among the first three hundred codes approved by the act, sixty-two contained elements on illegal copying of design, mostly in fashions, leather, and textiles. The NRA launched a public movement of support of labeled garments. On October 12, 1933, Eleanor Roosevelt and her daughter attended the public launch of the NRA coat and suit label. The new Coat and Suit Code Authority regulated the use of labels on garments and issued thousands of the new labels to New York factories. The event took place in a Seventh Avenue factory, Del Monte-Hickey, where the first two official labels were sewn into garments made for Roosevelt and her daughter. The Fashion Group launched a campaign, led by Roosevelt in her role as distinguished member, against sweatshops.[66]

In late November 1933, the Uptown Retail Guild of New York gave a dinner to honor Rentner at the Waldorf Astoria. Five hundred department store executives and other fashion retail professionals attended the party. P. A. O'Connell, former NRDGA president, enumerated the virtues of the NRA in a speech. The NRA had brought their business from the red back into the black, curbed cutthroat competition, and eliminated child labor. The codes were not perfect, conceded O'Connell, but this was an opportunity for the American fashion business to get rid of, in his terms, "the economic banditry" and "the stampede of price cutting." Rentner closed the series of speeches by underlining the necessity to encourage artistic detail in the public, rather than dependence on mass production.[67]

The guild, in its action to eradicate illegal copying of original fashions in the United States, established its own system of registration as a guarantee of the protection of original designs. Fashion originators could register a sketch or even a description of a design with the guild. The National Federation of Designs Inc. was in charge of keeping the designs registered by the guild, for a six-month term, and its clearinghouse was the Design Registration Bureau. Foreign designs and licensed copies of foreign designs could not be registered. For that reason, this registration system can be perceived as an incentive to create American originals rather than buying French originals. Fines paid by enterprises for infringement of the rules of the guild were redistributed not to the plaintiffs but to charitable associations. At the end of 1935, the guild had 250 members. There were between 12,000 and 12,500 cooperating retailers, in thirty-two states. In 1936, the guild registered between 40,000 and 50,000 designs per year.[68]

From its inception, the guild set up contracts with retailers stating that the retailers would not buy or sell designs obtained from copyists. In 1936, the guild examined the tariff law and launched an investigation in order to make sure that none of its members resold original Paris couture garments to model renters. It sought to establish cooperation among French couture, American manufacturers, and the American custom authorities in order to avoid loopholes in the haute couture imports, like, for example, the designs imported as private belongings, while they were meant for reproduction in the country of arrival.[69] During the same period of time, the guild started to support lawsuits against New York sketching businesses, on the grounds that such services were illegal copyists of American designs.[70] In 1936, the list of red-carded retailers numbered four hundred throughout the United States. Strawbridge & Clothier, Bloomingdale's, and Filene's were all red-carded at some point. Filene's retaliated by starting a civil lawsuit against the guild. Filene's lost. Andrew Goodman remembered later the arguments over the Filene's lawsuit in the guild hearings. According to Goodman, the purpose of the guild was to protect the artists, but this did not make sense because of the derivative character of the fashion industry: "In this business copyrighting is ridiculous. By the time something is copyrighted it's dead. The legal protection for such a thing is cumbersome and unworkable. [. . .] In this country the person who is protected is the copyist."[71]

Opposition to the guild developed in two main groups of fashion professionals: the manufacturers of cheaper lines, and a part of the retail business.[72] The guild had refused to join forces with the NRDGA or the Associated Merchandising Corporation, the two major American retailers' associations. In January 1933, early in the guild's existence and before it opened up to lower-price manufacturers, the Washington NRDGA office started inquiring into the legality of the guild's activities. Rentner replied that the form of the guild's plans could be questioned, but not its objectives, because it did not restrict trade; however, red-carding, as practiced by the guild, was a form of restriction of trade. Rentner's main argument remained the protection of creativity.[73] Retailers then started attacking the guild from different ends of the lower-priced lines. The retailers' opposition grew with the guild's decision to protect cheaper lines—a departure from its original purpose. In the beginning, the guild had consisted of garment manufacturers in the price lines of $22.50 and up. It was eventually divided into six sections: dresses, coats, junior miss, sportswear, textiles, and protective affiliates. The latter was not full membership, but a special category reserved for manufacturers in the lower price ranges. The Dress Creators League had been incorporated on November 11, 1932, with the purpose of uniting manufacturers of dresses in the range of $10.75 to $16.75 against illegal copying. The guild lowered its threshold from $22.75, to accept members of the Dress Creators League as protective affiliates, in April 1935. Both associations remained distinct. In October 1935 the guild was extended again in the direction of lower-priced lines, asking the retailers of wholesale lines sold between $6.75 and $8.75 to sign an antipiracy statement. This last move would feed the controversy about the policies of the guild.[74]

In 1935, the US Supreme Court judged the NIRA to be anticonstitutional. Lawyer Sylvan Gotshal described the impact of the act on the fashion industry as mitigated. But this was not the end; the guild expanded once more, in the fall of 1936, gathering four hundred firms that produced dresses in the range of $4.75 and under. The guild at one point comprised 60 percent of American dress manufacturers. The Popular Priced Dress Manufacturers Group then filed a petition with the Federal Trade Commission to launch an investigation into the actions of the guild. The petition, which gathered the signatures of three hundred jobbers producing dresses at $4.75 and less, stated that the guild engaged in boycott and in illegal restraint of trade, and asked for the issue of a cease and desist order against it. Retailers of mid- and low-priced dresses feared they would lose in volume sales because of the guild's actions. Rentner's purpose was to "restore apparel to a position of prestige and profit-making that it had lost when the bargain basements were permitted to invade the *French rooms* or the *little shops*."[75] The French room alluded to Filene's, red-carded by the guild, while the little shop referred to Macy's. This raises the question of whether it was still possible to pay for design in the lower-end lines. The Fashion Group took up the discussion on the guild's action, deeming it a response to "the subject of national evils." Gladys Rhodes, chairwoman of the Fashion Group's discussion on the guild, noted that the topic was a subject that could "shake the Fashion Group apart,"[76] adding that the American creative effort was tied to the protection of national designs.

Paris Couturiers Going West

In 1935 the Fashion Group launched a major campaign, the "Fashion Futures" show. Fashion Futures presented the most recent realizations of the New York fashion industries, which during the first two editions of the event, in 1935 and 1936, were mostly copies or adaptations of Paris designs selected to fit the American market. In 1937, however, Dorothy Shaver proposed that Fashion Futures showcase American fashion design instead of French creations, under the title "American clothes for the American scene."[77] The 1937 edition was successful in terms of both advertising and sales. *Fortune* magazine argued that the best way to nurture homegrown American design would be to encourage a small network of socialites to become style leaders, as could be found in Paris, and gave the example of Hollywood actresses Norma Shearer and Joan Crawford as trendsetters. In 1932, Crawford appeared in a Letty Lynton dress—a white, lightweight dress with short, ruffled, voluminous sleeves—of which Macy's then sold half a million copies. Paris couturiers accepted that Hollywood had a powerful effect on fashion advertising. In the late 1930s, Crawford and the Duchess of Windsor were the public figures whose images sold the most dresses.[78]

Gabrielle Chanel, who had been a pioneer in the development of haute couture perfume and sportswear, was the first Paris couturiere to visit Hollywood, in 1929. Chanel was perceptive of the aesthetic qualities of the "less is more" factor. In 1921, she had named her first perfume by the number of its sample, Numéro 5. In 1923, when all couturiers were still choosing evocative names for their designs and perfumes, Chanel preferred to give a humble number to hers, a practice that was common only among the low-grade Paris manufacturers during the same period. In the years that followed, more couturiers imitated Chanel, starting to give numbers to their designs. Chanel's modern take on reproduction, her Model T dress, was advertised in a 1926 issue of US *Vogue*. The little black dress designed by Chanel was received as the fashion counterpart of the basic Ford car.[79] While most Paris couturiers went to New York, Chanel chose Hollywood as her first American destination, where Samuel Goldwyn gave her a contract to design costumes for movies developed by his studios. With her flair for simplicity, Chanel designed costumes for Barbara Weeks in *Palmy Days*, including black pajamas and a beige tailored suit, but their inconspicuous style seemed somewhat too plain onscreen.[80]

Chanel pledged to make regular trips to the West Coast, and she returned to Hollywood to work with Goldwyn in October 1931. Chanel sent one of her Paris *premières* ahead to prepare her work. Her clothes were presented on models whom the designer had picked herself in Hollywood. Still, in 1931, Gloria Swanson visited Chanel's Paris ateliers, where she had a full wardrobe made for her to wear on the Goldwyn-produced movie *Tonight or Never*. Despite the fact that her first contract was lucrative, Chanel pursued her collaboration with Goldwyn for only a couple of years. She reportedly had difficulties adapting to the movie stars' demands and refused to design anything outside of her own aesthetic ideals.[81] During those years, Chanel started drawing a limited number of products for the American market. In the spring of 1929, Chanel designed a glove to be issued by the firms J. M. Chanut & Co., Steinberger Bros., and Block Corp. of New York. The firms kept the Chanel glove design a secret until its release, as the publicity given to an earlier, similar attempt by the couture house of Worth had inspired massive copying and seemingly resulted in losses for Chanut and Steinberger. The new Chanel glove was therefore registered by the French Patent Office. Further, Chanel entered into a contract with Chanut to design a glove on a monthly basis.[82] Chanel occasionally developed similar operations with other firms. Chanel also developed prestigious products: in December 1932 she started her own line of jewelry, featuring diamond pieces in a 1932 Paris exhibition that attracted Picasso, Cocteau, Condé Nast, and numerous socialites.[83]

In France, Chanel added her own line of fabrics to the creation of original garments. She settled her factory in Maretz, a village in the north of France. Specialization in tweeds came first, but soon she also designed exclusive lines of silk prints. Since her designs needed to be copied accurately, to be replicated in the exact fabrics, this production was a way to recoup at least some of the profits supposedly lost in copying. In late 1932, Chanel hired American Winnifred Boulter to work on the advertising of Tissus Chanel. Her collections were diversified: in March 1933, for example, Chanel showed 180 models, all in different fabrics, most of which were Tissus Chanel. She tended to show original prints, like a *trompe l'oeil* line in 1934. At that time, her line of fabrics was extensive, featuring cotton velvet, synthetic satins, woolens woven with metallic thread, and multicolored jerseys.[84] With the creation of her own line of fabrics, Chanel capitalized on the copying of her designs. In public, Chanel tended to say that copying was a form of flattery. But Chanel's position was more complex: on several occasions, she sued counterfeiters of her designs, even teaming up with her colleague Madeleine Vionnet in the courts.[85]

Chanel was followed to Hollywood by other couturiers, including Schiaparelli, Molyneux, Rochas, and Lelong. Hollywood had its own designers, and some of them achieved fame, such as Adrian, and Edith Head, who were the most institutionalized of Hollywood designers and enjoyed a privileged relationship with the movie industry and the Academy Awards. As an emerging fashion city, Hollywood was a threat to New York for the title of American fashion capital. From the start, the presence of Hollywood actresses and the nature of cinema rendered Hollywood designs international. Lelong, on his way back to Paris in the winter of 1937, hoped that it would be possible for Paris couturiers and American industrialists to reach an agreement about royalties.[86] Hollywood lost the battle for the title of fashion capital to New York during the interwar period. A reason for this was that the movie industry imposed creative constraints on fashions. Sophie Gimbel, designer for New York's Saks Fifth Avenue, thought that the constraints of the screen were, to some extent, incompatible with the most innovative elements of fashion; she said that Hollywood was a "rein on fashion. . . . The determination of film stars to look beautiful first and smart afterward has discouraged freak fashions."[87]

New York was much closer to Europe geographically, which gave it an advantage in the fashion trade. The growing richness of the New York cultural scene, museums, and art collections also played an important role in shaping a fashion industry there.[88] Several French fashion designers settled in New York during the interwar period. A handful of them specialized in millinery, like Lilly Daché, and Gaston de Clairville, head of millinery for the Saks department store. A handful of Paris couturiers tried their luck in New York. One was Hélène Lyolène, a pseudonym for Hélène Pouterman. Born in Baku, she moved to Paris with her son in the 1910s as a refugee from the Russian Revolution. She tried various jobs in interior decoration, doll dressing, and fabric design before opening her own couture workshop in 1926. The quality of her work earned Lyolène a good reputation. Fabrics played an important role in her creative process, with the use of Rodier jerseys for day and lamé, moiré, and taffetas for evening. Lyolène draped, cut, and pinned everything herself. In the early 1930s, she started to take rather frequent trips to New York and designed for Macy's. She also created designs exclusively for the New York retailer James McCreery & Co.; Chicago-based Marshall Field & Co. would soon set up a similar arrangement with her. In June 1934, Lyolène closed her house at 16 place Vendôme. She told the French press that she was planning a long trip to the United States, including a stay in Hollywood, but on August 31, 1934, she filed for failure at the city of Paris, right before leaving for New York. She declared to the press that she felt an urge to settle in the United States but that her business in Paris had been good. After World War II, Lyolène worked again in Paris, as an employee for the couturier Jacques Heim, for whom she designed a line for young customers.[89]

The other well-known couturier who set up shop in New York during the late 1930s was Marcel Rochas, who had founded a limited liability firm in Paris in 1925. Rochas refused to be part of the Chambre Syndicale and of the Protection Artistique. To protect his designs, Rochas claimed to have adopted a very modern method: a fast-paced turnover of his collections. In the press, Rochas denounced the wide dissemination of fashion as running counter to the national interest.[90] In November 1936, Rochas sailed to New York with the plan of branching out. He inaugurated a branch in Manhattan, at 32 East 67th Street, between Madison and Park Avenues, on September 28, 1937. Nearby streets housed other American dressmakers, notably the couture house of Elizabeth Hawes. The branch was managed by Guy Guérin de Font-Joyeuse, and staff members spoke French. The shop offered dresses, coats, and suits, designed by Rochas in French fabrics, shown with shoes and hats of French design.[91] Rochas's first New York fashion show featured a hundred pieces, from simple sport suits to evening wear. Rochas told the French press, "There is no doubt I am taking big risks. . . . What I therefore bring to the American woman, is my production of original quality, in the original French fabric, and for the illusion to be more complete, I have endeavored to recreate in New York the same atmosphere, in the exact same setting as my Paris house."[92]

The Paris couturiers thought that Rochas was the first outpost of haute couture in New York, but their hopes were short-lived. On December 15, 1937, American customs agents raided the New York branch of Rochas. A federal grand jury was subsequently appointed to investigate Rochas, who allegedly had smuggled haute couture dresses, hats, and furs into New York City. The trial was carried out before Federal Judge William Bondy. Marcel Rochas stayed in Paris while his New York manager, Guérin de Font-Joyeuse, went to court as the main defendant. Over thirty witnesses, including a dozen customers, testified at the trial. Models had allegedly brought Rochas garments from Paris as if they were their own property. Rochas then sold these garments to private clients despite the fact that the New York branch had not paid custom duties upon their entrance into the country. Sales of these dresses did not appear in the firm's books. The court found Guérin de Font-Joyeuse guilty of the charges and sentenced him to one year plus a day in prison and five hundred dollars in fines.[93] The seventy-five Rochas garments and accessories seized by US Customs were publicly auctioned in September 1938; valued at a total of $8,397 in foreign value, or $13,085 in US domestic value, the items yielded only $6,200 at auction. Rochas closed permanently in New York but remained opened in Paris.[94]

The New York garment district had remained the undisputed center of fashion production in the United States, from which goods were exported to peripheral and international markets. The volume of business far surpassed what Paris fashion could do, even if Paris was the leader in terms of design. In 1937, the New York City area had an output of $332,300,798 in the dress business alone. In 1938, the city's coat and suit industry produced fifteen million suits, most of them priced between $6.75 and $39.50 (5 percent were in the bracket of $59.50 and higher). In 1939, dress manufacturers were dominant, with 1,300 businesses totaling 105,000 workers and an annual volume of some $400 million. The largest firms made $3 million to $4 million, while the average firm yielded an annual $300,000. New York's dress business counted for 84 percent of the total US dress production. The coat and suit manufacturers followed, with 82 percent of annual US production located in New York, amounting to a value of around $200 million. The New York garment industry of the late 1930s praised itself for having left behind the "specter of sweatshop." It was also the most unionized business in the country: 92 percent of American coat and suit workers were unionized.[95]

The Birth of the Welfare State

Couturier Pierre Gerber, director of the house of Callot Sœurs, became president of the Chambre Syndicale in 1930. These were times of economic war, said Gerber in his May election speech to the Paris couturiers, and as a specifically French industry, haute couture had a role to play in the fight against high tariffs and counterfeiting. In such times of crisis, added Gerber, the vocation of the Chambre Syndicale for philanthropy should be used to prevent class conflict. Two charitable societies took charge of the welfare of Paris haute couture: L'Avenir, presided over by Jacques Worth, and La Couture, headed by M. Clément, director of the house of Paquin. The Chambre Syndicale supported both societies with the budget to operate an office and to print information materials. Their welfare was otherwise left to the private initiatives of the haute couture houses. Many of them featured extensive facilities—at the house of Lelong, for example, a canteen distributed hundreds of hot lunches to employees every day. Some were known to offer good health care, like the house of Vionnet, which offered employees health care and dental care, and provided an in-house children's day-care facility.[96]

Gerber and his team also aimed to provide better education of the workforce as part of the profession's strategies to alleviate social unrest. This developed into the creation of the Ecole Supérieure de la Couture by the Chambre Syndicale, a task that the Chambre assigned to M. Dupouy, of the house of Dupouy-Magnin, who had begun his career as an haute couture worker. Dupouy had noticed how difficult it was for a young apprentice or a low-rank seamstress to acquire the knowledge necessary to rise in the hierarchy and become a *seconde* or *première d'atelier*. Dupouy and a small team composed of Chambre Syndicale members drafted an education program that included the cutting of *toiles* (raw linen proto-types), fitting, and drawing, as well as the study of color, ornament, aesthetics, and textiles. Classes took place on evenings and Saturdays, three times a week over two years. A primary school education certificate was a condition for enroll-ment. Upon Dupouy's presentation of this program, Madeleine Vionnet—who had begun working as an apprentice at the age of eleven—reacted with enthusiasm, especially about its emphasis on drawing and the history of costume, which she considered to be particularly important in couture education.[97]

In the 1920s, Paris couture firms still employed part of their workforces on short-term contracts. The seasonal workforce reinforced the stable base of workers during the high seasons. The Chambre Syndicale negotiated with the unions as to what kind of compensation should be offered to workers when short-term contracts came to an end.[98] In 1923, an important strike had resulted in an unusual measure: a lockout of workers from the haute couture workshops by their employers. The Chambre Syndicale had then signed an agreement that tied the workers' wages to the consumption price index. During these negotiations, the division between workers affiliated to Christian unions and those belonging to left-wing unions had been a weakening factor among the workforce.[99]

In the fall of 1931, France felt the full effect of the Great Depression, and the question of the couture workers' wages came back on the agenda. In September, the members of the Chambre Syndicale decided to write off the interunion agreement on wages from 1923, arguing that the Great Depression, competing foreign markets, and France's declining balance of trade made these conditions unsustainable. The only option left for haute couture to survive, argued the Chambre Syndicale members, was to lower the wages. But they could not agree on a method of doing so. Anticipating opposition, they considered two options: one was to go back to piecework instead of an hourly wage; the other was to offer more temporary contracts and use the threat of instability to govern the workforce. At the Chambre, however, some members remained skeptical about such measures, notably the Social Catholic Dupouy, who argued for dialogue. Dupouy explained that he had been a worker himself and thus felt that without a consensus with the labor unions, no agreement would hold.[100]

Four months later, the members of the Chambre Syndicale agreed that the wages should be aligned with the cost of living index. Simultaneously, the Chambre Syndicale worked on reducing its expenses. In January 1932, the cost of living index went from 565 in the third quarter of 1931 to 531. The Chambre Syndicale decreased the salaries in proportion, a measure effective January 30, 1932, in all the member firms. The employees' representatives had written their opposition to the Chambre Syndicale, but the employers answered that it was the only remedy against an increase in unemployment, because of both the economic conditions and the decrease in haute couture exports. The members of the

Chambre explained that they would rather lower the salaries than lay off workers. At the same time, the Chambre members retained the ability to offer bonuses to the most productive workers.[101]

At that point, the salary for a first hand, the top-ranked worker in charge of directing a couture workshop, dropped from 208.80 francs per week to 198. The difference in salary between an apprentice and a top-ranked worker was roughly fourfold—less of a wage disparity than observed by labor experts at the turn of the century.[102] Large strikes took place in the mid-1930s. The limited size of most couture firms, as well as the involvement of the workforce in the creative output of the firms, meant that negotiation and cooperation between the workforce and the management was more important in haute couture than in most other sectors of French economic activity.[103] Negotiations followed the mid-1930s strikes in order to find common ground between the socialist labor union Confédération Générale des Travailleurs (CGT) and the employers' Chambre Syndicale. One of the sore points was the pay for overtime. At-home work, which still existed in haute couture, also needed to be reconsidered. Divisions between groups of workers resulted in more complex negotiations, and the employers' syndicates took advantage of the divisions between the various unions. Historically, the Chambre Syndicale had had easier relations with the Christian unions than with the left-wing ones, and for some time, the Paris branch of the CGT refused to sit at the table with the Christian unions and the employers' syndicates.[104] As for the Chambre Syndicale, the main challenge was in respecting its own collective agreements. Lelong, who was elected president of the Chambre Syndicale in 1937, considered it unjust that some member houses respected and loyally applied their collective agreements, while other members did not. The mid-1930s in France have been characterized as the *grande peur*, the great fear of employers under the left-wing Front Populaire government.[105]

The French government signed the Matignon Agreements on June 7, 1936, followed by a series of laws on June 11 and 12, 1936, that limited the workweek to forty hours and gave every worker the right to two weeks of annual paid vacation. The Matignon Agreements were the major milestone in the construction of the French welfare state. The Chambre also decided on a general raise of 8 percent at every salary scale in haute couture. The Chambre Syndicale and the unions then set to the task of redefining their collective agreements, called conventions, and finalized new versions of their agreements in 1938. The Chambre Syndicale exited the Depression era deeply divided both on questions of the workforce and on the debate over repression of copying. At that point, the number of members had dropped to 104 haute couture houses, which together employed a total of thirteen to fourteen thousand employees.[106] As a consequence of the Matignon Agreements, prices of both manufactured garments and haute couture rose, but even then, France was still competitive. A dress that required fifty hours of work now cost forty-eight dollars to make in Paris and sixty-six in New York. In late September and early October 1936, American buyers were rushing their orders to benefit from the devaluation of the French franc before couturiers increased their prices. The devaluation measures on the French economy, effective from 1938, had positive effects that lasted for the next couple of years.[107]

Chapter 4

Fashion *in* World War II

B uy until it hurts" was the motto of the American buyers in the spring of 1939.
Despite the imminence of a declaration of war, Marshall Field & Co. reopened its office in the rue Scribe. The brothers Maurice and Ira Rentner,
designer Fira Benenson, Francis Thynne, commissionaire for Bonwit Teller, and a
group of buyers for Saks Fifth Avenue were all in Paris. Banks transferred securi-
ties, and couturiers moved their collections of precious furs out of town. All were
anxiously watching Hitler's every move, hoping that peace was still possible. Facing
the international political tensions, and growing European competition in the fashion
business, the American trade welcomed the efforts of Paris couture to maintain a
high standard.[1]

German businessmen with sympathies for national socialism described the
French fashion business as completely infiltrated by the Jews and blamed the
Paris firms for disseminating immoral fashions, encouraging decadence, and dis-
turbing women from their most important duties, like motherhood. The Nazi regime aimed to supplant Paris couture with its own fashion industry, based in
Berlin and Vienna and led by an ad hoc German Fashion Institute. During the
interwar period, Germany had also, as had most other occidental countries,
pleaded for protectionist consumption. In 1938, however, the German outerwear
industry still spent an estimated 800,000 to 1,000,000 marks annually on Paris
designs, a sum deemed outrageous by the relevant German authorities. Patriotic

disapproval did not keep prominent German fashion houses from visiting the Paris collections.[2]

Discrimination against Jews in the garment trades accelerated in Germany until, in January 1939, the textile and clothing manufactures were made *judenrein*—cleansed of the Jews through Aryanization of their businesses. German entrepreneurs took over Jewish businesses from their former owners, who, in the best cases, fled abroad. Most left for England or America, where they started up workshops and factories. In New York, the local Jewish philanthropic societies gathered at the initiative of Henry Ittleson, president of the Commercial Investment Trust, to launch fund-raising efforts to help central European refugees.[3]

Franco-American Alliance against Piracy

In Paris, the members of the Chambre Syndicale focused their attention on two American importers, Ellerbe Wood and Elsie Cobin. Wood, an American citizen, arrived in Paris at the end of April, introduced by the trade press as a "New York model importer." She stayed until mid-May to study the French glassware and pottery market for future business. She also went to London. For more than a decade the Chambre Syndicale had tried to prove that Wood was a model renter traveling to Paris in order to supply American copyists with haute couture designs. The so-called model renters bought haute couture designs in Paris and rented them for copying to overseas manufacturers, a practice tolerated in America but viewed as unacceptable among Paris couturiers. Cobin, the other famous model renter, was listed among the passengers on the *Aquitania* on a transatlantic trip to France in February 1939, right on time for the new collections. The Chambre Syndicale denounced the model renters as copyists to the Ministries of Foreign Affairs and of Commerce. Earlier that year, a group of leading Paris couturiers had held a private conference with members of Rentner's guild to discuss the project to undercut the counterfeiting business. Rentner had threatened that the importers blacklisted from the shows should be barred from the Paris shows. But while *Women's Wear Daily* opened its columns to Rentner's opinion, the authoritative trade paper announced in the same pages the collection presented by Cobin in her New York showroom, describing at length the dresses by Lanvin and Piguet, and by London couturier Victor Stiebel. Most manufacturers could not afford to travel to Paris or to subscribe to expensive authorized services like the Tobé Report. These manufacturers needed information sources like Wood and Cobin in order to design their collections.[4]

Rentner was still a major actor among the garment district's entrepreneurs. He had followed Paris design for decades.[5] For Rentner, design was not a national issue. His emphasis on the need to buy Paris originals for authorized reproduction did not contradict his desire to see American designers developing their own creativity. The Fashion Originators Guild of America, which Rentner had founded the previous decade, was undergoing a new phase of confrontation with the American public authorities. In April 1939, the guild appealed a petition of the Federal Trade Commission (FTC) attesting that the guild was illegal because it attempted to create a monopoly. The FTC, however, added that the purpose of the guild was immaterial, because determining whether a garment was a copy or an original belonged to the immaterial realm. This decision of the FTC against the guild surprised Paris couturiers, who had had no doubt that the guild would win its appeal.[6] The guild responded that its policies were intended to suppress the evils of the industry, the worst of them being piracy; that its membership was voluntary; that its program was commensurate to the aims pursued; that the association was fairly administered; and that its objective was neither monopoly nor boycott. Copyists, argued the guild, competed on a price basis, cutting down costs by bidding the assembling work to contractors, whose only option was to lower the costs at the expense of the workforce.[7]

In May 1939, the guild and the French Protection artistique des industries saisonnières (PAIS), founded by Vionnet and her lawyer Trouyet, announced that they were joining forces to offer a common plan to check the deliveries of haute couture garments suspected of having been bought on behalf of model renters. The PAIS expected the guild to police the American market.[8]

The major novelty of 1939 was the opening of the transatlantic commercial airlines: the American Clipper and the British Caribou made the trip in twenty hours. David Nemerov, vice president and general manager of the New York department store Russeks, advertised his plane travel back to the United States with a selection of Paris fashions.[9] Upon arrival in New York, he was greeted by a delegation of Russeks colleagues and three mannequins "who staged an impromptu fashion show at the hangar. They exhibited the six models brought back by Mr. Nemerov on the Clipper. . . . Mr. Nemerov pointed out that the models being exhibited were shown in Paris four days ago, and would be on display in his store within one week, thereby saving from three to four weeks in presentation to the American public."[10]

The new airplane services offered faster communication between France and the United States, but the Paris commissionaires and couturiers agreed not to use the planes to deliver their international clients' purchases. Instead, they gathered all their shipments on the *Normandie*, departing August 22. Travel did not seem dangerous. The American embassy in Paris had not given any warning except to avoid Poland, and Paris was quiet. Fira Benenson, buying for Bonwit Teller & Co., along with designers Hattie Carnegie, Dorothy Couteaur, and Lilly Daché, traveled back to the United States on that same ship. The president of IBM, Thomas J. Watson, was sailing with them and, upon return to New York, commented on the absolute need to avoid another war. Also interviewed upon their return, Benenson and Daché were convinced of the imminence of war but thought that it would have little effect on the couture trade. Blackouts were frequent during their travel. Sending cablegrams was forbidden, and the ship sailed much farther north than its usual route.[11]

The Phony War (September 3, 1939–May 10, 1940)

Between September 3, 1939, and May 10, 1940, the Paris fashion industry was caught in the immobility of the so-called Phony War: war was declared, but nothing moved. Lucien Lelong, president of the Chambre Syndicale, was in charge. The number of firms with membership in the Chambre Syndicale had risen, from 122 in 1937 to 150 on December 31, 1939. The sizes of these enterprises were very diverse. The French Ministry of Labor proceeded through several changes on the collective conventions that had redrawn the organization of labor in 1936 and 1937. In September 1939, the number of hours worked per week went from forty to forty-five, without a pay change. The next month, the ministry decided that additional hours would be subject to a levy, or tax (*prélèvement*). In November, the ministry altered the scheme of paid vacations to establish social obligations in wartime.[12]

Lelong was mobilized on August 28, 1939, as lieutenant of the Third Cuirassiers, along with a number of other Paris fashion-business figures well known in American circles: Patou's manager Raymond Barbas, Balenciaga's manager Wladzio Jaworowski d'Attainville, commissionaire Raymond Schloss, and Associated Merchandising Corporation manager Edouard Leon. Lelong put the activity of Chambre Syndicale in the hands of its secretary, Daniel Gorin. The school of the Chambre Syndicale closed its doors. Barely ten days after the mobilization, Lelong was demobilized and sent back to business. American journalist Kathleen Cannell judged that Lelong owed his early release to the French government. Lelong reopened his haute couture house and went back to work as president of the Chambre Syndicale. Rentner sent him a cable expressing on behalf of the guild that the Chambre Syndicale should persist in its efforts amid the wartime difficulties.[13]

On September 12, Lelong gathered the committee of the Chambre Syndicale to examine possibilities of resuming activity. Before profit, he wanted to keep everyone at work, some twenty-five thousand people, of whom between a third and a half then worked in ammunition factories and on farms. Couture house Bruyère employed its personnel on rotation to avoid laying off some of them. To journalist Edna Woolman Chase, Lelong cabled in late September that it was "too soon to give you valuable information. Am doing utmost to find financial and commercial solution. Allowing for the reopening of houses and the living of thousands of women." Chase answered in front of the New York Fashion Group later that month: "Fortunately for American business, this season the French Openings had all taken place before the war started, which was very considerate of Mr. Hitler, and have made a special effort this season to give us enough trends and variety to last us for some time. . . . Besides, there is always something about the psychology of war that seems immensely stimulating to love and to fashion. Men in uniform always stir the feminine emotions, and women in love always want to look their loveliest—so naturally, the beauty parlors flourish and the dressmakers prosper."[14]

The Chambre Syndicale members started considering options for relocating their couture activity, and they deliberated on which provincial town would be better suited: Cannes, the spa city of Vichy, or Biarritz, where most couturiers had a branch. Biarritz was close to the Spanish market, where the rising star of Paris couture, Balenciaga, had a foreign branch. Couturier Jacques Heim relocated a part of his Paris work force to Biarritz. Lyolène was hesitant as to whether she should pursue working in Biarritz or enroll in the Red Cross. At that point most of the American women working in Paris haute couture houses as saleswomen or in public relations left to work in the *défense passive* or at the American Hospital.[15]

In early October 1939, after demobilization, 90 percent of Paris haute couture houses were closed for commercial purposes. The rest had resumed short-term activity, reopening with reduced staff. Lelong analyzed the situation of the couture businesses as follows: couturiers were to remain liable for paying taxes, social costs, and commercial costs, while altogether they had extended credit, yet unpaid, to private clients for a hundred million francs, which was irrecoverable. Lelong expected that the cost price of the unexploited collections, the missing clients, and the loss of foreign markets would prevent couturiers from making profit as usual. Lelong and the Chambre Syndicale lobbied the government. The Ministry of Finance extended the due dates for couture houses' payment of taxes. The tax on war profits would be calculated on net instead of gross benefits. The Banque de France granted discount terms (*facilités d'escompte*) to the suppliers of the couturiers. The Chambre Syndicale also obtained a delay on the payment of damages to its unemployed workers, arguing that the situation was exceptional for the enterprises. During these negotiations, Lelong insisted that his main objective was to minimize risk.[16]

At that point, the government asserted that it was a national duty and an absolute necessity to maintain the peaceful activities of the country and that couture was one of its most important export industries. At the general assembly meeting of the Chambre Syndicale on October 6, 1939, Lelong stated that "opening one's house can be considered an act of national duty."[17] Paris couture houses gradually reopened. Lanvin sent a cable to the US office of *Vogue:* "My house remains open and I am at the disposal of my American Clientele." The school of the Chambre Syndicale reopened its doors in October with 30 students; half a year later there were 250.[18]

Paris thus quickly reorganized. Many firms had decided to show a midseason collection: Alix, Lanvin, Molyneux, Patou, Paquin, and Piguet. Lelong, who was reluctant to organize midseason shows, still showed thirty silhouettes in early November. He then showed what he called his first wartime collection at Christmas, also in smaller numbers than usual, including designs in red, white, and blue.[19] The press deemed the styles as normal, with just a few more nods at military style. Molyneux showed to crowded Paris salons tailoring in "RAF blue" and "alert blue," a shelter ensemble, warm pajamas, and evening gowns designed for the American market.[20] A few couturiers showed dresses made to be worn over corsets, as they had been reintroduced the previous season in Paris by Mainbocher, who had delegated their production to corsetmaker Madame Détolle. These corsets were made of whalebone, laced up in the back, with padded hips. Sophie Gimbel, who directed the French salon of New York department store Saks Fifth Avenue, endorsed them as very comfortable.[21]

Most of the ready-made dress shops in the Champs-Elysées neighborhood stayed opened. Their owners were keen on advertising that they were French. Some of the shops owned by central European and Jewish refugees were closed, but others remained active, like the Valron and the Rosemonde businesses, which made beaded dresses for the American market, and Toutmain, the popular ready-made dress business owned by Isidore Berthe.[22] Despite optimistic discourses and strategies, the workers in haute couture felt the wartime strain. To provide work to all, the Chambre Syndicale arranged for couture workers to make uniforms for the French army. Just after demobilization, Lelong negotiated with the Ministry of Labor and the Military Commissariat to produce military embroideries and hospital equipment. The Ministry of Labor decided that seamstresses would produce uniforms, caps, lightweight carryalls, and blankets. The manager of the military equipment department confirmed the order, renewable on a three-month basis, of ten thousand wool jackets, ten thousand cotton jackets, and ten thousand pairs of wool trousers. Arguing that haute couture ateliers were ill equipped for this work, the firms decided that the seamstresses should do their work at home, under the regime of regulated domestic labor. The project was then enlarged, from haute couture to all French clothing industries. A nonprofit, the Association Interprofessionnelle, handled organizational aspects. Its board was composed of representatives of all the syndical chambers of French clothing industries.[23]

In response to the demand, the Chambre Syndicale founded its own society, the Société Anonyme Ateliers d'Equipement Militaire de la Couture Parisienne (hereafter, the Ateliers), on December 7, 1939, with a capital of 175,000 francs. Gorin directed the board of the Ateliers, and its members represented the French firms Lanvin, Lelong, Molyneux, and Paquin Ltd. The Ateliers received the raw materials, distributed them to the workers, and controlled the deliveries. Salaries were paid only upon delivery. The military equipment department paid the price of the work (*façon*): 80 percent went to the workers, 15 percent to social, tax, and overhead costs, and 5 percent to the Association Interprofessionnelle. By supporting this initiative, the Chambre Syndicale pursued a twofold aim:

keeping its employees at work, and, while avoiding potential departures for war and its industries, keeping them available for a reprise in haute couture. In November 1939, 550 haute couture workers contributed to the Ateliers. At that time, the Chambre Syndicale hoped that this would help put back to work most of the six thousand haute couture workers who were then unemployed. The Ateliers remained active until June 1940, when they closed and handed over all their remaining stocks to the occupation authority.[24]

Madeleine Vionnet showed in April 1939 a half-season collection of fashions partly inspired by Navy uniforms. After the show, she announced her retirement. The initial plan was that her chief designer, Marcelle Chaumont, would succeed her. Among Vionnet's investors, Martinez de Hoz planned to continue his financial interest in the house, but Bader withdrew his participation in her capital. Vionnet closed her doors permanently in June, which coincided with the expiration date mentioned in the foundation act of her firm. Instead of taking over the house of Vionnet, Chaumont opened a limited liability with 100,000 francs in capital and some of the sales personnel and heads of workshops from Vionnet at a new location, 19 avenue George V, in January 1940. Other former Vionnet employees founded haute couture houses. Charles Meuwese, a Dutchman who designed suits at Vionnet, joined with Augustine Paravy to open Charles Montaigne on the rue Royale in 1940. His official founding deed of 1943 mentions a capital of 900,000 francs. The third firm opened by Vionnet employees was the SA Mad Carpentier, opened by Adèle Clerisse (known professionally as Suzanne Carpentier) and Madeleine Mazeltos on the rue Jean Mermoz with the modest capital of 20,000 francs. Carpentier had her capital raised to 1,400,000 at the end of the occupation, in 1946.[25]

In the spring of 1939, American buyers enjoyed the shows but also noticed the sandbags on Paris streets, the evening blackouts, the restrictions on heating, and the meatless days. Germany and Italy already followed textiles and clothing rationing schemes, but France had so far avoided such constraints. All houses but Chanel had reopened. Chanel closed her couture operation and would return to haute couture fifteen years later, in 1954. However, her brand remained strong through the war years with the production of cosmetics, perfumes, and fabrics through the branches Tissus Chanel and Chanel Parfums.

The Chambre Syndicale negotiated with United States Lines to obtain fares on ships bound for the United States starting January 11, 1940, in order to deliver purchases from the summer 1940 haute couture collections to the American buyers on time. Identical talks took place with the French Merchant Marine. The Chambre Syndicale obtained from the railway company SNCF a direct train between Paris and Lisbon, an additional sleeping car for American buyers on the Paris–Genoa train, and regular Paris–Genoa plane service from Air France. Also, in order to facilitate communications with the United States, the Chambre Syndicale obtained an improvement of the conditions of transit through both Italy and Spain. The commissionaires fixed the dates of shipping and delivery according to the delays in transportation. In February 1940, problems arose with the blockade of Genoa by an inter-Allied committee, which prevented the shipping of American orders that were supposed to leave on the *Conte di Savoia* on February 20. The financial advisor to the French embassy in Washington, DC, Hervé Alphand, intervened in person so that the ship could leave on time. During that season, part of the haute couture industry hoped that the wartime censorship of the media would help them curb the copyists' business. However, this was naive optimism, as the censorship officers responded that the control of style piracy was not in their jurisdiction.[26]

In March 1940 the French government issued decrees to regulate prices and consumption, notably by way of food-rationing cards, and haute couture was left untouched. Between January and April 1940, the Chambre Syndicale made more than two hundred contacts with and visits to the French Ministries of Commerce, Finance, Labor, Justice, and Education. In April, Chambre Syndicale members bestowed on Lelong full responsibility for the industry during the exceptional period created by warfare. The French government appointed Lelong as head of a unit within the Ministry of Information in charge of developing French luxury businesses. In a meeting on April 2, the PAIS, the association active in the protection of design, was liquidated and its activities absorbed by the Chambre Syndicale. Paris couturiers expected that Lelong would use his connections with the British and American garment and fashion industries to facilitate exports. Lelong announced that "no amount of terrorizing by the Nazis would deter them from showing their midseason collections and carrying on."[27]

On April 6 and 7, the Chambre Syndicale organized a show—of creations by Alix, Lanvin, Lelong, Molyneux, Paquin, Patou, Piguet, Rouff, and Worth—under the patronage of the French ambassador in The Hague, at the Carlton Hotel of Amsterdam. Profits from the show were to benefit French soldiers. A similar benefit was organized in New York, featuring designs from thirteen Paris couturiers, who created living tableaux of Paris featuring models designed especially for the occasion; as with other creations for the United States, the couturiers preferred to reserve the exclusivity of Paris designs for their private and corporate clients. Edna Woolman Chase chaired the event. Gowns modeled by the debutantes and young women of New York society were auctioned to a crowd of New York retailers who bid between $150 and $700 per dress. The highest amount went to purchase a Lanvin hoop-skirted design of black-and-gold floral fabric, auctioned off by Saks Fifth Avenue. All profits of the night went to the United Committee for French Relief.[28]

American Fashions

On March 20, 1940, Fiorello La Guardia, the mayor of New York, addressed several hundred fashion experts at the lunch meeting of the New York Fashion Group. Fashion was still reserved for the higher class in Europe, said La Guardia. In America, conversely, women from farms to big cities expected fashionable dresses, which opened a gigantic market to the industry. Paris had not fallen yet, but the time was ripe to believe in New York designers: "It is getting to be a habit to hire designers by the hour or sometimes by the day and it is simply disgraceful! You just can't expect creative work to be successful and to be beautiful if the creator is working under the stress of economic problems. A good designer ought to be employed by the season, at least." La Guardia insisted that American designers should be trained in styles and art history, as they were in Paris, but that they should focus first on adjusting to the economic conditions of America, where New York alone was a market of two million people.[29]

Sportswear was an important source of inspiration for American fashions. In 1939 women's trousers made a breakthrough, and the American trade press promoted them as a new part of "conventional fashions," another form of activewear in peaceful times, supported by designers like Elizabeth Hawes. In Paris and London, women wore trousers too because they were warm and were easy to wear on the streets and in the shelters during air raids. The question that La Guardia asked was, Could the United States become an independent fashion producer? American fashion professionals were keen on proving that their industry was self-sufficient, and to do so they used a historical comparison with the situation on the eve of World War I. For example, in terms of dyes, the United States had in 1914 been dependent on Europe for 90 percent of its supply; now, the Americans were fully autonomous. Since 1936, textiles had become second to food in US production. In 1938 the US textile industry produced (in decreasing order) cotton, wool, rayon, and silk. The United States became the first source of nylon stockings worldwide during wartime. Corsets, gloves, and leather goods, including shoes, were also mainly manufactured in the United States for the domestic and international markets. Puerto Rico became the United States' main source for handmade lingerie merchandise, replacing most of the French imports. The idea of a self-sufficient America in fashion and textiles gained strength during wartime.[30]

Occupied Paris

The Phony War ended on May 10, 1940, with the invasion of France, Belgium, Luxembourg, and the Netherlands by Germany. New York entrepreneurs sent cables to Paris to express their sympathy and their hope that haute couture would carry on. German bombing of the airport in Lyons raised concerns among businessmen. The American buying offices in Paris were, over the next few days, reduced to a skeleton staff. Paris couture houses remained opened, and there was no movement of evacuation similar to what had happened in September 1939. The Chambre Syndicale urged its members to remain at work and to keep their employees at their posts.[31]

In New York, the fashion business greeted this business-as-usual policy warmly and kept sending orders to Paris during the last days of May. The *New York Times* reported, "*The chief,* as M. Lelong is affectionately called by his staff, is continuously being called upon for advice. . . . This quiet courage reassures everybody."[32] In early June, Alice and Bertram J. Perkins—Paris correspondent to *Women's Wear Daily* and Fairchild's European editor, respectively—were among the last Americans to leave Paris for New York on the SS *Manhattan*. Paris was rather empty when they left, like on a summertime Sunday, thought Alice Perkins, but most businesses had remained opened. The Perkinses went to say goodbye to Lelong, who was in his studio creating new designs and was sure to receive continued orders from American clients.[33]

On June 14, 1940, the Germans entered Paris. Bombing threats led to the signing of a cease-fire that same day. Three days later, Marshal Philippe Pétain called the French to stop fighting. The French-German armistice was signed in the forest of Compiègne on June 22. Bertram Perkins wondered whether Paris couture would accept an offer from the Nazis. On June 26, the Fashion Group started its usual New York lunch meeting with a "grab-bag party" that yielded $1,262 in donations for French war relief. Most in the audience had traveled regularly to Paris over the past decades, but they did not want to have anything to do with Paris business under Nazi rule: "Should the Parisian couture be ground under the domination of Nazi Germany, America will have no traffic with the former, regardless of the hurt which might accrue to the innocent people, it is maintained. Every instinct of the American people, let alone the garment trades, revolts against aiding in any manner the economic advancement of the totalitarian powers, it is reminded." The New York fashion businessmen firmly opposed the argument of a "lesser evil" policy—the idea that keeping the French at work in industries other than armament justified working under the Nazis. In the last days of June, the US presidency decided to stop trade with Germany and with the occupied territories.[34]

Protecting American Design

In June 1940, while the influence of Paris receded in the background, the Fashion Originators Guild of America went back to the US Circuit Court of Appeals to appeal the cease and desist order it had received from the FTC. The guild's attorney, Milton C. Weisman, asked the court of appeals to set aside the FTC judgment and consider the following question: "Copying of styles may be legal in some instances, but are copied styles legal when designs fall into the hands of thieves who deliberately break into the plant of a garment manufacturer in order to get such styles for reproduction?" Weisman added that the FTC had previously declined to examine evidence of the copying of designs; further, he elaborated on the different forms of bribery and fraud that such copying entailed. Weisman used the word *thievery* to qualify design copying, while Judge Augustus Hand preferred to say that "the whole system involved breaches of trust everywhere." They also discussed whether the guild was a club with selective membership, to which Weisman replied that all were welcome to join.[35]

American opponents of style protection, which included the Popular Priced Dress Manufacturers Group, believed that piracy was a driving force for economic growth. They ultimately won the battle against the guild, on the grounds that it red-carded the retailers that promoted copies. Such boycotts were considered violations of the Sherman and Clayton Acts. In July 1940, the US Circuit Courts of Appeals issued a negative verdict in the guild's case. The guild thus had to comply with the cease and desist order issued four years earlier by the FTC. The guild subsequently survived with reduced numbers.[36]

In September 1940, the New York fashion industry became vocal about leadership. The US edition of *Vogue* triumphantly advertised a cluster of American designers: "For the first time in history—America makes the mode! Can America design? Can America lead fashion? *Vogue* says, YES!"[37] Higher-end fashion businesses in New York increasingly created their own designs as the supply of Paris creations dried out. They added designs from London, especially tailored suits, coats, and sportswear.[38] Dorothy Shaver, vice president of Lord & Taylor and a pioneer of American fashion design campaigns, urged American manufacturers to develop their own creations. Shaver reminded her colleagues that America was a unique mass market, where prices had decreased during the interwar period while the New York garment district had improved in terms of working conditions. Coordination of colors and styles was central to American retail, stated Shaver.[39]

Sylvan Gotshal—a New York lawyer and a vibrant advocate of design protection from the interwar period—founded the American Council for Style and Design (ACSAD) in 1940. Retailers, manufacturers, and designers supported the association. Gotshal announced a four-point program. The first was to establish New York as the fashion center of the world. Second was to protect originality in design, which delved into Gotshal's longtime concerns. Third, the ACSAD aimed to serve as a clearinghouse for design. Gotshal suggested that it follow the lead of the French PAIS in that US originators register their designs with the ACSAD, as a replacement for the guild, tarnished as it was by the FTC's cease and desist order. The fourth was the creation of a new ACSAD trademark to promote American design.[40]

Corporatist Couture

In Paris, merchandise at the Hermès shop sold out within the first days of the occupation. At Lanvin, German officers bought perfumes and couture for their wives. Soldiers purchased fashionable merchandise in the department stores using occupation reichsmarks. An American diplomat, upon his return to New York, described that the attitude of the Nazis in Paris was so correct that it was painful.[41] *Women's Wear Daily,* through the patchy information received from Paris, perceived the discomfort of most Paris couturiers: "There is comment in some French circles that the way is now open for the resumption of business by some of the couturiers of French nationality willing to operate for the moment under totalitarian supervision. . . . Press dispatches refer to the general reopening of retail shops and buying by German troops of luxury and semi-luxury goods."[42]

As far as infrastructure was concerned, the situation was less dramatic than the German invasion had suggested. Over the summer, textile entrepreneur Paul Rodier traveled to the north of France to examine the situation of his production facilities scattered through three dozen villages where semiartisanal looms working for his firm were located. Most were still in working condition. South of Paris, most Lyons silk looms were intact, and stocks of materials were available. Silk manufacturers kept their stores open, ready to offer their stocks to couturiers.[43]

The situation of the export markets was more challenging. Belgium, the United Kingdom, the Netherlands, the United States, and Latin America were now closed to French goods. The dissemination of Paris fashion information for forecasting purposes had stopped, since cables could no longer be sent from the occupied zone to the United States. The British blockade affected the Mediterranean. Left within the reach of Paris couture were the markets of Switzerland, Italy, and Germany. On the domestic market, couturiers increasingly worked for the Paris theaters. Productions featuring haute couture costumes, at least for the leading roles, were commonplace during wartime.[44]

In August 1940, Lelong proposed to the Chambre Syndicale his plan for the reorganization of couture following the German occupation decrees. Lelong explained that "our entire executive and economic framework must be reconstructed" and that "there is no time to waste on tears and vain regrets for the passing of an order which has proven its obsolescence. New times demand a new technique." This technique was based on a corporatist doctrine, as Lelong put it: "That is the cornerstone of the new structure. . . . We must begin by organizing the various corporations. Economic reforms will follow."[45] The development of this collective project, he added, would encompass a rigid discipline and, after the

Chambre Syndicale accepted the new rules, a strict enforcement of professional control and of sanctions.[46]

In September and October 1940, Paris houses presented smaller collections. Despite the blockade of the French coast, cables about the Paris collections reached New York via Berlin and were avidly commented on in the US trade press, which featured detailed descriptions of the current collections and trends in colors, accessories, and hairstyles. Formal openings tended to be subdued or replaced with presentations by appointment. Lelong showed his winter collection to small groups of private clients, journalists, and buyers. Italian buyers placed orders at Lanvin, Molyneux, Paquin, and Rouff. One of the small groups attending Lelong's show was composed of German officers who gave their wives' measurements to the saleswomen, who in turn helped the officers choose clothes for them. American journalist Kathleen Cannell also saw the collection. In her report to the *New York Times,* she underlined the distinction of Lelong's silhouette. During that week Lelong announced that he had discontinued his Edition line, the longest lived of pioneering designer ready-to-wear lines. Molyneux had gone to the United States, where he declared that he was uncertain about the reprise of his French salons; in his absence, his Paris premises showed "a large Winter collection that includes rich and formal evening clothes. . . . The salons were so crowded that Field Marshal Hermann Goering and his staff said they would come back to see the collection another day."[47]

The occupation authorities set up a system of textile rationing. A minority of the Paris couture firms were given a regime of exemptions from rationing, called the *dérogation.* Selected haute couture houses received 60 percent of the volume of textiles they had used in 1938, a quota that could be adjusted later on. In February 1941, thirty-five houses benefited from the dérogation, then eighty-five, and then eventually sixty-five, which were authorized to present collections of at most seventy-five silhouettes. The Chambre Syndicale aimed with this scheme to spare the French workers unemployment or obligatory work in Germany.[48]

Couturiers under the Vichy Regime

At the beginning of the occupation, a large number of French men and women saw Marshal Pétain, who was a hero of World War I, as the savior of the country. Pétain took the leadership of a regime of occupation that settled in the spa city of Vichy, in the free zone of France, and actively collaborated with the German occupation authorities. In the magazine *L'Officiel*, advertisements for Marshal Pétain's charity Winter Help alternated with those for haute couture and perfume. Despite the restrictions, new fashion publications flourished in Paris, emphasizing a new vision of womanhood that praised natural looks and maternity as virtues for the new order. Fashions on display aligned with the "back to nature" discourses of the Vichy regime and marked a distance from luxury clothing, but did not emulate the American model of mass consumption.[49] Several spring 1941 collections in textiles, couture, and accessories showed the imprint of the marshal's propaganda. Bianchini-Férier created a silk fabric with a salient theme. The tricolor—for the flag of France and Pétain's Etat Français that had replaced the Republic of France—was present everywhere. Fashion photographers set their models in wheat fields replete with poppies, daisies, and cornflowers. The artisanal theme was prominent in the products displayed, honoring the extensive handwork deployed in the French lingerie, lace, and embroidery industries. The press underlined the aesthetic and national qualities of craftsmanship, but also the fact that it could constitute an additional salary for French housewives, in the line of Vichy's family policies. Fewer materials could give more work to Frenchwomen. Propaganda for Pétain was also on display on silk-square scarves, some of them printed with his portrait. Higher-end fabric manufacturer Colcombet printed his own scarves of the marshal.[50]

In 1940, Lelong adapted his views to the political context in which haute couture had to survive. He stressed the necessity of liberalism in April, but in late summer, he discussed the corporatist status of the Chambre Syndicale. Reform was fast. The law of August 16, 1940, marked the shift to a state-controlled economy. Couture was part of the Organization Committee of the Textile Industry, which was divided into branches, the tenth one of which was the Garment Committee. This committee included groups created by the Ministry of Production, and Lelong was appointed to chair Group I—the group that gathered the couture industries and that was to act as the leading group of all the other industries of the garment and textile branches in occupied France.[51]

From the summer of 1940 to early 1942, Lelong did not organize new meetings of the Chambre Syndicale. Meanwhile, the Vichy regime organized the status of French Jews in alignment to the Nazi regime. The decree of October 3, 1940, defined the status of Jews in occupied France and excluded them from a number of professions and, among others, from entrepreneurship. On October 18, 1940, another Vichy decree made the listing of Jewish enterprises mandatory. The Vichy regime proceeded to the Aryanization of Jewish firms, a process in which Jewish managers were systematically fired and replaced by Aryan ones.[52]

As mentioned earlier, Gabrielle Chanel closed her haute couture house in 1939. She had a love affair with a German intelligence officer, Hans Günther von Dincklage, with whom she spent most of the war in Switzerland. Chanel's perfume branch ensured her a comfortable amount of revenue during the war and beyond, until her return to haute couture in 1954. Following the occupation directives of May 20 and October 18, 1940, Chanel's perfume branch was subjected to the Vichy Aryanization policies. The Wertheimer brothers lost the direction of Chanel perfumes for the duration of the war; they fled to Brazil and then to New York. Aryan director Félix Amiot replaced them at the helm of Chanel perfumes. The Société Anonyme des Parfums Chanel had been constituted on April 15, 1924. During the war it had a capital of 4.2 million francs. Amiot owned the 380 shares that had previously been the Wertheimers' and would be returned to them after the war. Chanel owned 60 shares, and the SA La Financière owned the remaining 60 shares.[53]

Research has shown that the occupation regime of France pursued outright racist policies that aimed to suppress any Jewish direction in business. Examination of the registers of French companies for the wartime period confirms that the occupying authorities systematically pursued the politics of Aryanization in the Paris fashion industry. This was especially visible in the smaller couture firms and, even more so, in garment manufacturing. There were only a few cases of Jewish directors in haute couture. The Heims, who were Jewish and had to leave Paris, went to the South of France, in the part of the country that remained the free zone (*zone libre*) until November 1942. The Heims spent most of the war in Cannes. Another major couture firm put under German administration during the occupation was Molyneux. The firm's owner and most of its shareholders were British. Therefore, the occupation authorities considered it an enemy business and put it under the direction of two German administrators.[54]

The Chambre Syndicale set up a craftsmanship section in 1942. At the beginning of the war, only haute couture and manufacturers benefited from available quotas of fabrics. In 1942, this support for craftsmanship helped the small and medium couture firms survive despite the shortages. Being a member of the

Chambre Syndicale became mandatory, along with the application of the Charte du Travail, the labor rules decided by the Vichy regime. For this reason, the Chambre Syndicale membership reached an all-time high. The number of member firms rose from 150 in 1939 to 350 in 1941 and 500 in 1942.[55]

In January 1942, Lelong expressed critical views of what he called the "pseudo-liberalism" of the interwar French economy in which "the principle of an unorganized economy, without fulcrum, without relays, and sometimes without Chiefs has had grave consequences.—One had had to acknowledge it, then with courage apply vigorous remedies." During the same meeting Lelong pointed to a lack of unity among couturiers: "It would have been easier to restart from scratch. One had had to start from a bunch of mistakes, confusion, and sometimes, ill will." He then described his role, which was to "create a new order, it is to abolish disorder; it is reuniting the people practicing the same profession and speaking the same language; it is organizing the profession starting from the social ladder, gathering local syndicates on the regional level, then the national one; it is, lastly, to ensure the liaison between the various professions of Group I."[56] Lelong justified the prevailing place of haute couture in this organization by arguing that the creative skills it involves gave it leadership over all other garment industries. In January 1942, Group I comprised a total of 50,150 firms: 20,723 in couture, and the rest in millinery, lingerie, lace, tailoring, shirting, and fashion drawing. The total sales of Group I were worth 3,619,417,835 francs that year.[57]

In January 1942 Lelong explained the motives for his action: "After June 1940 our single preoccupation was to keep Paris Couture alive despite the innumerable difficulties it had to face. We have, with equal measure, maintained the contact with the French authorities as well as with the Occupation authorities, being inspired by our only concern of defending the profession's interests."[58] Lelong described his work as a continuous effort to keep the profession organized from 1936, which had been the year of the great strikes and of the Matignon Agreements. The relation between the couturiers and politics was subjected to changes over time, notably when it came to relations between the couturiers and the Vichy regime, and with the occupation authorities, that evolved in the population as well. Robert Paxton, in his study of Vichy France, underlines that the relations between the Vichy authorities and the Nazi occupiers and ultra-collaborationist groups in Paris were not static. The changes in the goals of production of the occupation regime, which from 1943 aimed again to raise the production of France at home, also nuance the supposed success of Lelong in keeping haute couture in France. Lelong, in his role of leader of the Chambre Syndicale, adapted to his environment. After this was established, Lelong found in the corporatist organization of labor that prevailed under the Vichy regime an opportunity to lead the entire couture industry of occupied France in a common direction.[59]

For the authorities of occupied France, haute couture exports were a matter of importance. The Ministry of Finance aimed to exchange couture products for foreign raw materials. As in the case of other luxury industries, the couture firms received supplementary quotas of materials in the form of textile points allocated in proportion to their exports. These quotas added to the ones derived from the dérogation system. Importing countries listed by the French Ministry of Finance in 1942 included Denmark, Finland, Norway, Portugal, Romania, Spain, Sweden, Switzerland, and Turkey. Most of these exports would be done through the free zone, which required planning with the authorities of the free and the occupied zones.[60] While Lyons was still in the free zone of France, Lelong organized a fashion show there in March 1942 to cater to the countries that could still import couture. In order to obtain the authorizations necessary to organize the show, Lelong used the semiformal network that the Nazi authorities had set up in the form of lunch meetings, called the Déjeuners de la Table Ronde. Lelong went to one of these lunches with the Nazi authority at the Ritz, place Vendôme, in February 1942. He used the occasion to ease the way for the Chambre Syndicale in receiving authorization to show in Lyons. Lelong would be reproached after the war for this participation, seen as an instance of collaboration with the Nazi authority.[61]

The cards delivered by the Clothing Organization Committee of Group I to haute couture customers give an indication of the number of clients during wartime. On September 15, 1941, there were 9,035 clients of Paris haute couture; there were 16,661 on March 15, 1942, and 13,629 in the spring of 1944. The Chambre Syndicale delivered the cards to private clients on the condition of the deduction of points on the regular clothing rationing card, and of the delivery of old clothes to the Secours National.[62] Firms that obtained the dérogation received 60 percent of the quantity of fabrics they had used in 1938. This percentage was adjusted to the consumption index of 1942 and 1943. In 1942 the Chambre Syndicale evaluated the textiles used in haute couture as 0.5 percent of the total textiles available in France. In 1943, a hundred tons of fabrics were used by Paris haute couture, of the forty-eight thousand tons of fabrics used in France that year.[63]

So far any firm could use the words *haute couture* as a brand name or to advertise its activities in Paris and abroad. However, in 1943, the Chambre Syndicale created a legal definition of the term, to better protect its usage. During the postwar period this helped reinforce the position of the Chambre Syndicale when it sued competitors in the courts, at home and abroad, for unauthorized use of the term *haute couture*.[64] From 1943 onward, the Chambre Syndicale also organized its members into three categories: *couture création*—what is actually generally known as "haute couture"—was at the top; second was the category called *moyenne couture;* and third, a basic *couture* category. This ranking remained in use after the war.[65]

From Paris to New York

Fashion histories underline the fact that Paris fashions developed in near isolation from the rest of the world during the war. Women wore ever bigger hats, or turbans, whose eccentricity was thought to defy the Nazis. Recycling of older outfits gave way to new clothes made of patchwork or that were color blocked. The majority of the population had to make do and mend, and their creativity also contributed to changes in the fashion landscape. When Paris was liberated, the eccentricity of its fashions surprised many outsiders. Few had followed what was going on in Paris couture during the war years. Several studies have challenged the view of a Paris fashion milieu experiencing the war in isolation from most of the rest of the world. Occasionally Americans received information on Paris couture from private buyers. For example, on July 14, 1943, the *New York Times* published the story of Mary Costes, wife of a French air army colonel, who upon arrival in New York reported on Paris fashions. Costes explained that fashion firms remained opened to keep people at work and lift their spirits. She cited Balenciaga, Dormoy, Fath, Grès, Lelong, Paquin, Piguet, Rochas, and Rouff as the best-loved houses, and she opened her Paris-bought wardrobe to the journalist, who was surprised by the abundance of fabrics in Costes's tunic jackets and draped dresses. These clothes differed aesthetically from the American designs. The US War Production Board announced on March 8, 1942, the L-85 restrictions that rationed the use of fabrics in order to support the American war effort. These restrictions put limits on the use of materials in American fashions and resulted in a more utilitarian and practical definition of a garment.[66]

Few couturiers went to New York, either permanently or for long stays. Hélène Lyolène, who had become the director of the youth line Heim Jeunes Filles at the Paris house of Heim, was already committed to a transatlantic career. After several trips to New York, she planned a four-month stay there in the fall of 1939. She had to wait three months to obtain a Nansen passport and visa. In December 1939, she was hired by New York dressmaker Hattie Carnegie as a head of the youth department. Lyolène showed a quick mastery of the right mix of French training and American adaptation—including in her communication to her New York peers. She became a regular guest at the Fashion Group. She also conceded that working for mass manufacturing required the development of appropriate skills. Lyolène, in the summer of 1940, defined herself as a product of a transatlantic fashion industry and a citizen of the world. Elsa Schiaparelli was another case of a couturiere with a transatlantic life who ended up spending most of the war in New York, leaving her Paris firm in the hands of trusted managers. Similarly, Bruyère, another well-esteemed Paris couturiere, resettled in New York for the war.[67]

In October 1939, Mainbocher's 250 Paris employees had all been conscripted or sent off for war duty. In his view, "New York was slated to be the world's fashion capital and . . . Paris is finished—at least for a long time." He closed his Paris business and reopened in New York, in October 1940, at 6 East 57th Street. The couturier filed for incorporation in Albany on September 18, 1940, under the category of "apparel," with a capital of $100,000 in a thousand shares. Mainbocher had a reputation of financial probity. In the mid-1950s his business still brought an annual 5 percent to his stockholders. He was warmly received in the United States and gave his first show at Hotel Astor on November 30, 1940.[68] Virginia Pope, chief fashion editor of the *New York Times*, commented that it was just like a Paris showing. Mainbocher imported Paris fashion culture when in his first New York show he emphasized wasp-waisted silhouettes based on corsets produced in collaboration with the American mass manufacturer Warner. Mainbocher also showed two dirndls, the traditional German peasant's costume appropriated in Nazi Germany and revisited by haute couture that season, in his fall 1941 collection.[69]

In 1942, Mainbocher was commissioned to design the "visible" uniform of the women's US Navy reserve for eleven thousand women. The navy chose him because he was born in the United States and had the ability to tailor as a Paris

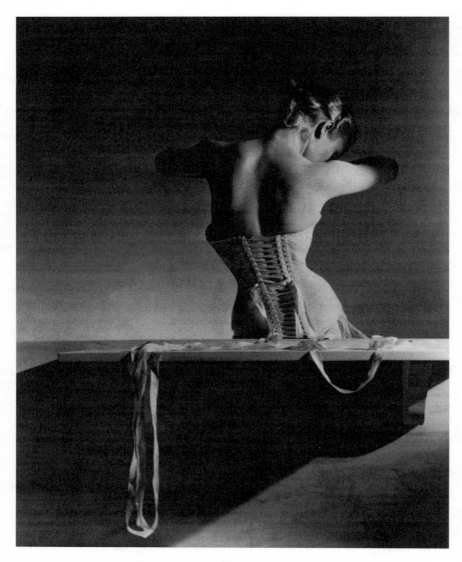

FIGURE 4.1 From the late 1930s and into World War II, couturiers created hourglass lines worn with corsets, which were again in fashion for a few years. The photograph by Horst P. Horst, titled *Mainbocher Corset*, from August 1939, is one of the most famous fashion pictures of the twentieth century. It also celebrates the work of an American couturier in Paris, Mainbocher, a year before he closed his Paris firm and resettled in New York.

Horst P. Horst/Getty Images.

couturier. Mainbocher (see Figure 4.1) never reopened in Paris and remained active in New York until 1971. During the postwar period, he hired Natalie Paley,
former wife of Lucien Lelong and now a Hollywood actress, to manage his public
relations.[70]

Cases such as Mainbocher, Bruyère, Lyolène, and Schiaparelli made the outbreak of World War II a turning point in the internationalization of French couture. While Rochas had failed to settle in New York in 1938, these couturiers
were pushed to leave by the outbreak of the war, and to go produce their own
lines in America. Bruyère and Lyolène did not seek to incorporate in the United
States but rather used other business structures to sell their products under contract with American firms. They aimed to produce lines oriented to the needs
and desires of their American clientele. Both clients and fashion journalists saw
this as a gesture of acknowledgment toward an American culture of design rather
than an imposition of an aesthetic from abroad.

New York fashion professionals had an important infrastructure and market
to support their industry. In 1940, the total annual estimated volume of the American women's fashion industry, including millinery and shoes, was \$3.5 billion.
This figure could be broken into subcategories, of which dresses made
\$461,576,477 annually. The American domestic market at that time numbered
132 million people. The volume of business created by the New York garment
district far surpassed that of Paris couture: "Exact figures of profit have always
been hard to obtain in the Paris couture industry, but it is doubtful if any Paris
couturier ever made as much money in his business as a successful Seventh
Avenue manufacturer or any of the leading specialty shops of the 57th Street
type."[71]

New York fashion professionals observed in 1940 the need to develop an
authority that would have a stabilizing effect on styles. For Stanley Marcus, one
option was to set up a "central casting bureau" for American fashion designers,
which he compared to the practices used for the selection of actors in Hollywood.
The American fashion publications should play a central role to offer consumers
an impression of coherent fashion trends and to avoid chaos in design offerings.
Alfred Chandler had observed a lack of central management in the nineteenth-
century American textile industries.[72] In the 1940s, nothing had changed: fashion
forecaster Tobé shared the view that American fashions needed a clearinghouse
for fashion manufacturers. Tobé also argued that New York needed more social

occasions to foster higher-end dressing and that wealth was the dominant factor: "Style has always followed the *wealth line of the world.*"[73]

During the war years New York mayor Fiorello La Guardia multiplied his public appearances with the objective of promoting the New York fashion industries. La Guardia involved the press and the industry in his project of making New York the world's fashion center. In 1943, La Guardia named former police commissioner Grover P. Whalen chairman of the Mayor's Committee on the World Fashion Center. In 1944, the works of that committee developed into a plan for erecting the World Fashion Center in New York City, within a quadrangle defined by Broadway and 6th Avenue, at the height of 27th and 28th Streets, to be occupied by six to ten large buildings and an auditorium. Estimated costs were by then between $88 million and $126 million. Although wartime conditions slowed down the project, it eventually developed into the New York Fashion Institute of Technology, which opened its doors in 1944.[74]

The Profits of Couture

For the majority of the population, in France as elsewhere in the West, rationing and shortages made dressing a challenge. Despite these circumstances, haute couture thrived and couture sales multiplied fivefold between 1941 and 1943.[75] In the meeting of the Chambre Syndicale general assembly in January 1942, Lelong asked if the couturiers had known in July 1940 that a year and a half later they would be over five hundred thriving firms. Information about the economy of couture during the war can be found in the archives of the Comités de confiscation des profits illicites (Committees for the Confiscation of Illicit Profits), following the decree of October 18, 1944. The Comités de confiscation closely examined the accounts of firms active since September 1, 1939, for any undue profits from the enemy and, in such cases, determined whether the profits should be paid back to the French Treasury. The Comités de confiscation examined the accounting of hundreds of firms, and its archives include a handful of cases in the fashion industry. Two of the firms investigated were the perfume operations opened by the houses of Chanel and of Patou to produce and retail branded products.[76]

The firm Jean Patou Parfums, founded in 1925, became in 1932 an SA that was a distinct legal entity from the haute couture house. Couture and perfume kept going strong under the management of Raymond Barbas, who had succeeded founder Jean Patou after his death in 1936. The Comités de confiscation examined the business of Patou Parfums in France. In 1930, Jean Patou had opened an American firm to sell his perfumes in the United States; during that decade, it was directed by Lieutenant-Colonel Jacques de Sieyès, a member of the cabinet of General de Gaulle. In June 1940, Sieyès gave the Gaullist movement in New York the opportunity to use the Patou office at 730 Fifth Avenue as the first headquarters of the French Resistance in New York. In France, however, the French firm Patou Parfums sold cosmetics and perfumes to the enemy. After the war, the management at Patou argued that they had tried as much as possible to slow down such sales, but the Treasury inspectors remained unconvinced. Before the war, in 1939, Patou Parfums had sold 1 percent of its product to Germany, but at its highest pitch, in 1943, sales to Germany reached 33 percent of Patou's perfume production. In 1945 the Comités de confiscation ruled that Patou Parfums had to pay to the French Treasury 5,502,862 francs in illicit profits, in addition to a fine of 500,000 francs.[77]

In Paris, both Chanel Parfums and Patou Parfums sold products, especially bottles of perfume and boxes of cosmetic rice powder, to enemy and occupied countries. While these sales yielded significant profits, the argument made by both firms was that they had been made under constraint during the occupation. Chanel Parfums had published substantial advertising in the German press of occupied Paris during the war, which was interpreted as evidence that sales of Chanel had not been constrained. Chanel Parfums' volume of export to enemy countries amounted to 9.05 percent of the firm's sales. These enemy countries of export were, first, Germany, then Hungary, Bulgaria, and Finland. Chanel also exported to territories occupied by the Germans, notably to Alsace-Lorraine, Belgium, and Norway. The Comités de confiscation stated that Chanel Parfums had sold to the enemy and had made sales with balance cash payments (*vente avec soulte*). For these reasons, Chanel received in 1947 the injunction to pay the French Treasury a recovery sum amounting to 4,255,592 francs and, further, to pay a fine of 1,000,000 French francs.[78]

Two haute couture houses also appear in the archives of the Comités de confiscation: Jeanne Lanvin and Maggy Rouff. Jeanne Lanvin was the founder (in 1909), owner, and designer of a well-established firm on the Faubourg Saint-Honoré. One of the most respected fashion entrepreneurs of her time, Lanvin received the Legion of Honor in March 1926. Lanvin herself, as well as her managing director Jean Labusquière, had been at the forefront of the international visibility of Paris couture during the 1930s, working to organize shows abroad and to represent Paris couture at the 1937 and 1939 World's Fairs. In 1939, Labusquière joined the staff of General Charles Huntziger, Vichy's commander in chief of land forces and minister of defense since September 6, 1940. Labusquière died in the crash of Huntziger's plane on November 12, 1941.[79]

In the early hours of the occupation, Lanvin reopened with a reduced staff. Wives of high-ranking German officers who paid in occupation reichsmarks were among her clients.[80] During the war, two firms carried Lanvin's brand: the haute couture house and Lanvin Parfums, which had its own perfume factory. Jeanne Lanvin had unique taste and creativity, grounded in her love for art history. She also had a strong relation with the only child she had with Count di Pietro, Marguerite Marie-Blanche, who became a well-known musician and socialite. Marie-Blanche married Count Jean de Polignac and became known as a socialite by the name Marie-Blanche de Polignac.[81] From early on, Jeanne Lanvin dressed her daughter and designed mother-daughter ensembles that Paris society women admired and that made Lanvin's fortune. The image that became Lanvin's signature, and the logo of her perfume Arpège, was composed of the silhouettes of a mother and a daughter in art deco style. On the basis of her first private firm, Lanvin founded the private firm Lanvin-Fourrures-Lanvin-Parfums on December 1, 1925. From this company, she founded the Société Anonyme Jeanne Lanvin on January 1, 1927, with a capital of 15 million francs, divided into 30,000 shares of 500 francs each. Of these, 29,353 shares were in the hands of the Lanvin family: Jeanne Lanvin owned 22,363 shares, Jean Gaumont owned 833, Maurice Gaumont, Gabriel Lanvin, and Emile Lanvin owned 750 shares each, and Marie-Blanche de Polignac owned 3,907. The inspector of the French Treasury who examined Lanvin's accounting after the war noticed that even though Lanvin was a public company, it had a very strong character of a family firm.[82] In 1935, in the aftermath of the Great Depression, the general assembly reduced the capital of the SA Jeanne Lanvin to 7.5 million francs.[83] In 1943, the board doubled the capital of both the haute couture firm and the perfume firm, which brought the capital of the couture house back to its pre-Depression level. The operation was realized by incorporating reserves and distributing to each shareholder one free share for each that they previously owned. Jeanne Lanvin, now in her mid-seventies and in declining health, transferred ownership of her couture firm from herself to her daughter. Ownership in 1943 was divided among Marie-Blanche de Polignac, who held 53,208 shares; Maurice Gaumont, 1,582 shares; Jean Martin and Je(h)an Gaumont, 802 shares each; and Camille Lanvin and Emile Lanvin, 1,500 shares each. Lanvin couture created and sold fashionable garments for women as well as tailoring for men and women, hats, furs, luxury leather goods, and branded gifts. In addition to its Paris headquarters, the firm had a branch in Biarritz and one in Cannes, and it opened a branch in Deauville on July 14, 1946.[84] In January 1943, an extraordinary general assembly raised the capital of the SA Lanvin Parfums from 1.25 to 5 million francs, an operation realized by the incorporation of reserves. Even if we take into account that the French franc devaluated during wartime, the capital did not depreciate during the conflict.[85]

Two departments, couture and tailoring, composed the haute couture SA Lanvin. The biggest sales were in couture. Lanvin was an atypical case in haute couture, as it produced garments for both women and men earlier than other firms. Lanvin's aggregated couture and tailoring sales amounted to 29,937,584.68 francs in 1939. In 1942, sales rose to 64,473,121.30 francs, and in 1945, to just over 100,000,000 francs. Adjusted for inflation, these figures show stable sales value throughout the war.[86] Principal Treasury inspector Lucien Faure noted that it was a known trend that French haute couture firms systematically—and not only during wartime—hid 20 percent of their sales. As far as the inspector had been able to document, this was the case at Lanvin, and he therefore added 20 percent to the figures calculated for the profits that Lanvin made during the war.[87]

In peacetime, textile manufacturers would grant haute couture houses an advance on the fabrics to be used for the season ahead. For couture houses, advance credit on textiles could ensure a firm's survival, should a bad season occur. During the war, Lanvin was one of the houses that benefited from the dérogation from rationing. The war stock figures show that the house did fairly well, with a total value of couture stocks of 1,591,534.10 francs in 1938, 6,892,761.65 in 1943, and 10,682,412.55 in 1945, which, even if we consider that the franc lost three-quarters of its value over the occupation, still shows a considerable increase in the value of stocks during the war. To this was added the stock of the tailoring department, which amounted to 4.7 million francs in 1945, and of furs, a little over 1 million.[88] The inspectors who examined Lanvin's accounting in 1949 found proof that the firm had not declared the entire price of its textiles stocks, which often appeared in the books for half of their sales value. The accounts of Lanvin show that despite the penury created by the war, which required a system of rationing in order to organize French consumption, the firm continued to acquire materials—the sources of which are unspecified in the archives.[89]

The officers in charge of the Comités de confiscation inquiry examined Jeanne Lanvin's way of life. As an entrepreneur in charge of a luxury firm, she had built for herself a corresponding lifestyle. According to her biographer, her most important success, in both social and affective terms, was her only daughter's marriage. Jeanne Lanvin owned a private property in Paris and two secondary residences, themselves composed of several villas. She also employed seven servants full time for her private service. The inspection by the Treasury found that she spent 1 million francs per year, on average, for her private expenses during the war.[90] When Jeanne Lanvin died, on July 6, 1946, her daughter took over the firm, and the administrators of her two companies, the haute couture house and the perfume firm, filled out the *déclaration de profits illicites* (declaration of illicit profits). The Treasury officers, on behalf of the Comités de confiscation, looked at profits made by the haute couture firm during the war to determine what proportion was the result of tax fraud and sales to the enemy. In 1950, the firm Lanvin, now directed by Marie-Blanche de Polignac, had to pay 3,194,183 francs to the French Treasury.[91]

During the occupation years, most clients of haute couture were private. The press reported on the German officers and the war profiteers—also called, in French, BOF, for *beurre-oeufs-fromage* (butter-eggs-cheese), the products through which many made their fortunes on the black market—who regularly attended the haute couture shows. In the absence of client files for wartime, however, information remains scarce. The clientele of couture was not systematically examined by the tax officers of the illicit profits commission. Perfume sales were better documented and show that Lanvin Parfums sold to the German wholesale firm De-Vau-Ge, with which Lanvin was already doing business before the war.

The Comités de confiscation also inquired into the wartime activity of haute couture firm Maggy Rouff SA, founded in 1927 under the name Société Anonyme ROUFF-COUTURE. In 1929 the shareholders transformed the firm into a new SA Maggy Rouff, with 1 million francs of capital. Pierre Besançon, the husband of head designer Maggy Rouff, was the president and the sole board member of the firm. The new SA Maggy Rouff went through a complex recapitalization in 1939. A new limited liability, Haute Couture et Fourrure Maggy Rouff 1939, with a capital of 100,000 francs, was added to the old firm. The new limited liability registered losses during war, until 1944, but it paid important license fees for the exploitation of the Rouff brand to the old SA. The Treasury inspectors in charge of examining Rouff accounts mentioned in their report that they found the accounts of the firm particularly confusing and that in all likelihood the accounting was not truthful. The inspectors set to the task of determining Rouff's real profit figures. They estimated that at its highest point the firm had most likely made an extra 100 to 120 percent on the declared sales. The total amount in sales actually made by the house of Rouff during the war was therefore 159,947,198 francs, according to the French Treasury. Additional reports to the inquiry mentioned that the wife of Otto Abetz, German ambassador to Vichy France, was a client of the firm. The firm had also exported merchandise to Belgium, Italy, the Netherlands, Spain, and Switzerland during the occupation years. The house of Rouff contested the conclusions of the committee and requested another report. That report underlined that most of the occupation clients of Rouff had been war profiteers. Further, it noted that Rouff employees demonstrated that although they did not enjoy the occupation clientele, they had pursued their work because they had no other choice. The case of Rouff was closed without further inquiries.[92]

The fifth and final case in the illicit profits files, the limited liability firm Etablissements Pierre Cazaux & Co., documents a ready-made clothing manufacturer situated outside the luxury neighborhoods, at 17–19 Cité Voltaire, in the 11th arrondissement of Paris. The firm made functional clothes and uniforms. At the beginning of the war, it turned out thousands of uniforms per year for the French army. After Paris fell, Cazaux received orders from the German army and the civilian markets. In total, the firm produced 76,000 pieces in 1941 and 113,000 pieces at its peak in 1943. Sales by Cazaux totaled between 14 and 31 million francs per year during the conflict. The Comités de confiscation investigated the business of Cazaux at the end of the war. A note from its manager, Henri Darnat, underlined that the firm had engaged in a form of passive resistance by slowing down the deliveries of uniforms to the German authorities. In 1948, the committee handed over its report, which concluded that the firm had to pay the French Treasury the sum of 169,916 francs, representing illicit war profits. No fine was added to the judgment.[93]

Of the cases examined by the Comités de confiscation, some of the firms had to pay part of the profits they had made during the war to the French Treasury. From the moral perspective, these firms were not considered guilty of illicit operations with the enemy. The sales and benefits of Lanvin show that, in a context where haute couture was cut off from most of its international markets, profits thrived. At Lanvin, the amount of sales made during the war suggests that the enterprise kept a significant share of its old clientele, and found new clients as well. It remains difficult to assess the proportion of German occupiers and of war profiteers among the clientele in the absence of client files. Considering the extant sources and the volume of sales, it is reasonable to conclude that several Paris couture houses and some of their branded perfume divisions sold to private clients indiscriminately, regardless of their nationality or their profession, reaching a wide clientele that included personnel from the German occupation authorities, Nazi officers, German wholesalers in cosmetics, and war profiteers.

Lelong's Responsibility

Lelong's relation to the occupying authorities has been debated since the war. Critique from within appears in the meeting minutes of the Chambre Syndicale. In late November 1944, the general assembly of the Chambre Syndicale had not met in nearly two years—its meetings had been replaced by committee meetings. The November 1944 meeting opened, as usual, with the reading of a series of reports: on the financial situation of the syndicates, on the haute couture schools, and on the situation of employees. Lelong then read a program of action proposed by the committee of the chamber for the months ahead. After reading, he opened the floor. A long-term member of the Chambre, M. Dupouy, then read a report that criticized the management of the Chambre Syndicale. There is no indication in the meeting minutes whether this report had been written solely by Dupouy or in agreement with other members. Dupouy's intervention contested the validity of the decisions made by the Chambre Syndicale during the war. It addressed critiques of the organization committee of the Chambre and, especially, contested the principle and application of the dérogation, the policy ascribing quotas of textiles to the haute couture houses in wartime. Dupouy further contested the report made by Lelong on the Chambre's internal finances and the organization of its schools. He finished by demanding the establishment of a provisory committee that would set up a *comité d'épuration* (postwar purge committee).[94] Another member of the Chambre, Ms. Alexandre, in charge of representing the small and medium couture houses, read another report that in part echoed Dupouy's critiques, especially against the dérogation system, in which the small and medium couture firms asked why some firms had received much higher quantities of fabric than others.[95]

Other Chambre Syndicale members reacted to these critiques and defended Lelong's work. M. Becquart then spoke, asking members to set aside personal dissent that was, he argued, in part informing Dupouy's views.[96] M. Mola, who chaired the Nice Region couture association, pointed out that Lelong's policies had helped defend the small and medium couture houses. More important, he mentioned, "the fact that Monsieur Lelong had obtained the dérogation from the Germans was fully approved by the Resistance. It was that much less for the Germans to have."[97] In terms of the decision-making process within the organization, Lelong replied that he was surprised to be accused of dictatorship, since no important decision had been taken without gathering all thirty members of the commissions representing all the nuances of the opinions in the Chambre Syndicale.[98] Lelong also addressed the technical points raised by his fellow members. He saw his work for the Chambre Syndicale as a continuation from 1937, when he had worked to keep the members together in times of social unrest and internal dissent.[99] At the end of the meeting, the whole committee of the Chambre Syndicale resigned.[100] A year later, in 1945, Lelong handed over the leadership to Jean Gaumont-Lanvin, director of the house of Lanvin, who was elected his successor.[101]

Chapter 5

Global Haute Couture

n the postwar years, Paris couture experienced a last golden age that coincided with a time of prosperity that the economist Jean Fourastié called the "thirty glorious years."[1] Haute couture was the symbol of French economic and cultural success, and the symbol of haute couture was the house of Christian Dior, forming a virtuous circle in which the nation and the designer helped with the branding of one another.

In the summer of 1946, Christian Dior was a young and little-known designer soon to meet Henri Fayol Jr., manager for the French textile magnate Marcel Boussac, "the king of cotton." The son of a clothing manufacturer, Boussac was the owner of the Boussac Group, composed of sixty firms around the Comptoir de l'Industrie Cotonnière (CIC). The Boussac Group included the most modern French factories and made 10 percent of the domestic market's share of cotton textiles. In 1952 it produced 132 million meters of fabric, for a total in sales that reached 70 million French francs. Boussac was the richest man in his country—and among the best breeders of thoroughbreds in the world. He was looking for a young talent to take over an older couture firm he had owned since 1937, the house of Gaston. Fayol set up the meeting between the two men. Dior sat before Boussac and told the king of cotton that he was not interested in carrying on the older firm. Boussac then offered Dior 10 million French francs to start one on his own. Dior, afraid, withdrew from the negotiations; because he was a superstitious man, he went to consult with two different fortune-tellers. After hearing what they had to say, Dior sealed the deal with Boussac.[2]

The Foundation of Dior

The house of Dior was incorporated in October 1946 as a limited liability company for ninety-nine years with a capital of 5 million French francs, an unusually high sum for an haute couture firm. Dior dreamed of a small haute couture house catering to an exclusive clientele—a laboratory of style focusing on the design innovation that he thought was much needed after the long stagnation caused by the war. Boussac also offered Dior one of his own managers, the director of finance Jacques Rouët, who had no experience in haute couture but proved excellent on the job. Initially, Dior employed eighty-five employees in three workrooms. He hired a team of skilled women. Some of the best members of Lelong's staff went on to manage the workshops and sales at Dior, bringing their experience and networks to the new firm.[3] On February 12, 1947, when Dior showed his first collection, consumer goods were still rationed and the salons where the models walked were not well heated. One of the models was shown in a tailored suit called Bar, with a full skirt made of black Boussac fabric and a fitted jacket of white Chinese shantung. American fashion journalist Carmel Snow immediately commented that this was a "New Look." Although the striking design of Dior's Bar was not entirely new—the houses of Lelong, Mainbocher, Rochas, and Fath had shown wasp-waisted silhouettes with longer skirts as early as 1938—the influence of his creations on the ready-to-wear industry was soon global in its scope.[4]

During the war, the production of garments had been limited by tight textile quotas. For example, the skirts had never been shorter, barely hiding the knee. Because of the New Look's stark contrast with the styles necessitated by postwar shortages, its early adopters were seen as scandalous and exposed to public insult. In the United States, three hundred thousand women responded by joining the Little Below the Knee Club, whose protests consisted of publicly cutting long skirts shorter to acknowledge the ongoing fabric quotas. Unfazed, Dior told the American press, "We want to forget all about the war."[5]

Dior had initially wanted to become an architect, and a phase of experimentation in his youth found him managing an art gallery, traveling, and training as a *modéliste*. In 1938, he worked at the house of Robert Piguet, where he was credited for designing Café Anglais, a fashion hit at the time. Then Dior went on to train at Lelong, where he further learned the techniques of couture alongside another promising talent, Pierre Balmain.[6] In his own firm, Christian Dior's work for a collection started two months before a show. He was very self-aware regarding his creative process, and his autobiography offers a balance of creative vision and commercial sense. From his time as an aspiring architect, Dior had developed a sense of proportion that he readily transferred to the human body. His work with other designers had also made him aware of the constraints and technicalities of his trade. Dior always maintained an acute sense of his responsibilities for "the subsistence of 900 people that I would risk if I drew one collection wrong."[7]

When he started working on a collection, Dior drew six hundred silhouettes. These were sent to the workrooms, where the first hands used them for cutting *toiles*, or prototypes in raw cotton linen. Dior then reviewed the toiles and kept some 220 models. The materiality and colors of fabrics had a profound influence on his work. Every garment was fitted several times, and Dior rejected those that proved unsatisfying until he was down to 180. The use of raw materials and investment in working hours for each haute couture collection were staggering—about twenty-two miles of raw "toile," 9,750 yards of fabric, and, over the six weeks leading up to the presentation of the collection, hundreds of working hours on the 180 dresses of the collection. The total costs of a collection measured in the tens of millions of French francs.[8]

Early on, the Dior firm aimed to control the channels of dissemination of fashion designs. The management worked to know the corporate buyers better and asked them to sign contracts that specified the conditions of reproduction of Dior originals. Such contracts specified that authorized reproduction of Dior should only be sold above a certain price. Buyers, noted Dior in his memoirs, were tireless. They had a photographic eye that allowed them to see all of the interesting details in a collection: "They often come with their *premières*, whose memory is excellent. After the collection, they come back. They spend entire hours touching, turning over, palpating, stripping the garments." Despite such behavior, relations between the couturier and his buyers were amicable. Dior commented, "They buy the best they can, we sell the best we can."[9]

Forty percent of Dior's corporate buyers were American, and so were between 30 and 40 percent of his private clients.[10] Manager Jacques Rouët ensured that every purchase was recorded, which in turn provided information as to which types of designs were in greatest demand and to which markets those designs were going. Interwar couturiers used bound ledgers to record sales in chrono-logical lists.[11] Statistical methods were considerably modernized in postwar France, and Dior's administration used a system of mobile sheets that allowed analysts to correlate data on sales. Employees made notes on the files dedicated to each design, adding clients' feedback and thoughts on what should be modi-fied in the future.[12]

Behind the scenes was a whole team. Dior's financier, Rouët, was the equiva-lent of Boussac's right arm, Henri Fayol Jr., who had studied Frederick Winslow Taylor's organizational methods in the United States in the 1920s and then pur-sued a career in finance and, after the war, in the Boussac Group. Fayol became an important contributor to the theory of management. Fayol and Boussac met weekly to discuss the Dior business, and never in the presence of the designer. They were both members of the Conseil National du Patronat Français (CNPF). Boussac had great influence in the CNPF, especially regarding prices of goods and workforce compensation, as he sought to protect the French textile and gar-ment industries from competition from other markets, especially Italy and its cheaper labor force.[13]

The new house of Dior embraced an image of modernity. The narrative of Dior as introducing a rupture with the past, in marketing as well as aesthetics, en-dures in numerous studies on the designer that insist on the fact that Dior had refused to take over the more ancient house of Gaston. But the history of the Boussac Group shows that the new haute couture house had deep roots.[14] Boussac built up Dior's capital from assets already in his possession. The limited liability Société Gaston, now ended, brought a capital of half a million and the building containing the actual house itself, 30 avenue Montaigne, with the right to take over its commercial lease. Furthermore, the assets transferred from the house of Gaston to the house of Dior comprised the name, merchandise, and clients of the old house. Even its furniture and the equipment from its workshops were brought to Dior. The value of the assets transferred from Gaston to Dior totaled 2,706,000 French francs. The rest, or a bit less than half of the 5 million in capital of Chris-tian Dior, was brought in by the Boussac Group and by other societies within the group: the Filatures de Thaon, the Filatures et Tissages de Nomexy, and the Société Anonyme Anciens Etablissements Ziegler.[15]

Christian Dior was appointed sole manager of the firm for an unlimited dura-tion, though his contract specified that it could be terminated for legitimate causes.

Christian Dior owned no share in the society, but he would later receive a share in Christian Dior Parfums. Boussac examined the question of the name of Dior, its possible uses, and its future, particularly given that the Dior firm had been set up for ninety-nine years upon Christian Dior's appointment. The management and Boussac said that they had received all of the appeasements as to using the name of Dior and as to the future of their new brand.

The fact that Dior was a single man—in this case, an accepted term to denote that Dior was gay—and apparently not interested in descendants was part of the assessment. To complete the directorial team at Dior, Rouët received the powers delegated to him by Boussac; in addition, an administrator and an accountant had Boussac's mandate to manage the finances of the new company. One administrator from each of the firms CIC, Nomexy, Thaon, Ziegler, and Pierre Clarence, the society that took over the assets left by the house of Gaston, attended the yearly general assembly of the Dior firm.[16]

French Haute Couture in the Oxygen Tent?

Dior had an unusually high capital, whereas most other haute couture firms in Paris were smaller and struggled to adapt to the postwar context. The 1946–1948 period of austerity following the occupation was a challenging time. Costs associated with the workforce rose due to the institution of employment regulations; this, added to inflation, made French fashion less competitive than ever. Eastern European markets were lost behind the Iron Curtain.[17] Raymond Barbas, president of the Chambre Syndicale, described the difficulties then faced by haute couture: the rising prices of fabrics, social cost of the workforce, and creation costs. High overhead, including rising rents in the center of Paris, further contributed to a difficult situation. Strikes had been endemic in couture, with a postwar peak of activity in 1949, and Christian Dior deplored the negative image this strife presented to foreign buyers visiting Paris. In early 1951, the Chambre Syndicale took pride in reaching a long-sought agreement with the workers' union CGT, a leftist union close to the French Communist Party with which an increasing number of haute couture workers were affiliated. Yet the Chambre Syndicale resisted the tide of change, even if the advent of mass consumption and the development of the welfare state were making haute couture a thing of the past. Joseph Schumpeter, whose seminal book on the topic was published in 1942, used the notion of creative destruction to describe the way new firms succeeded—and therefore contributed to eliminating—obsolete ones.[18]

Against all odds, Paris haute couture survived and even experienced a new golden age. Boussac himself managed to maintain an immense empire in textiles, a branch of industry that everyone considered to be in decline in postwar France. Haute couture houses nonetheless struggled to pay their staff and to maintain a client base. Ultimately, the issue attracted the attention of the French government. What would it take to keep haute couture going as a flagship for the French industries? Could haute couture secure enough resources from private groups, like the Boussac Group, or would public investment be necessary to guarantee the future of the industry? The intervention of the state in the rescue of haute couture evokes the image of the oxygen tent that Schumpeter used to illustrate the artificial maintenance of an industry even in the context of declining profitability and aggressive competition from mass production. During the immediate postwar years, the Chambre Syndicale lobbied the Assemblée Nationale, the CNPF, and the domestic textile industry to obtain support for haute couture. This effort developed in two directions. The first was an attempt to obtain a tax exemption, or a favorable tax policy. During the 1950s, as a result of these efforts, the Chambre Syndicale managed to remain exempt from the value added tax, which amounted to 20 or 22 percent on the retail price of goods. The second was an attempt to secure from the state a direct subvention for haute couture. Unlike the manufacture of Sèvres porcelain and other creative industries, haute couture had never been a state monopoly, though it had benefited from state support. After the war, analysts continued to celebrate the ability of haute couture to add so much value to so little material and deemed it worthy of further government investment. The government developed a project to directly help the haute couture industry through support for research and development. This process was initiated a few months before the establishment of the Commissariat général au Plan, directed by Jean Monnet.[19]

The government implemented a label identifying the haute couture houses as "Couture Création" in decrees of April 6, 1945, and June 6, 1947. In the summer of 1945, the Chambre Syndicale published the first ranking criteria for firms wishing to be registered as Couture Création in directories of commerce and professions. A ministry briefing of 1945 defined Couture Création as the work of haute couture firms, which were forbidden to outsource design and production.

Firms had to be accepted by a commission of selection and control composed of members of the Chambre Syndicale. A series of criteria applied to the firms. They had to present two annual collections of at least sixty designs. The selling of original creations in couture, furs, or hats had to represent at least 75 percent of the total turnover of the firm. Each house had to employ a minimum of thirty permanent workers on a full-time basis, of whom at least twenty had to be involved in production. To guarantee eligibility, all firms were required by the government to have paid their dues to social security.[20]

In 1952, Paris couture received an initial subvention of 400 million French francs from the Encouragement Fund for Textile Production in France (Fonds d'Encouragement de la Production Textile). The funds behind the Couture Création subventions distributed by the state came from the tax on the French textile industries. The French textile industrialists expected a return on their investment, and it is therefore not surprising that the firms receiving a subvention were asked to ensure that less than 10 percent of the textiles used in their designs, and in the genuine reproductions they made for their private clients, be foreign textiles.[21] Creation was a costly process in terms of both material and working hours. The French Union of the Textile Industries (Union des Industries Textiles) remained willing to help haute couture, because it was still considered the best advertising for the French textile exports. A special commission within the union met to discuss the amount that should be given to each haute couture house.[22] The commission concluded that the subvention should be used to advertise haute couture and to pay for the creativity process in preparing the collections. The cost of making a collection, for the bigger houses, was an estimated $150,000 to $200,000 in today's currency. Couturiers received a grant in cash of $16,800 to $33,600.[23]

In 1952, Raymond Barbas, on behalf of the Chambre Syndicale, asked the French state secretary of economic affairs to renew the industry subvention because haute couture was a source of invisible exports and excellent advertising for French textiles in the context of heightened international competition. In the following years, the subvention averaged 200 million French francs annually and covered 30 to 40 percent of the haute couture firms' textile needs.[24] Government support was motivated by the certainty that haute couture had to remain in Paris and that the industry would disappear without help. Some Chambre Syndicale member firms were too small to be part of Couture Création. Because the framework behind the category was more restrictive than the industry's general practice, the line between the world of haute couture and mass distribution was crossed on occasion as well.[25]

Paradoxically, Dior, who reawakened the haute couture industry after World War II, was also the couturier who contributed the most to undermining the older structure of Paris haute couture as a cluster of local firms—because he became the center of a multinational luxury conglomerate—and to the introduction of more industrialized practices. Boussac had bought the haute couture firm Gaston in 1937 and then used most of its assets to build up the Dior concern. With what was left of Gaston, Boussac founded another firm, called Pierre Clarence, which produced a hybrid between couture and ready-to-wear. It made sense for Boussac to capitalize on the diversity of his group: Dior was a higher-end style laboratory, most of the firms in his group manufactured mass-market textiles, and Clarence bridged high and low. In the 1950s, the Pierre Clarence firm applied for the classification Couture Création in order to receive an haute couture subvention from the government, but the standard inquiry carried out to validate Clarence's application revealed ambiguities in its production. The evaluator mandated by the government found that the workers at Clarence commonly used an overlock stitch machine for the finishes and that the buttonholes on some dresses were done by machine and not by hand, as was expected in haute couture. While machines were present in haute couture houses, their use was limited to a few tasks. On their second visit, the evaluators discussed the machine-made finishes with Clarence's director. In the end, Clarence received a subvention that year—even as other firms did not, because either their production was deemed too mechanized or they did not produce all of their collections in-house. The Clarence episode is not unique and demonstrates one of the ways in which haute couture found itself trapped between seemingly contradictory strategies. Allowing mechanization would deprive couturiers of government funding even if it were perfectly appropriate to adapt to changing clients and markets.[26]

The firms accepted into the Couture Création category in 1954 were a diverse group, ranging from one-person enterprises to a handful of companies employing several hundred workers between the administration and the workshops. The firm with the highest capital was Balenciaga, whose founder was then one of the great architects of the fashion industry along with Christian Dior. The biggest firms offered slightly more prestigious positions and higher salaries, especially at

Balenciaga, Balmain, Dessès, and Dior. The postwar period was marked in general terms by a return to the dominance of men in the profession, whereas the interwar period had been the golden age of women designers. Couturiers acknowledged that they depended on governmental subvention and that, without this help, the few houses that would have survived would be working under foreign auspices. While couturiers continued to lobby the French government, resignations from the Chambre Syndicale far outnumbered new applicants. By the mid-1950s, Couture Création houses together presented upward of four thousand original designs made with French textiles every year, even as the number of beneficiaries of subvention diminished after an initial increase: from forty-five in 1952 to twenty-four in 1960. Many closed shop, however, including the houses of Agnès-Drecoll, Lafaurie, Lelong, Piguet, and Rochas. Perfume and cosmetics subsidiaries generally outlasted the haute couture houses. In 1959, haute couture entrepreneurs employed just twenty thousand people in France, only a tenth of the two hundred thousand workers in Philippe Simon's count of 1931.[27]

Prewar ready-to-wear manufacturers based in France had been kept out of the haute couture shows, which only opened their doors to foreign manufacturers. The Chambre Syndicale justified this rule as necessary to safeguard the prestige of haute couture, but it generated numerous problems. In 1944, the Chambre Syndicale drafted the Paris-Province agreements that opened the haute couture houses to French manufacturers and retailers, provided they received a buyer's card. These contracts were intended to create additional revenue by selling haute couture on the domestic market and to offer guarantees to provincial buyers that their right of reproduction would not be undercut by lower-grade manufacturers. Paris couturiers started applying these agreements in 1947. The prevention of piracy was an acknowledged part of the plan, at home but also abroad. The Chambre Syndicale hoped that, in the near future, similar contracts would be made between haute couture and the foreign markets. In 1957 the Chambre Syndicale planned a "one million dollar dream pact"—an agreement between the top fifteen Paris couture houses and American manufacturers that "would be the end of the couturiers' difficulties."[28] While this remained a distant possibility, the Paris-Province agreements had immediate results, in the form of additional domestic net revenue in the coffers of haute couture. A total of eighty-seven domestic buyers purchased originals for an amount of 44,880,000 French francs in 1948. In 1957, domestic sales to French corporate buyers reached their peak, with a total of 76 million French francs from a total of seventy-nine buyers. Subsequent years show stable figures ranging between 60 million and 70 million French francs per year.[29]

Strategies of couturiers to prevent so-called piracy also progressed considerably during the postwar years. The Artistic Property Service of the Chambre Syndicale de la Couture Parisienne was now directed by Rouët, who coordinated the antipiracy activities of the whole profession.[30] Dior figured as both a leader and an example to follow. The service's chief legal adviser was Suzanne Dreyfus-David, a pioneering woman member of the Paris bar.[31] Repression remained the most important response of Paris haute couture to unwanted copyists at home and abroad. The Chambre Syndicale frequently sued as a private plaintiff, along with member firms. As protective practices evolved, new questions arose—for example, the Chambre Syndicale made the case to the police for the need to work together. The Sûreté Nationale helped the Artistic Property Service by sending officers and an inspector to complete the seizures at the copy houses. In 1947 the service and the French police raided six medium-size and small couture houses in the cities of Lyons, Lille, and Bordeaux, seizing and affixing seals on 548 sketches, eighty-four paper patterns, thirty-five toiles, and twenty-two counterfeited designs. Those six firms admitted to making over 21 million French francs in counterfeited trade. At the request of the Committee of the Fédération Nationale de la Couture, the litigation was settled through an amicable agreement, with the six copyists agreeing to pay an aggregate sum of 725,000 francs in damages. The Artistic Property Service often handled cases through such transactions, and only a few had to be abandoned that year as well, either because the seizures were handled badly or because the costs of litigation were too high. Other cases were amnestied because of the insufficiency of income to pay the penalties.[32]

The Conquest of the Americas

The couturiers sought to pursue a similar policy abroad. One major change took place in the postwar years: the Paris couturiers eventually surmounted the obstacles that had discouraged most of them from opening branches outside France. The house of Dior was the leader in this new phase of the internationalization of haute couture. Christian Dior New York, the first overseas branch of Dior, opened in October 1948 as a "wholesale salon" located at 730 Fifth Avenue.[33] The salon's decor displayed the same architectural design details that were considered to be part of the visual identity of the Paris haute couture house: Louis XVI chairs, white moldings, and fabrics and carpeting in light "Dior gray." Two times a year, in June and November, Dior presented 130 exclusive models in New York that were different from the Paris collection. Specially designed by Dior for New York, these garments were sold wholesale and reproduced in American sizes. Their prices varied from $135 to $300 for tailored suits, $125 to $400 for afternoon and cocktail dresses, and $225 and above for evening dresses. Twice a year, Christian Dior went to New York with two or three of his managers and stayed for a month at the Hotel Pierre to design the American collection with American retailers in mind. Dior showed his first New York collection on November 8, 1948. "Dior, at opening, *copies himself*," commented Virginia Pope of the *New York Times*, adding that "it is strictly Dior."[34]

Nearly all of the Paris couturiers regularly toured the United States and set up contracts to design for American manufacturers, but few of them were able to establish permanent overseas branches. Most Paris couturiers who had tried to settle in New York during the interwar period failed in short order. Those earlier attempts had often suffered from a lack of investment, from high tariff barriers, and from the severity of the US Customs authority. Couturiers had been more successful with their American perfume ventures. Boussac knew that he wanted to open a Dior branch in the United States, but instead, in 1946, he first turned his attention to South and Central America, preparing to create four societies: Rosine Deltour Mexico, Tisgar Fabrics Mexico, Rosine Deltour Argentina, and Tisgar Fabrics Argentina. Deltour was conceived as a ready-to-wear manufacturing operation, and Tisgar as a textile manufacturer. In September 1946, Boussac transferred $50,000 to the Lloyd Bank Trust in Mexico to constitute the capital of his society Rosine Deltour SA Mexico, incorporated on September 13, 1946. Initially, half of the capital was supposed to belong to a series of local businessmen, but all of them signed documents acknowledging that they were acting on behalf of Boussac, who was the effective owner of the whole capital of the firm, minus two shares. He used the same process to set up Tisgar Fabrics, Inc., incorporated on January 9, 1947, with a capital of $10,000, and for the creation of the two Argentinian societies. As outlined in their statutes, the goal of these societies was to manufacture ready-to-wear for the South American markets.[35] But the societies Deltour and Tisgar never got off the ground. Both firms were relocated to New

York immediately after their constitution, and Boussac promptly transferred the capital of these societies to set up Rosine Deltour Inc., New York. Finally, the name of this society was changed in 1948 to Christian Dior New York, now with a capital of $50,000, constituted with one hundred shares entirely in the hands of the CIC. Christian Dior had remained apart from the whole process and did not own shares in his American couture firm.[36]

In the spring of 1948, Boussac hired Ellen Engel, a New York–based lawyer, to help set up Dior in the city. During World War II, Engel had been active on the War Committee with Anne Morgan, the daughter of banker John Pierpont Morgan. Engel had also worked on the promotion of the Théâtre de la Mode, the traveling exhibition of dolls set up by the Chambre Syndicale in 1945–1947 as the medium to promote haute couture abroad during textile rationing. Engel's first task was to scout the city's real estate market and find a suitable location for the New York haute couture house.[37] Engel shaped the contractual relations between the Dior firm and the American market. When "making its own copies," Dior New York tried to gain control of the dissemination of Christian Dior's designs. But in so doing, Dior took haute couture out of the Paris cluster and risked diluting the prestige of his brand name.[38] The managers of the American branch were well aware of the complications for haute couture of going wholesale. Would it lose its symbolic capital, its reputation for exclusivity, quality, and innovation within tradition?[39] Coping with this hazard was Engel's task. On July 9, 1948, she sent a long letter to Rouët from her office at 1757 Broadway, around the corner from the most exclusive New York fashion establishments of 57th Street. The letter laid out in detail the optimal way to launch the Dior collections in the United States. Her first point was that the Dior New York wholesale designs should be sold under the name of Dior, not another brand name.[40]

Engel then presented an in-depth discussion of the Dior brand itself in its most concrete iteration—that is, the fabric labels sewn into the garments. The question was, Should Dior originals be labeled in a consistent way all over the world? Should the Dior firm sell predetermined series of Dior labels to the American manufacturers that bought Dior originals in Paris, along with the right to reproduce them for their domestic markets? Interwar Paris couturiers had never systematically resolved these issues, leaving them open upon the development of the international Dior concern.[41] Engel was certain that Dior should not sell in the United States under a name other than his own, but his clients were sure to question why some Dior (the haute couture, or Paris, dresses) was more expensive than other Dior (the wholesale New York line). This was the objection raised by the American trade press regarding Madeleine Vionnet's wholesale line, which had retailed under the name Eva Boex in the 1920s. Dior lines received Dior labels, but the labels clearly differentiated among those lines. Despite all the caveats she placed on her preparatory research, Engel had sketched out what would become the first royalty system for Dior.

Dior faced a challenge when he had to communicate about these various lines, all designed and gathered under his brand name. He insisted that he did not provide copies of his haute couture designs to the American markets but instead sold other ready-to-wear designs under the Dior New York label. Launching a ready-to-wear line in New York was viable only if the firm was able to convince the US market that it was selling Dior ideas there. But Dior's haute couture clientele also had to be reassured that the Paris production retained its primacy. Adapting to customers across product lines represented a balancing act. Ideas were translated into the American line, but, as Rouët explained to the Boston public during a Dior conference tour in 1958, the garments produced in Paris ateliers were handmade and therefore unique. The quality of haute couture was impossible to reproduce exactly, and this lent the Dior brand its particular prestige: "Our technique has practically not varied for centuries. . . . This will not change and if we should one day abandon hand work, a specific notion of quality, without any other equivalent in the world, would come to disappear along with us."[42] The system drafted by Engel repurposed the traditional haute couture practice of asking corporate buyers to pay a security deposit that also represented a minimum guarantee of purchase. In Paris, where many American buyers kept traveling to see the haute couture of Dior even though they now had ready access to his wholesale dresses, Engel advised that couturiers should ask for higher sums than before. The Chambre Syndicale similarly advised that corporate buyers pay a guarantee of purchase prior to their admission to the shows. At Dior the requirement was 100,000 French francs, or approximately $300.[43]

The Dior New York wholesale dresses followed the general direction of the haute couture collection, but were adapted for machine production and ready-to-wear clients. The manufacturing work was done in New York, but not in the 730 Fifth Avenue building that hosted the prestigious showroom.[44] The other Paris haute couture houses that had branched out to New York had so far imported, at least in large part, goods made in Paris; we saw that this caused repeated problems for couturiers with the American customs officials and even, in the case of Rochas, the failure of the American branch. Dior adopted a different strategy and embraced the Seventh Avenue way of doing things. Dior's wholesale line was made in New York first by Jack Sommerfield, who was previously at Ben Reig, Inc., and then, starting in 1952, by new technical and production manager Vincent J. Coppola, previously from cloak and suit manufacturers Deitsch, Wersba, and Coppola, who were known for their high-quality production. Coppola established a special workroom with fifty employees on Eighth Avenue. Dior New York would, over the next decade, become completely integrated into the New York garment district, as fashion expert Bernard Roshco observed: "Between 36th and 37th Streets is 498, the fourth of Seventh Avenue's quartet of top addresses. Top-priced firms on these premises include Ben Reig, Maurice Rentner, and a branch of the Paris house of Dior, Christian Dior New York. A dress or suit bearing one of these labels is likely to sell for more than $200." Dior integrated an industry where employees switched posts and transferred skills among the higher-grade manufacturing workshops.[45]

From 1947 onward, the house of Dior researched the better manufacturers and retailers in the United States.[46] Dior cultivated quality suppliers and retailers. Hattie Carnegie, the New York entrepreneur mentioned in Chapter 3, created her own high-end lines in addition to copies of French fashions priced at $39.50 and up. Dior salesperson "D.S." noted in the Dior list that Carnegie was "alright to sell." It was a "very good house to keep," according to Yvonne Minassian, the director of American sales at the Paris house of Dior and the best saleswoman in the firm.[47] But Halpert, a prominent Seventh Avenue manufacturer that made good-quality dresses retailing for $22.75 and up and bought at Dior for 120,000 francs of original designs in 1948, was noted as "to eliminate." In New York, a Dior salesperson concluded that the firm "should definitely not sell [to Halpert]; he is now making Jacques Fath's American collection."[48] Although Dior did not systematically pursue exclusivity contracts with American manufacturers, this note reveals a sense of competition—Fath was one of the first Paris couturiers to follow in the footsteps of Dior regarding overseas expansion strategies.[49]

Dior staff members engaged in similar conversations about retailers. For example, they discussed whether they should sell to the New York retailer Russeks, which purchased designs from Dior Paris. Russeks's owner David Nemerov was known to show his haute couture purchases literally as he stepped off the plane in New York. Copies of the French designs were, in the mid-1950s, available to buy within three weeks.[50] At Dior, the salespeople were furious, and one of them concluded that Dior "*definitely* should not sell them. They exploit Dior's name at very cheap prices to give to cheap mfg to copy; . . . well-dressed New York women resent seeing cheap copies of Dior's Paris collection in Russeks." On the other hand, Minassian described Russeks as a "good house, client to see."[51] Such a case shows room for discussion in evaluating clients, even if they were pioneers of faster fashions like Russeks. Buyers had to sign an agreement with the couturier that set the terms under which they would be authorized to reproduce their purchases. In 1948, Lucien Le Lièvre, Dior's legal counsel, declared that the firm would not allow corporate clients to buy Dior designs with US reproduction rights to retail dresses bearing the Dior name for less than $69.95.[52] On average, a Paris original cost $800, while an American knockoff could cost anywhere between $10 and $100. A high-quality authorized reproduction of haute couture was much more expensive: at Bergdorf Goodman, in the mid-1950s, the price of a French design custom made with a legal authorization for reproduction would start at $500. The list of Paris originals that Bergdorf bought for the 1954–1955 winter season totaled sixty-eight designs, of which ten were by Dior, ten by Balenciaga, seven by Hubert de Givenchy, seven by Jacques Griffe, five by Nina Ricci, four each by Alix Grès and Mad Carpentier, three each by Fath and Balmain, two each by Patou and Dessès, and one by Chanel. This list reflects the favorites of haute couture buyers at the time, who went first to Dior and Balenciaga, then to the others.[53]

Dior was the first French fashion firm that thoroughly studied the US market, from the very foundation of its American branch. The sales staff visited department stores throughout North America in order to survey how they displayed Dior-branded products—perfumes and, in some cases, dress reproductions—in what numbers, whether the light was good, which competing brands were nearby, and whether the sales staff was competent and dedicated enough to push the sales of Dior products. New York was still where it all happened. In 1955, Manhattan and its immediate surroundings were responsible for $3,355,955,000, or 65.7 percent of garment sales in the nation. Of the 169 American medium- to high-grade retailers and manufacturers listed by Dior's sales services in 1949, only twenty-seven were located outside New York.[54]

Adaptive Intellectual Property Rights Strategies

Dior New York engineered a worldwide expansion and the licensing of branded products on an unprecedented scale. Already in October 1946, Dior had opened a Paris boutique that sold gifts, scarves, gloves, perfumes, and its own seasonal collections of some fifty models of beachwear and holiday clothing. The decision to develop licensing for an increasing number of boutique products was a result of the success of the New York branch. In France, licensing agreements were signed in 1947, with the founding of Christian Dior Parfums Paris Ltd. and for furs; in 1950, for ties and shoes; in 1951, for hosiery; and in 1954, for men's wear. In the United States, Christian Dior Perfumes, New York, and Christian Dior Hosiery were both founded in 1949. In 1955, Dior set up a licensing agreement with the firm Henkel and Grosse in Pforzheim, Germany, to manufacture and sell Dior's costume jewelry worldwide. To centralize the relationships among the various Christian Dior companies and associated firms, a new company, Christian Dior Export, Inc., was launched in 1951. It monitored the establishments abroad and the Dior licenses.[55] The name Dior unified the various societies. It was registered in France as an international brand for the first time in 1948, and subsequently dozens of names of tie-in products, licenses lines, and logos were registered by Dior and his managers.[56] Dior also registered patents in France, the United States, and other secondary markets to protect the most technical of the firm's innovations, a majority of which were in the realm of perfumes and cosmetics.[57]

The Paris house of Dior keeps large albums that index the "codes" of the house—that is, fixed aesthetic symbols of Dior's designs that are in constant use. Examples of codes include the houndstooth pattern, the lily of the valley motif and scent, the very pale gray identified as "Dior gray," the cane work, and a peculiar model of Louis XVI chair.[58] Such codes were incorporated not only into garments, accessories, and perfumes but also into the decoration of Dior establishments around the world, conferring unity to the brand in the same way that all Tiffany stores around the world feature the company's precise shade of pale greenish blue. In the United States, the Lanham Trademark Act of 1946 made it possible to extend, for example, the protection of the Tiffany brand to such distinctive signs as the "Tiffany blue," the white ribbon on its blue boxes, the font of the branded logo, and the decoration of Tiffany stores. The protection of such brand-identity markers corresponds to the domain of intellectual property rights known as *trade dress*. In the absence of any protection for design copyright in American law, some lawyers argue that trade dress would allow for the effective protection of a fashion designer with a distinctive (registered) identity. But implementing features protected by the trade dress law in garment designs necessarily required an excessive standardization in the form. While the trade dress remained too limited to protect fashion design entirely, Dior made astute use of the codes. For example, in his first perfume, Miss Dior, launched in 1947, Dior had the bottle packed in an oval-shaped box covered in his favorite houndstooth pattern. As the composition of a perfume is not protected by intellectual property law in France, codes nonetheless allow for reinforcement of the brand identity of the fragrances. Such codes had long been used by haute couture houses to ensure the transmission of design and brand from generation to generation.[59]

The Société des parfums Christian Dior was founded in 1948, the same year as the New York branch. The capital of the French perfume branch was initially 5 million francs, raised to 13 million in 1951. The compared profits of haute couture and perfume were, in each case, of 3 million in 1948, then the net profits of haute couture remained higher until 1953, when haute couture yielded 30 million francs, and perfumes' net profits were nearly threefold that sum. The growth of perfume continued, and in the early 1960s Dior Parfums was making an annual 200 million francs in profits, and haute couture a quarter of this. Couture was losing its client base while the profits from perfumes buttressed the expansion of the Dior brand.[60]

The Dior empire kept growing, itself a part of the gigantic Boussac Group. The company C. D. [Christian Dior] Models was founded in London in 1952. Dior London workrooms received designs from both the haute couture Paris line and the ready-to-wear New York line and then reproduced them for the UK market. After losses in 1954, the London company became a branch of Christian Dior Paris. It catered to all the British dominions except for Australia, which was the subject of a special contract signed in 1952 between Christian Dior New York and the Sydney firm House of Youth for the manufacturing and selling of exclusive reproductions of Christian Dior New York designs. A similar agreement was set up in Canada, between Christian Dior New York and retailer Holt Renfrew, in 1951. In Mexico in 1950, in Cuba in 1951, and in Chile in 1952, the company selected an upper-class department store and arranged an exclusive contract with it for the legal reproduction of Dior Paris haute couture and Dior New York ready-to-wear designs. In 1953, Dior opened in Caracas; Christian Dior Venezuela, Inc., was housed in another replica of the avenue Montaigne Dior boutique. The Venezuelan house sold only garments from the haute couture collection, created in Paris and reproduced by hand in the Caracas ateliers of the house. Because of the oil boom, a luxury sector quickly developed in Caracas, and the jeweler Cartier and another Paris couturier, Pierre Balmain, also branched out there at this time. A second branch of the Dior conglomerate, called Christian Dior Del Sur, opened in Caracas to handle the financial aspects of Dior's businesses in the Americas. These operations would later be transferred to Curaçao and Panama.[61]

In the second half of the 1950s, the Dior conglomerate set up a system of royalties in which the various overseas branches of Dior could pay the Dior Paris haute couture house a royalty for the know-how created at the headquarters. Sums varied over the years. For the year 1956, a peak year in the decade for royalties, the total royalties paid to the Société Christian Dior by overseas branches in 1956 was 23,579,280 French francs.[62] In extending branded licenses all over the world, Dior represented an innovation in developing a commercial realization of the intangible assets of haute couture.[63] To describe such intangible assets, Rouët used—perhaps for the first time—the word *immateriality* at the conference he held in Boston in 1958 on the influence of Dior.[64] A couture house, observed the financial director, was first and foremost a laboratory for aesthetic research, and this mission of creativity brought with it the high costs of experimentation and risk taking. The ready-to-wear dresses designed in Paris for the New York branch were different in quality from the haute couture production, but, with its licensing agreements, the Dior group had finally turned this reality to its advantage. The Dior firm, which was nicknamed the "General Motors of Fashion," was featured in the car company's advertising.[65]

Transatlantic Pursuits

Boussac, Rouët, and Dior created a global empire for the Dior brand. Other couturiers followed in their footsteps and developed their own overseas ventures, agreements with American manufacturers, and global beauty brands. They also did not forget the problem of piracy. Couturiers allied against the imitators, and in so doing they were often supported by the Chambre Syndicale. Its Artistic Property Service handled dozens of cases of piracy during the 1950s and increasingly treated such offenses not as isolated cases but as networks. In the 1920s, couturiers often prosecuted copyists together; this became standard practice during the postwar period. It then made sense to coordinate antipiracy activities under the auspices of the Chambre Syndicale. In this way, in 1949, New York–based model renter Elsie Cobin, whom Paris couturiers had wanted to see thwarted since the 1930s, was successfully sued. The affair was resolved through a negotiated agreement. Because the case involved so many haute couture houses, Rouët, as chair of the Artistic Property Service, proposed that the money paid by Cobin be, after expenses, equally divided among the members of the Chambre Syndicale. The numerous legal cases waged by Paris couturiers against pirates in various parts of France increasingly pointed to international networks. In 1950, the Artistic Property Service sued the Maison S. Guattari, on the Cours de l'Intendance in Bordeaux. The firm had workshops employing twenty-five people and did not make contracts with Paris haute couture. Guattari obtained its originals through various intermediaries that included a Paris-based embroidery firm. The Guattari case exposed a network that went all the way to several South American countries. A raid performed with the help of a local representative of a Paris couturier revealed that Guattari traveled to Morocco and was supplying copies to the markets of the French protectorate.[66]

On March 12, 1952, the Paris couturiers' lobbying efforts resulted in the approval of the Loi réprimant la contrefaçon dans les Industries Saisonnières de la Parure et de l'Habillement, also known as the Loi Saunier, after Claire Saunier, the senator who proposed the project. Saunier had been a member of the Resistance during World War II; she was then a senator from 1946 to 1948 and served as a member of the government commission in charge of national education, fine arts, sports, youth, and leisure.[67] The haute couture initiative was put in her hands by Vincent de Moro Giafferi, who had prepared the first drafts of the law with members of the Artistic Property Service. The Chambre Syndicale had been ready with an initial text in 1945, but voting on it was delayed because the protection of haute couture intellectual property raised issues for intellectual property rights in general. The text of the law of 1952 was endorsed by Edgar Faure, the adjunct to the state secretary of the budget. The Commission on Justice and Legislation of the French National Assembly then adopted it, in a vote of thirteen to nine.

The consequences of this law for the French couturiers included the reorganization of the protection of creativity and an increase in the penalties handed out to
copyists, including the closing of their businesses and jail sentences for repeat
offenders. The text seemed to have the desired dissuasive effect as, barely a year
later, the Artistic Property Service estimated that piracy was on the decline in
France.[68]

The signing by a great number of countries of the Universal Copyright Convention of Geneva took place a bit later that year, on September 6, and made the
protection of fashion design more straightforward throughout Europe. Belgium
and Italy were now able to work directly with France to curb piracy. The United
States signed the convention but chose not to include fashion within the scope of
its own copyright law. Compared with the US law, then, the French law seemed
very protective of fashion, but the couturiers still considered it insufficient. The
Artistic Property Service of the Chambre Syndicale increased its activity during
the 1950s. Inquiries could lead to seizures that were conducted with the help of
the Sûreté Nationale. In 1952, the service conducted 124 inquiries and made
thirty subsequent seizures. The lawsuits concluded in the year 1952 alone yielded
a total of 2 million French francs in damages, which was divided among couturiers whose designs had been copied or counterfeited. The year's other cases produced amicable agreements generating another 4 million French francs for the
Chambre Syndicale members.[69]

Despite—and because of—this increased surveillance, piracy would stop
where repression hit, only to reappear elsewhere. Networks of copyists had gone
global, and the work of repressing piracy had to follow them overseas. Before the
Treaty of Rome set up the common market policy, the Chambre Syndicale filed
lawsuits in Belgian, German, Spanish, and Swiss courts, and its Artistic Property Service worked tirelessly to build up the international case law. In 1954,
the Chambre Syndicale contacted the Bureau International de la Protection Industrielle in Bern and obtained international registration for its members' production. Registering designs cost a moderate 1,500 French francs per year for a multiple registration of two hundred designs that would be protected in ten European
countries and North Africa. Finally, the Milan Conference on November 11, 1955,
included an encouraging discussion with the Italian authorities, who were also
worried about increasing fashion counterfeiting at a time when the Italian fashion
industry was gaining international success.[70]

While haute couture was making progress in unifying its European antipiracy strategies, the man to capture on the other side of the Atlantic turned out to be Frederick L. Milton. During the 1950s, the *New York Times* identified five major sketching agencies on Seventh Avenue—that is, firms that illegally sold sketches of haute couture designs to fashion manufacturers and retailers. The most famous of them was run by Milton, who was listed in the Manhattan directory as a designer.[71] The Chambre Syndicale, which organized the Paris fashion shows, decided that the distribution of press materials, pictures, and sketches of the collections would be prohibited for thirty days after the shows. Then came the official release date, when the press and buyers had official access to new haute couture designs for buying, reproducing, and selling. The Chambre Syndicale had a hard time enforcing this sanction, though this was no surprise—Paris couturiers had for decades tried to catch the sketchers and model renters that fed information to copyist networks. Milton illegally obtained sketches from the Paris haute couture shows. He sent out his sketches of haute couture designs five days after the fashion shows, using cable transmission. A thousand subscribers each paid Milton $1,000 a year to obtain the new haute couture designs twenty-five days before their official release dates. Journalist Nan Robertson defined sketching services as "the pirates . . . that peddle bootleg drawings of Paris fashions on Seventh Avenue before the official release date and before the French clothes bought legally arrive in this country."[72]

On October 26, 1955, four Paris couturiers—Christian Dior, Geneviève Fath, the house of Lanvin, and the house of Patou—held a press conference at the house of Dior on the avenue Montaigne. In front of an audience of international journalists, they announced that they were collectively suing Milton. The four couturiers filed the lawsuit in New York City, charging Milton with style piracy, trademark infringement, and unfair competition and asking for a total of $1.35 million in damages.[73] The plaintiffs accused Milton of profiting from information illegally obtained from Paris since 1948, even though the Fashion Institute of Technology archives list Milton's service as an operation beginning in 1940.[74] Inquiries revealed that Milton sent agents posing as retailers, manufacturers, and journalists. Along with Milton, the defendants included two Manhattan photography studios. The court proceedings also alluded to a host of unspecified "conspirators" who had contributed to copying haute couture designs without authorization.[75] Attorneys Cleary, Gottlieb, Friendly, and Hamilton represented the couturiers.

Today a leading global law firm, the Manhattan-based concern was the first American law firm to settle in postwar Paris in 1949. Jacob H. Gilbert represented Milton. Gilbert was a lawyer and a representative in the New York State Congress from 1951 to 1960. A Democrat, he also represented the Bronx in the US Congress from 1960 to 1971.[76]

The plaintiffs thought that Milton's venture was fraudulent, but American entrepreneurs were divided on the question of how to interpret the practices of Milton and other sketchers, which made prosecution difficult.[77] Some entrepreneurs, including Maurice Rentner, thought that working from sketches was a "poor way to copy" and that the only way to understand the garments was to go to Paris to see and touch the originals.[78] Other American manufacturers valued Milton's services and considered him a legitimate source of information, along these lines: "Last year, United States buyers legally brought back more than $1,500,000 worth of Paris originals. Reports are that this year's purchases will total an even larger sum. How does it happen? How is it that the majority of the 4,000 clothing makers on Seventh Avenue, the nation's wholesale garment center, never go to Paris? Yet most of the four billion dollars worth of clothes they make every year have something of Paris built into them—in shape, in details or both."[79] For low-grade manufacturers, designers depended on sketchers' services like Milton's for novelty and admitted that "we copy a new neckline treatment or another detail [from the sketches]."[80]

In October 1955, the *New York Times* interviewed Milton, who said that the case had no merit. Milton asserted that he was a creative designer and, in this respect, often had the privilege of anticipating the Paris collections: "Mr. Milton said, his styles for a given season are *usually half a year ahead of the Paris presentations.*"[81] In so doing, he turned the argument regarding anteriority on its head, and he accused Dior and the other plaintiffs of being the copyists of his own sketchbooks. The American court did not accept this argument. Supreme Court Justice of New York Henry Clay Greenberg took a very firm position and condemned Milton's activity on moral grounds within the American legal framework. The judge noted that the four plaintiff couturiers had adopted a system to defend their creations against copying. He then noted that Milton and his employees had violated the conditions of entry to their showings, copied the designs under cover, and sold the results to people who were not authorized to see them. Although fashion designs were not protected by copyright in the United States,

Milton was selling not garments but drawings and sketches, which were better protected.[82]

In response to Greenberg's decision, Gilbert tried to have the lawsuit dismissed on the grounds that the facts had been insufficiently documented. Greenberg ruled that the lawsuit should not be dismissed and stuck to his argument against Milton.[83] Dior and the three other plaintiffs, Justice Greenberg noted, had reputations as leading fashion designers, and this allowed each of them to design unique dresses that "represent the product of his special skill and genius."[84] Greenberg insisted that this originality had earned Dior his excellent commercial reputation, and he therefore veered toward the protection of the trademark to better articulate his judgment: "In the exploitation of such designs [the] plaintiff has incurred great expense, has acquired a reputation and good will of value and has acquired valuable property rights in its good will and reputation, and its names *Christian Dior* and *Dior* have become well and favorably known in France, the United States and throughout the world."[85] The designs, according to Greenberg, had been appropriated by the defendants through an "unlawful conspiracy" between Milton and the intermediaries he used between Paris, Vienna, and New York, and even today, such a charge has the ability to increase a penalty.[86] Greenberg ended with a plea for the moral conduct of one's business enterprise.[87]

What were the costs of piracy? Being by definition an illegal business, fashion piracy is hard to quantify exactly in terms of profits for the copyists or costs to the couturiers. According to the Chambre Syndicale, piracy cost "hundred millions of francs" annually. In the late 1950s, the management at Dior estimated that around one-quarter of the firm's income was lost to piracy each year. In 1959, the *New York Times* gave the figure of $20 million as an estimation of the annual losses to Paris couture from piracy. Considering that Dior was responsible for 5 percent of all French exports, such figures made fashion piracy an *affaire d'Etat*, and eradicating it became an objective of the government. Of course, if one accepts the *New York Times* journalist Nan Robertson's estimate that American buyers legally purchased $1.5 million of Paris originals per year while Seventh Avenue manufacturers were producing clothes to the tune of $4 billion a year, France's influence on worldwide fashions becomes relative. Even in the Dior era, the influence of France paled in comparison with the profits generated on Seventh Avenue.[88]

The Appellate Division of the Supreme Court of the State of New York thus refused to dismiss the lawsuit, which went ahead.[89] In 1956, Milton and his co-defendants presented their claim that protection of couturiers had no basis in American law.[90] Justice Greenberg upheld the right of the Paris couturiers to protect their creations.[91] To the paradox that emerged from the fact that the couturiers asked to retain the right of exclusivity of their designs even as they advertised them for all to see, Greenberg replied that the care with which couturiers regulated their fashion shows, and the fact that they published fashion plates for restricted purposes, showed their intention to retain control of the originality of their designs.[92] The fight against unfair competition was the principle that allowed Justice Greenberg to construct his case, despite the asymmetries between the French and American legal systems. The Milton lawsuit was expensive for both the plaintiff couturiers and the Chambre Syndicale, which supported them. In addition to the couturiers' individual bills, the accounts of the syndicate in 1958 list payment to the law firm of Sylvan Gotshal of 347,024 French francs for the first round of the Milton lawsuit and 167,559 for the second part of the trial.[93] It had ended in a victory—or so the members of the Chambre Syndicale thought.[94] Yet the Milton case was not over yet.

The French law on artistic and literary property, passed on March 11, 1957, was the next important step in copyright protection, one that had been eagerly anticipated by the French couture industry since the interwar period as a replacement of the law of 1909.[95] The Chambre Syndicale lobbied the French government to ensure that the law of 1957, which reformed authors' rights, would not undo the protection granted to the seasonal industries. Thanks to this intervention, the text protecting the applied arts was included in the new law, thereby giving fashion industrialists protection for their creations.[96] Under this new legal regime, penalties for copying fashions included up to a two-year jail sentence in France.[97] Case law, however, could limit the protection of fashion designs to a single season in many cases, even though fashion experts thought that items such as the classic Chanel suit, for example, should be protected for much longer. The Artistic Property Service went to work on the French appeals court (Cour de Cassation) to secure longer-term protection for fashion designs.[98] At the end of the decade, the service's report was extremely optimistic, even remarking on a quasi-total withdrawal of copying in France.[99] In 1957, a dozen cases of counterfeiting pursued by the Chambre Syndicale and its members yielded a total of 3 million French francs in penalties, as well as 25 million in damages.[100]

The End of Dior?

The year 1957 also marked the tenth anniversary of the Dior firm. The business that Christian Dior had envisioned as a creative little house had become a multinational corporation. Global sales of the Dior enterprises—including couture, ready-to-wear, licenses, and perfumes—totaled $17 million in 1956 and $22 million in 1957.[101] Christian Dior designed the Paris and New York collections and controlled the products resulting from every licensing agreement. He had a good team, excellent managers, and skilled *modélistes*. Among them was a particularly capable young man named Yves Mathieu Saint Laurent, born in Oran, Algeria, in 1936. Still, the pace of the collection seasons and the need to be constantly creative took a toll on Christian Dior. He had always spent part of the year in the countryside to recuperate, but his heart was weak. The little couture house that he had intended to be the postwar laboratory of style had become an empire that had started to devour him.[102]

On October 24, 1957, Christian Dior died of heart failure in Montecatini, Italy, where he was on vacation. He had become so central to the fashion industry that his peers all felt the loss deeply, both personally and professionally. Jacques Heim commented: "Now that Dior is dead, the spotlight turns on Balenciaga. But all of us, the whole couture, must get down to business. We have to work harder and be more efficient to save the future of French high fashion."[103] Maurice Rentner, asked by the American trade press who could possibly succeed Dior, replied that it was too soon to know. Rentner added that a designer's success depended on individual creative abilities, but also on the ability to recruit talented teams and help them grow. Rentner himself suffered from a stroke in March 1958 and died in July.[104] Within a few months, two of the most important fashion entrepreneurs of the twentieth century, Dior and Rentner, one French and the other American, had gone.[105]

Let us now return to the Milton piracy lawsuit, which kept going despite the death of Christian Dior, the main plaintiff. In 1959, while the case was still pending in the State of New York Supreme Court, Viennese journalist Helene Kastner-Srubar, who used the pseudonym Mariavera, was caught red-handed by the French police sketching illegally in Paris couture houses for Milton.[106] She was "charged by the French police with being a secret agent of the Milton Fashion Service of New York."[107] This brought to light a whole complex of sketchers and copyists based in central Europe. The couture houses accusing Milton of his malfeasance added the members of this new network to the list of his so-called co-conspirators. Details then surfaced about the network of informants that Milton had built up between Paris, central Europe, and New York. The network was exposed with the help of the communication companies Western Union Telegraph Co., Commercial Cable Co., and RCA Communications, Inc. The defendants, once again, denied all charges.[108] The case was eventually resolved in 1962 through a negotiated agreement. That same year, the French government phased out its postwar aid program to haute couture. Haute couture houses engaged in piracy lawsuits now had to carry out the inquiry work themselves instead of relying on the Artistic Property Service of the Chambre Syndicale, which had been downsized for lack of funding. Couturiers could still consult with Suzanne Dreyfus-David, the lawyer appointed by the Chambre Syndicale to work on intellectual property rights, for a standard fee.[109] The couturiers who had founded the four Paris companies that sued Milton were all dead in 1962, when the case eventually reached its conclusion. Although the four couture houses did not obtain the damages they had sought, it was still considered a victory, because Milton was found guilty and had to cease all of his activities. The lawsuit also built up helpful case law on the other side of the Atlantic. Far from being a failure, these cases demonstrated the maturation of fashion intellectual property rights strategies. Going to court was costly and exhausting. Most entrepreneurs preferred to try to solve problems through negotiated agreements that were cheaper and faster and could still generate relevant sums of money.[110]

The Milton case did not go so far as to make a significant mark on US copyright law. Over the decades since, there have been many initiatives to establish better protections for fashion design in the United States, but unlike in France, fashion design remains unprotected today in the US copyright law. In 1957, within the time span of the Milton case, a new design piracy bill was discussed in Congress. The draft bill included a system of registration that was adapted to fashion design, and it was supported by major players in the American fashion industry. Oleg Cassini, who designed many outfits for Jackie Kennedy, publicly voiced his support of the bill. Other voices were skeptical—designer Tom Brigance, for example, thought that the line between creativity, adaptation, and copying was a very fine one, probably too fine to make protection relevant. British-turned-American virtuoso designer Charles James, who had in the past been fiercely protective of his designs, "declared himself in favor of piracy" rather than the new bill in the trade paper *Women's Wear Daily.* What really mattered to the industry, he insisted, was not the protection of a design but the protection of the brand of the couturier.[111]

Piracy lawsuits were not restricted to relations between Paris and New York. Even as the four Paris couturiers were suing Milton, American firms were also filing suits against local competitors for piracy. In 1955, American manufacturer Lilli Ann Corp., known for its high-fashion dressmaking advertised in *Vogue* and *Harper's Bazaar,* sued Jones Store Co. and Mercantile Store Co. for piracy, asking for $2 million in damages.[112] The field of fashion intellectual property rights was maturing in the United States as well. The Milton case shows that it was possible to build case law in the United States despite an incomplete legal framework for the protection of fashion design. Justice Greenberg managed to advance the argument of unfair competition while underlining the powerful trademark protection that characterized Paris couture. While Paris couturiers still experienced great difficulties and, in the United States, met with failure in trying to persuade legislators to internationalize the copyright protection of their creations, they had, over many decades, built a strong brand capital that would from that point forward be the strongest asset in their intellectual property rights portfolios.[113]

From Local to Global

From that very first "New Look" show in 1947, Dior positioned himself as the leading trendsetter for women's fashions internationally. He regularly sparked fashion *revolutions:* clear changes of style that drove retailers and consumers to discard previous fashions and adopt new ones. In August 1953, barely six years after the scandalous long skirts of the New Look, Dior surprised his clients yet again by being the first to return to shorter hemlines. He did it in such a way that it was not perceived as a return to 1940s styles but instead seen as a new development in fashion. The change impacted the whole industry, including underwear and hosiery, because foundation garments had to follow Dior's new silhouettes.[114]

With its licensing agreements, the house of Dior was the first French firm to fully turn fashion copying to its advantage. The previous chapters have clearly shown the limits encountered by haute couture when trying to set up shop beyond borders.[115] Dior was not the first multinational enterprise to be set up by a Paris fashion entrepreneur. On the one hand, haute couture had always been an international affair, as is clear from the cosmopolitanism of its entrepreneurs and buyers, its retail practices, and the trafficking of its products all over the world. On the other hand, the capital of haute couture, including all of its workshops and salons, remained in Paris until at least 1946 and was still French in the postwar years. Before World War I, an early movement toward the internationalization of haute couture took place with the founding of branches outside Paris, notably in New York and London. This raises the question of whether the Dior-driven globalization of haute couture might have happened earlier, had the global economy not contracted as a result of the Great Depression. In addition, it must be said that Dior was not the only French fashion entrepreneur to venture into the American market. Vionnet had come close to success there. The lesser-known house founded in Paris by the French Boué sisters managed to branch out more durably to New York. When Boué Sœurs's Paris activity grew sluggish during the Great Depression, the New York branch kept going and remained active even into the postwar period. In addition, the American societies founded by French couturiers to sell their perfumes on the other side of the Atlantic, such as Lelong, Inc., proved to be long-lasting ventures. Finally, a small group of French fashion entrepreneurs and designers migrated to the United States in the interwar period, and a handful more on the eve of World War II.[116]

When Dior opened a house in New York in 1948, he was not the first one there, but he would be the first to thrive. Dior turned experimentation into strategy and opportunity into a system. Boussac's backing was essential, as he provided capital, oversight of all investments, and management for the Dior firm. The experiences (and failures) of the aforementioned international predecessors played a role in the culture of transatlantic fashion entrepreneurship. Balmain, who had trained at Lelong along with the young Christian Dior during the war, tried to expand his new couture house overseas in the postwar era, but he did not have the benefit of a capitalization as large as Dior's.[117] The successes of Dior underline the return of men to the forefront of haute couture entrepreneurship. The interwar period had been the era of women entrepreneurs, even in overseas ventures. Now, it was the turn of men to dominate the business again, as had been the case in the nineteenth century. It is notable that the legal profession, which had become a necessary expertise in the haute couture industry, featured a generation of prominent women on both sides of the Atlantic, exemplified by the skills of Dreyfus-David in Paris and Engel in New York.

The time was ripe for a bolder move overseas—historians have long described the backwardness of French business in this era. David Landes, in a seminal article of 1949, observed that French business enterprises had conservative structures characterized by familial capital, a lack of external funding, and stout traditionalism.[118] While Landes was writing primarily about the nineteenth century, he drew plenty of connections between his work and features of the French economy in his day, which coincided with Dior's rise to fame in Paris couture. The French economy was bouncing back after the war, trying to replace obsolete industrial structures and seeking strategies for expansion and modernization.[119] The luxury expert Claude Rouzaud, in 1946, wrote that the power of haute couture lay in its capacity to add great value to a very small quantity of material.[120] Landes himself underestimated the value of innovation and creativity, as historians have consistently noted when debating his view of the backwardness of French entrepreneurship.[121]

Dior seemed revolutionary when he presented his New Look to the world's press and buyers in the avenue Montaigne salons, yet his collection was buttressed by the century-long experience, know-how, and symbolic capital of the fashion ecosystem. Paris haute couture had been the most prestigious fashion brand for a century or more. Though rejuvenated by Dior, it was still not known whether French fashion would succeed in becoming a global business.

Chapter 6

One World *of* Fashion

Couturiers resumed their travels at the end of World War II. To anticipate future external markets, Paris couturiers had collectively organized an exhibition of fashion dolls called the Théâtre de la Mode, which traveled through Europe and the United States in 1945 and 1946 to reawaken interest in haute couture. Added to this traveling haute couture was a new genre of exchange, thanks to missions of productivity dedicated to the fashion industry, beginning in 1948 with a group of sixteen fashion industrialists headed by the French leader of manufacturing, Albert Lempereur. The group visited New York and San Francisco to study retail and manufacturing. In the United States, these missions of productivity were organized as a part of the Marshall Plan—the European Recovery Program of humanitarian aid, developed by US secretary of state George Marshall, that aimed to limit communist influence and provide access to consumer goods in Europe. The Marshall Plan was an enterprise of seduction of the French, who were renowned for their anti-Americanism. Industrialists from any domain traveled to the United States within the framework of these missions, which had the effect of amplifying transfers of technology and culture from the United States to Europe. Some missions were industry themed; others centered on a category of industrial actors, like the American unions, for example. Until World War II, a majority of American garment industrialists had found inspiration in French design, originating primarily from Paris haute couture. Important garment designers in America included Hattie Carnegie, Elizabeth Hawes, and Claire McCardell, who, despite their relentless creativity, remained less well known than their French counterparts. In the framework of the productivity missions, the direction of influence seemed to flip, as the French fashion world was eager to learn of American techniques. The Marshall Plan offered Paris fashion industrialists the opportunity to increase their travels to America. But instead of Paris couturiers, it was the French media professionals and ready-to-wear entrepreneurs who filled the spots on these missions.[1]

America's Garment Industries through the Eyes of the Visitors of 1952

Eleven French garment industrialists set out on a tour of New York, Boston, and Chicago on the mission of November and December 1952, which was focused on women's wear. The group was composed of six women and five men. Three of them worked for the Société Parisienne de Confection, one of the largest garment manufacturers in Paris and the main production plant for the department store Galeries Lafayette. Two group members worked for Etablissements Lempereur, one of the most important ready-to-wear firms in France. The group, assisted by translators, visited employers' syndicates, trade unions, professional schools, an advertising agency, a bank, industrial sites of production, and over twenty garment manufacturers.[2] In their report that followed the tour, the mission members underlined both the similarities and the differences between the French and US garment industries. They were interested in labor conditions in the United States and in the structure, management, and technology of the firms there. In 1952, the garment and textile trades were the second-largest source of economic activity in the United States. Two-thirds of US garment production was concentrated in New York, still the undisputed fashion center of the country. Because of financial pressures, however, some of the firms were looking to relocate outside the city, to other US locations where the unions were less powerful and wages were lower. The French mission noted that in New York three-quarters of all garment workers were women and that the profession employed numerous foreigners; the most recent census indicated that 51 percent of New York garment workers were Italians, 32 percent were Jews (mostly from Germany and Poland), and 17 percent were of other nationalities, including Americans. In San Francisco, another important manufacturing hub, the majority of garment workers were from Mexico.[3]

All members of the 1952 mission were highly interested in labor conditions. The structure of the industry had remained very similar to what it was before the war, although the number of firms had decreased during the Great Depression. In the early 1950s the United States contained over three thousand garment manufacturing firms. As before the war, they were divided between manufacturers and subcontracting firms that competed for orders. These firms formed groups organized by type of garment and by price category. The French travelers noted the importance of labor unions in organizing the US workforce, whose rights were based on the 1935 Wagner Act, completed by the Taft Hartley Act of 1947. The powerful International Ladies Garment Workers' Union, which was founded in 1900 and, in 1952, federated some four hundred thousand members across the United States and Canada, had no equivalent in France. The union occupied multiple social roles. The high quality of dialogue between the unions and the trade syndicates made a strong impression on the French mission members. The workweek was thirty-five hours, with very limited options for paid overtime. Working two shifts was forbidden. Working at home was also forbidden, while it was still common in France. Employees were given six official days off per year, but the mission members noted that salaries were high enough that most workers could afford to work less than fifty weeks per year.[4]

The goal of the French mission was to understand why the American garment manufacturing industry was so much more productive than the French one, and the members identified a number of factors to explain it. American workers were better paid and enjoyed a greater level of trust and dialogue with their managers. Education was of a high standard, as the French group observed when visiting the Fashion Institute of Technology in New York. The French mission members found important reasons for high productivity in the methods of the American firms. Workshops were organized so as to minimize the distances that workers had to walk during the workday. The sewing machines were not new, but high-quality scissors, other cutting devices, and smaller machines for finishing, all placed judiciously on the tables, were clever additions that helped save time. Measuring the time needed for each operation allowed management to distribute tasks among workers efficiently. Similarly, finishing techniques for basting hems, reinforcing backs, and making belts were particularly efficient and gave good results. Although the French mission members did not use the word in their report, their observations show a much greater degree of Taylorism in the US production than in France. Their conclusions, however, should be considered alongside the fact that the group visited only a selection of American firms in large unionized centers. Sweatshops were endemic in America as in Europe, and numerous workshops remained outside the unions. Observations by social workers and labor historians mitigate the impression that labor conditions were so much better in the United States than they were in France.[5]

The mission of 1952 observed somewhat paradoxical features in the fashion media. In the United States, sales personnel had already become, as it would generalize later in the twentieth century, quite minimal, and this was a low-paid, low-status job in the mass fashion retail. Advertising was a driving force in the largest consumer market in the world, but the brands of textile and garment manufacturers were still usually separate from the brand of the retailer. This was the most important difference between the French and the US garment industries. In contrast, the French fashion business had managed to build stronger brand identity. The French mission members returned home convinced of the backwardness of their own ready-to-wear industry and of the need to adopt American methods.[6]

The 1955 Mission and the Creation of the French Fashion Coordination Committee

In 1955, the Marshall Plan funded a new mission of productivity aimed at the fashion business, with a focus on relations between the industry and the media, a theme that had raised great interest during the 1952 mission. The 1955 mission was, again, composed of eleven French delegates led by Lempereur, president of the firm Etablissements Lempereur and of the largest employers' syndicate in French ready-to-wear, the Fédération des Industries du Vêtement Féminin. Most other members of the delegation worked for the fashion media. The US Department of Commerce established the program and its itinerary, which went again to New York and then, this time, to Wilmington, Delaware; Dallas, Texas; and California, where the group visited San Francisco and especially its garment center, the largest in the country after New York and Los Angeles.

In New York the mission of 1955 visited Fairchild Publications, publisher of the trade newspaper *Women's Wear Daily;* the offices of the *New York Times* and of Condé Nast, the publisher of the US edition of *Vogue* fashion magazine; and the offices of *Harper's Bazaar.* The French delegation visited the offices of the most important style consultancies: Amos Parrish & Co., Inc., and Tobé. They also visited the Fashion Group, which had remained the most important association of women in the US fashion business, with its base in New York and numerous local chapters across the United States, and now around the world. The 1955 mission seemed to discover the work of Tobé, Parrish, and the Fashion Group as trend brokers, even if all three organizations had been founded between 1927 and 1929 to connect the textile, manufacturing, retail, and media industries in US fashion (see Figure 6.1).[7]

The French mission group found that the ranges of clothing offered to the US public were narrower than in France but of very good quality for their price. This was a consequence of the project of an American fashion democracy that aimed to offer current clothes of decent quality at affordable prices in greater numbers. In the mid-1950s, 85 percent of American women bought their clothes ready-to-wear, compared with less than 40 percent of French women. The US Department of Commerce, along with American department stores, had taken the initiative of measuring the population for clothing, and it kept updating and completing these measurement campaigns. And yet, even in the United States, the standardization of sizes remained one of the most important challenges to the industry, as Andrew Goodman explained to the Fashion Group. As a consequence, added Goodman, clients requested a lot of alterations, which were the costlier expense for the ready-to-wear business.[8]

As a contrast, the goal of fashion in France was to create difference, or even snobbery, noted the French manufacturing experts. In 1904 German sociologist Georg Simmel had defined fashion as attire that allowed the wearer to both blend in and stand out. Fashion was a system of both inclusion and exclusion. If we examine this definition with the report of the 1955 French mission of productivity in mind, the French fashion industry then was still trying mostly to help its consumers stand out, while the US fashion industry aimed for its consumers to blend in. The Lempereur mission further noted that the main selling argument of the US garment industry was to allow all strata of consumers to be in fashion, and that this sociological trait contributed to fostering a higher demand for and a faster rotation of the merchandise offered in the stores. The attraction of cheap, well-made clothes in large series was, noted the visitors, very powerful to the consumers. On average, American women bought four times more clothing than their French counterparts in 1955.[9]

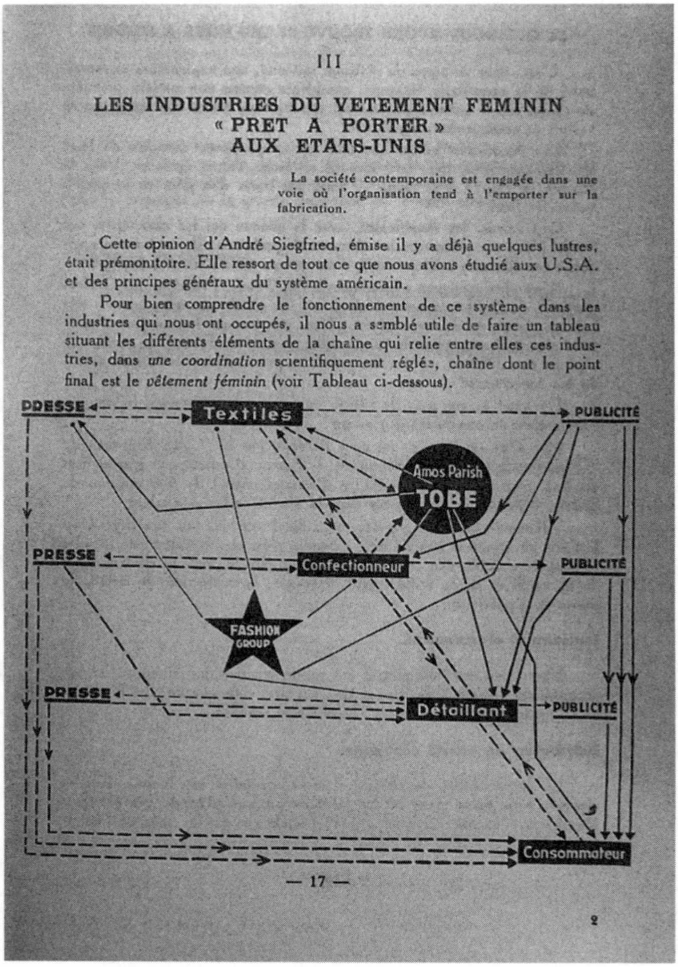

III

LES INDUSTRIES DU VETEMENT FEMININ
« PRET A PORTER »
AUX ETATS-UNIS

La société contemporaine est engagée dans une voie où l'organisation tend à l'emporter sur la fabrication.

Cette opinion d'André Siegfried, émise il y a déjà quelques lustres, était prémonitoire. Elle ressort de tout ce que nous avons étudié aux U.S.A. et des principes généraux du système américain.

Pour bien comprendre le fonctionnement de ce système dans les industries qui nous ont occupés, il nous a semblé utile de faire un tableau situant les différents éléments de la chaîne qui relie entre elles ces industries, dans *une coordination* scientifiquement réglée, chaîne dont le point final est le *vêtement féminin* (voir Tableau ci-dessous).

— 17 —

2

FIGURE 6.1 The coordination of the US fashion industries, as represented in the report of the 1955 French mission of productivity to the United States.

Les Relations entre les Industries et la Presse de Mode aux Etats-Unis, *mission d'études, mai 1955, supplément à la revue* L'Industrie du vêtement féminin *(Paris, May 1956), Archives Nationales de France, AJ 81.64.*

The mission of 1955 stopped in Wilmington, Delaware, to visit the textile plants of DuPont de Nemours, a firm founded in 1802 at the same location as a gunpowder mill. After merging with Dow Chemical Company in 2017, it became DowDuPont and the largest chemical conglomerate in the world; then, in June 2019, it split into three companies: Dow (dedicated to commodity chemical production), DuPont (specialty chemical production), and Corteva (agricultural chemicals). Over its history DuPont had specialized in explosives, automotive parts, and, shortly before the Great Depression, polymers, which resulted in the firm's accession to a leadership position in the development of manufactured fibers.[10] Paris couturiers, and the fashion industry more generally, had started to experiment with manufactured fibers during the interwar period, and they pursued tests in this domain during World War II, pushed by the need to provide replacements for the natural fibers that had become rarer as a result of the requisitions and penuries of the war economy. But wartime consumers tended to be highly critical of these wartime substitute fibers, called *ersatz* in the jargon of the occupation years. Overall, fabrics made with these fibers seemed more prone to wrinkle, thinner, and less soft than the natural fibers they aimed to replace, notably wool.[11]

This view had shifted by 1955, however, as the members of the French mission reported on the "miracle fibers" that the United States had developed very actively from wartime onward. Cotton still dominated and was used for 86 percent of ordinary mass-produced garments. The production of cotton was, correctly, expected to develop even further. But in the mid-1950s, 60 percent of the higher-grade dresses, which retailers sold as units, were made of rayon and fibrane, two popular manufactured fibers. The use of nylon was on the rise. Not only was nylon used as a replacement for silk in stockings, but it was also blended with other fibers to create more resistant fabrics of much easier care: nylon dried faster than natural fibers and did not need ironing. In 1954, reporting on the state of French fashion consumption at a Fashion Group meeting, Goodman stated that the nicest gift one could bring from America to a European woman was still a pair of American nylons. France also produced nylons by then, and the main manufacturer of nylon there was Rhodiaceta, a firm founded in 1922 in Paris as a branch of the chemical group Société des Usines Chimiques Rhône-Poulenc. Rhodiaceta had four manufactures outside of the capital, including one in the north of Lyons. In 1939 Rhodiaceta acquired from DuPont the exploitation license of nylon for

Belgium, France, Spain, and Switzerland. Using American machinery, Rhodiaceta started trial production of nylon from 1941 onward and intensified it during the postwar era. In 1949 Rhodiaceta produced one thousand tons of nylon, and in 1955, ten thousand tons. During the decade of the 1950s, Rhodiaceta's production enjoyed a growth rate that was double that of the other chemical specialties within the Rhône-Poulenc group. The firm developed a series of partnerships and participations in firms at the international level, notably in Italy and Brazil. Manufactured and blended fibers had become the norm. Their easy care was the most important sales argument in the industry.[12]

The French industrialists who visited the United States were impressed by the quality of the fit of ready-made clothes purchased off the rack. Availability, affordability, and washability were all essential criteria to the American wardrobe. The French visitors were also impressed by the separates, those flexible and wearable pieces that could be worn together or mixed and matched with other clothes: skirts, blouses, jackets, and, increasingly, women's trousers. American designers including Elizabeth Hawes and Claire McCardell had made of the separates a fashion that was elegant and comfortable. The functionality of shapes aimed to accommodate active women, whether they worked inside or outside the home. American fashion experts and sociologists praised the fashion democracy that succeeded on their domestic market. Budgets, however, remained limited, and sociologists of the postwar period showed that middle-class women who lived with their families on a budget of $2,000 per year afforded for themselves one $30 ensemble per season, and not more.[13] The popularization of fashion in America relied on the experience of the trend bureaus in all fashionable merchandise, whether clothing, accessories, or household goods. Expertise on color forecasting developed in the United States with the formation of the Textile Color Card Association of the United States (TCCA), which in 1915 published its first color card, for spring 1916. The TCCA changed its name to the Color Association of America in 1955 and is still active to this day. In 1930, a group of British industrialists founded the British Color Council Ltd., which would merge with the Council of Industrial Design in the early 1970s.[14]

Since the late 1920s the development of the fashion forecasting services by consultants such as Tobé and Amos Parrish drew the interest of American retailers. While Tobé's business kept flourishing, in the mid-1950s she increasingly contributed to the institutionalization of her profession. At that time, she was writing a weekly column, "Tobé Says," that was published in more than forty newspapers, including the *Herald Tribune*. She founded the Bosses' Dinner, an event gathering dozens of retailers, where she presented the most prestigious award in the field. In 1956, she started to fund a series of endowed lectures in retail, which bore her name, in the Master of Business Administration program at the Harvard Business School. The content of the lectures was then published in a series of short volumes used to teach graduate programs in business administration at dozens of American universities and colleges. The lectures continued until Tobé's death, in 1962. Two years earlier, in 1960, US senator John F. Kennedy had appointed Tobé a member of the National Committee on Business and Professional Men and Women.[15]

The French ready-to-wear manufacturers were curious about the place that consultants like Parrish and Tobé occupied in the US fashion industry. As a conclusion to its American travels, the group led by Lempereur came to think that the French fashion industries needed a sort of clearinghouse or unifying group to offer trend direction. To this end, in 1955 they established a coordination committee of the fashion industries in Paris.[16] The goal of this committee was to conduct a harmonization of the materials, colors, and sizes used at all levels of the French textile, fashion, and leather industries. The Chambre Syndicale de la Couture Parisienne had shown interest in the work of the TCCA during the interwar period, but it took three decades for this interest to develop in practice. The creative hegemony of haute couture was partly replaced by a larger array of designers, some still in haute couture, as well as others who worked for garment manufacturers and retailers. To all of them, the coordination committee offered information on the trends, from the fibers to the media.[17]

The French missions of productivity pinpointed the need for magazines to present a vision of fashion that was both glossy and approachable. The idea that fashion was relatable was the mainstay of *Elle* magazine, a French fashion weekly founded in 1945 by journalists Marcelle Auclair and Hélène Gordon-Lazareff, who had spent the entire war in America. Gordon-Lazareff was born in Russia to a Jewish family who had fled the 1917 Revolution to resettle in France. With Pierre Lazareff, her second husband and the founder of the daily *France-Soir* in 1945, she became highly influential in the Paris media milieu. *Elle* offered women a bridge between high and low fashion and coverage of society topics with a focus on lifestyle. The staff aimed to have a realistic approach to fashion while keeping strong links with the desirability of design. Along with other titles, such as *Le Jardin des Modes* and *Marie-France, Elle* played an essential role in the French postwar transition to ready-to-wear. The magazine promoted both the idea of smarter fashions created by the manufacturing industry and the dissemination of haute couture design to larger strata of consumers through the publication of authorized paper patterns and designer ready-to-wear.[18] At the same time, haute couture took up the task of adapting to changes in clothing production. During the late 1940s Jean Gaumont-Lanvin worked on the project of a limited popularization of haute couture that the Chambre Syndicale realized in June 1950, under the name of the Couturiers Associés, which linked the couturiers Carven, Dessès, Fath, Paquin, and Piguet to seven French manufacturers. Every season, each couturier in the group committed to create seven designs made by the manufacturers without limitation in numbers. Retailers of good standard then sold the clothes in twenty-five French provincial cities under the collective label of Couturier Associé added to the designer's name. These garments matched the current fashions in an "understated rather than overstated" way. Dresses retailed for between 25,000 and 45,000 francs, or about $75 to $115.[19]

The New York fashion industry shared with Paris manufacturers methods of batch production and flexible specialization. The industry everywhere rested on the human hand, with important differences in the extent and the management of mechanization. But Paris and New York still had different approaches to branding. The manufacturer who made a collection of dresses did not always give his name to the line, and often sent entire collections anonymously to department stores and specialty shops, where the retailer's name, and sometimes but not always the manufacturer's name, would be added to the label as the brand of the garment.[20]

A deficit in brand image still plagued the New York garment firms, but haute couture was in an increasingly difficult position. A few months after Christian Dior passed away, in September 1958, Jacques Heim (who had become president of the Chambre Syndicale de la Couture Parisienne) was in New York after a five-year absence and commented that the spotlight now turned on Balenciaga. The fashion system was changing fast. After the war, Lelong had resumed his travels to the United States and his good relations with his American buyers. There, his perfume business expanded; as early as 1947, he bought a twenty-five-story tower in Chicago, at the corner of Madison Street and Michigan Avenue, for $2.3 million in which to house his cosmetics and perfume operations, Lucien Lelong Inc., which also had offices in Paris, New York, and Los Angeles. The next year, in 1948, Lelong closed down his couture operation. He announced that his retirement was due to illness, and never came back to haute couture. But his American perfumes and cosmetics firm continued to thrive, and, in 1953, beauty multinational Coty acquired a controlling share of Lucien Lelong Inc. In 1958, Lelong died from illness after a decade in retirement. The Chambre Syndicale saluted his memory and his efforts during the war to keep the personnel of haute couture at work.[21]

Several prominent couturiers were ready to revive the creativity of haute couture after Dior. Heim had cited the name of Balenciaga, who had been part of haute couture's return to prosperity in the late 1930s. The couturier—born Cristóbal Balenciaga Eisaguirre in 1895 in Getaria, a small town on the Basque coast not so far from the French border—had started his first haute couture house in San Sebastián in 1917. He fled Spain for Paris during the civil war and in 1937 opened his haute couture house as a limited liability firm, with a capital of 100,000 francs, at 10 avenue George V. He owned his Paris firm along with two managers: fellow Basque Nicolas Bizcarrondo and Frenchman Wladzio Jaworowski d'Attainville, who was also the great love of Balenciaga's life. Balenciaga opened a retail branch in Biarritz. In addition, he was a part owner in three independent ready-to-wear establishments, in San Sebastián, Madrid, and Barcelona, called Eisa B. E. Costura, for which Balenciaga designed more affordable collections than for his Paris house. Balenciaga's capital grew to 200,000 francs in 1946, then 30 million francs in 1960. During the 1950s, the houses of Balenciaga and Dior were the firms that had the highest capital in Paris couture, sold the most expensive designs, and paid the highest salaries to their premières and cutters—more than double what workers in similar posts were paid by most other couture firms.[22] Balenciaga was an extremely precise tailor who could sew very well. He innovated technically and creatively but, unlike Dior, did not aim to regularly launch commercial revolutions through a change of line. Balenciaga's relation to volume was avant-garde, and his fashion related to the body in a visionary manner—a term often used to describe his work. Many of Balenciaga's creations could be worn on all types of bodies. Balenciaga did not limit himself to dressing thin, model-stereotype women. Maybe more than any other couturier of his time, he managed to balance beauty and wearability, creating clothes that were warm or allowed freedom of movement when needed. In his approach to movement and real bodies, Balenciaga acknowledged the designs of Vionnet as having a profound influence on him. At the same time, he announced futuristic shapes that would be picked up by the next generation of couturiers, notably Pierre Cardin and André Courrèges, whose wife, Coqueline, was a former seamstress at Balenciaga. His influence remained important later in, for example, the production of the Japanese and Belgian fashion avant-gardes, notably with couturiers like Dries Van Noten, Martin Margiela, and Yohji Yamamoto.[23]

Diverse talents were emerging in haute couture, including such names as Pierre Cardin and Hubert de Givenchy. Jacques Heim could now announce that the future of haute couture was bright. He thought that Cardin, who showed a sensitivity for pop and futuristic lines as well as a great sense of business innovation, seemed best able to capture the spirit of the times, even more so than Dior's gifted apprentice, Yves Saint Laurent. Cardin became the spearhead of the aggressive licensing strategies adopted in France by couture firms including Dior and Saint Laurent, in Italy by leather goods firm Gucci, and in the industry generally. These firms developed diverse practices of licensing. Cardin took the licensing of his haute couture name to an extreme, with branded goods extending from women's dresses and men's suits to bath towels and ashtrays. Everyone could buy a little bit of an haute couture name. The obvious danger was that this strategy would erode the image of the brand. This happened to Cardin, who never completely regained the image of a luxury brand after overlicensing to mass production starting in the 1960s.[24]

A small group of couture houses were eager to internationalize. Pierre Balmain, who had apprenticed at the house of Lelong at the same time as Dior, left Lelong to open the limited liability firm Pierre Balmain in May 1945. An essential difference was that Balmain had a more modest capital than Dior. Balmain traveled to New York in the fall of 1946 to study the American market, and signed a contract to design a range of products for the Californian department store I. Magnin. Balmain told the US press that he believed in closer ties between New York and Paris and that he was planning to expand his business into a line of informal clothing and separates. In 1949, Balmain started his first ready-to-wear line in the United States, manufactured in the New York garment district. He returned in 1950 to tour America and vacation in Florida with his mother, who acted as his model and muse. She presented Balmain's separates, travel fashions, and evening wear to the American public. Balmain hired Ann McGarry, former fashion coordinator at Neiman Marcus, to handle his firm's public relations. In 1952, he started designing his own New York wholesale collections, in partnership with New York manufacturer Maria Krum. In 1955, he received the Neiman Marcus fashion award for distinguished service in the field of fashion, a prestigious distinction that Dior had received in 1947.[25]

Jacques Fath was another couturier who enjoyed being at the forefront of internationalization. He had started his business in 1937 with a rather modest capital of 25,000 francs. Fath went through a tremendous phase of activity during the occupation years and increased the capital of his firm to 100,000 francs in 1942. He started licensing as early as 1947 and tripled his sales between 1947 and 1949. In 1950, he again increased the capital of his firm, to a whopping 20 million francs—then among the largest in haute couture. Fath transformed his business, which included a perfume line, into a société anonyme in 1951. He signed an agreement with American manufacturer Halpert, known as the best but also the toughest in the New York garment district, for whom Fath designed two yearly collections, which were sold in more than a hundred American cities. Halpert paid Fath on a royalty basis. The agreement with Halpert brought Fath into competition with Dior, who developed wholesale couture manufactured by other New York garment firms. Fath's success was cut short by illness, however, and he died of leukemia in 1954. His couture operation closed in 1957, but his perfume brand remained active and was eventually integrated into the L'Oréal Group in 1992.[26]

In the 1950s, Paris couture also had its eye on the French colonies. The interwar Algerian dailies and magazines featured the fashion shows that Paris couturiers, notably Lelong and Patou, organized in Algeria's main cities with the aim of finding clients among the wealthiest strata of the colony. The Paris couture firms discontinued such fashion shows in the French colonies during World War II, for the most part. Then, during the postwar years, a new crop of couturiers emerged in Algeria's most important cities. Some of these names became famous as they resettled in Paris to study and begin a career, Yves Saint Laurent being the most famous of them. Others remained lesser known, like Michel Tellin, born in Algeria in 1933. Tellin had started designing early and used to say that, when still a child, he had sent sketches to Lelong, who was favorably impressed. Tellin studied the fine arts and then settled in a couture house in Algiers in 1954. Three years later, Tellin opened a Paris branch, on rue de Ponthieu. Both of his establishments, in Algiers and Paris, offered haute couture and ready-to-wear clothing. As a consequence of Algeria's war of independence, which took place from 1954 to 1962, Tellin fled from Algiers to focus on his Paris activity (see Figure 6.2). Later on, in 1977, he designed clothes for the crowning ceremony of the Central African Republic dictator Jean-Bédel Bokassa. Tellin developed a second career as a sculptor before falling into oblivion. He died in 1989.[27]

Couture and the Nation

The postwar period was characterized by the development of a large program of nationalization of companies by the French state. Haute couture firms remained in private hands, but in order to give subventions to haute couture houses, the French Ministry of Economy and Finance mandated the commission Couture Création to investigate whether the Paris haute couture houses that operated to the letter of the 1947 Paris-Province agreements would be eligible. Jacques Heim, whose house had opened in 1930, claimed that ready-to-wear was not a legitimate output for the Chambre's members. Yet, in his own firm, Heim was an early promoter of haute couture spin-off lines. He had debuted his Jeunes Filles (junior misses) collection of couture, adapted for youthful customers, in 1936 and hired as an in-house designer Hélène Lyolène, who had extensive experience in New York. Heim failed in his first attempt to license a branded line in the US market, in 1946. In the 1950s, he divided the Heim firm into two companies: Heim SA and Heim Actualités, which produced ready-to-wear collections. But Heim liquidated this second firm in 1954 and placed all of its operations under the firm Heim SA, which oversaw the haute couture and two ready-to-wear lines, Heim Jeunes Filles and Heim Actualités. At the end of that year, Heim claimed that his house had reverted to its focus on haute couture and abandoned all previous ready-to-wear and wholesale lines. In February 1955, the leadership of the Couture Création, in charge of attributing support to the Paris couture houses, paid an impromptu visit to the Heim workshops and asked to see the full collection that was hanging on the rails. The government-appointed visitors checked the finishing of all the garments to make sure they met the standards of perfection expected in haute couture. The assessment was positive. Heim fulfilled the criteria and received a subvention; the application form for this is shown in Figure 6.3.[28]

In his position as president of the Chambre Syndicale, Heim was particularly exposed to the contradictions faced by Paris couture. Even at Dior, the most

paris couture—fall and winter

Tellin, Newest Paris Couturier, Also Youngest

PARIS BUREAU

PARIS, Aug. 26. — Michel Tellin's designing career started when he was eight. He sent a batch of sketches to Lucien Lelong from Algiers where he was born and brought up. The couturier, then at his peak, wrote back to Tellin, without realizing his age, saying he'd be happy to see him when he came to Paris.

Tellin had already been sketching for a year, having become interested by watching his mother run up her own things. A young woman with advanced ideas about fashion, which she gave to her son, she couldn't find what suited her in North African shops.

Now at 24, he has his own couture house in Paris, combined with ready-to-wear operation plus a similar setup in Algiers. He retails only from his own houses for the moment, but plans general distribution from next season on.

Painting is his hobby and his clothes reflect the rounded spherical effects, the reds, blues, blacks which he favors. He belongs to the school of young futuristic designers emphasizing movement in clothes. Hats, shoes and costume jewelry accompanying his models are also designed by him.

Tellin stopped regular studies to go to the Beaux Arts in Algiers, where he has had several painting exhibitions. Five years ago he came up to Paris to study fashion designing; he sold sketches and toiles to the Paris couture.

A year later he returned to Algiers, worked as a men's wear shop salesman.

His own couture house in Algiers came next, three years ago. Then he started bringing the collection up to Paris, showing it at the George V.

Finding a good location is hard in housing-shortaged Paris; he's finally found suitable headquarters in the little house Rue de

Ponthieu previously occupied by milliners Svend and Maud Roser.

Tellin's own sketch illustrating the short tunics over slim skirts, high waistlines which he likes.

Chiffon overblouse with a wide draped sash ending in long floating panels gives this model a dressed-up touch. Dark and peacock blue combine in the floral pattern done on warp print satin for the tunic and skirt, on silk chiffon for the overblouse.

(Model copyrighted, reproduction forbidden.)

Dark haired, handsome Michel Tellin is one of the youngest newcomers to the Paris Couture. Twenty-four years old, he heads couture and boutique ready-to-wear operations in both Paris and Algiers.

FIGURE 6.2 Couturier Michel Tellin started his career in Algeria before launching his brand in Paris.
Women's Wear Daily, *August 27, 1957, p. 18.*
© Fairchild Publishing LLC.

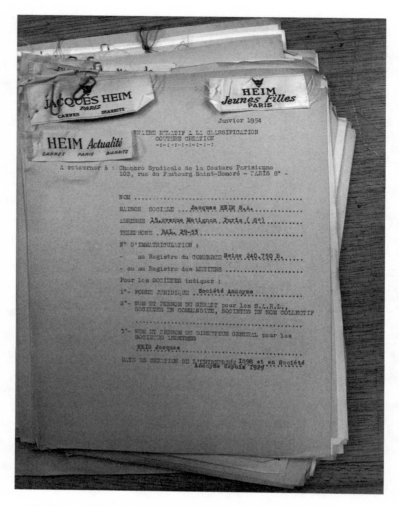

FIGURE 6.3 The application of the firm Jacques Heim for an haute couture subvention in 1954 shows the various tags used for the firm's different branded lines.
Archives Nationales de France, AJ F12.10505.

successful haute couture house of the postwar period, after four private fittings on a client the couturier was working at a loss; in some cases, the client needed up to eight fittings before her garment was ready. Haute couture was on its way to becoming a rarefied craft, with little or no profitability. Yet instead of letting the industry undergo creative destruction, the French government decided to support it financially. The challenge was to set up criteria of eligibility. To receive financial support, haute couture firms had to respect restrictive conditions of craftsmanship that prevented them from entirely modernizing their production techniques. The situation was easier for the couturiers who had established a separate firm to produce and sell their perfumes, as the existence of a separate company or a distinct perfume division did not prevent the couture branch from receiving the government subvention.[29]

A group of Paris couturiers benefited from government support for a decade, from the early 1950s to the early 1960s. There were few newcomers among these firms, with the notable exception of Gabrielle Chanel. Chanel, while she was not yet close to the age of retirement in 1939, had seemingly shut down her haute couture operation permanently and retained a 10 percent share in her perfume business.[30] She reopened her haute couture house after a fifteen-year hiatus, in 1954, and received a subvention from the Couture Création in 1955. Her comeback collection of 1954 was received coldly by the buyers, maybe because she did not seem to have renewed herself creatively very much. But soon, Chanel's couture was praised again. Her knit and tweed suits perfectly answered the needs of women active at work and featured prominently in the fashions shows of Paris designs presented in the United States. The New York Fashion Group called her work "the Chanel look," emphasizing that her clothes were "relaxed" and comfortable, an increasingly important quality in the American marketplace. In 1957 Chanel was invited to the United States, where she received the prestigious Neiman Marcus Award at the flagship department store in Dallas, Texas. The American trade press followed her visit closely and published complete descriptions of her personal travel wardrobe. At seventy-three, Chanel was a fashion icon in the United States.[31]

A Constellation of Fashion Centers

During those years, two major competitors to Paris rose to prominence: Great Britain and Italy. Great Britain had always been important in the fashion markets, and it was an essential actor in the early internationalization of haute couture. Throughout the interwar period the British fashion industries offered the highest-quality, most sought-after sportswear and women's wear, including very high-quality woolens. In 1936, eighteen prominent British fashion designers, including Norman Hartnell, the House of Reville, and Victor Stiebel, showed fashions together for the first time in order to better reach their foreign markets, especially American buyers. The group took as an example the Fashion Originators' Guild of America in setting the agenda for the international dissemination of their designs. In 1942, a group of these prominent London entrepreneurs founded the Incorporated Society of London Fashion Designers, which would continue to represent the interests of British designers during the postwar era. Aesthetic concerns had remained central to British couturiers throughout the Depression and the war, as Britain experienced stricter rationing policies than France. Major British tailors and couturiers returned to the stage during the postwar era. Essential to the vitality of their businesses was, as in the earlier period, the presence of the British court. The reach of several of these entrepreneurs was international. Most prominent among them was Royal Warrant holder Norman Hartnell, who had opened his business in London in 1923 and gone on to design a number of dresses for Queen Elizabeth II, including her wedding gown in 1947 and her coronation dress in 1953. Hartnell developed from London a business model that was the closest to Dior's reach on international markets. Dior and Hartnell knew each other and showed mutual admiration.[32]

The Italian fashion industry developed toward haute couture, capitalizing on high-quality craftsmanship, excellent creative taste, and prices that were less than half those in Paris. Several clusters of firms developed in a constellation of fashion cities: Milan, Florence, Rome, and Turin. Prestigious Italian haute couture firms—including Roberto Capucci, the Sorelle Fontana, and Simonetta in Rome; Germana Marucelli and Jole Veneziana in Milan; and several others—attracted an international clientele. In the United States, retailers and the Fashion Group showed sustained interest in Italian design from the postwar period that would not abate. Most Italian firms regularly showed their designs at Palazzo Pitti in Florence from 1951, when Giovanni Battista Giorgini organized a first collective event, aimed at attracting foreign buyers. The sector of retail, and especially the department store La Rinascente founded by the brothers Bocconi in Milan in 1865, had paved the way for the fashion expertise of the postwar era. Middlemen such as Giorgini, who was already active in the commissionaire trading of Italian fashions during the interwar period, were able to build an excellent atmosphere for foreign buyers. Giorgini took international buyers to visit sites in addition to the fashion shows at Palazzo Pitti, which still today hosts the world's most significant event in the domain of men's wear. The Italian fashion entrepreneurs of the time capitalized on the historical narrative of the Renaissance to build a prestigious image of Italy's fashion industries and augment its symbolic capital. The growing expertise of Italian textile firms, the creative renewal of the important cluster of high-end textile mills in the region of Lake Como, and the development of a thriving men's wear sector contributed to build a hinterland for the fashion industries of northern Italy. Milan eventually came out of the small group of Italian fashion cities as the long-term center for the industry and to this day is one of the world's four major fashion cities, along with London, Paris, and New York.[33]

The most important fashion-business innovator of this era, however, appeared at a distance from the four big fashion cities. It was the Swedish retail chain Hennes & Mauritz, founded by Erling Persson in his hometown of Västerås, in central Sweden, in 1947. Persson started outsourcing the production of garments internationally in order to provide mass fashions for women, and soon also for men and children. In this sense, Persson aimed to give Europeans a concrete iteration of the model of a fashion democracy. Persson expanded first to Norway, in 1964, then to an increasing number of countries, to draw a global map with the Hennes & Mauritz (H&M) stores. Since launching its initial public offering in 1974, Persson's family firm has become a global brand. Persson's son and grandson succeeded in managing the global empire that placed the founding family among the world's top fortunes. The H&M model was founded as a small shop in a moderately sized Swedish town, contemporary with the foundation of the house of Dior, which assumed the transformation of haute couture into a global luxury business. The global expansion of H&M, based on the relocation of production, was at the forefront of the massification of the fashion business that took place in the last quarter of the twentieth century.[34]

Intellectual Property Rights in the Era of European Integration

During the postwar era, haute couture took the path of global luxury branding. The industry might have instead chosen to remain a local cluster of artisans focusing on savoir faire, like the Italian leather goods craftsmen or the Swiss watchmakers. To understand the process of their building strong brand identities, it is useful to turn again to the history of the couturiers' approach to intellectual property rights. France enjoyed a legal regime that was very protective of intellectual property rights, more so than that of Germany, Belgium, Italy, Luxembourg, and the Netherlands, the other five countries in the European Economic Community (EEC), or the Common Market, created by the Treaty of Rome in 1957 and in effect from 1958.[35]

In this context, the Chambre Syndicale developed efforts across national boundaries to repress counterfeiters. The rewriting of the Chambre Syndicale's rules in 1943 and 1944 allowed for strict legal regulation of the use of the term *haute couture*. Over the next two decades, the Chambre Syndicale as a private plaintiff, and the couturiers as individual firms, closely watched the use by competitors of a large number of Parisian phrases and symbols associated with haute couture and French national identity. The couturiers managed to secure restrictions on the use of terms like *Paris, Belle France,* and *Champs Elysées* and symbols like the Eiffel Tower when used on fashion products that were not made in France. Couturiers sued counterfeiters of the Paris brand at the global level, obtaining injunctions in Belgium, Italy, and other countries.[36] In an April 1959 meeting of the United Nations Educational, Scientific, and Cultural Organization (UNESCO), French fashion entrepreneurs advocated a double protection for author's rights and applied arts, as a continuity with the previous French intellectual property rights, which France managed to retain thanks to significant lobbying efforts. European integration harmonized the laws in member countries and made it easier to pursue counterfeiters, along lines similar to those of today. The new challenges that emerged, then, were related to the protection of European brands in a globalizing world.[37]

French couturiers, including Dior manager Jacques Rouët, aimed to facilitate the proof of ownership of an original design as intellectual property and to raise the penalties meted out to counterfeiters. The Chambre Syndicale lobbied authorities within the EEC to protect fashion innovation. Economic integration among the six member countries laid the foundation for a new pan-EEC law on related intellectual property rights, drafted in 1962, which unified rules for the Inner Six.[38] At the international level, the haute couture firms had the opportunity to register their designs with the International Registration Bureau in Geneva, but it seems that the practice was not common among the couturiers, as shown in the answers to a detailed questionnaire to all members of the Chambre Syndicale sent in February 1962. Several couturiers thought that the number of countries covered, which did not include North and South America, was too small for the measure to be effective. The French law on brands (of December 31, 1964) limited the protection of brands for a ten-year period, after which an unexploited brand entered the public domain. With this rule in mind, the Chambre Syndicale advised couturiers to register their brands or to renew their older brands if they did not want to lose future possibilities for their exploitation.[39]

The Chambre Syndicale in New York

The Chambre Syndicale used a part of the state subventions to haute couture to help disseminate Paris haute couture abroad. Those funds enabled the establishment of a Chambre Syndicale office in New York and paid for the services of New York–based legal counsel specializing in intellectual property. Jacques Heim continued to establish connections between the fashion businesses in Paris and New York during his term as Chambre Syndicale president from 1958 to 1962.[40] In 1958, the communication office of the Chambre Syndicale hired an Anglo-American press agent, Marjorie Dunton, and additional public relations staff. Heim proceeded to realize his ambition to set foot in New York, marking a change with regard to the history of the Chambre Syndicale, whose presidents had always refused to relocate, even in wartime. While the Chambre would indeed remain in Paris, the purpose of its New York branch was to develop connections with the American press, expand networks, and organize fashion shows for buyers around the country. The travel time between Paris and New York was down to eleven hours, bringing the two cities closer than ever.[41]

Heim commissioned the consulting firm Gallup to conduct a survey of the American clientele of haute couture houses. Gallup conducted the poll on a sample of 713 elite American women whose annual household incomes were $7,000 or higher or who were listed in the Social Register, a directory of elite US families. Heim had tasks planned for the Chambre Syndicale in New York: to provide American buyers and manufacturers with information on the activities of French couture, to increase the numbers of American buyers and manufacturers going to Paris for the shows, and to help them buy more French couture productions from the United States.[42] Heim hired the services of the consulting organization of Edward Gottlieb to handle communications. The Manhattan law firm of Sylvan Gotshal, a pioneering expert on intellectual property, was in charge of all questions related to the protection of the intellectual property rights of the Paris couturiers in New York. Heim hired Baroness Monique de Nervo, a French society woman married into the industrialist Louis-Dreyfus family, who had previously acted as the style ambassador representing the interests of French glove producers in the United States (see Figure 6.4). De Nervo, assisted by a bilingual secretary who was fluent in English and French, was responsible for the New York office. She alternated two months in Paris with four months in New York in the service of the promotion of Paris haute couture among high society.[43]

The New York office coordinated the actions of French couturiers in America. It used its operational funds to pay for transatlantic travel, the costs of Gotshal's legal services, and the Gottlieb organization's fees for public relations. Heim organized a ten-day visit to the United States in 1958 with a series of ambitious goals that included the development of American TV projects, the organization of package trips to Paris for American personalities, the creation of a special label and a royalty system, the reorganization of the press and buyers' passports, and the training of American stylists in Paris. The New York office was the most important item in the 1958 accounting of the Chambre Syndicale, with a debit of 4,708,255 French francs. Chambre Syndicale members estimated that the increased purchases of haute couture designs by American retailers were proof that the investment in a New York office had yielded immediate returns. On January 31, 1958, the Fashion Group paid unanimous homage to Paris couture in one of its lunch meetings, at which 250 guests had gathered. Heim interpreted all of these elements as evidence of the success of the New York office, whose activity continued during the next year. Costs were still the most important item of the Chambre Syndicale accounting but had considerably diminished after the implementation year.[44]

However, in 1961, the French government shifted the program of subventions to haute couture that it had begun ten years earlier and, during the next years, help to the industry was pursued along different lines. During the intervening decade, the European Recovery Program and the French government had supported the French ready-to-wear industry, which benefited from close analysis of the reasons for the success of American manufacturing. The development of the French synthetics industry was another technological step that had had a determining influence on the French production of fashions for the masses. As a consequence of the end of the government's financial support, the Chambre Syndicale had to operate with a reduced budget. The Chambre's committee calculated that the help from the subventions would sustain its communication services until

The Leather Glove Producers
of France
take great pleasure in introducing

Madame Monique de Nervo

*Ambassadress for
French Leather Gloves*

*who has come directly
from Paris to report
the "Fashion Story"
during her tour of fine stores
in 17 U. S. cities*

This season's program by Madame de Nervo will feature:

★ **A Fashion Accessory Clinic for Customers**
(highlighting gloves as an integral part of the costume)

★ **A Sales Training Session for Store Personnel**
(to be held from 6 to 7:30 p.m. during an informal party)

High points of these events will be the
Paris Fashion report, discussion of color,
texture, and length in French leather
gloves, the new "overnight" washability,
and dramatic ways of

SELLING
PROMOTING
WEARING

*FRENCH
LEATHER
GLOVES*

Madame de Nervo has just completed her visit with
William H. Block in Indianapolis
and
Neiman-Marcus in Dallas
and looks forward to working with

Neiman-Marcus	Houston	Sept 27
Halle Bros	Cleveland	Sept. 29, 30, Oct. 1
J. L. Hudson	Detroit	Oct. 2, 3, 4
Rich's	Atlanta	Oct. 6, 7, 8
Scruggs Vandervoort Barney	St. Louis	Oct. 9, 10, 11
Carson Pirie Scott	Chicago	Oct. 13, 14, 15
I. Magnin & Company	San Francisco	Oct. 17
I. Magnin & Company	Seattle	Oct. 27
The Crescent	Spokane	Oct. 28, 29
May-D&F	Denver	Oct. 30, 31, Nov. 1
Levy's	Memphis	Nov. 3, 4, 5
Woodward & Lothrop	Washington, D. C.	Nov. 6, 7, 8
Bonwit Teller	Philadelphia	Nov. 10, 11, 12
Filene's	Boston	Nov. 17, 18, 19

**FIGURE 6.4 Monique de Nervo promoted
the French gloves industry in the United
States.**
Women's Wear Daily, *September 26, 1958, p. 11.*
© *Fairchild Publishing LLC.*

1964. The Chambre canceled its contracts with de Nervo (seen wearing Jacques Heim in Figure 6.5), Gottlieb, and Gotshal, and it closed the New York office.[45]

Subventions could not reverse the process of creative destruction that haute couture was experiencing at that time. The industry was having difficulty attracting young talent. The school of the Chambre Syndicale was unable to maintain its enrollment numbers. Teachers reported that they struggled to sustain the quality of training, and that most students at the beginning of the 1960s were no longer able to reach the level necessary to become a skilled worker called a *première main;* rather, many women preferred office work, hairdressing, or other manufacturing professions.[46] Haute couture firms faced economic challenges, including inflation, increases in the costs of social welfare and in rent, and growing foreign competition, first and foremost from Italy. The members of the Chambre Syndicale considered taxes to be crushing. They lobbied the French government for discounts on the cost of social security and the high rents in Paris. In 1961, after two years of discussions between the trade unions and the couturiers represented by the Chambre Syndicale, all parties signed a new labor convention that aimed to maintain social peace in the haute couture industry.[47] Despite such mutual efforts, nothing could be done about the changing structure of the market. The number of clients willing to buy and able to afford made-to-measure garments was diminishing. Haute couture did not vanish, but it developed a different form of existence. The French government kept making excellent use of haute couture as a diplomatic tool. Charity galas and balls featured haute couture shows. It had become a tradition to offer a private haute couture presentation to the wives of foreign heads of state visiting France. Other prestigious events, like the debutantes ball held either in Versailles or at the Paris Opera at Palais Garnier, enjoyed a symbiotic relationship with the haute couture industry. Heim, as Chambre Syndicale president, hoped that the funding for such events could be secured in order to reaffirm the prestige of haute couture. Prestige would remain, but at the cost of a reconversion of the industry in brand value, while the making of haute couture itself was increasingly reduced to a symbolic part of France's fashion industries. The production of haute couture dematerialized and was converted into brand value.[48]

Branded luxury goods including perfumes and accessories generated strong market value. But numerous haute couture firms closed their couture operations during the 1950s and 1960s. Fath died in 1954. Another still-young founder of

FIGURE 6.5 Monique de Nervo directed the bureau of the Chambre Syndicale de la Couture Parisienne in New York. Here she is photographed for promotional purposes, wearing an ensemble by couturier Jacques Heim.
Karen Radkai / Getty Images.

a couturier and perfume firm, Marcel Rochas, died in 1955. His widow, Hélène Rochas, liquidated the couture operation in 1957 but kept the perfume division, which US multinational Procter & Gamble bought in 2003. Procter & Gamble tried several times to relaunch Rochas as a couture or demi-couture firm, but its success remains uncertain. Haute couture, increasingly carried out at a loss, preserved craftsmanship and realized profits from spin-off products such as perfumes, cosmetics, accessories, and ready-to-wear. Paquin Ltd., the only one of the Paris couture firms that remained a British society throughout its existence, took over the house of Worth in 1954. Worth continued to operate under its own name, until Paquin and Worth wound down the business in 1956. From the couturiers who had trained with Vionnet, only Charles Montaigne lasted until the 1970s, closing in 1972. Mad Carpentier liquidated her business in 1950. Marcelle Chaumont closed her doors as a result of bankruptcy in 1953. In 1968, the American buyers perceived the closing of the haute couture house of Balenciaga as highly symbolic in regard to the changing times and student revolution happening on the streets of Paris. In the long term, the inclusion of the remaining haute couture firms in luxury holdings shows that bespoke haute couture could survive as a laboratory of styles. Haute couture was on its way to becoming part of the French cultural heritage, a movement that can also be identified as the patrimonialization of haute couture. When the French government decided to restart a program of subventions to haute couture in 1968, the strategy of rebranding haute couture as heritage was under way.[49]

The Rise of the Stylists

Heim, during his tenure as the president of the Chambre Syndicale, understood that the development of the boutiques of couturiers and of designer ready-to-wear lines could help the haute couture firms survive. This time, however, creativity did not happen so much in the boutiques of the couturiers as in the offices of the stylists, a new group of consultants and designers who had taken up the task of creating innovative fashions. Most of them were young women with higher education degrees. Several of these stylists started their careers as consultants for French department stores, in charge of increasing the stores' fashionability. A pioneer in the new affordable French fashions was Ghislaine de Polignac, who was well connected and had started her career as a public relations officer for Cardin. The Galeries Lafayette then hired Polignac in 1952 to reinvigorate its fashion quotient, and for this reason Polignac came to be regarded as the first French stylist. Other department stores, especially Monoprix and Prisunic, sought to develop lines of clothes, accessories, and home furnishings that were both affordable and aesthetically pleasing. This movement of democratization of style, known as "beautiful for all," was a landslide. It became the direction followed by the generation of professionals who founded the first French style bureaus. Among them, Claude de Coux founded her consultancy Relations Textiles in

1958. Maïmé Hentsch-Arnodin, who had previously completed her education in engineering, went to work as a fashion consultant for the magazine *Jardin des Modes* and for department store Le Printemps, along with colorist Primrose Bordier. Arnodin fostered the work of new, up-and-coming designers including Emmanuelle Khanh, Christiane Bailly, and Gérard Pipart, who worked in close collaboration with the ready-to-wear manufacturers situated in the Paris district of the Sentier. Some of them, notably Khanh, also designed collections in collaboration with American manufacturers. The stylists' goal was to elevate the work of these older manufacturers and use their know-how to make fashions that were attractive to young consumers. In the years surrounding 1968, several trend bureaus opened in Paris. Arnodin, with her colleague and new life partner Denise Fayolle, founded consultancy Maïmé Arnodin Fayolle International Associés, best known as Mafia. Two other stylists, Françoise Vincent-Ricard and Danielle de Diesbach, founded the Promostyl trend consulting office. These consultancies formed as a result of the networks that connected the Paris department stores, the manufacturing district of the Sentier, and the French fashion magazines. They built on the expertise of their predecessors, including sample firm Claude Frères, textile consultant Fred Carlin, and Tobé. The new fashion consultants of the 1960s were well aware of the work of their American counterparts, and an important network for the new generation of Paris fashion stylists was the Paris branch of the American association for women fashion professionals, the Fashion Group. The Paris branch of the Fashion Group was founded in the late 1950s, and its activity gathered speed over the following decades. As haute couture had become a more male-dominated profession during the postwar period, it is quite logical that the stylists, who were primarily women, found a network in the Fashion Group.[50]

Most of the stylists were working women, often educated and with a background in the bourgeoisie. These stylists were acutely aware that they were conducting the last and most important revolution in French fashion—one that took it out of the realm of the elites. When researching this book, I met one of them, Françoise Vincent-Ricard, who insisted both on her contribution to design and that she also had taken French fashion out of its centralization in Paris by working toward the development of the brands that claimed the label "Mode Côte d'Azur," or fashions for the Riviera. The Riviera designers, including the French firms Tiktiner and Jacques Esterel, among others, had echoes of the Californian sportswear by designers like Louella Ballerino, Mabs of Hollywood, and, especially, Claire Mc-Cardell. All of them aimed to create affordable and outdoorsy clothes. One of the style's early icons was actress Brigitte Bardot, who, for her wedding to Jacques Charrier in 1959, broke the rules by wearing a dress from Esterel cut in a pink-and-white-check cotton fabric called *vichy*. Young consumers found it acceptable to participate in important occasions wearing clothes produced in series and in a cheap fabric. Bardot, not only in her sartorial choices but furthermore in her films and interviews, rebelled against the old generation.[51]

By launching the Mode Côte d'Azur, a small group of entrepreneurs including Esterel and Vincent-Ricard contributed to a deprovincialization of the French fashions not made in Paris. In addition, counterfeiting did not seem to be such a threat to these entrepreneurs, who created fashions of the moment as a part of a culture of leisure. A parallel movement took place on the other side of the channel. British fashion industrialists captured the spirit of the times equally well, making small-batch production fashionable. Recent research has shown the importance of the London set, but also of the secondary cities from Brighton to Leeds, where youth adopted the newest fashions by making extensive use of mail-order catalogs and sewing clothes at home from paper patterns.[52] In 1960s London, a new crop of boutiques including Barbara Hulanicki's Biba, Lee Bender's Bus Stop, and Mary Quant's Bazaar offered midtier fashions that the designers created at home or in the back of their shops. Two fashion entrepreneurs, Mary Quant in London and André Courrèges in Paris, simultaneously invented the miniskirt, a design revolution that signaled that the sexual liberation movement was on and that fashion was happening on the street rather than behind the doors of the couture salons. In the boutiques, when a dress sold well, it went out of stock quickly, due to limited production capacity and difficulties of reordering fabric promptly. The young entrepreneurs perceived that this weakness could built up desirability, making their shops permanent cultural hubs where customers dropped in just to see what was on display that weekend. The boutiques' tie-in lines of accessories, homeware, and cosmetics were often better restocked than their fashion lines, and that allowed them to expand their brand visibility by retailing the nonclothing products on international markets.[53]

Critical observers noted that the rise of Paris manufacturing and stylists took place in a symbiotic relationship with the small firms of the Sentier, a neighborhood of the Paris Right Bank where small, narrow old houses were packed with crammed workshops that were difficult to access and prone to fire hazard. The structure of the Sentier resembled workshops in the New York garment district, including a significant presence of immigrant workers. Research on the Sentier activity underlines the opacity in its chains of production, the numerous subcontractors that tended to foster clandestine labor, and the omnipresence of tax fraud on a small scale. These methods of production were contemporary to the rise of throwaway fashion that began in the early 1960s. Shorter clothing life cycles had a huge impact on production, as the solidity of seams and fabrics, and even a garment's comfort, no longer really mattered. During the 1960s, fashion firms in Europe and in the United States, but also in the countries situated behind the Iron Curtain, started making paper dresses decorated with fashionable and often photographic prints. These dresses were the peak of ephemeral fashion, but the fad for paper as a clothing material did not last.[54]

American Fashion on the Map

Blue jeans became fashionable in the late 1940s. In May 1948 youth fashion was the topic of a meeting of the New York Fashion Group, where fashion correspondent Mary Burdell introduced the topic by describing the young women wearing blue jeans and white socks and borrowing flannel shirts from their fathers as the stereotypical "bobbysoxers." Burdell linked the look both to sports clothes and to beauty purchases in cosmetics. From then on, the youth market became a staple topic in the meetings of the biggest association of American fashion professionals. The Fashion Group discussed youth especially in relation to American fashion retail in clothes, sports clothes, and beauty products for college women.[55]

Denim fabric dyed in indigo for men's and women's garments has a long history in the United States. Its origin is uncertain, possibly to be found in the "toile de Nîmes" from the southern French town that produced it from the seventeenth century. It was used for items of clothing as diverse as work overalls for men, work jackets for men, and women's skirts and dresses. The fabric faded naturally—stonewashing the fabric to increase its faded effect was an invention of the second half of the twentieth century. American garments were made fashionable by the US soldiers stationed in Europe as a consequence of World War II. American movie and music culture that was exported to 1950s Europe lent a decisively fashionable luster to the blue jeans and white T-shirts worn by actors such as James Dean and Marilyn Monroe. Jeans remained a symbol of marginality, rebellion, and even delinquent behavior through the 1950s and 1960s in the United States as well as in France; from the margins, though, they demonstrated very clearly that fashion had changed direction. Fashion was no longer expected to trickle down, from the elites to aspirational consumers. As shown by Pierre Bourdieu, who was contemporary to this phenomenon, fashion was now issued from multiple directions of emulation at the same time. Such a change seemed to promise consumers greater equality of access to fashionable clothing and increased freedom in using fashion as self-expression. It was in the 1970s that the consumption of jeans really took off in France. The most-sold brand of jeans in Europe then, and for several decades after, was Levi's; a Californian firm, Levi's was a trademark registered in 1873, when innovator Levi Strauss and Jacob Davis also registered a US patent for the riveting of fabric that was characteristic of their jeans. A clothing item deemed typically American, jeans were now on their way to leave the margins behind and to become a staple of mainstream fashion.[56]

During the same decades, American fashions institutionalized. In the mid-1950s, New York's new mayor, Robert F. Wagner, revisited the ambition to put the city on top of the fashion world. For several decades, industrialists such as Maurice Rentner, in his role as president of the Fashion Originators' Guild of America, had organized collective shows that displayed clothing designed in Paris and in New York. The Fashion Group also showed designs from the collections several times per year and organized thematic shows. New York's department stores had a century-long history of organizing their own shows.[57] Mayor Wagner's public support of the fashion industry contributed to its legitimization. A series of milestones confirmed the industry's institutionalization in New York. Several specialized schools and graduate programs aimed to educate competent professionals in all areas of the industry. A good example of this endeavor is the opening in 1944 of the Fashion Institute of Technology. New York museums started showing fashion exhibitions more regularly from wartime onward, without a distinction of the designers' nationalities. Further institutionalization developed in American fashion with the creation of several prestigious awards to distinguish both businessmen and designers, notably the Neiman Marcus awards, created in 1938, and the Coty award, established in 1942. The former was open to European and American designers and entrepreneurs, while the latter was specifically intended for designers in the United States. New York was now the world fashion center, wrote *New York Times* journalist Virginia Pope in 1952. English, Italian, Swiss, Spanish, and French fashion buyers visited the city, and this accumulation of influences made New York grow stronger as a creative center. Such a "foreign invasion" of New York, added Pope, had started in 1948 with the opening of Dior's American branch. Then Fath had settled there, delegating his production to garment district manufacturer Halpert. Next came Jean Dessès, whose haute couture firm received financial backing from shipping magnate Aristotle Onassis. And then occasional visitors designed collections in New York and worked with Seventh Avenue manufacturers, including Balmain, Schiaparelli, and Antonio Canovas del Castillo, who had taken over the house of Lanvin.[58]

Excellent American dressmaking was fostered not only by institutions but also by affluence, in which the US First Ladies could play a prominent role: they were expected to choose American over European fashions to wear. Particularly scrutinized for her elegance was First Lady Jacqueline Bouvier Kennedy. Very fond of Chanel, she bought some of the designer's creations but also, more often, had them emulated by excellent American designers, most notably Oleg Cassini. She also relied on the services of one of the most accomplished fashion designers and technicians of her era, Ann Lowe, the African American couturiere who made Kennedy's wedding dress. A virtuose technician, Lowe remained for a long time in the shadow of other designers. A possible reason for this was that Lowe was African American, and also that, as she charged less than most of her competitors for work of equal or better quality, she struggled financially. However, fashion historians are reviving the importance of her work, the extreme quality of her craftsmanship, and her influence on American couture.[59]

On December 6, 1956, Mayor Wagner made New York Fashion Week official with a public presentation at city hall. Wagner understood that the fashion industry added almost a billion dollars annually to the city's economy. In comparison, Paris haute couture made an estimated $13 million a year, of which roughly half was from private clients, both domestic and international. The value of Paris couture purchased by private US clients totaled $1.2 million per year. The French customs evaluated that France exported for 350 million francs of haute couture patterns and garments in 1948, and for 660 million in 1955. This was less than 5 percent of the French exports of textiles to the United States.[60] American fashion expert Bernard Roshco noted that some Seventh Avenue manufacturers sold more merchandise on the domestic market than all the couturiers together sold globally. Making Fashion Week official added one element to the institutional construction of New York as a major fashion center, toward the goal, underlined by Wagner, of making it the fashion center of the world.[61]

Despite the challenges, the US fashion industries also managed to make some progress in the protection of their designs. The first goal in this project was to protect textile design. In 1954, copyright protection became available on a limited scale in the United States to the designers of textiles "incorporating artistic designs," who were allowed to register their work at the US Copyright Office. The US Supreme Court had resisted this for some thirty years, and indeed, the US Copyright Office would be hard-pressed to confirm not only the novelty of a textile design but also its artistic quality. The procedure for protection consisted of filing an application at the office, with a four-dollar fee for each item registered. Protection extended from the date of filing, if the design was unreleased, or from the start of distribution of the registered item. This decision promptly raised the question of who would do the anteriority research. Another unclear issue was the definition of a work of art. The trade press noted that these questions would have to be answered by a Supreme Court ruling.[62]

This textile-related decision brought with it hope for a revision of US copyright legislation that would be favorable to the fashion industries. Sylvan Gotshal, who had been since the interwar period a staunch advocate of the inclusion of fashion in US copyright law and served the office of the Chambre Syndicale in New York, thought that this new step could resolve issues dating back to the early 1920s. America, he thought, should follow the example of the European countries, which had proved that strong copyright legislation could be used to protect fashions. Gotshal's view was that there was a need in the United States for the protection of original designs, above and beyond the textile designs covered by the new US law of 1954.[63]

Protecting textile designs was a step in the right direction, but fashion design— the creativity in the cut, color, and material of a garment—was not yet the object of US law. In the 1950s, the Fashion Originators' Guild of America was still active, with the same agenda of advancing its antipiracy stance. One of its supporters was Stanley Marcus, who, in a 1955 address to another association, the Fashion Group, defended creation against standardization because, in his own words, "there is no price tag on good taste." Marcus also noted what he considered to be the economically destructive effects of design piracy. Because the issue of protecting fashion designs under US copyright law remained unresolved in the 1950s, some industrialists wondered whether patent law could be of use; however, it proved to be too slow and expensive for the needs of fashion innovation.[64]

The New York garment district consisted of small and medium-size enterprises, of which few were public. These manufacturers thrived by selling to the department stores: Bergdorf Goodman, Bloomingdale's, Lord & Taylor, Macy's, Ohrbach, and many others. Despite the idea that the business of the fashion manufacturers was volatile, some of the earlier names in New York luxury fashion managed to last, like Hattie Carnegie, Lily Daché, Nettie Rosenstein, and Maurice Rentner. Some also succeeded in transmitting their know-how to a new generation, like Rentner, who trained among other talent Bill Blass, a prominent name of the next generation. The names of American fashion entrepreneurs gained traction in the American market. Among the couture designers of New York, Charles James, Sophie Gimbel for Saks, Mainbocher, and Leslie Morris for Bergdorf Goodman captured public attention as major designers.[65]

Experts agreed that branding was the weak point of the US fashion industrialists. They noted that the homegrown New York entrepreneurs struggled to build luxury brands, even though New York was home to Madison Avenue, the world's center of the advertising industry. The United States had no equivalent to Hermès, the fashionable French maker of luxury leather goods, and yet younger firms managed to address a wider consumer base. In this respect, the American answer to Hermès was the New York–based brand Coach. Miles and Lilian Cahn founded the leather goods workshop Coach on 34th Street in 1961, and hired Bonnie Cashin, a Californian designer who had started her career in sportswear in the New York garment district. Cashin brought to Coach her sense of simplicity and practicality and her taste for color. Her design principles were already well in place when the New York division of the Fashion Group invited her to present her work in 1953. She showed only three designs on mannequins that day. Before the small show, she explained her vision of the industry and her hope to see better integration between the work of the manufacturer, the designer, and the retailer. This disconnect indeed was one of the most striking differences between American garment manufacturing and Paris couture. But Cashin did not aim to produce high-luxury garments and accessories. Instead, she thought that necessity was the overarching principle of the creation of any good design. Designs should be made for movement and for travel, Cashin said, as she herself enjoyed traveling.[66]

American ready-to-wear strived to adjust to what industrialists interpreted as the demands of their domestic market, and especially of working women.[67] Anne Klein imposed herself as an entrepreneur able to answer such demands. Born Anne Kline, she started her career along with associate Frank Adams at a New York garment district manufacturing firm called Junior Sophisticates in 1951. There she designed collections of dresses called "unfitted," made to fall comfortably and casually on the body. Klein herself liked to tell journalists that youth was a state of mind and neither a size nor an age. As an individual, Klein was small-featured and found that the offerings of department stores for women with her physical characteristics were insufficient, forcing her to the junior misses department, in which the clothes were designed for college girls and, she thought, either too casual or too cute for working women. Klein set to the task of designing clothes that would allow petite women to be taken seriously in the workplace, as she herself wanted to be. She strived to design for active American women, for whom she made affordable and versatile fashions. She was a pioneer in designing functional and elegant shirtdresses, sober and simple suits, and other options for career wear.[68]

The Battle of Versailles

In 1973, New York star publicist Eleanor Lambert and Chateau de Versailles curator Gerald van der Kemp organized and staged the "battle of Versailles," a prestigious show in which both Paris and New York designers took turns showing their creations at the Palace of Versailles. One pioneering American designer, Elizabeth Hawes, showed her fashions in Paris, in 1931. Hawes was at that time getting settled as a designer in New York and thought that it would be a good idea to promote her original designs in Paris. Her show was well attended, but it was met with astounding silence in the French press. Discouraged by the cold reception of her work, Hawes never again tried to show in Paris. After Hawes, the exception was Mainbocher, who successfully opened an haute couture firm in Paris during the interwar period.[69] The concept of the battle of Versailles was therefore quite symbolic to the inside circles of the fashion profession. It also took the unusual form of a confrontation between two teams of five designers each. The French team showed first, followed by an interlude that included a dance number by Liza Minelli, star of the movie *Cabaret*. Her great friend Andy Warhol was in the audience, as well as a plethora of stars including actresses Elizabeth Taylor and Marisa Berenson. Haute couture clients were also well represented in the audience. The Sun King, Louis XIV, had on occasion ship battles organized for his pleasure over the waters of the Versailles complex. This time, the battle was transatlantic in a metaphorical manner: designers from France and from America faced off with their talents on the catwalk set up in Versailles. The French team featured the finest works by trendy, up-and-coming Paris couturiers Marc Bohan for the house of Dior, Pierre Cardin, Hubert de Givenchy, Yves Saint Laurent, and Emanuel Ungaro. According to the audience, the French show was good but a bit slow, even somewhat pompous and overdecorated. After Minelli's appearance, the American designers sent their models down the catwalk. The diverse group of five US designers included Bill Blass, the already popular successor of Maurice Rentner; Stephen Burrows; Halston, who was the favorite couturier of New York nightlife; Anne Klein, who had brought along a young assistant named Donna Karan; and Oscar de la Renta. The five New York couturiers had had to work with limited means. They had brought together thirty-six models, and with the limited budget most models did not receive more than $300 for the event. The clothes were simple, many of them long, flowing, pull-on dresses in very bright colors. The music was powerful, and the models walked fast and danced in a minimalist decor. Full of energy, the American show blew the audience away. Press accounts on each side of the Atlantic gracefully credited the other side with winning that amicable battle, but for many in the audience, the Americans succeeded to a greater degree in representing the spirit of the times.[70]

Chapter 7

End *of* the Century

O ver the final decades of the twentieth century, fashion finalized its transformation into a mass-market industry. Manufacturing kept relocating to new places of production where wages were lower and where fashion could contribute to creating employment and growing the local economy. Fashion production had moved from the West and its hubs, like the New York garment district, to regions where wages were cheaper, in southern Europe, then to the southern US states, and then farther abroad, to North African countries, Turkey, the Caribbean countries, and Asia. Facing this race toward ever-cheaper manufacturing hubs, the Western countries aimed to limit overseas production of textile products, including fashionable garments and accessories. From 1974 until 2004, the Multi-Fiber Arrangement (MFA) created favorable conditions for low-cost countries to export manufactured garments to the West while aiming to impose some limits by way of quotas of exports of goods by categories and by countries.

Faster Fashions

Important technological advances impacted the fashion industries during the nineteenth and twentieth centuries. Innovations in textile looms changed the speed and quality of yarn and fabric production. Several patents had already offered increasingly precise versions of the zipper by World War I. The interwar period was a time of innovation in manufactured fibers. In 1958 the chemical firm DuPont invented Lycra, one of the most important technical revolutions in modern clothing. Before that, couturiers like Madeleine Vionnet had to rely on the bias cut to create fluidity and reduce constriction in garments. Lycra eventually allowed for garments to stretch around the body. In the last decades of the twentieth century, the integration of flexible materials into jeans manufacturing rendered denim fabric more comfortable and changed the way jeans were designed and worn. Possibly the most important element in the mechanization of clothing has been in the development of knitting machines, which are increasingly automated, allowing for new business models. A pioneering model is that of the Japanese group Fast Retail, and especially its brand Uniqlo, which has aimed to offer minimalistic, good-quality garments for everyone. Uniqlo's model is based on lowering costs thanks to, notably, the automation of knitting machines, although Uniqlo offers not only knits but also tailored garments for everyday life.[1]

To make garments, however, the sewing machine is at the core of fashion production—at least for any clothes assembled with seams, which includes knits (for example, most classic T-shirts and sweaters) as well as tailored clothes. To be assembled, fabrics need to be guided through a sewing machine by human hands. Since the invention of the sewing machine in the mid-nineteenth century, technology has been stable, with far less innovation in the technological realm than in the realm of design novelty. In other words, the fashion industry offers from this vantage point an example of what David Edgerton, a historian of technology, calls the "shock of the old." Like the bicycle, the sewing machine is an innovation whose utility has endured for over a century and a half. The most significant change in the technology of the sewing machine was the replacement of the treadle with electricity, which allowed the machines to be operated faster, but fundamentally the technology has remained the same, and it is still possible to use old sewing machines to make clothes that may or may not have a high fashion content.[2]

Independently from the machinery, seasonal novelty in designs, shapes, colors, and materials has therefore been the most important driver of garment changes. These changes appear quite limited, in a sense, because garments retain certain functional features: a bodice, sleeves, and a skirt or legs. Scholars interested in the sociology of fashion, notably the French linguist Roland Barthes, have theorized the acceleration of fashion cycles, which is a central factor to the growth of the fashion industry. In the West, a consequence of this was that sewing became undervalued, considered a chosen hobby instead of an economically sound activity. Faster fashions also meant that, in turn, entrepreneurs had little incentive to buy sophisticated machines able to perform specialized operations such as finishing or complex embroidery motifs. Fast changes in fashions meant that simpler machines were the safest investment in production.[3]

The next most important technological development in the fashion industry was the adoption of the just-in-time methods that originated in the production of cars, especially by Japanese firm Toyota. Such methods allow for rather light tools of production, subcontracting, and fast decision-making on reorders, which was key in solving the problem of restocking. Provided the general economic climate remained stable, just-in-time methods could alleviate the problem of remaining stocks that Alfred D. Chandler had already identified as the main challenge for department stores selling fashionable merchandise in the previous century. Fashion firms emulated these methods by using software systems to plan manufacturing optimally, with the goal of reducing stocks and addressing the demand. Pioneers in these methods include Uniqlo, founded as Ogori Shoji Co. Ltd. by Tadashi Yanai in 1963, and retailer Zara, founded by Amancio Ortega and his first wife Rosalia Mera in 1975. In 1979 Zara became part of the Inditex Group, Industria de Diseño Textil SA, also founded by Ortega and Mera, who expanded the firm from their home base, A Coruña, a small seaport town of Galicia in northwestern Spain, far from the fashion capitals. Ortega picked up the fashion revolution where the 1960s stylists and their boutiques had left it. These innovative 1960s entrepreneurs had made fashionable and affordable garments for immediate purchase and use. Clients would frequently change in the shop and leave with their new dress on. The boutiques met with difficulties in restocking the most successful designs and colors and thus were often out of stock. The development of specific IT programs, and their integration into the fashion chain of production, allowed for more precise and faster responses to consumers' demands. At Inditex, the mother company of Zara, the management and design teams can make rapid decisions based on data gathered from consumers' purchases, source the necessary materials, and run the production at high speed. Logistics are central to the holding's success. Today, the fast-fashion groups that developed these IT systems in the first place can get a fashionable new garment from the drawing board to the shop floor in thirteen days.[4]

This method allows firms to offer fashionable garments while their designs are still trendy and for affordable prices. However, this system is not immune to criticism, especially on two grounds. The most challenging point is the use of sub-contracting, which is also the most enduring feature of the fashion industry. Sub-contracting creates pressure on the costs and, in turn, on the workforce; in addition, due to the complexity of fashion supply chains, the retailer can lose sight of labor conditions and therefore fail to enforce necessary controls over places of production. The other contentious point in this process is the reproduction of trends. Fashion is a derivative industry, which points to the nature of fashion itself. As sociologists including Georg Simmel and Gabriel Tarde had already pointed out in the nineteenth century, fashion itself is imitation, as wearers want to emulate trends and to wear them as well. Most haute couture creative entrepreneurs tried over the course of the twentieth century to protect their innovations and thus reap the rewards of the dissemination of their creative designs at home and abroad, especially in the United States. This was a daunting task, and it became even more so as the speed of communication increased. Indeed, the incorporation of just-in-time methods into garment production made reproduction quasi immediate.[5]

Fast fashion completed the democratization of fashion, but the concept of fashions for all needs to be considered carefully. Histories of the consumption of secondhand fashions show that even in the affluent West, some strata of consumers could not afford—or did not want—to buy new, even at a low price point, and had to rely on charity secondhand garments to make ends meet. The democratization of fashion was a long-term process that developed alongside the rise of the ready-to-wear industry and in which fashion stopped being purely a luxury and became a commodity.[6]

Tension between higher-end and mass consumption that was already present between Paris and New York during the earliest decades of the twentieth century kept growing as the fashion industry reached new stages of globalization, especially from the 1960s. This tension developed into a series of more complex relationships, as the creative centers of fashion and the directions of emulation multiplied.[7] Critics confronted faster fashions, especially from the side of the designers who often feared unsolicited copying of their work by the largest retail chains. Large firms have addressed the problem in various manners. One approach, called masstige, consists of mass fashion firms hiring higher-end designers to create co-branded manufactured collections. Swedish retailer Hennes & Mauritz (H&M) popularized this strategy of aligning a mass fashion brand with a high-end designer at the end of the twentieth century.[8] Another strategy is to offer important lines of basic garments, which the so-called fast-fashion chains do. These lines can also be produced farther away from the firm's headquarters, as they renew more slowly. The most successful fast-fashion firms offer an efficient combination of these "slower" classic and basic pieces along with items that closely follow the latest trends and are manufactured much closer to the home base of the firm, often in the West.

Machines today are operated by men and women who may be working far from the headquarters of retailing firms. Fashion is an important source of employment worldwide. Competition between contractors at the local level keeps labor prices down, but sourcing from distant locations is a challenge for workers and for firms. At the beginning of the twentieth century, clothing was manufactured largely in urban centers, close to the firms that worked on image, media, and value creation. Paris was the center of design and of bespoke women's fashions; London was the center of tailoring, sportswear, and woolen clothing; and New York emerged as the world's most dynamic manufacturing center. In these major cities, unions and activist groups, including consumers' leagues, worked hard to gain more control over the conditions of production. They denounced the use of *sweated labor*—that is, the exploitation of low-paid, often immigrant, women and children working in tenements and insalubrious buildings, which remained endemic. The German Jewish workers of nineteenth-century New York were replaced by successive waves of immigrants: Polish and Russian Jews, Italians, Chinese, and Puerto Ricans.[9]

Another process took place: the relocation of garment production from Western countries to Asia, the Caribbean basin, North Africa, and, after the fall of the Iron Curtain, to former Soviet-bloc countries. The places of production shifted both to allow for lower costs and as reactions to policies of quotas and of trade barriers that governments set up with the aim of preserving their national industries.[10] Much of garment manufacturing work can be, and for a long time has been, subcontracted. Contractors had to compete for orders and, therefore, were often prepared to press their workers to offer cheaper and faster deliveries. Such competition remained prominent not only in manufacturing domestically but also when it relocated overseas, which limited the ability of the retailers and manufacturers giving orders to supervise the conditions of labor in distant workshops.[11]

From the 1970s and 1980s, new trade agreements allowed manufacturing-intensive countries to use low wages as a competitive advantage in garment exports. New countries, notably Hong Kong, Taiwan, and South Korea, outpaced northern European countries, the United States, Canada, Australia, and New Zealand in the flow of cheaper merchandise. Lower wages, longer hours, and local production of textiles allowed the new places of production to offer fashionable goods for retail sale in the West. In an attempt to limit competition, the low-cost manufacturing countries and the Western importers negotiated trade agreements within the framework of the General Agreement on Tariffs and Trade (GATT). The MFA, for instance, aimed to limit the production of low-cost fashions and its effect on older places of production, but experts observed that bypassing or cheating on the import quotas of garments was common. In some cases the arrangements did not achieve the desired effect and, instead of protecting fragile producers, ended up penalizing other producing countries (for example, in the case of Greece in southern Europe). The end of the MFA on January 1, 2005, resulted in a boom in the lower-cost garment industry, despite the negotiation of new bilateral agreements.[12]

Especially from the 1970s, the consequences of the offshoring of production became perceptible in the old manufacturing centers in Europe and in the United States, where entire regions lost thousands of manufacturing jobs. In terms of employment, the countries that had developed a comprehensive welfare state were penalized in comparison with those that had not done so.[13] Contemporary fashion industries, characterized by flexible specialization and rapid response, are characteristic of post-Fordist economies. Areas in the West that had traditionally specialized in fabric and garment manufacturing converted part of their activity into creation, design, and media, often supported by governmental programs aiming to compensate for losses in manufacturing jobs. Even designers based in Japan or Belgium, for example, found that showing in Paris or New York was still the best way to be acknowledged as a global brand. While London, Milan, New York, and Paris remained gatekeepers of the fashion business, they would be joined in this role by Shanghai, Tokyo, and a growing number of other cities, whether in Africa, in India, or in Scandinavia.[14]

In the West, many of the original production centers and their abandoned sites, or neighboring cities, became postindustrial creative centers. Multiple actors contributed to make such reconversions possible: city and state officials eager to reignite activity in dormant regions, designers attracted by cheaper rents, the last firms left behind, and new entrepreneurs. Governments at city and state levels developed programs of recovery and of subventions. As they had earlier in the history of the fashion business, governments were eager to support the industry.[15]

A Consumers' Revolution

Fashion mass production provides many people with entry-level jobs, but, as its critics suggest, this mode of manufacturing can result in difficult labor conditions and, in the worst cases, grave labor accidents. This touches especially the countries where safety regulations are not enforced, often for reasons of corruption. Bangladesh has been particularly affected by such accidents. A turning point in the late twentieth century was the December 1991 Saraca factory fire in the suburbs of Dhaka that killed twenty-five women and children. Mass labor unrest and union creation followed the Saraca fire. The Clean Clothes Campaign, a Dutch-founded alliance of nongovernmental organizations (NGOs) and labor unions, then researched dangerous labor conditions in Bangladesh. Despite these efforts, other accidents followed. The largest accident in the garment industry took place on April 24, 2013, when at least 1,134 people were killed as a result of the collapse of the Rana Plaza building in Savar, also in the suburbs of Dhaka. More than three thousand people were working in the building, producing apparel for various subcontractors. Among the survivors of the collapse, many were gravely injured. In the case of Rana Plaza, corruption in the construction sector had resulted in a disregard for building safety, which caused the accident. Several other accidents in apparel factories had occurred in the preceding months, and others have taken place since in various locations around the world.[16]

The retailers whose brand image was tarnished by the Rana Plaza disaster stated that they had not been fully informed of the conditions of production. Retailers subsequently engaged in reparation and developed corporate social responsibility (CSR) programs. The Rana Plaza collapse took on symbolic proportions because of both the magnitude of the number of victims and the excessive consumerism associated with the cheap fashions produced there. In numerous media discourses, mass fashion became synonymous with guilt. Economist Pietra Rivoli and *New York Times* journalist Adam Davidson have described low-wage garment factories as a part of an economy's "T-shirt phase": a phase that developing economies have to go through in order to provide low-cost jobs to large groups of people, before reaching a stage of prosperity that will result in better jobs and better wages. The T-shirt phase is expected to take place for a limited period of time and to be gradually replaced by more qualified and higher-paid forms of employment, as can be observed in, for example, some parts of China, where low-cost manufacturers coexist with workshops that employ more qualified workers. As far as fashion manufacturing is concerned, however, the research of labor historians and social scientists tends to show that sweated labor comes back in waves, including in the fashion hubs of the West. But numerous low-cost-production countries—notably Bangladesh, Cambodia, and Pakistan—also seem to experience challenges in leaving the T-shirt phase. Regions in these countries are slow to meet a prognosis for increased qualified labor, while deadly accidents continue to occur, and workers' protests on labor conditions are often met with repression. An important issue that arises here, as examined by econo-mists including Joseph Stiglitz, is the need for establishing a precedence of tran-sition to democratic regimes as a precondition for further development.[17]

In some of the world's most affluent countries, new discourses encouraging restrained, responsible consumption have risen to prominence in the media and often translate aesthetically into minimalist styles. An important question for the actors involved, from producers to consumers, is whether global fashion retailers should divest from economies that produce low-cost fashions at a risk to the workers. Most of the actors involved tend to agree that it is better for multina-tionals to avoid doing a "cut and run" on their orders when production disregards labor codes. Liesbeth Sluiter of the Clean Clothes Campaign writes that NGOs generally encourage multinationals to stay and work with the local contractors, the unions, the government, the International Labor Organization, and the NGOs to improve conditions at the local level and to develop a cooperation paradigm based on furthering dialogue among all these actors.[18]

Recent studies have tried to evaluate the costs that the consumer would have to pay in order for workers in low-cost-production countries to receive a minimum wage and a basic welfare safety net. According to these studies, such a change may result in an increase of less than a dollar per garment on the sales floor.[19]

To the ethical dilemma of labor in distant places of production has been added the environmental question. Analyses of the environmental impact of the fashion industry tend to show that it is the second most damaging industry after fossil fuels. In response, new business models are emerging, based on, for example, the recycling of materials and the renting of clothes. Newer places of production, among which some of the most prominent are currently in Africa (for example, in Ethiopia), that are engaging in garment production in order to grow their economy also need to benefit from the renewed attention to conditions of labor.[20]

But newer technological change may upset the fashion system that has prevailed for the past 150 years. Over this time span, garment assembly has consistently demanded that human hands guide the fabric through the machine. The knitting industry, with the development of automated looms, had gone as far as possible in reducing human interaction, but most garments still need to be assembled (for example, with side seams), and this procedure has so far resisted automation. Being a soft material, fabric is very difficult for a robot to manipulate. Most recently, innovators have come up with "sewbots": robots that may replace the human hands needed to push the fabric through the machine and control its course. An important component of this innovation is the development of a method for the nonpermanent stiffening of fabrics, which are plunged into a bath of polymer-based chemicals that stiffen when dried; then, a sewbot can effectively replace the human hand and assemble the stiffened fabric. The assembled garment is then plunged into a new bath to rinse out the stiffening product and, once dry, sent for finishing steps. The high cost of the sewbots signifies that such methods have thus far remained uncompetitive in comparison with a human workforce. Similarly, comparisons of costs suggest that 3-D textile or knit printing machines have remained marginal in fashion production. These new developments in the automation of fashion production have the potential to become the most innovative breakthrough since the development of the sewing machine in the nineteenth century and the development of IT systems for just-in-time production in the late twentieth century. Whether these new innovations can be commercialized remains to be seen. As a further consequence, while automation may relieve some of the physical strain on garment workers, it would likely result in a new cycle of significant job losses in places where workers are particularly vulnerable. Most recently, the effects of the Covid-19 induced pandemic have resulted in losses of employment for vulnerable groups in the industry, and revealed the fragility of the people who work for it without having control on its chains of production.[21]

Paris and New York as World Fashion Cities

Despite the upheavals in fashion production briefly described above, Paris and New York have remained centers for the fashion industries at a global level. The two cities alternate in the top place in the global rankings of fashion cities, followed closely by London and Milan. New York's slight advantage, according to sociologist Frédéric Godart, may be due to the preeminence of English in global communications, with Paris being a very close second. As an important part of the haute couture houses' activity has been absorbed by larger luxury groups, it is relevant to note that New York, despite the fast growth of the Asian markets, remains to this day the top market for the purchase of luxury goods in the world. Furthermore, and despite the relocation of fashion production to distant places, Europe remains the second-largest exporter of clothing worldwide, behind China. To this day, the symbiotic relation between Paris and New York remains a global window (see Figure 7.1), along with the two other fashion capitals of London and Milan, to which buyers and journalists from around the world flock to learn of the new trends.[22]

The Chambre Syndicale de la Couture Parisienne, the main employers' syndicate that has brought together couturiers since 1868, remains in existence as a prestigious group whose members create collections at least twice a year and show them on live models in suitable venues. For most couturiers, affording such conditions of production has become a challenge, which explains why membership in the trade syndicate over the past decades of the twentieth century, and today, has numbered only a couple dozen firms. The oil shock of 1973 marked a downturn in the production of haute couture and its consumption by a small international elite of clients. That same year, the Chambre Syndicale was integrated into a larger structure, the Fédération de la Haute Couture et de la Mode (Federation of Haute Couture and Fashion), that included men's wear and designer ready-to-wear, two branches that had become staples in the high-fashion industry. The Chambre Syndicale increasingly included guest members, higher-end designers, and couturiers who showed their collections in Paris. In 1988, the Chambre Syndicale welcomed its first American member, African American designer Patrick Kelly. Born in Mississippi in 1954, Kelly rose to prominence for the quality of his designs, and the prestigious US manufacturer Warnaco commissioned him

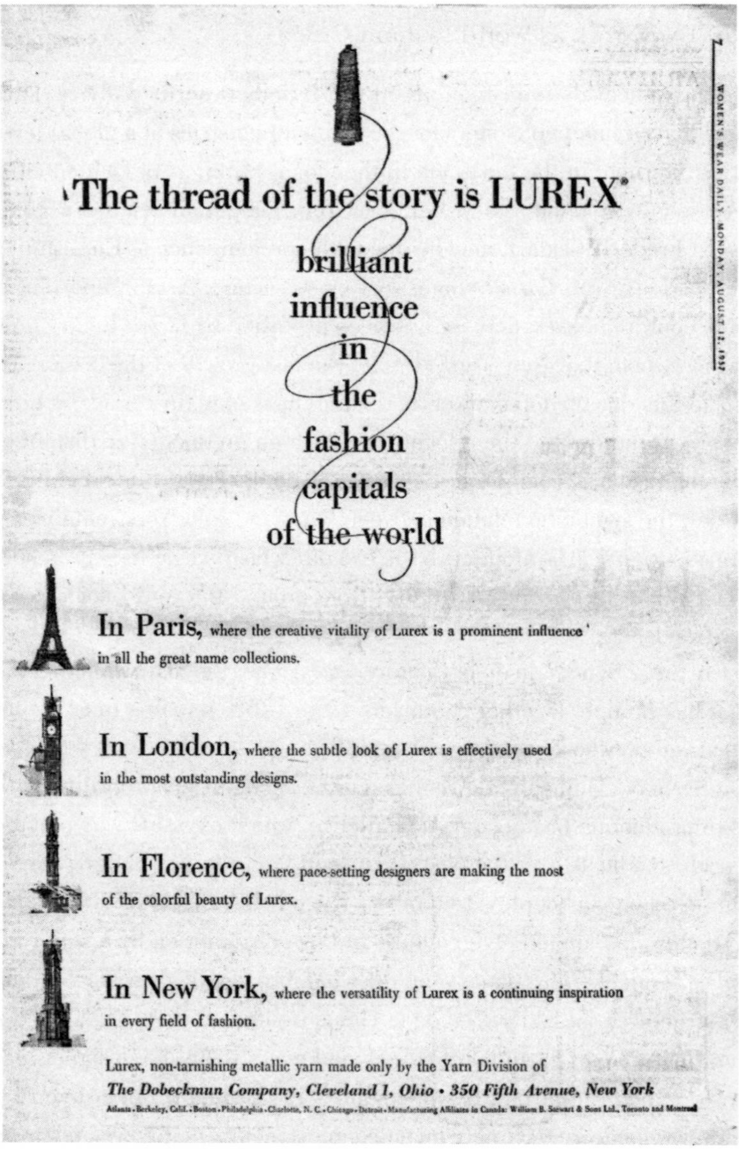

FIGURE 7.1 In this advertisement for a yarn company, Florence is featured as one of the "Big Four" fashion capitals, a title that subsequently went to Milan.

Women's Wear Daily, *August 12, 1957, p. 7. © Fairchild Publishing LLC.*

to design lines for manufacture. Kelly moved to Paris in the 1970s on the sug-
gestion of his friend Pat Cleveland, a star model who had walked the runway at
the 1973 battle of Versailles show. Kelly employed dramatic tailoring and designed flowing dark dresses. He was also a collector of African American mem-
orabilia, and as such he decoded and reinterpreted stereotypes of African American culture such as minstrel shows and blackface representations. His designs
conveyed multiple critiques of stereotypes of America but also of ironical distance from Paris cultural symbols including the Eiffel Tower and *Mona Lisa*.
Kelly's inclusion in the ranks of the Chambre Syndicale shows both the positive
reception of his critical views and the openness of the Paris fashion milieus to a
postmodern understanding of the reinterpretation of its own image. Kelly died of
AIDS-related complications in 1990, as the epidemic took a significant toll on
the creative professions, including the fashion business.[23]

Licensing and the Renovation of Couturiers' Ready-to-Wear

Dior and several of his peer couturiers added licensed lines to their haute couture workshops. The case of Dior, then the most important French luxury firm in
the United States, shows that the development of licenses cast a wide net over
international markets. After Christian Dior's premature death in 1957, the firm
kept the designer's name, which had become brand capital over the first decade
of the firm's existence.[24] Dior was succeeded by Yves Mathieu Saint Laurent, best
known as Yves Saint Laurent. Saint Laurent, born in Oran in 1936, moved to
Paris in 1953 and was trained in the school of the Chambre Syndicale, where he
learned the techniques of haute couture. Saint Laurent apprenticed at Dior at the
side of another promising talent of the same generation, Karl Lagerfeld. In 1957,
when Christian Dior died unexpectedly, Boussac and Rouët chose Saint Laurent,
then just twenty-one, to take over the haute couture house. The press and the
buyers praised Saint Laurent's creativity as much as his respect for the spirit of
the master, but this was only a short-term creative respite for the house of Dior.
In 1960 Saint Laurent was called as a conscript to serve in the French military
and sent to Algeria amid the decolonization war that lasted from 1954 to 1962.
At the time, the press focused on Saint Laurent's military service as a dramatic
loss for fashion culture. Boussac terminated Saint Laurent's contract allegedly
due to his absence. Meanwhile, the young designer, who found conditions in the

army unbearable, was sent back to Paris and hospitalized for a depressive episode.

Once released, Saint Laurent, along with his partner in life and in business, Pierre Bergé, opened the Yves Saint Laurent haute couture house in 1961 with the funding of American financier Jesse Mack Robinson, who retained his investment in the firm until 1966. Like Dior before him, Saint Laurent surrounded himself with a small court of managers and muses. He developed a strategy of diversification in lines and in prices with the opening of Saint Laurent Rive Gauche, a boutique selling designer ready-to-wear, in 1966. Saint Laurent moved his boutique to the trendier Left Bank (Rive Gauche) of the Seine, a location aiming to appeal to younger consumers, thereby announcing a renewal of the clientele. In addition, a Saint Laurent Rive Gauche boutique opened in New York in 1968 and in London in 1969. Saint Laurent Rive Gauche is often credited as the first example of a ready-to-wear line designed by a couturier, but there had been earlier attempts, including the Lucien Lelong Edition line and Christian Dior—New York line. One can debate whether Lelong Edition can be called ready-to-wear. The Edition workers used sewing machines but finished pieces by hand with great care and offered fittings to the clients. In the case of Dior, production was delegated to high-quality garment manufacturers in New York. This shows a succession line of fashion innovators who strived to protect the prestige of couture and at the same time foster the emergence of branded ready-to-wear. Saint Laurent committed to designing ready-to-wear with pride, affirming that he wanted to "do Prisunic" (referring to the name of an iconic low-price department store in France). He aimed to make some pieces affordable to high-street consumers. He also innovated with dressing working women, for whom he created sleek pants suits and dress suits, as well as trousers adapted from a men's tuxedo for evening wear. An obsolete French law that forbade Frenchwomen to wear trousers was partially lifted in 1892 and again in 1909 for the practice of sports but was not fully abolished until 2013. The law had long been forgotten by the time Saint Laurent was designing, but women's trousers carried a subversive charge for a long time.[25]

Saint Laurent pushed the boundaries of the language of fashion in many domains, as was apparent in the relationships he drew between fashion and eroticism, fashion and exoticism, and fashion and addiction. In 1968, the year of the May revolution, he designed voile blouses to be worn without a bra. The transparent fabric aimed to reveal bare breasts, although the blouses were mostly worn under a jacket, thereby nuancing the effect of nakedness. When actress Monique Van Vooren wore one of these blouses at the Biltmore Theater in New York for the opening of *Hair*, the ensemble created a stir. Journalists compared it to the recent fashion innovations of American designer Rudi Gernreich, credited with inventing the monokini. Saint Laurent brought new aesthetic codes to the fashion industry. The transparent blouse sexualized couture in a novel manner. Saint Laurent also integrated exoticism in the language of his clothes with fabrics and shapes borrowed from Asia, from Africa, and from colonial imagery. He sought to diversify the profiles of models who showed his clothes, hiring African and Asian women as star models. Christian Dior before him had shown some diversity with his models, of whom a few were of mixed origin from Asia and North Africa, but at Saint Laurent the image of the women wearing the designs became much more diverse than what haute couture was used to. With the launching in 1977 of the perfume Opium and its advertising campaigns, Saint Laurent brought yet another important, durable, and, in this case, highly controversial element to the language of the fashion industry: the culture of drugs and addiction, to which both the name of the perfume and the slogans and imagery of its advertising campaigns represented the consumption of opium. The theme of drug culture was adopted by some other global fashion and luxury brands, keeping such images alive in ad campaigns and contributing to distinct stereotypes in fashion advertising.[26]

After Saint Laurent's departure from the house of Dior in 1960, the Boussac Group moved designer Marc Bohan—who had worked for Dior London's ready-to-wear line since 1958—to a new assignment as head designer of Dior's main women's lines. To this, Bohan added a new men's line for Dior in 1970. In addition, the general management of the group assigned one person to be the head designer for Dior New York; this position was held successively by Hubert Latimer, Guy Douvier, Gaston Berthelot, and Dominic Toubeix. Dior's managing director, Rouët, kept working for the brand for two decades after the death of its founder. In the mid-1970s, Rouët visited the New York headquarters and moved the financial arm of the global company from Curaçao to New York. He also used his time in the United States to produce a complete assessment of the licenses of Dior in America. Having done this, he recommended more extensive quality controls regarding the US production. The large number of American licenses had eroded the prestige of the Dior brand, and Rouët understood that it was time to redress the licenses.[27] Dior's management knew the importance of compromises between aesthetic and commercial considerations when it came to the brand's use in overseas markets.[28]

Dior's business model sourced creation in Paris and located the reproduction processes abroad. The firm opened branches in a number of countries in the 1950s and 1960s—including Australia, Cuba, Great Britain, the United States, Venezuela, and similar locations—to serve wealthy clients. Dior sold branded ready-to-wear in most of its international outposts. A few select branches, especially in Latin America, had their own workshops where local workers made exact reproductions of the Paris headquarters' haute couture garments. Before the postwar era, the Paris couturiers had tended to keep production in France. Haute couture entrepreneurs wanted to keep their know-how and their work domestic. The process of regulating the label *haute couture* developed at the same time that the French manufacturers gained access to haute couture shows for the authorized reproduction of designs. Postwar, couturiers delegated manufacturing tasks to licensee firms at home and abroad with an eye on the quality of production and the demand on international markets.[29]

During the postwar era, a group of pioneering firms, including Dior, established a system of royalties for Paris haute couture at the international level. For several decades this had been attempted by couturiers, notably Poiret and Vionnet, who contributed to reinforce the immaterial rights of haute couture, but did not succeed in establishing a stream of revenue from royalties. A consequence was that lawyers gained a place in the management of haute couture and luxury firms. The aim of a royalty system was to enjoy the profits from investments made by couture in the design of their branded products. Branding took on increasing importance in the intellectual properties portfolios of haute couture firms (see Figure 7.2).

The US market, especially, appeared as a space to conquer, but couturiers generally lacked the financial capital required to do so. Setting up licensing agreements was the haute couture industry's response to the long-standing difficulty experienced by Paris couturiers when they wanted to protect the intangible assets of their brands overseas. Boussac's financial investments provided the house of Dior with the means to launch licenses and expansion—the main reason why Dior succeeded where most of his predecessors had failed in the US market.[30]

FIGURE 7.2 In February 1951, the French edition of
Vogue published a portfolio on haute couture that
represented only the labels of the haute couture
houses. Jacques Griffe, who had worked for
Madeleine Vionnet before launching his own house,
also used a thumbprint on his branded labels. The
Vogue portfolio exemplifies the dematerialization of
haute couture and its conversion into brand value.
© Vogue *Paris.*

When firms moved the production of their branded lines out of Paris, they did
so intending to choose manufacturers carefully and to monitor quality. The management of Dior, chaired by Rouët, set up a special contract for each manufactured line bearing the Dior brand. The firm registered the subtle variations on
the Dior brand for each line with the national and international brand registration offices. In the earliest years of the brand, Christian Dior and his close team

of assistants—especially Mitzah Bricard, who was in charge of accessories—reviewed each product proposed for licensed lines for its quality, taste, and coherency with the brand before giving the seal of approval.

In the United States, the firm Christian Dior New York, in the footsteps of the work initiated by in-house lawyer Ellen Engel, developed a comprehensive portfolio of intellectual property rights that can be summed up under the following categories: trademark and patent protection, general counsel activities and corporate organization, certified public accountant responsibilities, and licensing and related contracts. During the 1980s, Dior delegated the work related to trademark and patent protection in the United States to Amster, Rothstein and Ebenstein, a law firm specializing in trademark protection. Dior's general legal counsel in America was the firm Windels, Marx, Davies and Ives, vested with the task of preparing the meetings of the board of directors and of stockholders. Dior New York also worked with a certified accountant, M.R. Weiser & Co., in charge of financial statements and licensing audits. The lion's share of the legal work for Christian Dior New York was taken up by the management of the firm's licenses. During the 1970s and 1980s, the legal arsenal for fashion intellectual property rights had matured. American firms in high fashion and designer ready-to-wear now preferred to settle cases by transaction. Litigation in the United States was notoriously expensive, and the outcome was often unpredictable.[31]

Christian Dior New York set up its licensing agreements following a specific five-step process. First, the firm used a model license agreement produced by Windels, Marx, Davis and Ives to draw up a standard license contract. On this basis, Dior (which was the licensor) and the licensee entered into a negotiation process to determine the limits on net wholesale price deductions, on the royalty rate, and on minimums. Second, Dior and the licensee agreed on an automatic renewal of the license contract and on the possibility of adjusting the contract upon renewal. Third, licensees could in some cases request an extension of the contract, even when renewal had not been included as an option in the original agreement. A fourth step was that, in case of any dispute over the license agreement, the parts would write complementary letters, about the date of the payment of royalties, for example, or to define creative matters like the approval of product styles and advertising. A fifth step concerned sublicensing—that is, when a licensee contracts all or part of production for a license to a third party.[32]

Usually a license agreement made for Christian Dior New York consisted of a document of more than twenty pages in which the relations between the licensor—that is, the Dior New York headquarters—and the licensee were presented in detail. The license contract also specified the geographical area covered by the licensee. Items produced by the licensees to be retailed under the Dior brand automatically became the property of Dior. The main reasons why licensing contracts were so long and required such legal groundwork was that the production of licensed goods encompassed the use of Dior's brands, logos, and images. At that point in the firm's history, Dior was a multinational that owned several brands and logos, small variations of which represented the various products and branches of the firm: Christian Dior, Christian Dior New York, Christian Dior Original, Christian Dior–C.D. models, Christian Dior Créación, and so on. Each of these Dior-related trademarks was the property of the mother firm, the Société Anonyme Christian Dior in Paris. The firm registered its brand under various trademarks and service marks—Christian Dior, Dior, CD, and others—with the registration bureaus in France, in the United States, and, at the international level, in Switzerland.[33]

The first license contracted by Dior for the US market was set up in 1949 for Dior-branded men's neckties. While the Paris haute couture salons kept creating elite products for a rarefied clientele, licenses aimed to bring good quality to a wider base of middle-class clients. Finding the best manufacturers was a priority for the Dior executives. An important challenge was to keep the quality of the licensed products consistent with the haute couture lines, brand image, and overall production. However, management's attention to the licenses gradually relaxed, especially after Christian Dior died. Dior headquarters kept most of the existing licenses going, even though some of the resulting products were considered outdated in purpose or design, or lacking in aesthetic interest.[34]

Twice a year, Christian Dior and his core team used to sit around a table and examine the products designed by the firm's licensees. Then the designer and his management team offered recommendations on the quality, aesthetics, and prices of the branded products. The designers who succeeded Christian Dior at the Paris headquarters continued to approve the new collections designed by the licensees. They had a directive role over the aesthetics and the final word on the products. The license contracts outlined that licensees ought to respect Dior's goodwill and prestige. In addition, licensed merchandise sold at the retail level had to match the highest standards of luxury. But the relationship between Dior and its licensees was an ever-evolving process that relied on mutual understanding by all parties. Over the 1960s and 1970s, Boussac's management became less attentive and the firm's licensing strategy started showing weakness; the Paris headquarters' work shifted toward a policy that brought royalties into Dior's treasury and only occasionally required any changes to be made to the licensed lines. This resulted in a dilution of the brand's prestige.[35]

Boussac's Decline

From the 1960s, Marcel Boussac was unable to renew the management of his group strategically. His group continued to produce cottons with classical patterns, which an increasing amount of consumers thought to be old-fashioned, while his competitors were going strong with synthetic textiles and products made in Italy and in various Asian countries. The Boussac Group was deeply anchored in the north of France, which, along with neighboring Flanders in Belgium, was historically a major center of textile production. In the context of changing textile policies, these regions could no longer keep up with the international competition, and their textile mills closed one after the other, leaving thousands of workers unemployed. The decline continued throughout the 1970s. Boussac closed a number of the textile mills in his group, and in 1973 he sold the prosperous perfume operation of Christian Dior to a group that specialized in alcoholic beverages, Moët Hennessy (then owned by Alain Chevalier), and that would merge with luxury leather goods firm Louis Vuitton (led by Henry Racamier) in 1987.[36]

Working women made up a significant share of American fashion consumers in the 1970s. Bill Blass, who had succeeded the veteran Seventh Avenue entrepreneur Maurice Rentner, and Anne Klein both designed great career wear. The New York nightlife crowd that gathered at Studio 54 and at Andy Warhol's Factory favored luxury evening wear designers like Halston but also appreciated vintage dresses that gave the wearer a unique look and artistic cachet. The trendy clientele was no longer interested in haute couture or in the type of wholesale couture that Dior had introduced in New York. In the mid-1970s, specialty stores like Jay Thorpe and New York's most famous couturiere, Hattie Carnegie, closed their doors. Department stores, including the prestigious Bergdorf Goodman and

Saks Fifth Avenue, closed their haute couture salons, where they used to display designs imported from France, with reproduction rights, and their own genuine reproductions or adaptations of Paris couture.[37]

Over the 1970s, the income from Dior's licenses in the United States did not grow much. In 1975, Christian Dior New York closed its wholesale couture salons. However, the SA Christian Dior—that is, the firm's Paris-based headquarters— kept the American licensing business of Christian Dior New York active. The firm capitalized on the name of the couturier to retain its premium place on the US luxury market. In the mid-1980s, the United States, which represented Dior's largest market, was responsible for around 40 percent of the conglomerate's global volume. At that time, the American market seemed unfavorable to haute couture, yet Christian Dior New York remained active after 1975 in managing some fifty Dior licenses there. That same year, Christian Dior licenses world- wide amounted to over 130 products. Dior was in the process of extending its retail operations, with the opening of several Dior retail stores in Switzerland, Germany, Belgium, Greece, and Monaco. Bohan, as the head designer of Dior haute couture in Paris, and his assistant, Cathy Khan, watched over Dior's li- censes. Khan visited New York for two weeks twice a year, during which time she examined all Dior-licensed women's lines. Bohan made sure the licensed women's wear aligned with Dior's Paris collections. In the second half of the 1980s Dior was particularly successful with suits and coats that retailed at Bergdorf Goodman, Bloomingdale's, and other prestigious department stores. The majority of Dior's licensed lines, however, consisted of men's wear lines. In nearly thirty years of presence in America, the Dior conglomerate had shifted its focus from producing women's designer ready-to-wear to catering to career men.[38]

The 1980s were a turning point, in which the Dior headquarters started to re- gain control over its licensed lines. In that decade, Dior pursued forty-five li- censing contracts in the US market in various fields: men's wear, women's wear, accessories, children's clothes, and home decor. The brand then had the largest dress shirt and tie business in the United States, selling licensed products in de- partment stores across the country. In addition, Dior was considered to be the "only major designer business in the US" for men's scarves and handkerchiefs. The manufacturer Warnaco—originally Warner Brothers Corset Company, founded in 1874—was the main licensor for Dior's men's wear in the United States, yielding sales of more than $100 million in 1988, of which the royalties paid to Dior totaled over $5 million, or 25 percent of the total royalties from Christian Dior's US operations. The Warnaco Group was taken over in 2013 by the largest American luxury group, Phillips-Van Heusen (PVH), owner of numerous brands, including Calvin Klein and Tommy Hilfiger, and the major competitor to Ralph Lauren, an iconic brand for classic American style.[39]

From Boussac to Arnault

The appointment of Dominique Morlotti as Dior's head of men's wear design indicated that the time had come for change. Morlotti, who occupied the position from 1983 to 1992, decided to redress the Dior licensed sportswear lines and, in so doing, to shift production from synthetic fibers and blends to wool and cotton, aiming to imprint a more European sensibility onto the products made for the US market. During his twice-yearly visits to New York to examine the licensed products, Morlotti offered licensees constructive criticism and prepared written benchmark reports.[40] In the 1980s, women's wear turned out to be the most difficult segment of Dior's business in the United States, where some of these lines registered losses. One of the sore points was the women's sportswear that Dior had licensed to Jones Apparel Group. In 1986 this line registered a loss amounting to $9 million in sales for the year. Dior headquarters determined that the loss was primarily a consequence of production problems, but a question also lingered over the greater exposure of Dior's system of international royalties to monetary fluctuations. To address potential production problems, Dior headquarters imposed new quality controls. Jones Apparel hired a new designer, who followed Bohan's directives; subsequently, within less than two years, the lines licensed by Jones for Dior registered a 15 percent increase in sales. At that point in Dior's history, the choice to keep a decently large number of licenses was coherent with the firm's overall strategy of financializing its haute couture brands and including them in holdings.[41]

Income statements from the 1980s show an overall growth in both US sales and US royalties for Dior, which may indicate that the firm's closer control of its licenses was the right strategy for business in America. During the 1980s, and through to 1992, the yearly royalties that Dior earned in the United States amounted to double the firm's net profit, or roughly 5 percent of Dior's total US sales.[42] At that point, most Dior-branded goods sold in the United States were licensed to domestic manufacturers for production. A limited number of Dior lines sold in America were made in Europe. For example, the Dior umbrellas for men and women were designed in Paris, then part of them was made in Italy, and another part in Asia—a strategy that is increasingly popular among the large luxury groups based in Europe today. Production of Dior-branded luxury leather handbags was licensed to the firm Guene in France, while some less luxurious leather goods were produced in Japan; Dior licensed its fabric handbags to US manufacturers.[43]

The management at Dior followed the activity of the clusters and sites of production and carefully analyzed the competition in the American market, where it catered not only to higher-end consumers but also to the middle class that shopped in the department stores. Management teams kept abreast of any technical advancements by licensees as well. For example, Dior licensed its men's hosiery lines to manufacturer Camp, a division of Union/Fruit of the Loom. Men's hosiery was characterized by machine-intensive production. The reason Dior was able to grow its market share in this domain, explained the management, was that Union/Fruit of the Loom had enough capital to buy the latest technology in machinery, thereby keeping its production for Dior competitive, especially for knit products. Diversification of manufacturing and adaptation to local markets were major factors in the most successful of Dior's licensed lines.[44]

During that same period, Boussac proved unable to remedy the financial situation of his group, despite the closure of several of its textile firms and cutbacks in employee numbers. Boussac, a holding that included the house of Dior since the foundation of the haute couture firm in 1946, had to file for bankruptcy in the French courts. Several French firms showed interest in acquiring Dior, which—despite the brand's aging image, in comparison with Yves Saint Laurent, for example—remained the biggest and most prosperous French brand to have emerged from the business of haute couture. The French right-wing government of Valéry Giscard d'Estaing was not prone to interventionism, even in the ailing textile sector, but in the case of the selling of a business of the magnitude of Boussac's, the French authorities were eager to ensure that the buyer would be able to redress most of the group's firms. Two buyers remained in the last round: Maurice Bidermann and the Agache-Willot Group. Bidermann, born Maurice Zylberberg in Belgium, was the child of Jewish immigrants from Poland. He was a garment manufacturer producing for licensed brands, including Yves Saint Laurent and

André Courrèges. Pierre Bergé, the main financier and manager behind the Saint Laurent brand, was a part of Bidermann's bidding team. Bidermann would further develop his group internationally, including in the United States, with ownership of Calvin Klein men's sportswear and Ralph Lauren women's wear. But the French court deemed Bidermann too small to successfully absorb the Boussac Group, and the sale went to the four Willot brothers (Bernard, Jean-Pierre, Régis, and Antoine), who in the 1960s had founded a textile group specializing in medical bandages in Roubaix, the heart of the textile region of northern France. The Agache-Willot Group bought the Boussac Group in 1978 for 700 million francs. But the aging textile sector of the North kept accumulating losses, and the group, again, was unable to repair its finances. Agache-Willot filed for bankruptcy three years later.[45]

Bernard Arnault was an entrepreneur from northern France who joined his father at the helm of holding Ferret-Savinel, later called Férinel, a French leader in the construction of holiday real estate. Born in Croix, a commune adjacent to Roubaix, Arnault succeeded his father in 1978 and then spent three years trying to develop the family real estate business in the United States, where he became well acquainted with American methods of management. Arnault then moved back to France and bought the Agache-Willot Group in 1984. He set to the task of redressing the ailing group. To do so, Arnault sacrificed the firms that were unprofitable and did not match the profile he had in mind for his holding. In this process, a significant number of the group's smaller firms were closed, and numerous other firms downsized. The group laid off thirty-six hundred workers in 1985, bringing its total number of employees below ten thousand.[46] Among the group's remaining firms, the largest included furniture business Conforama, Paris department store Le Bon Marché, and Dior, still the most high-profile brand in the holding. On this foundation, Arnault built the world's largest luxury group. An essential step was the challenging and complex process through which he took control of Moët Hennessy Louis Vuitton (LVMH), an outcome that was achieved in 1990 and that revealed Arnault's tactical brilliance. Over the course of these events, Arnault managed to obtain the support of the left-wing French government led by Prime Minister Laurent Fabius. Licensing had become the core element in strategies of international expansion of haute couture brands that reconverted into luxury brands. Arnault limited the expansion of the licenses and then undertook several reorganizations of the brand's portfolio. The group maintained its specialization in luxury, but Arnault's investments represented an important diversification in agriculture, real estate, and supermarkets.[47]

During the phase in which Dior was integrated into the LVMH holding, its control over licensees evolved into a much more hands-on approach. LVMH monitored markets while aiming to realign the Dior brand with the highest luxury standards in terms of taste and means of production. In so doing, LVMH did not adopt a one-size-fits-all approach; to the contrary, the group carefully selected and revived some licenses on the basis of comparative assessments of various global markets. This strategy resulted in diversified product lines, as can be seen in the case of Dior-branded fashion watches. In the United States, Dior licensed its watches to the producer Memox, with the end product targeting middle- and upper-class consumers and retailing from $250 to $600 in department stores. The American Dior watches were conceived to be more middle-class products than the Dior-branded watches sold in Europe. This difference between the high-luxury lines sold in Europe and the somewhat more affordable luxury line sold in the United States appeared consistently in the transatlantic strategies of Dior. This was in part the result of the analysis waged at Dior headquarters, but also the result of a concept that had originated much earlier: that Paris offered more luxurious products, and that mid-luxury dominated in the US market.[48]

Selling Dior in the United States

The licensing business of haute couture went hand in hand with new developments in branding and advertising. When Dior was integrated into the LVMH group in the mid-1980s, the brand commissioned the full-service agency Chiat/Day Advertising, located on Fifth Avenue in New York, to design its US advertising campaigns.[49] When Morlotti visited the United States, he systematically met with Dior's licensees and visited Chiat/Day's client service. Dior budgeted around $4 million per year for advertising, 70 percent of which was paid for by Dior's forty-six licensees, and the rest by Dior's head office. The licensing contracts included an advertising clause in which the licensees agreed to spend a set amount of the volume they made for Dior on advertising. Most importantly, this budget was reserved for national campaigns, which would result from a concerted effort between Dior and the licensees. In the second half of the 1980s, the Dior headquarters worked to unify its advertising aesthetic. A result was the greater use of the Dior codes, certain traditional Dior symbols used to identify the brand, notably in the lifestyle advertisements realized by Chiat/Day. The agency conceived a worldwide campaign featuring the Louis XVI medallion chair, a staple of Dior's salons since the beginning. The agency reinvented these codes and aimed both to give them a universal appeal and to make them consistent across the globalizing markets that hungered for Paris-branded luxuries. In line with the campaign, Dior headquarters encouraged all licensees to include the Louis XVI chair in their displays and advertisements, with the clear aim of reinforcing the brand's visual identity.[50]

Christian Dior also had its own in-house public relations service that managed, among other tasks, the relationships between the licensees and the trade press. The functions of this office included calling journalists to announce the new collections and organizing the lending of Dior merchandise, especially haute couture items, to the American press for editorials and photo shoots. Dior's PR office took charge of the insurance and the transport of these loans. Another role of Dior's PR service was in the organization of prestigious events. Dior delegated the organization on the ground, in the case of the largest galas, to the New York–based agency Harriet Weintraub and Associates, which specialized in events for the luxury business, especially in the realms of fashion and real estate. Weintraub took charge of the galas that Dior held for several hundred guests at the Stephen A. Schwarzman building of the New York Public Library at 42nd Street, situated in Bryant Park, which remained a major site for the events of New York Fashion Week.[51]

While Dior was on its way to becoming a part of the global luxury business, the LVMH group increasingly secured premium retail locations. Real estate prices rose during the 1980s' real estate boom, and numerous retailers in the luxury sector had to abandon their original locations on Fifth and Madison Avenues. Dior was doing well and even dominated in some sectors of the US luxury markets, notably in men's wear, which allowed for an ambitious strategy in terms of retail spaces. Dior opened a boutique in 1989 in Waikiki, Hawaii, which was a prized shopping destination, and another boutique in 1990 on Madison Avenue, an old bastion of luxury that was accessible to only the most successful brands in the American market: the US-based Donna Karan, Ralph Lauren, and Fred Leighton; French luxury firms Balmain, Cartier, Yves Saint Laurent, and Sonia Rykiel; and the Japanese Kenzo Takada, who would sell his brand Kenzo to LVMH in 1993. Italian luxury entrepreneurs Giorgio Armani, Valentino Garavani, and Gianni Versace were also present among this group of high-end luxury firms. Most in this group were from Europe or, like Kenzo, had long settled in Europe, and industry insiders tended to perpetuate the notion that luxury was still a European rather than an American specialty.[52]

The Refoundation of Luxury into Global Groups

Under brand founder Christian Dior, the firm had focused on innovating in women's haute couture, with a few licenses in men's and women's accessories, beginning with neckties. Couturiers established luxury licenses first in the United States and then in other countries; Japan, for instance, was another pioneering market for luxury licenses. In Japan, Dior had held an exclusive contract since 1953 to sell its haute couture lines through a legal reproduction agreement at the department store Daimaru, based in Osaka. Then, under the aegis of Rouët, in 1964 Dior entered into a licensing agreement for the production of its ready-to-wear and cosmetic lines with Kanebo, a Japanese multinational that had started as a cotton spinning company in 1887. The lines were designed at Dior head-quarters in Paris and produced in Japan by Kanebo. Rouët had been aware of the importance of the Japanese market from the 1950s, and he aimed to hybridize the tastes of France, the United States, and Japan for that market. Most of the sales and revenue grew outside of Christian Dior's original expertise. In the United States, the brand proved remarkably adaptive in its development of men's wear and accessories, which grew steadily during the 1970s and 1980s. Meanwhile, women's wear was in an era of casualization. When Arnault and his LVMH holding took over Dior, an urgent task was to tidy the business of licenses; too numerous, and unmonitored, they could threaten the prestige of the brand name and weaken its sales. The integration of the house of Dior into the LVMH group produced comparative data that allowed a refining of strategies in the context of globalization, including in terms of pricing differentiation. To survive in the United States, Dior developed a three-pronged approach characterized by shutting down a portion of the brand licenses, modernizing the brand's advertising, and acquiring competitive retail locations. Dior advertised an increasingly unified image that aimed to flow seamlessly across cultures.[53]

As demonstrated by recent research on luxury groups, Arnault aimed to strike a balance between centralized and decentralized features for the LVMH brands on the path to making luxury global. At the turn of the millennium, Dior was one of the LVMH group's most profitable brands. Arnault has gradually sold or divested from the nonluxury brands, while diversity—with products ranging from wines to perfumes and couture—is at the core of the holding's ability to make luxury one of the most profitable sectors of its entrepreneurial activity. This is what happened in the conversion of the Dior firm from a haute couture salon to a global luxury brand. Dior lost some prestige when it entered global markets for licensed goods, but it was able to regain this prestige in the long term. Other brands, most notably couturier Pierre Cardin, never fully recovered from overlicensing: the Cardin brand name had 350 licensed products in 1977 and 540 in 1982. Cardin had also been a pioneer in the project of designing couture for all; and for his attempts to democratize, he was temporarily expelled from the Chambre Syndicale. But Cardin seems to be the exception. Another heavyweight in luxury licenses, the Italian firm Gucci (now a part of the second-biggest French luxury group, Kering), has also recovered from a period of overlicensing that was contemporary to Dior's. Yet another example is the British brand Burberry, which experienced some turbulence before regaining a foothold as a midrange global luxury firm. Examination of the longer-term history of the house of Dior, combined with analysis of the economy of haute couture, shows that it is when luxury started catering to much wider strata of consumers that it achieved profitability. At the end of the twentieth century, the luxury industry was dominated by three holdings, all based on the European continent: LVMH, Kering, and Richemont. LVMH is the most important, and its president, Arnault, is among the world's richest individuals. The acquisition by LVMH of Tiffany & Co., a jewelry brand that symbolizes American luxury, was under way when I was finalizing this book. It is the most expensive transaction ever conducted by Arnault, who may therefore acquire a top brand in jewelry, the only domain of luxury where he had not yet established leadership. This would consolidate the strength of the LVMH holding in comparison with other luxury conglomerates and notably Richemont, which holds a strong position in jewelry. The potential purchase of Tiffany & Co. by LVMH appears as a symbol of the dominance of France over the United States as far as the luxury industry is concerned.[54]

Luxury is a global business, and in the recent decades luxury holdings have grown considerably, notably in Asia and in the Middle East. The two closest competitors to Arnault are, however, based in Europe. Kering is (since 2013) the name of the French group founded by Francois Pinault in 1963 as Etablissements Pinault and then called Pinault-Printemps-Redoute (PPR). The group initially traded in timber but then branched out into the department store and mail-order business with French giant La Redoute and increasingly developed its luxury activities. By the turn of the millennium, PPR had acquired control of major luxury businesses—including Yves Saint Laurent, Balenciaga, Italian leather goods makers Gucci and Bottega Veneta, and French jeweler Boucheron—to which new brands have since been added. The Kering group has also developed an important portfolio of creative sportswear brands and is, especially in the person of son and successor Francois-Henri Pinault, involved in the visual arts through the Pinault Foundation. The Swiss group Richemont was founded in 1988 by a South African entrepreneur, Johannes Rupert. Richemont features fewer fashion businesses—notably, couturier Azzedine Alaïa, higher-end fashion designer Chloé, and leather goods firm Lancel—and has its core expertise in jewelry and watches, having acquired Baume & Mercier, Cartier, Jaeger-Le Coultre, Montblanc, Piaget, Vacheron Constantin, and Van Cleef & Arpels, among other notable brands.[55]

Luxury is also gaining a market share in the BRICS countries (Brazil, Russia, India, China, and South Africa) and, especially, in Asia. Large Asian cities—including Mumbai, Shanghai, and Tokyo—are capitals of fashion and luxury in their own right and foster creative design, even if numerous brands tend to adopt names for retail that sound French or Italian. An important question is whether the new luxury capitals will be able to develop global brand visibility in the face of the long history of French and other European cultural, and often also economic, dominance.[56] Alongside these important players, fashion groups were established in Asia in the 1980s, including the Japanese Fast Retailing Company (founded in 1984) and the Chinese Metersbonwe Group (1995). Both have acquired an impressive assortment of brands over the past decade that stretch from basic fashion to masstige and designer lines. As far as luxury is concerned, cases like Shanghai Tang show the challenge of integrating the aesthetic heritage of pre-Maoist design into modern luxury. Entrepreneur David Tang founded the luxury brand Shanghai Tang in Hong Kong in 1994, intending that it would be the answer to the haute couture houses. The brand sells luxury silk garments, accessories, and higher-end ceramics. The firm aims to be creative in terms of fashion designs, and its aesthetics gesture toward the Republic era, after the end of the Qing dynasty in 1912, especially as far as women's fashions are concerned. This choice allows the brand to veer away from the uniformity of the Mao era, as well as from controversial imperial ideals of beauty—for example, the practice of bound feet. Tang found shapes from the 1920s and 1930s to emulate within a historical repertoire that nods to both modern capitalism and luxury, while still looking to the past. Despite the high quality of the brand's products, Shanghai Tang faced creative struggles; in response, the management chose to hire Western designers. In 1998, the Richemont group bought Shanghai Tang. In 2017, the head of Richemont died, and shortly after, David Tang died as well. It is still too early to know which direction the brand will take in terms of design. A group of anthropologists including Lisa Rofel and Sylvia Yanagisako, who studied the interactions of Italian designer firms and Chinese manufacturers, have shown that all players in the industry identify European-ness as warranting good taste and fashionability, thereby denying the Chinese producers the ability to gain complete independence from European sources in terms of design content. Such studies seem to underline a phenomenon identified in the United States more than half a century before. It is not an inability to design that plagued American or Chinese entrepreneurs, but rather a lack of assertiveness as designers. In other words, prejudices, rather than design or taste, remained a problem.[57]

The Persistence of Private Luxury in the Fashion Industry in the New Millennium

Some luxury groups—for example, Chanel—have remained privately owned well into the twentieth century. In the quarter century following the mid-1980s the global value of the luxury sector grew ninefold, from $20 billion to $180 billion. Globalization was an essential factor in the growth of luxury, which is a group of industries notoriously difficult to define, composed as it is of higher-end market segments rather than of specific products. Haute couture firms, which were at the forefront of fashion design until the 1960s, became the jewel in the crown of the luxury groups. To this day, clothing and footwear companies dominate the luxury business as far as profits are concerned. Financialization offers greater security to the couturiers, whose profession is vulnerable to economic and political crises, and the large groups have often understood the need to preserve the creative freedom of the head designers in their haute couture houses, which has been analyzed in the case of LVMH in terms of centralized decentralization. Seen from the perspective of the creative designers, such an equation may still reveal the challenge of remaining creative in an independent manner while also resisting the great pressures of the industry, as the recent changes of designer at Dior, for example, show.[58]

Over the final decades of the twentieth century, most haute couture firms either wound down or were integrated into luxury holdings. While the three most significant of these groups are based in Europe, groups based in Asia, notably in China, and the Middle East are increasingly investing in luxury firms and acquiring stakes in Western luxury firms. Apart from very small-scale craftsmanship or start-ups, it has become extremely challenging to develop a creative, high-end haute couture operation outside of the financialization of the luxury business. Even couturiers considered to be exceptionally creative and independent have sought at least partial funding from the luxury groups. An important example is Paris couturier Azzedine Alaïa, born in Tunisia in 1935, who trained as a tailor at Christian Dior. Alaïa's unique creative talent and vision brought him success as a Paris couture house, especially from the 1980s, and he always managed to retain a private clientele smitten by his sleek designs and impeccable technique. Alaïa was known to want to remain a smaller, independent couture house that in most cases refused to retail in department stores, and yet he reached out for funding, initially in the early 2000s to the Italian group Prada, from which he bought himself out. In 2007 the Richemont group bought a stake in Alaïa, who until his death in 2017 worked to retain his creative freedom.[59]

Among the luxury brands that, for now, remain on their own amid a general movement of concentration in large holdings are Chanel and Hermès. Founded in 1837, Hermès originally specialized in luxury leather goods, and it has since developed a wider luxury fashion business. During the interwar period the brand hired designers, often with a cosmopolitan background, to design lines of clothing and scarves—notably its famed silk *carrés*, or square scarves; one such hire was stylist Lola Prusac, an immigrant from Poland who worked for the brand from 1925 to 1935. Prusac went on to open a small, eponymous haute couture firm and to secure membership in the Chambre Syndicale. Hermès had a long history as a powerful brand, with its core specialization in leather goods, which became central to the luxury industry after both haute couture and hats lost market share. Indeed, central to luxury fashion was the production of made-to-measure clothes and hats. When it became apparent that haute couture houses were increasingly conducting fittings at a loss, handbags became the core of production for luxury and fashion firms, as they were statement-making goods yet did not necessitate any fitting, thereby cutting the made-to-measure costs. A similar principle applied to the scarves and small jewelry in which Hermès specialized in addition to its expertise in leather goods. The longevity and status of Hermès made it a symbolic brand of French luxury—and one in which the LVMH group wished to acquire a majority stake. Starting in 2002, LVMH began to buy shares of Hermès silently through derivatives, until the holding owned 14 percent of Hermès in 2010. LVMH's strategy sounded alarm bells at the agency Autorité des Marchés Financiers (AMF), the French authority on financial markets. While LVMH kept augmenting its share in Hermès, the agency suspected that LVMH would attempt an equity swap and thus acquire a majority of the private group. The French state, through the AMF, intervened to prevent this from happening. Hermès had gone public in 1993, but the family resisted the acquisition and in the process received the support of the French government.[60]

Chanel is another important case of a luxury firm built on haute couture and perfume that has remained privately held. In 1983, twelve years after the death of founder Gabrielle Chanel, Karl Lagerfeld—the son of a German business family and designer for his eponymous brand and for the Italian label Fendi— took over as head designer of Chanel. Today, Chanel is still a private group, owned by the brothers Alain and Gérard Wertheimer, grandsons of cofounder Pierre Wertheimer; it comprises the Chanel brands, including couture and perfumes, and a group of other small luxury firms. Besides the Chanel brand itself, the private group led by the Wertheimer family has, over the past decades, consistently pursued the enterprise of acquiring smaller, mostly Parisian artisans. These small firms pursue their activities as decentralized elements under the helm of a special division of the Chanel Group called Paraffection (the French term *par affection* meaning "as a token of affection"). This branch now includes embroidery house Lesage (formerly Michonet, founded in 1858), flower maker Guillet (1869), feather artisan Lemarié (1880), bootmaker Massaro (1884), glove maker Causse (1892), hat maker Maison Michel (1936), embroidery firm Montext (1939), costume jeweler Robert Goossens (1953), and Scottish knitwear firm Barrie (1903). The communication of the Chanel Group reveals that such an operation is more an enterprise in conservation, aiming to preserve these artisanal firms from creative destruction, than a strategy to acquire full control over suppliers. As such, the group offers these small firms the means to survive within the helm of the Chanel group. For the first time in 108 years, the house of Chanel published its results in June 2018: $1.86 billion profit after tax for the year 2017. Shortly after, in 2019, head designer Karl Lagerfeld died after thirty-six years as the creative head of the firm.[61]

The integration of haute couture into the luxury groups, and the process of expansion of these groups, which experts often describe as a process of financialization, happened at the same time that the status of haute couture was changing—a change accurately described as patrimonialization. Haute couture has become a rarefied craft that is still a laboratory of style as well as a tool to advertise and lend authenticity to branded luxury products. This luxury has become, at least in some segments of accessories, cosmetics, and perfumes, accessible to increasingly large numbers of consumers. Haute couture has, in the meantime, found a growing place in museums. Important museums have historically featured prominent costume and textile galleries. Yet, a symbolic moment occurred in 2000, when the Solomon R. Guggenheim Museum in New York mounted the exhibit *Giorgio Armani: A Retrospective*. The Italian couturier was considered the first to have received treatment equal to that of an artist—that is, in the high arts such as painting and sculpture. The show sparked controversy, as it brought into question the traditional boundaries between art forms. Most couturiers did not describe their couture work as art, although many of them practiced fine arts in addition to haute couture. By the turn of the millennium, commerce was entering the museums and, to some observers, bore the risk of threatening their independence—Armani had himself donated $15 million to the Guggenheim at the time of his show. Numerous couturiers have since been granted a retrospective in major museums around the world, and fashion has become a staple of exhibitions that also tend to generate record levels of visits.[62]

Consumers of garments and accessories produced by the brands in the luxury groups are in search of objects that qualify as timeless, classic, and, often, good investments. Many of these items have reached this status in the most literal sense. A tweed jacket from the house of Chanel, a quilted bag from the same haute couture house, or a leather handbag from the house of Hermès can bring a higher price when sold as a vintage object than when sold as new. This phenomenon shows that luxury objects, even those made by fashionable brands, have often become timeless classics. The consumer who seeks to invest will buy such an object to enjoy for several seasons and most likely pass it on to the next generation. As a statement, such objects need to be easy to recognize, and so from this vantage point, too, luxury objects can be quite static. For most, fashion has migrated out of the realm of luxury.[63]

Conclusion

n 2016, management consulting firm McKinsey published its inaugural report on the fashion business, called *The State of Fashion*.[1] The report forecast the growth of newer markets, especially in Russia, Asia, and Africa, and mapped out new and emerging fashion capitals in China, the Middle East, and Latin America. This report was also, to some extent, the result of an industry panic. For the first time since the end of World War II, growth in the fashion business was slowing down, and new ways of consumption were becoming mainstream (for example, renting luxury clothing and accessories instead of buying them new). Consumers were also increasingly buying clothes secondhand, including in middle-market segments—a practice previously (although not exclusively) limited to the less affluent strata of society. Other consumers either bought less clothing or stopped buying new clothes and accessories for months. Such consumer behaviors had thus far been restricted to activists but, over the past few years, when McKinsey started examining the problem, had come to have a wider impact. Reasons for such changes were multiple, including a long-distance solidarity with the workers subjected to risky conditions of labor, and environmental concerns. To this was added, in 2020, a pandemic that had the effect of further slowing down fashion consumption and resulted in higher numbers of bankruptcies for fashion firms. As a consequence, the fast pace of growth in the fashion industries is slowing down—a pace that may have seemed unstoppable to the garment industry manufacturers in New York and the Sentier manufacturers in Paris over the past century.

During the twentieth century, fashion shifted from the elites to the masses. It remained an industry centered on the process of endless novelty. While the sewing machine remained at the heart of innovation, fashion entrepreneurs and designers kept the innovation constant, feeding themselves to the great variety of cultural sources they could find in cultural and economic capitals, in fashionable resorts, in their travels, and in galleries and exhibitions. Paris and New York offered the designers close contact with cultural sources, with the art world, and with wealth, all of which were important in nurturing the fashion industry at least until haute couture started to fade during the 1960s.

The word *fashion* finds its origins in the making *à façon* (literally "custom making") of made-to-measure, personalized dress. Over time the increased precision in sizing also allowed consumers to purchase ready-made clothes. The process of dressing was, among nearly all consumers and for most of the last century, a personal mix of old and new, higher and lower design content, machine-made and homemade or customized. The generation of the baby boomers, who endorsed the youth fashions of the 1960s and abandoned the direction of haute couture, still sewed many of the items in their wardrobes at home on their own sewing machines. It is only during the last quarter of the twentieth century that the sewing machine became an item reserved to a hobby and that the provenance of worn clothes was entirely off the rack. This way of consumption, in the greater picture, may only be a brief historical moment, as new habits of consumption have gained traction in recent years.

Rapid changes in consumption and in markets have made the fashion firms quite vulnerable. American marketing experts of the first half of the century found that the biggest risk to the industry was in anticipating the whims of the consumer. An entire profession of fashion consultants, capitalizing on trend risk, kept traveling across the Atlantic to find inspiration. American entrepreneurs Tobé and Amos Parrish sought to provide affordable translations of Paris haute couture for the masses in the United States. During the postwar period, the delegation of French manufacturers headed by Albert Lempereur along with other study travels funded by the Marshall Plan were inspired by Tobé's business to modernize the obsolete French ready-to-wear industry.

For most of the century, at least until the 1960s—from the time of Charles Frederick Worth to the early careers of Pierre Cardin and Yves Saint Laurent— haute couture provided direction to the fashion industry, a hundred-year system in which haute couture ruled and was admired by fashion-conscious consumers all over the world. Paris directed the trends, but the role of markets was essential in adopting, adapting, and disseminating them. In comparison with the economic weight of New York's garment district, which reproduced trends for the largest consumer market in the world, the economic output of Paris fashions was modest. And yet, to this day, the largest holdings in the so-called fast-fashion system, as well as the most important luxury holdings, are based in Europe. Examining Paris fashion helps us to understand the endurance of the industry in Europe, even in times of seemingly irresistible Americanization.

Fashion did not happen in Paris or in New York but between the two countries, as a common enterprise born of the circuits of exchanges. The fashion trade could follow several routes. Retailers, buyers, commissionaires, forecasters, photographers, sketchers, and journalists all played a role in the dissemination of fashion that took an increasingly nonmaterial form throughout the century. Equally powerful were both authorized and nonauthorized channels of dissemination. For an entrepreneur based in the United States, traveling to Paris was an expensive investment. Diverse kinds of networks offered Americans access to Paris design without having to spend money on traveling. Subscriptions to the well-received forecasts delivered by Tobé or Amos Parrish were less than half the price of a trip to Paris. Yet another option was to rely on sketching services that delivered unauthorized drawings after the release of the Paris collections, as Frederick Milton did.

The cluster of design innovators based in Paris lobbied legislators during the entire twentieth century to obtain more protection for fashion designs. Considering the derivative nature of fashion itself, which is a cultural system based on imitation, couturiers had few chances to curb copying, but they still spent a great deal of time and energy in suing all types of infringement on what they considered to be their intellectual property rights. Entrepreneurs of the early twentieth century, including Jeanne Paquin, Paul Poiret, and Madeleine Vionnet, made considerable efforts to curb the makers of substitute products in France and in the United States. Vionnet started winning an increasing number of cases and integrated intellectual property into her strategies to assert her authority on the domestic market, thereby sending some of her direct competitors out of business. Couturiers entertained close ties with the high arts, and Poiret tended to view himself as an artist. Vionnet, who was the most stringent advocate of high intellectual property rights for couture, defined herself not as an artist but rather as a craftswoman. Whichever way they defined their trade, this generation of couturiers fostered a marketing of authenticity and contributed to the luster of Paris as a cultural capital. The symbiotic relationship between haute couture and tourism was well known by the governments at both the state and city levels and thus the governments provided continuous help to haute couture in the forms of tax reductions and subventions.

The haute couture trade was international from the outset. In Paris, Madame Roger, arguably the first entrepreneur to offer the mix of design and retail that would come to define the industry, offered services in French and English to a domestic and international clientele with refined tastes. In New York, couturiers Lucile and Boué Sœurs were immigrants with a cosmopolitan background and branch stores on three continents. This dynamic of exchange was fueled by the political upheavals of the twentieth century and the successive waves of immigrants who settled in both fashion capitals, supplying the trade with some of its most innovative entrepreneurs. The fashion trade fostered success among an unusually high number of women and gay individuals engaging in international business. The figure of the fashion designer as an entrepreneur was a powerful branding tool. What this history shows, however, is that behind the most successful designers stood the discreet figures of skilled managers, most often trained in economics or in law. The right mix of creativity and finance was to be found more frequently in a duo than in one single entrepreneur. A delicate balance of creative freedom and economic soundness remains one of the most important challenges of the industry to this day.

The internationalization of the firms themselves was a slow process. The accounting of Jeanne Paquin, for instance, shows that fashion, as a trade, was very sensitive to economic and political crises. The system of credit that haute couture offered for a long time to its clients, and that was rooted in the practices of the ancien régime, also weakened the treasury of early couture. After a few years of internationalization of the haute couture firms between Paris, London, and, to a lesser extent, New York, World War I had the effect of sending most of these international firms back to their domestic markets. World War I did not put a halt to the exchanges between Paris and New York fashion entrepreneurs, buyers, and clients, but the branching out of firms came to a halt. Few Americans tried to reverse the tide of Paris fashion. Among those who did was the extremely successful Main Bocher, born in Chicago and a former journalist at US *Vogue*, who became a much-appreciated Paris couturier until World War II sent him back to the United States.

During those years, the volatility of the New York garment district firms increased. The devaluation of the French franc in the 1920s had a negative impact on the international commerce of haute couture that was only aggravated by the Great Depression. An early attempt at financialization of haute couture by the banker Georges Aubert, who was associated with the Ponzi schemes of the French bank Oustric, failed spectacularly and resulted in a greater unwillingness of the haute couture profession and financiers to trust each other. On both sides of the Atlantic, the Great Depression and the tariff wars put a quasi-complete halt to the internationalization of couture and garment firms. Those that survived generally downsized by laying off personnel, who in turn often reacted to untenable living conditions with social unrest. The social measures engineered by the Front Populaire in France and the New Deal in the United States were central in redressing the trade as well as in providing some surveillance of the conditions of production. In New York, Maurice Rentner—known as the dean of the garment district, who had started his career with the foundation of several nonunionized shops—launched a movement of legitimization of US fashion under the auspices of a professional association, the Fashion Originator's Guild of America, that aimed to authenticate the garments, provide stronger brand identity, and curb recurring sweatshop production. Rentner managed to obtain the adhesion of a majority of firms in the garment and fashion business of New York, but he came under scrutiny for infringement to fair competition. The FTC issued a cease and desist order to the Fashion Originator's Guild of America, considerably weakening its position in the long run and curbing any attempt at building an intellectual property rights system in the United States that would be equivalent to the one in France.

Fashion entrepreneurs never stopped traveling across the Atlantic. American entrepreneurs went to find inspiration in Paris even when their budgets for buying haute couture designs with official reproduction rights had diminished. In turn, Paris fashion entrepreneurs went to the United States to study the market; there, they sold less haute couture than designs for clothes and accessories, and, increasingly, perfumes and cosmetics. While Paris couturiers stopped opening haute couture branches in the United States during most of the interwar period, they did open American perfume branches. The restrictive rules of the Chambre Syndicale, intended to keep the production and retail of haute couture in Paris, did not forbid the couturiers from manufacturing and retailing branded perfumes and cosmetics in the United States and elsewhere, and the couturiers who did so were very well received. The attempts of Paris couturiers to produce their own lines of ready-to-wear clothes were less convincing, apart from Lucien Lelong, whose Edition line—launched in 1934, and more demi-couture than ready-to-wear—was met with success.

World War II was in many respects a time of exceptions in the fashion industry. Although some ties remained between Paris and New York, especially through the media and through private individuals, the US fashion entrepreneurs refused entirely to trade with firms working under the occupation of the Nazi regime. Most couturiers in Paris managed to keep their businesses open during the war, as well as most of their branches in the French province resorts. Lelong, who during the interwar period had been an ardent supporter of exchanges between Paris couture and the US fashion trade, took charge of the fashion industries now under control of the German occupation authorities. Lelong managed not only to obtain an exemption from the war-rationing policies for a group of several dozen haute couture firms but also to secure quantities of primary materials that allowed them to remain open and keep their personnel at work. In 1943, the Chambre Syndicale negotiated legal protection for the name *haute couture*. Paris couture, despite being cut off from major foreign markets, remained profitable during the occupation by selling both to clients in the neutral countries and to the occupier. Restrictions and rationing imposed on American garment production by the US War Production Board limited the creative ambitions of the industry there, starting in 1942, but the city of New York nonetheless strengthened its position during the war years. In 1943, Mayor Fiorello La Guardia inaugurated the New York fashion center, and the Fashion Institute of Technology opened its doors to students the following year. Indeed, New York's status as the world's fashion capital gained momentum during World War II.

During the occupation, Paris haute couture firms sold their products to clients, in most cases whatever their origins and politics. Only a handful of these firms were investigated after the war for illicit profits. Yet the Vichy regime systematically excluded Jewish entrepreneurs from business life, subjecting their firms to a process of Aryanization in which the Jewish owners were replaced by Aryan ones. In haute couture, this was the case for Jacques Heim, who managed to escape and to hide for the rest of the war in the South of France. Entrepreneurs with an "enemy" background—for example, British entrepreneurs, such as couturier Edward Molyneux—were also excluded. Numerous smaller entrepreneurs, especially the less affluent ones, were unable to escape the racist policies of the Vichy regime and many of them were sent to the concentration camps. After Paris was liberated, on August 25, 1944, it seemed clear that the city had lost its hegemony over women's fashion design.

After the war, the fashion trade questioned Lelong but did not condemn him, rather recognizing that he had kept most of the industry's workers employed, thereby allowing them to avoid obligatory work in Germany. What Lelong could have done for the communities persecuted during the war was the topic of few discussions. Lelong, however, stepped down from his leadership functions and opted for early retirement. While rationing remained in place for many long months after the war, a tangible reality for populations on both sides of the Atlantic, a question for the fashion trade was whether Paris couture would regain its former prominence. Christian Dior, a relative newcomer who had trained with Lelong among other couturiers, became the figurehead of the postwar resurgence of Paris design. Most importantly, Dior benefited from large capital investments by a pioneer in French textile and garment manufacturing, Marcel Boussac. Equipped with large cash reserves and excellent managers, Dior branched out to New York, Great Britain, Australia, and South America. His firm produced mainly clothes, accessories, perfumes, and cosmetics abroad, thereby avoiding the problems with US Customs that had plagued many of his predecessors, such as Boué Sœurs and Marcel Rochas. An elaborate system of investments mediated through the intermediary of Central and South American firms also helped Boussac transfer capital to the United States more easily than if coming directly from France. Dior succeeded where the others had failed in establishing an haute couture multinational. Furthermore, Dior established a system of licenses and of royalties that contributed to the circulation of profits between branches and the mother ship in Paris. So far, the Paris fashion industry had remained a local cluster fostered by a rich hinterland supplying high-quality materials and by international commerce. After more than three decades, the Chambre Syndicale de la Couture Parisienne finally decided to sell haute couture for reproduction to French domestic manufacturers and department stores, which resulted in millions in additional revenue.

Within the Boussac Group, the house of Dior thrived until the premature death of Christian Dior in 1957, ten years after the foundation of the firm. Maurice

Rentner died that same year. Numerous cases in this book demonstrate the endurance of the family business at both ends of the fashion industry. Whether producing mass-manufactured garments for all or luxury goods for the few, family remains central both in the methods of management and in the patterns of transmission of ownership.

The newer business models that followed in the footsteps of New York garment district entrepreneurs and aimed to offer affordable fashions to all were retail firms. The most innovative of them emerged in rather peripheral places. Fast-fashion firms achieved global success with the development of IT systems that enabled fast responses to consumer demands, thereby avoiding delays in restocking and allowing copies of a piece seen on the catwalk to appear on their shop floor in less than two weeks. With two types of firms, the slower-paced H&M and the faster-paced Zara, the fashion industry achieved the democratization of its production. However, their methods of production relied on the relocation of much of their production, thereby often resulting in a loss of control over labor conditions at their suppliers. For this reason, such models of production came under scrutiny at the end of the century. The initial ideal of democratic fashions found itself confronted with the race to the bottom that characterizes the globalization of manufacturing. Increasingly, overproduction and overconsumption of fashion engendered by easy access to cheap clothing became part of the critique of these large chains during the recent decades.

With the advent of the welfare state, the conditions of haute couture production changed drastically, rendering the industry obsolete. It no longer responded to the needs of nearly all market segments, and design now emerged from new generations of creators who worked for the ready-to-wear industry. Stylists could be found in Paris but were equally thriving in the other Big Four cities of London, Milan, and New York, as well as other fashion cities. Haute couture became a rarefied craft that justified the authenticity of the branding of ever-increasing accessories, perfumes, and cosmetics. The French government offered several financial assistance programs to haute couture, marking the industry's entry in a process of patrimonialization, a form of museum industry and cultural diplomacy. The concentration of firms in large holdings allowed them to conduct the pursuit of haute couture at a loss. In this phase, Dior remained a leading example, as the ailing Boussac Group was taken over by, first, the Agache-Willot Group and, subsequently, industrialist Bernard Arnault, who redressed the business of Dior and made it the flagship of his luxury holding LVMH—which today is the world's largest luxury group, followed by Kering, also based in France, and the group Richemont, based in Switzerland. The fashion market is changing fast as a result of challenging times for the environment, the health of workers, and production, which may result in further changes for the luxury industries, in which couture has found a safe haven.

Notes

Introduction

1. Claudia d'Arpizio, Federica Levato, Daniele Zito, and Joëlle de Montgolfier, *A Time to Act: How Luxury Brands Can Rebuild to Win*, Luxury Goods Worldwide Market Study, Fall–Winter 2015 (Boston: Bain, 2015); Kerry A. Dolan and Luisa Kroll, "Forbes 2016 World's Billionaires: Meet the Richest People on the Planet," *Forbes*, March 1, 2016, https://www.forbes.com/sites /luisakroll/2016/03/01/forbes-2016-worlds-billionaires-meet-the-richest-people-on-the-planet /#4a85aa7c77dc; "Global Fashion Industry Statistics: International Apparel," Fashion United, n.d., https://fashionunited.com/global-fashion-industry-statistics, accessed June 1, 2017; "New Maloney Report: Americans Spent Nearly $380 Billion on Fashion in 2015," Rep. Carolyn B. Maloney (website), September 6, 2016, https://maloney.house.gov/media-center/press-releases/new-maloney -report-americans-spent-nearly-380-billion-on-fashion-in-2015.

2. Michael B. Miller, *The Bon Marché: Bourgeois Culture and the Department Store, 1869–1920* (Princeton, NJ: Princeton University Press, 2018); Rosalind Williams, *Dream Worlds: Mass Consumption in Late Nineteenth-Century France* (Berkeley: University of California Press, 1982); William Leach, *Land of Desire: Merchants, Power, and the Rise of a New American Culture* (New York: Vintage, 2011); Vicky Howard, *From Main Street to Mall: The Rise and Fall of the American Department Store* (Philadelphia: University of Pennsylvania Press, 2015); Emily Remus, *A Shopper's Paradise* (Cambridge, MA: Harvard University Press, 2019).

3. Nancy L. Green, *Ready-to-Wear and Ready-to-Work: A Century of Industry and Immigrants in Paris and New York* (Durham, NC: Duke University Press, 1997); Andrew Godley, *Jewish Immigrant Entrepreneurship in New York and London, 1880–1914: Enterprise and Culture* (New York: Palgrave, 2001); Mary Lynn Stewart, *Dressing Modern Frenchwomen: Marketing Haute Couture, 1919–1939* (Baltimore: Johns Hopkins University Press, 2008); Caroline Evans, *The Mechanical Smile: Modernism and the First Fashion Shows in France and America, 1900–1929* (New Haven, CT: Yale University Press, 2013).

4.   Christopher Breward and David Gilbert, eds., *Fashion's World Cities* (Oxford: Berg, 2006); Sven Beckert, *The Monied Metropolis: New York and the Consolidation of the American Bourgeoisie, 1850–1896* (Cambridge: Cambridge University Press, 1993); Emmanuelle Loyer, *Paris à New York: Intellectuels et artistes français en exil, 1940–1947* (Paris: Grasset, 2005); Bernard Marchand, *Paris, histoire d'une ville, XIXe–XXe siècle* (Paris: Seuil, 1993); Saskia Sassen, *The Global City: New York, London, Tokyo* (Princeton, NJ: Princeton University Press, 1991); Tyler Stovall, *Paris Noir: African Americans in the City of Light* (Boston: Houghton Mifflin, 1996); Richard Caves, *Creative Industries: Contracts between Art and Commerce* (Cambridge, MA: Harvard University Press, 2000).

5.   Philip Scranton, *Figured Tapestry: Production, Markets and Power in Philadelphia Textiles, 1855–1941* (Cambridge: Cambridge University Press, 1989); Philip Scranton, *Endless Novelty: Specialty Production and American Industrialization, 1865–1925* (Princeton, NJ: Princeton University Press, 1997); Regina L. Blaszczyk, *Imagining Consumers: Design and Innovation from Wedgwood to Corning* (Baltimore: Johns Hopkins University Press, 2001); Regina L. Blaszczyk, ed., *Producing Fashion: Commerce, Culture, and Consumers* (Philadelphia: University of Pennsylvania Press, 2007); Regina L. Blaszczyk, "Aux couleurs franco-américaines: Quand la haute couture parisienne rencontre la confection new-yorkaise," *Le Mouvement social: Revue d'histoire sociale* 221, no. 4 (2007): 9–31; Alfred D. Chandler, *Scale and Scope: The Dynamics of Industrial Capitalism* (Cambridge, MA: Harvard University Press, 1994).

6.   Richard Kuisel, *Capitalism and the State in Modern France: Renovation and Economic Management in the Twentieth Century* (Cambridge: Cambridge University Press, 1981); Hubert Bonin and Ferry de Goey, eds., *American Firms in Europe, 1880–1980: Strategy, Perception and Performance* (Geneva: Droz, 2009); Victoria de Grazia, *Irresistible Empire: America's Advance through 20th Century Europe* (Cambridge, MA: Belknap Press of Harvard University Press, 2005); Marie-Laure Djelic, *Exporting the American Model: The Post-War Transformation of European Business* (Oxford: Oxford University Press, 1998); Daniel T. Rodgers, *Atlantic Crossings: Social Politics in a Repressive Age* (Cambridge, MA: Belknap Press of Harvard University Press, 2000); Philippe Roger, *L'ennemi américain: Généalogie de l'anti-américanisme français* (Paris: Seuil, 2002); Jan Logemann, *Engineered to Sell: European Emigrés and the Making of Consumer Capitalism* (Chicago: University of Chicago Press, 2019).

7.   Roland Barthes, *Système de la mode* (Paris: Seuil, 1967).

8.   Green, *Ready-to-Wear.*

9.   Paul Bairoch, *Victoires et déboires: Histoire économique et sociale du monde du XVIe siècle à nos jours*, 3 vols. (Paris: Gallimard, 1997); Suzanne Berger, *Notre première mondialisation: Leçons d'un échec oublié* (Paris: Seuil, 2003).

10.   Stephanie Lake, *Bonnie Cashin: Chic Is Where You Find It* (New York: Rizzoli, 2016); Alexandra Palmer, *Dior: A New Look, a New Enterprise (1947–1957)* (London: Victoria and Albert Museum, 2009).

11.   Sara Beth Marcketti, "Design Piracy in the United States' Women's Ready-to-Wear Apparel Industry: 1910–1941" (PhD diss., Iowa State University, 2005).

12. Caves, *Creative Industries;* Walter Friedman and Geoffrey Jones, "Creative Industries in History," *Business History Review* 85, no. 2 (2011): 237–244.

13. Jonathan M. Barnett, "Shopping for Gucci on Canal Street: Reflections on Status Consumption, Intellectual Property, and the Incentive Thesis," *Virginia Law Review* 91, no. 6 (2006): 1381–1423.

14. Caroline R. Milbank, *New York Fashion: The Evolution of American Style* (New York: Harry N. Abrams, 1989).

15. Bibi Zorina Khan, *The Democratization of Invention: Patents and Copyrights in American Economic Developments, 1790–1920* (Cambridge: Cambridge University Press, 2005); Valerie Steele, *Paris Fashion: A Cultural History* (Oxford: Oxford University Press, 1988).

16. Lourdes M. Font, "International Couture: The Opportunities and Challenges of Expansion, 1880–1920," *Business History* 54, no. 1 (2012): 30–47; Véronique Pouillard, "The Early Globalization of the Fashion Business" (paper presented at the Business History Conference, Denver, Colorado, March 31, 2017); Véronique Pouillard and Waleria Dorogova, "Couture Ltd.: French Fashion's Debut in London's West End," *Business History,* published online February 20, 2020.

17. Betty Kirke, *Madeleine Vionnet* (San Francisco: Chronicle Books, 2012), 9.

18. Jean Allman, ed., *Fashioning Africa: Power and the Politics of Dress* (Bloomington: Indiana University Press, 2004); Linda Welters and Abby Lillethun, eds., *Fashion History: A Global View* (London: Bloomsbury, 2018); Parminder Bhachu, *Dangerous Designs: Asian Women Fashion the Diaspora Economies* (London: Routledge, 2004); Tereza Kuldova, *Luxury Indian Fashion: A Social Critique* (London: Bloomsbury, 2016); Douglas Bullis, *Fashion Asia* (London: Thames & Hudson, 2000).

1. The Early Internationalization of Haute Couture

1. Léonore database, Jacob Jeanne Marie Charlotte, 19800035/1481/72058, Etat-civil, Extrait du Registre des Actes de Mariage, Ville de Saint-Germain-en-Laye, année 1891, n. 17, Archives Nationales de France, Paris (hereafter cited as FNA); *Encyclopaedia Universalis,* s.v. "Paquin," by Catherine Ormen, accessed January 16, 2016, https://www.universalis.fr/encyclopedie /paquin/.

2. Véronique Pouillard, "A Woman in International Entrepreneurship: The Case of Jeanne Paquin," in *Entreprenørskap i næringsliv og politikk: Festskrift til Even Lange,* ed. Knut Sogner, Einar Lie, and Håvard B. Aven (Oslo: Novus Forlag, 2016), 189–210.

3. Nancy Green, *Ready-to-Wear and Ready-to-Work* (Durham, NC: Duke University Press, 1997); Olivier Saillard, ed., *Fashion Mix: Mode d'ici, créateurs d'ailleurs* (Paris: Flammarion, 2014); Thorstein Veblen, *The Theory of the Leisure Class: An Economic Study of Institutions* (New York: Macmillan, 1899); Christopher Bayly, *The Birth of the Modern World, 1780–1914: Global Connections and Comparisons* (Oxford: Blackwell, 2004), 238–239; William Leach, *Land of Desire: Merchants, Power and the Rise of a New American Culture* (New York: Vintage Books, 1993).

4. Camille Doublot, *La protection légale des travailleurs de l'industrie du vêtement* (Paris: L. Larose, 1899), 9–11.

5. Thierry Maillet, "Histoire de la médiation entre textile et mode en France: Des échantillonneurs aux bureaux de style (1825–1972)" (PhD diss., EHESS, Paris, 2013); Regina Lee Blaszczyk, *The Color Revolution* (Cambridge, MA: MIT Press, 2013), 31.

6. Doublot, *La protection légale*, 11–12; "Le Roi de la Mode," *Le Gaulois*, March 11, 1895, p. 1; Chantal Trubert-Tollu, Françoise Tétart-Vittu, Fabrice Olivieri, and Jean Marie Martin-Hattenberg, *La Maison Worth (1858–1954): Naissance de la Haute Couture* (Paris: Editions la Bibliothèque des Arts, 2017).

7. Ryan Lampe and Petra Moser, "Do Patent Pools Encourage Innovation? Evidence from the Nineteenth-Century Sewing Machine Industry," *Journal of Economic History* 70, no. 4 (2010): 898–920; Andrew Godley, "Selling the Sewing Machine around the World: Singer's International Marketing Strategies, 1850–1920," *Enterprise & Society* 7, no. 2 (2006): 266–314.

8. Trubert-Tollu et al., *La Maison Worth*, 188–189.

9. Jacques Makowsky, *Histoire de l'industrie et du commerce en France* (Paris: Editions d'Art et d'Histoire, 1926), 118; Trubert-Tollu et al., *La Maison Worth*; E. J. Scott, "Fried or Truffled Couture? Debunking the Myth That House of Worth Was the Sole Domain of the Ultra-Wealthy" (paper presented at the conference Nouveaux regards sur la Haute Couture parisienne, de 1850 à nos jours, Institut National d'Histoire de l'Art, Paris, March 24, 2017).

10. "Discours de M. Aine," *Bulletin de l'Association Générale du Commerce et de l'Industrie des Tissus et des Matières Textiles*, March 21, 1914, p. 669; Robert Plantel, "La toilette féminine en 1897: La grande couture parisienne et les industries françaises qui s'y rattachent," *Le Figaro*, special supplement, August 19, 1897, pp. 1–2; Doublot, *La protection légale*, 41–58; Jean-Pierre Hirsch, "Revolutionary France, Cradle of Free Enterprise," *American Historical Review* 94, no. 5 (1989): 1281–1289; Alain Plessis, *Naissance des libertés économiques: Liberté du travail et liberté d'entreprendre. Le décret d'Allarde et la loi Le Chapelier: Leurs conséquences, 1791–fin XIXe siècle* (Paris: Institut d'Histoire de l'Industrie, 1993).

11. "Société Dœuillet, Limited. 16 and 18, Place Vendôme, Paris," H661, Société Ch. Drecoll, Archives Nationales du Monde du Travail (Roubaix) (hereafter cited as ANMT); Susan North, "John Redfern and Sons, 1847 to 1892," *Costume* 42, no. 1 (2008): 145–168; Susan North, "Redfern Limited, 1892 to 1940," *Costume* 43, no. 1 (2009): 85–108; Geoffrey G. Jones, *Multinationals and Global Capitalism: From the Nineteenth to the Twenty-First Century* (Oxford: Oxford University Press, 2005); Mira Wilkins, *The Emergence of Multinational Enterprise* (Cambridge, MA: Harvard University Press, 1970).

12. "Company Meetings. Paquin, limited," *Financial Times*, n.d., 1900, n.p., H672, ANMT; Paquin, Memorandum of Articles of Association, London, 1904, 9, H672, ANMT.

13. Paquin, Memorandum of Articles of Association, London, 1904, 1, H672, ANMT; Paquin, Ltd., Report, 1897, 1–4, H672, ANMT.

14. "Les couturiers en actions [*sic*]," *Le Globe*, December 31, 1903, Press clippings file, H642, Beer, ANMT; *La Ville Lumière: Anecdotes et documents historiques, ethnographiques, lit-*

téraires, artistiques, commerciaux et encyclopédiques (Paris: Direction et administration, 1909), 90; Mathilde Héliot, "La maison de couture Beer" (master's thesis, Université Paris-Sorbonne, 2016).

15. Incorporation documents, File BT 31/17380/83458, Martial and Armand & Co., Ltd., British National Archives, London (hereafter cited as BNA).

16. Plantel, "La toilette féminine."

17. Paquin, "Company Meetings. Paquin, limited," *Financial Times*, n.d., 1900, n.p., H672, ANMT.

18. Louis Magné, "Robes et Manteaux," *Le Courrier de la Bourse et de la Banque*, December 3, 1903, Press clippings file, H642, ANMT.

19. Pouillard, "Case of Jeanne Paquin," 205; Paquin, Limited, press clippings file, March 1908, H672, ANMT; Emile Laurier, "Douze millions de frivolités," *Le Figaro*, April 26, 1907, p. 1.

20. File Maison Agnès, H632, ANMT.

21. Waleria Dorogova, "Boué Soeurs," in *The Berg Encyclopedia of World Dress and Fashion: Global Perspectives*, ed. Joanne B. Eicher and Phyllis G. Tortora (London: Bloomsbury, 2017), accessed 20 August 2020; Foundation of a company limited by shares, May 21, 1906, BT 31/17764/88838, BNA; Copy of register of directors or managers of Boué Sœurs limited, October 18, 1906, BT 31/17764/88838, BNA.

22. "The Story of John Barker & Co Ltd, Kensington, London," version 2, April 2007, University of Glasgow Archive Service, http://www.gla.ac.uk/media/media_91174_en.pdf.

23. Ch. Drecoll, press clippings file, H661, ANMT; "Société G. Beer Limited," *Le Répertoire financier*, November 4, 1909, n.p., H642, ANMT; Dœuillet, press clippings file, H660, ANMT; Véronique Pouillard, "The Rise of Fashion Forecasting and of Fashion Public Relations, 1920–1940: The History of Tobé and Bernays," in *Globalizing Beauty: Consumerism and Body Aesthetics in the Twentieth Century*, ed. Hartmut Berghoff and Thomas Kühne (New York: Palgrave, 2013), 160.

24. Claire Haru Crowston, "The Queen and Her 'Minister of Fashion': Gender, Credit, and Politics in Pre-revolutionary France," *Gender & History* 14, no. 1 (2002): 92–116.

25. Andrea Colli, *The History of Family Business, 1850–2000* (Cambridge: Cambridge University Press, 2003), 10.

26. Nancy Troy, *Couture Culture: A Study in Modern Art and Fashion* (Cambridge, MA: MIT Press, 2003), 131–133; Mary E. Davis, *Classic Chic: Music, Fashion, and Modernism* (Berkeley: University of California Press, 2006), 38–47.

27. Georges Aubert, *La finance américaine* (Paris: Ernest Flammarion, 1910).

28. Dœuillet, printed document "Societe Dœuillet, Limited," November 11, 1907, 2, H660, ANMT; Dœuillet, foundation act, BT 31/18149/94098, BNA.

29. Dœuillet Ltd., Prospectus, July 1907, H660, Dœuillet, ANMT.

30. Maison Agnès, bulletin, June 13, 1913, H632, Agnès, ANMT.

31. Maison Agnès, press clippings file, H632, ANMT.

32. Maison Agnes, H632, ANMT.

33. Subfile 1914, "Maison Agnès," Supplément à la France économique et financière, March 28, 1914; "Maison Agnès," *La petite cote de la Bourse, Journal financier quotidien,* March 13, 1914, p. 1; "Maison Agnès," *Guide de la Bourse et de la Banque,* February 7, 1914, Maison Agnès, H632, ANMT.

34. Dœuillet file, H660, ANMT; Martial and Armand & Co., Ltd., BT 31/17380/83458, BNA.

35. "Les Couturiers en actions [*sic*]," *Le Globe,* September 31, 1903, H642, Beer, ANMT.

36. "Company Meetings. Paquin, limited," *Financial Times,* n.d., 1900, n.p., H672, ANMT.

37. H632, Agnès, press clippings file, ANMT.

38. "Paquin Limited," 1908, H672, ANMT.

39. Paquin Ltd. Report, London, February 25, 1913, H672, ANMT; Martial and Armand & Co., Ltd., BT 31/17380/83458, BNA.

40. Alfred D. Chandler, *Scale and Scope: The Dynamics of Industrial Capitalism* (Cambridge, MA: Harvard University Press, 1994), 59–61; "Prosperous Paquin, Ltd.," *Financial Times,* March 19, 1903, n.p., H672, ANMT.

41. "Prosperous Paquin, Ltd."

42. Véronique Pouillard, *Hirsch & Cie Bruxelles (1869–1962)* (Brussels: Editions de l'Université Libre de Bruxelles, 2000), 50; Werner Sombart, *Luxury and Capitalism* (Ann Arbor: University of Michigan Press, 1967), 88, 170; "Prosperous Paquin, Ltd."; "Paquin's Sundry Debtors," *Financial Times,* March 10, 1905, n.p., H672, ANMT; Erika Diane Rappaport, *Shopping for Pleasure: Women in the Making of London's West End* (Princeton, NJ: Princeton University Press, 2001).

43. Makowsky, *Histoire de l'industrie,* 112; H672, ANMT; *Archives commerciales de la France,* August 28, 1897, p. 1085.

44. Makowsky, *Histoire de l'industrie,* 118.

45. Paquin Ltd. Reports, London, March 4, 1910, 1, and February 25, 1913, 1, both H673, ANMT; Jose Blanco F., Patricia Kay Hunt-Hurst, Heather Vaughan Lee, and Mary Doering, eds., *Clothing and Fashion: American Fashion from Head to Toe,* vol. 1 (Santa Barbara, CA: ABC-CLIO, 2016), 24; Lourdes M. Font, "International Couture: The Opportunities and Challenges of Expansion, 1880–1920," *Business History* 54, no. 1 (2012): 38–39; Angel Kwolek-Folland, *Incorporating Women: A History of Women and Business in the United States* (New York: Palgrave, 1998); Valerie Steele, *Paris Fashion: A Cultural History* (London: Bloomsbury, 1998).

46. Joy Spanabel Emery, *A History of the Paper Pattern Industry: The Home Dressmaking Fashion Revolution* (London: Bloomsbury, 2014), 60–71.

47. Green, *Ready-to-Wear;* Morris De Camp Crawford, *The Ways of Fashion* (New York: G. P. Putnam's Sons, 1941), 171; Helen Everett Meiklejohn, *Dresses: Impact of Fashion on a Business* (New York: McGraw-Hill, 1938), 343; Saskia Sassen, *The Global City: New York, London, Tokyo* (Princeton, NJ: Princeton University Press, 1991), 4.

48. Meiklejohn, *Dresses,* 314–315.

49. Crawford, *Ways of Fashion,* 14; Meiklejohn, *Dresses,* 326.

50. Meiklejohn, *Dresses*, 304; "Rentner Dies," *Women's Wear Daily*, July 8, 1958, pp. 1, 19, Resseguie Collection, Baker Library, Harvard Business School, Boston (hereafter cited as BL, HBS).

51. "Interview with Ira Rentner, younger brother of Maurice Rentner," interview by Mildred Finger, New York, August 31, 1982, 85, Oral History Project of the Fashion Industries, Fashion Institute of Technology, New York (hereafter cited as FIT).

52. Meiklejohn, *Dresses*, 312–313; Green, *Ready-to-Wear*.

53. Meiklejohn, *Dresses*, 321.

54. "Interview with Arthur Jablow," interview by Mildred Finger, New York, May 14, 1982, 20, and "Interview with Selma Frankel, daughter of Maurice Rentner," interview by Mildred Finger, New York, August 31, 1982, 30, both in Oral History Project of the Fashion Industries, FIT; "Rentner Dies," *Women's Wear Daily*.

55. Susan A. Glenn, *Daughters of the Shtetl: Life and Labor in the Immigrant Generation* (Ithaca, NY: Cornell University Press, 1991); Alice Kessler-Harris, *Gendering Labor History* (Champaign: University of Illinois Press, 2006); Gus Taylor, *Look for the Union Label: History of the International Ladies' Garments Workers' Union* (New York: Routledge, 2016).

56. Green, *Ready-to-Wear*, 155–158.

57. Bertram J. Perkins, "Glimpses of Paris," *Women's Wear Daily*, April 26, 1939, p. 4.

58. The Fashion Group Inc., Wednesday afternoon, September 27, 1939, Biltmore Hotel, New York, 18, box 73, folder 6, Fashion Group International Archive, Special Collections, New York Public Library (hereafter cited as FG, NYPL).

59. The Fashion Group Inc., Wednesday afternoon, September 27, 1939, Biltmore Hotel, New York, speaker Edna Woolman Chase, 29, box 73, folder 6, FG, NYPL.

60. The Fashion Group Inc., Wednesday afternoon, September 27, 1939, Biltmore Hotel, New York, 29, box 73, folder 6, FG, NYPL.

61. "Le Syndicat de Défense de la Grande Couture Française et des Industries qui s'y Rattachent," *Le Style parisien, revue mensuelle*, 1915, pp. 23–25; "Chambre Syndicale de la Couture: Séance du Comité du 18 mars 1914," *Bulletin de l'Association générale du commerce et de l'industrie des tissus et des matières textiles*, April 15, 1914, p. 696.

62. Font, "International Couture," 38–39; Marlis Schweitzer, "American Fashions for American Women: The Rise and Fall of Fashion Nationalism," in *Producing Fashion: Commerce, Culture, and Consumers*, ed. Regina L. Blaszczyk (Philadelphia: University of Pennsylvania Press, 2008), 130–149; Niki C. Lefebvre, "Beyond the Flagship: Politics and Transatlantic Trade in American Department Stores, 1900–1945" (PhD diss., Boston University, 2016), 61.

63. "Paquin Ltd., London. Review of the Years' Business," *Financial Times*, March 25, 1914, reprint folio, n.p., H672, ANMT; Caroline Evans, *The Mechanical Smile: Modernism and the First Fashion Shows in France and in America, 1900–1929* (New Haven, CT: Yale University Press, 2013), 70–71; M. Putois, "Questions de jurisprudence: Robes et manteaux," *Revue mondiale, économique et financière*, February 28, 1911, p. 261, H672, ANMT.

64. Palmer White, *Poiret le magnifique: Le destin d'un grand couturier* (Paris: Payot, 1986), 115–117, 239–242.

65. John Bayley Swinney, *Merchandising of Fashions* (New York: Ronald Press, [1942]), 40; Troy, *Couture Culture.*

66. Troy, *Couture Culture*, 212, 217.

67. Paul Poiret, "First News of French Fashion Syndicate's Official Plans," *New York Times*, January 23, 1916, p. 2; Sophie Kurkdjian, *Lucien Vogel et Michel de Brunhoff, parcours croisés de deux éditeurs de presse illustrée au XXe siècle* (Paris: Institut Universitaire de Varenne, 2014), 166–167; Mary Lynn Stewart, "Copying and Copyrighting Haute Couture: Democratizing Fashion, 1900–1930s," *French Historical Studies* 28, no. 1 (2005): 103–130; Troy, *Couture Culture*, 302, 311.

68. Schweitzer, "American Fashions," 130–149; Troy, *Couture Culture*, 269–274, 281; Poiret, "First News," 2.

69. Plantel, "La toilette féminine," 2.

70. Pouillard, *Hirsch & Cie Bruxelles.*

71. "Tribunaux: Le procès Ch. Drecoll-Montaillé," *Le Matin*, July 16, 1916, p. 2; "La Maison de Couture Ch. Drécoll," *Bulletin de la Ligue anti-allemande: Organe de défense des intérêts économiques français et coloniaux*, August 1, 1916, pp. 6–7; "Ch. Drecoll Limited," *Le Journal des transports: Revue internationale des chemins de fer et de la navigation*, May 13, 1911, p. 248.

72. Félix Belle, "Chronique des Tribunaux: Le procès de la maison Drecoll. Deuxième audience," *Le Gaulois: Littéraire et politique*, July 9, 1916, pp. 3–4; "Les Tribunaux: La maison Drecoll contre M. Aine-Montaillé, président du syndicat," *L'action française, organe du nationalisme intégral*, July 14, 1916, p. 1.

73. Jean-Claude Daumas, "Marcel Boussac, 1889–1980," in *Dictionnaire historique des patrons français*, ed. Jean-Claude Daumas (Paris: Flammarion, 2010), 120–122.

74. *Bulletin de l'Association Générale du commerce et de l'industrie des tissus et des matières textiles*, December 17, 1913, p. 167.

75. Maude Bass-Krueger, "From the *union parfaite* to the *union brisée:* The French Couture Industry and the *midinettes* during the Great War," *Costume* 47, no. 1 (2013): 28–44; "L'audience: La grève des midinettes," *Le Matin*, July 27, 1918, p. 2; *Statistique des grèves et des recours à la conciliation* (Paris: Ministère du commerce, de l'industrie, des postes et des télégraphes, 1921), vi–vii.

76. Plantel, "La toilette féminine," 1–2.

77. *Bulletin de l'Association Générale du commerce et de l'industrie des tissus et des matières textiles*, December 17, 1913, p. 167.

78. Philippe Simon, *La haute couture: Monographie d'une industrie de luxe* (Paris: Presses Universitaires de France, 1931), 93–94.

79. Chanel documentation file, The Costume Institute's Irene Lewisohn Costume Reference Library, Metropolitan Museum of Art, New York; Bertram J. Perkins, "Newer Couturiers Finding Place in Fashion Sun," *Women's Wear Daily*, February 11, 1929, p. 4; Myrbor advertisement, *L'Officiel*, January 15, 1923, pp. 18–19; Myrbor advertisement, *L'Officiel*, October, 1923, p. 51; *L'Officiel*, March 15, 1923, cover page; Claire Zalc, *Melting Shops: Une histoire des commerçants étrangers en France* (Paris: Perrin, 2010), 163.

80. "Paquin, Limited," *Information*, March 25, 1914, H672, ANMT.

81. H672, press clippings file, ANMT; Patricia Tilburg, "Mimi Pinson Goes to War: Taste, Class and Gender in France, 1900–1918," *Gender & History* 23, no. 1 (2011): 101.

82. Mary Louise Roberts, *Civilization without Sexes: Reconstructing Gender in Postwar France, 1917–1927* (Chicago: University of Chicago Press, 1994); Christine Bard, *Les Garçonnes: Modes et fantasmes des années folles* (Paris: Flammarion, 1998); Edmond Goblot, *La barrière et le niveau: Etude sociologique sur la bourgeoisie française moderne* (1925; Paris: Presses Universitaires de France, 2010), 1–3; H672, press clippings file, ANMT.

83. "Ch. Drecoll., Ltd.," 1922, H661, Ch. Drécoll, ANMT.

84. Molyneux & Cie, société à responsabilité limitée au capital de 1,400,000 francs, Paris, 1919, H1351, Molyneux, ANMT.

2. Branding Haute Couture

1. "Jeunes mariés," *Fémina*, June 24, 1932, p. 34; "Grands mariages," *Le Monde Illustré*, January 25, 1936, p. 83; *Vogue* (Paris ed.), May 1, 1926, p. 26; *L'Officiel*, February 1930, p. 32.

2. Twelfth Criminal Court of the Seine, December 30, 1921, D1U6 001654, City of Paris Archives (hereafter cited as CPA).

3. Kolleen Guy, "Rituals of Pleasure in the Land of Treasures: Wine Consumption and the Making of French Identity in the Late Nineteenth Century," in *Food Nations: Selling Taste in Consumer Societies*, ed. Warren Belasco and Philip Scranton (New York: Routledge, 2002), 34–47; Martin Bruegel and Alessandro Stanziani, "Pour une histoire de la *sécurité alimentaire*," *Revue d'histoire moderne et contemporaine* 51, no. 3 (2004): 7–16; Alessandro Stanziani, "Information, Quality, and Legal Rules: Wine Adulteration in 19th-Century France," *Business History* 51, no. 2 (2009): 268–291.

4. Alessandro Stanziani, "Wine Reputation and Quality Controls: The Origins of the AOCs in 19th Century France," *European Journal of Law and Economics* 18, no. 2 (2004): 149–167; Kolleen Guy, *When Champagne Became French: Wine and the Making of a National Identity* (Baltimore: Johns Hopkins University Press, 2003), 139–144.

5. Valérie Marchal, "Brevets, marques, dessins et modèles: Evolution des protections de propriété industrielle au XIXe siècle en France," *Documents pour l'histoire des techniques* 17 (2009): 8; Gabriel Galvez-Behar, *La République des inventeurs: Propriété et organisation de l'innovation en France (1791–1922)* (Rennes: Presses Universitaires de Rennes, 2008), 210.

6. Hermine Valabrègue, *La propriété artistique en matière de modes* (Paris: Librairie générale de Droit et de Jurisprudence, 1935), 83.

7. Twelfth Criminal Court of the Seine, 1921, CPA: "avec quelques modifications d'ordre secondaire qui n'ont été entreprises que pour dissimuler l'imitation."

8. Betty Kirke, *Madeleine Vionnet* (San Francisco: Chronicle Books, 2012), 118.

9. Ibid., 221.

10. Twelfth Criminal Court of the Seine, 1921, CPA: "le résultat d'une expérience et d'un travail personnel, qu'ils joignent le plus souvent, à leur élégance, à leur goût très sûr, un cachet d'originalité indéniablement esthétique qui les individualise." Valabrègue, *La propriété artistique*, 105; Marie-Christine Piatti, "Le droit de la mode" (unpublished presentation, Fashion History seminar, Institut d'Histoire du Temps Présent, Paris, April 28, 2006), 3–7.

11. Twelfth Criminal Court of the Seine, 1921, CPA.

12. Nancy L. Green, *Ready-to-Wear and Ready-to-Work: A Century of Industry and Immigrants in Paris and New York* (Durham, NC: Duke University Press, 1997), 104; Solange Montagné-Villette, *Le Sentier, un espace ambigu* (Paris: Masson, 1990).

13. Designs by Miler Sœurs were published alongside haute couture designs from Jane Regny, Claire Any, and Martial et Armand in *Vogue* (Paris ed.), July 1930, p. 67.

14. James Laver, *Dress: How and Why Fashions in Men's and Women's Clothes Have Changed during the Past Two Hundred Years* (London: John Murray, 1950); Barbara Vinken, *Fashion Zeitgeist: Trends and Cycles in the Fashion System* (Oxford: Berg, 2005), esp. 41–59; Marc Desley, "Modèles de grande couture," *Le Radical*, December 10, 1921, p. 3; Twelfth Criminal Court of the Seine, 1921, CPA; "Vionnet Wins in Case against Style Copyists," *Women's Wear Daily*, December 31, 1921, p. 1.

15. "The Dressmakers of France," *Fortune*, August 1932, p. 75; Kirke, *Madeleine Vionnet*, 30; Caroline Evans, *The Mechanical Smile: Modernism and the First Fashion Shows in France and America, 1900–1929* (New Haven, CT: Yale University Press, 2013), 168n62; Pamela Golbin, *Madeleine Vionnet, puriste de la mode* (Paris: Les Arts Décoratifs, 2009), 26, 292; Mary Lynn Stewart, "Copying and Copyrighting Haute Couture: Democratizing Fashion," *French Historical Studies* 28, no. 1 (2005): 112, 128.

16. Claude A. Rouzaud, *Un problème d'intérêt national: Les industries du luxe* (Strasbourg: Librairie du recueil Sirey, 1946), 115.

17. Ibid., 116.

18. Naomi Lamoreaux and Jean-Laurent Rosenthal, "Legal Regime and Contractual Flexibility: A Comparison of Business's Organizational Choices in France and the United States during the Era of Industrialization," *American Law and Economics Review* 7, no. 1 (2005): 28–61; Béatrice Touchelay, "Statistiques et secret des affaires," in *Dictionnaire des patrons en France*, ed. Jean-Claude Daumas (Paris: Flammarion, 2010), 944–949; Hubert Bonin, *Les banques et les entreprises (1919–1935)*, vol. 2, *Les banques françaises de l'entre-deux-guerres* (Paris: Plage, 2000), 198; Philippe Simon, *La haute couture: Monographie d'une industrie de luxe* (Paris: Presses Universitaires de France, 1931), 128.

19. "Dressmakers of France," 75; Rouzaud, *Un problème d'intérêt national*, 122; Pierre Vernus, *Art, luxe et industrie: Bianchini-Férier, un siècle de soieries lyonnaises* (Grenoble: Presses Universitaires de Grenoble, 2006), 100–104; Morris De Camp Crawford, *The Ways of Fashion* (New York: Putnam, 1941), 194; Werner Sombart, *Luxury and Capitalism* (1913; Ann Arbor: University of Michigan Press, 1976), 87–88; Simon, *La haute couture*, 26–27; "Dressmakers of France," 76, 78.

20. Emmanuèle Peyret, "Les Callot, de filles en aiguille," *Libération*, July 25, 2015, http://www.liberation.fr/cahier-ete-2015/2015/07/22/les-callot-de-filles-en-aiguille_1352094;

Kirke, *Madeleine Vionnet*, 32; Nancy O'Bryant, "Facets of Madeleine Vionnet's Cut: The Manipulation of Grain, Slashing, and Insets," *Clothing and Textiles Research Journal* 11, no. 2 (1993): 32–33; Nancy O'Bryant, "Insights into the Innovative Cut of Madeleine Vionnet," *Dress* 12, no. 1 (1986): 80; "Couturiers Who Count," *Women's Wear Daily*, June 26, 1931, p. 4; Golbin, *Madeleine Vionnet, puriste*, 29; Caroline Rennolds Milbank, *Couture: The Great Designers* (New York: Stewart, Tabori & Chang, 1985), 63.

21. Georges Le Fèvre, *Au secours de la couture (industrie française)* (Paris: Editions Baudinière, 1929), xviii–xix; Mary Lynn Stewart, *Dressing Modern Frenchwomen: Marketing Haute Couture, 1919–1939* (Baltimore: Johns Hopkins University Press, 2008), 128–129; Nancy Troy, *Couture Culture: A Study in Modern Art and Fashion* (Cambridge, MA: MIT Press, 2003), 234–251; André Allart and Paul Carteron, *La Mode devant les Tribunaux: Législation et jurisprudence* (Paris: Librairie de la société du Recueil Sirey, 1914), 3–6.

22. *Gazette du Palais* 1 (1920): 178; Valabrègue, *La propriété artistique*, 100.

23. "Dossier de Légion d'Honneur d'Adolphine Marie Berthe Gerber, born in Paris 10 February 1857," LH/1121/31, database Léonore, FNA; Stewart, *Dressing Modern Frenchwomen*, 7.

24. Kal Raustiala and Christopher Sprigman, "The Piracy Paradox: Innovation and Intellectual Property in Fashion Design," *Virginia Law Review* 92 (1996): 1687–1777; Kal Raustiala and Christopher Sprigman, *The Knockoff Economy: How Imitation Sparks Innovation* (Oxford: Oxford University Press, 2012), 19–55.

25. Valabrègue, *La propriété artistique*, 100.

26. *Gazette du Palais* 1 (1920): 178; Valabrègue, *La propriété artistique*, 100–101: "Il n'est pas possible que deux personnes absolument étrangères et ne travaillant pas ensemble puissent arriver, à l'aide d'un document, à combiner un modèle dont les ressemblances sont aussi saisissantes."

27. Angel Kwolek-Folland, *Incorporating Women: A History of Women and Business in the United States* (New York: Palgrave, 1998); Geoffrey J. Jones, *Beauty Imagined: A History of the Global Beauty Industry* (Oxford: Oxford University Press, 2010); Malia McAndrew, "A Twentieth-Century Triangle Trade: Selling Black Beauty at Home and Abroad, 1945–1965," *Enterprise and Society* 11, no. 4 (2010): 784–810; Catherine Omnès, *Ouvrières parisiennes: Marché du travail et trajectoires professionnelles au 20ᵉ siècle* (Paris: Edition de l'Ecole des hautes études en sciences sociales, 1997), 33–34; G. Frèrejouant du Saint and Eugène Godefroy, "Dessins et modèles.—V. Contrefaçon.—Propriété littéraire et artistique. Chapitre I. Généralités et notions historiques," in *Répertoire général alphabétique du droit français*, ed. G. Frèrejouant du Saint and Eugène Godefroy (Paris: Recueil Sirey, 1926), suppl. t. 5, 342; Anne Chanteux, "Les inventives: Femmes, inventions et brevets en France à la fin du XIXᵉ siècle," *Documents pour l'histoire des techniques* 17 (2009): 90–97; Bibi Zorina Khan, *The Democratization of Invention: Patents and Copyrights in American Economic Development, 1790–1920* (Cambridge: Cambridge University Press and NBER, 2005), chaps. 5 and 6.

28. Kirke, *Madeleine Vionnet*, 32–33; Milbank, *Couture: The Great Designers*, 160; Madeleine Vionnet & Cie, acte sous seing privé, July 5, 1922, and April 4, 1923, D31U3 002083, CPA; Sylvie Aubenas and Xavier Demange, *Elegance: The Séeberger Brothers and the Birth of*

Fashion Photography, 1909–1939 (San Francisco: Chronicle Books, 2007), 99; Michael Miller, *The Bon Marché: Bourgeois Culture and the Department Store, 1869–1920* (Princeton, NJ: Princeton University Press, 1981), 54–55; David Landes, "French Entrepreneurship and Industrial Growth in the Nineteenth Century," *Journal of Economic History* 9, no. 1 (1949): 45–61; Lamoreaux and Rosenthal, "Legal Regime and Contractual Flexibility"; Michel Lescure, "Les entrepreneurs européens à la fin des années trente," *Revue économique* 5, no. 2 (2000): 336.

29. Société Madeleine Vionnet, livres des ventes, April–November 1924, July–November 1928, and October–November 1937, Union Centrale des Arts Décoratifs, Paris (hereafter cited as UCAD).

30. Paul Johnson, *Creators: From Chaucer and Dürer to Picasso and Disney* (New York: HarperCollins, 2006), 227; O'Bryant, "Innovative Cut of Madeleine Vionnet," 73–86; Kirke, *Madeleine Vionnet;* Golbin, *Madeleine Vionnet, puriste,* 50–51.

31. Madeleine Vionnet & Compagnie, Acte sous seing privé du 15 juin 1919, July 5, 1922, D31U3 002083, CPA; Maison Vionnet, Collaborateurs: correspondance, presse, copy of Louis Dangel's work contract, 1–3, Madeleine Vionnet boxes, Documentation Center, UCAD.

32. John Palfrey, *Intellectual Property Strategy* (Cambridge, MA: MIT Press, 2012), 11; Robert Mouquet, "Points de droit," *L'Officiel de la Couture et de la Mode,* January 1922, p. 28.

33. *Le Temps,* September 19, 1920, n.p.

34. Ibid.

35. Mouquet, "Points de droit," 28; Stewart, *Dressing Modern Frenchwomen,* 7; Marc Martin, *Trois siècles de publicité en France* (Paris: Odile Jacob, 1992), 114, 117; Gilles Feyel, "Prémices et épanouissement de la rubrique de fait divers, 1631–1848," *Les Cahiers du Journalisme* 14 (2005): 26–28; Dominique Kalifa, "Usages du faux: Faits divers et romans criminels au XIXe siècle," *Annales: Histoire, Sciences Sociales* 54, no. 6 (1999): 1345–1362; Jürgen Habermas, *Strukturwandel der Öffentlichkeit* (Frankfurt: Hermann Luchterhand Verlag, 1962), chap. 6; Nadège Sougy, "Imitations, composition et renouvellement de l'offre, XVIIe–XXe siècles," *Entreprises et histoire* 78 (2015): 7.

36. "Les Etrennes des contrefacteurs," *L'Officiel,* December 1921, p. 15; "Avis divers: Les Etrennes des contrefacteurs," *Le Temps,* December 8, 1921, n.p.; Sarah Newman and Matt Houlbrook, "The Press and Popular Culture in Interwar Europe," *Journalism Studies* 14, no. 5 (2013): 640–650; Stewart, *Dressing Modern Frenchwomen,* 123; Florence Brachet Champsaur, "Madeleine Vionnet and the *Galeries Lafayette:* The Unlikely Marriage of a Parisian Couture House and a French Department Store, 1922–1940," *Business History* 54, no. 1 (2012): 48–66; "Têtes mises à prix," advertisement, *Le Temps,* March 16, 1921, p. 5.

37. Copy of the Madeleine Vionnet brand registrations, Madeleine Vionnet boxes, UCAD; Emmanuelle Serrière, "The Invention of the Label," in *Paris Haute Couture,* ed. Olivier Saillard and Anne Zazzo (Paris: Flammarion, 2012), 28.

38. Troy, *Couture Culture,* 331, 42–47; Champsaur, "Vionnet and the *Galeries Lafayette,*" 48–66; "Sliding Price Scale for Boex Copies of Vionnet's Models," *Women's Wear Daily,* November 21, 1921, p. 21; Palmer White, *Poiret le Magnifique: Le destin d'un grand couturier*

(Paris: Payot, 1986), 117; Stéphane Lacroix and Emilie Bénéteau, *Luxe et licences de marque: Comment renforcer l'image et les résultats financiers d'une marque de luxe* (Paris: Eyrolles, 2012), 18–19; "Les Etrennes des contrefacteurs," 15; Hillel Schwartz, *The Culture of the Copy: Striking Likenesses, Unreasonable Facsimiles* (New York: Zone Books, 1996), chap. 2; "Avis divers: Les Etrennes des contrefacteurs."

39. "Sliding Price Scale," 21.

40. Véronique Pouillard, "Managing Fashion Creativity: The History of the Chambre Syndicale de la Couture Parisienne during the Interwar Period," *Investigaciones de Historia Economica/Economic History Research* 5, no. 2 (2015): 1–16; Georges Lefranc, *Les organisations patronales en France du passé au présent* (Paris: Payot, 1976); Michel Offerlé, *Sociologie des organisations patronales* (Paris: La Découverte, 2009), 14.

41. Richard Kuisel, *Capitalism and the State in Modern France: Renovation and Economic Management in the Twentieth Century* (Cambridge: Cambridge University Press, 1981), 21–22.

42. Alexandra Palmer, *Couture and Commerce: The Transatlantic Fashion Trade in the 1950s* (Vancouver: University of British Columbia Press, 2001), 14; Claire Lemercier, "Looking for *Industrial Confraternity:* Small-Scale Industries and Institutions in Nineteenth-Century Paris," *Enterprise and Society* 10, no. 2 (2009): 304–334; Claire Lemercier, *Un si discret pouvoir, aux origines de la Chambre de Commerce de Paris, 1803–1853* (Paris: La Découverte, 2003), 212–238; Alain Chatriot, "Les ententes: Débats juridiques et dispositifs législatifs (1923–1953); La genèse de la politique de la concurrence en France," *Histoire Economie et Société* 27, no. 1 (2008): 7–22; Luca Lanzalaco, "Business Interest Associations," in *The Oxford Handbook of Business History*, ed. Geoffrey G. Jones and Jonathan Zeitlin (Oxford: Oxford University Press, 2007), 294; Offerlé, *Sociologie des organisations patronales*, 62–86.

43. Didier Grumbach, *Histoires de la mode*, 2nd ed. (Paris: Edition du Regard, 2008), 30; Committee meeting minutes, July 27, 1937, Chambre Syndicale de la Couture Parisienne Archive (hereafter cited as CSCPA); L. Lelong to M. Cognet, Paris, November 18, 1937, 2, CSCPA; Michel Offerlé, "L'action collective patronale en France, 19e–20e siècles: Organisations, répertoires et engagements," *Vingtième siècle: Revue d'histoire* 114 (2012): 89.

44. Lemercier, "Looking for *Industrial Confraternity*," 322–326; Elodie Voillot, "Imiter sans copier, imiter pour créer: Les détours de la contrefaçon dans le bronze d'art au XIXᵉ siècle," *Entreprises et Histoire* 78 (2015): 49–50; *Bulletin de l'Association Générale du commerce et de l'industrie des tissus et matières textiles*, January 1932, pp. 4–8.

45. Yuniya Kawamura, *The Japanese Revolution in Paris Fashion* (Oxford: Berg, 2004), 60–69; Grumbach, *Histoires de la mode*, 90–103; Committee meeting minutes, May 30, 1933, 1, CSCPA; Questionnaire relatif à la classification couture-création, January 1952, Maison Marcel Rochas, 1, F12 10504, FNA.

46. Because it gathered such a diverse spectrum of luxury industries, Dangel's association can be positioned as a predecessor to the Comité Colbert (http://www.comitecolbert.com/), founded in 1954 to represent the French luxury industries.

47. Simon, *La haute couture*, 153–154; "Nouvelles diverses. France. Contre les voleurs de modèles," *La Propriété industrielle*, May 31, 1923, p. 70; "Association pour la défense des 'arts plastiques et appliqués' en France et à l'étranger," n.d., 2, Collaborateurs: correspondance, presse, Maison Vionnet, Madeleine Vionnet boxes, Documentation Center, UCAD; Christine Senailles, "Lutter contre la copie," in *Madeleine Vionnet: Les années d'innovation* (Lyons: Musée des Tissus, Paroles d'Aube, 2002), 9–12; "Paris Anti-Copyist Society Renews Its Activities," *Women's Wear Daily*, February 28, 1923, p. 20; Maison Vionnet, Collaborateurs: correspondance, presse, Exposition 1925, Madeleine Vionnet boxes, Documentation Center, UCAD.

48. Simon, *La haute couture*, 156–157; "Nouvelles diverses," 70; "Association pour la défense des arts plastiques et appliqués," UCAD.

49. Bertram J. Perkins, "Glimpses of Paris: Paris Group Would Join Germans to Fight Piracy," *Women's Wear Daily*, June 18, 1929, p. 5.

50. "Nouvelles diverses," 70.

51. "Paris Anti-Copyist Society," 20.

52. "Paris Anti-Copyist Society," 20.

53. Simon, *La haute couture*, 155; Marcel Plaisant, *De la protection internationale de la propriété industrielle: Collected Courses of the Hague Academy of International Law* (Leiden: Brill, 1932), 458–459; Perkins, "Glimpses of Paris," p. 5.

54. Champsaur, "Vionnet and the *Galeries Lafayette*," 52; Golbin, *Madeleine Vionnet, puriste*, 36–47.

55. "Un luxe bien français," *Le Petit Parisien*, January 30, 1924, p. 2. The same advertisement appeared in *Le Figaro*, January 31, 1924, p. 2.

56. Adrian Johns, *Piracy: The Intellectual Property Wars from Gutenberg to Gates* (Chicago: University of Chicago Press, 2009), 124–125; Carla Hesse, "The Rise of Intellectual Property, 700 B.C.–A.D. 2000: An Idea in the Balance," *Daedalus* 131, no. 2 (2002): 26–45; David Lefranc, "The Metamorphosis of Contrefaçon in French Copyright Law," in *Copyright and Piracy: An Interdisciplinary Critique*, ed. Lionel Bently, Jennifer Davis, and Jane C. Ginsburg (Cambridge: Cambridge University Press, 2010), 55–79; Susan Scafidi, *Who Owns Culture? Appropriation and Authenticity in American Law* (New Brunswick, NJ: Rutgers University Press, 2005), 18.

57. Eugène Soleau, *De la protection des modèles d'art appliqués à l'industrie, loi française du 11 mars 1902* (Paris: Imprimerie typographique Charles Blot, 1902).

58. Du Saint and Godefroy, "Dessins et modèles.—V. Contrefaçon," suppl. t. 5, 337.

59. Stewart, *Dressing Modern Frenchwomen*, 113–115; Evans, *Mechanical Smile*, 63–64.

60. Simon, *La haute couture*, 156–157; P.-P. Martin, "La protection des Dessins et Modèles," *La France active: Organe de toutes les formes de l'activité nationale*, February 15, 1932, p. 114; Rouzaud, *Un problème*, 145.

61. "Loi sur les dessins et modèles du 14 Juillet 1909," *Journal Officiel de la République française*, July 19, 1909, pp. 7761–7763; "Loi du 14 juillet 1909 sur les dessins et modèles," *Legifrance*, accessed December 1, 2013, http://www.legifrance.gouv.fr/affichTexte.do;jsessionid=B36E87CFB5DC433BD5B7AFD39FB2183B.tpdjo13v_3?cidTexte=JORFTEXT000000315081

&dateTexte=19920702; Du Saint and Godefroy, "Dessins et modèles.—V. Contrefaçon," suppl. t. 5, 340–341; Allart and Carteron, *La Mode devant les Tribunaux*, 3; Stephen P. Ladas, *The International Protection of Literary and Artistic Property* (New York: Macmillan, 1938), 67–369; Piatti, "Le droit de la mode," 9.

62. Galvez-Behar, *La République des inventeurs*, 22–26; Khan, *Democratization of Invention*, 39–65; Piatti, "Le droit de la mode," 2, 3; Roland Barthes, *Système de la mode* (Paris: Seuil, 1967).

63. Khan, *Democratization of Invention*, 8–10.

64. *La Presse*, September 19, 1923, n.p.; *L'Humanité*, September 19, 1923, n.p.; Stewart, *Dressing Modern Frenchwomen*, 122; "Informations diverses," *Le Temps*, February 11, 1924, p. 3.

65. Twelfth Criminal Court of the Seine, 1921, CPA.

66. Elizabeth Hawes, *Fashion Is Spinach* (New York: Random House, 1938), 46.

67. Elizabeth Hawes archives x-149, box 1, folder 1, box proposals drafts and vita, Special Collections, Gladys Marcus Library, FIT; Hawes, *Fashion Is Spinach*, 38; Stewart, *Dressing Modern Frenchwomen*, 120–121; Bettina Berch, *Radical by Design: The Life and Style of Elizabeth Hawes* (New York: E. P. Dutton, 1988), 26; Martine Rénier, "La grande diversité des modes nouvelles," *Fémina*, April 1926, p. 5; Martine Rénier, "Dessous et revers de la copie," *Fémina*, June 15, 1931, pp. 7–8; Edmond Goblot, *La barrière et le niveau* (1925; Paris: Presses Universitaires de France, 1984), 19; Hubert Bonin, "La contrefaçon et les guerres industrielles: L'Union des fabricants et l'INPI acteurs de la lutte contre la contrefaçon," in *Fraude, contrefaçon et contrebande de l'Antiquité à nos jours*, ed. Gérard Béaur, Hubert Bonin, and Claire Lemercier (Geneva: Droz, 2006), 779.

68. Danielle Allérès, "La propriété industrielle dans l'univers du luxe," *Réseaux* 88/89 (1998): 4; Stephen Mihm, *A Nation of Counterfeiters: Capitalists, Con Men, and the Making of the United States* (Cambridge, MA: Harvard University Press, 2007), 352–359; Jonathan M. Barnett, "Shopping for Gucci on Canal Street: Reflections on Status Consumption, Intellectual Property, and the Incentive Thesis," *Virginia Law Review* 91, no. 6 (2005): 1381–1423; Jonathan S. Jennings, "Trademark Counterfeiting: An Unpunished Crime," *Journal of Criminal Law and Criminology* 80 (1989): 805–841.

69. Le Fèvre, *Au secours de la couture*, 93; André Beucler, *Chez Madeleine Vionnet* (unpublished typescript, 1932), bibliography, Madeleine Vionnet Boxes, UCAD.

70. Simon, *La haute couture*, 150.

71. William P. Carney, "Paris Plans Curb on Bootleg Styles," *New York Times*, November 8, 1931, p. E4; Christian Bessy, Benoît Demil, Régis Huguenin-Dumittan, Jean-Daniel Pasche, and Nadège Sougy, "Débat: Imitation et mondialisation à l'épreuve de Sisyphe," *Entreprises et Histoire* 78 (2015): 118; Simon, *La haute couture*, 142.

72. Bertram J. Perkins, "Klotz Deplores Inefficiency of French Style Piracy Laws," *Women's Wear Daily*, May 22, 1929, p. 1.

73. Beucler, *Chez Madeleine Vionnet*, 42.

74. "Pénibles étrennes," *L'Officiel*, January 15, 1923, p. 5; "Simple réponse," *L'Officiel*, December 15, 1922, p. 1; Hawes, *Fashion Is Spinach*, 40; Simon, *La haute couture*, 156–157.

75. "Pénibles étrennes," 5.

76. This phrase, meaning "of inferior race," was used to suggest in this case that a person was Jewish.

77. "La défense des couturiers," *Le Populaire de Paris: Journal socialiste du matin*, December 31, 1921, p. 2: "Madeleine Vionnet, couturière, intente un procès à deux de ses confrères, mais de petite race, à qui elle reprochait d'avoir copié ses modèles. N'eût-il point été scandaleux qu'une quelconque petite bourgeoise puisse exhiber, au Café du Commerce, la pelure au pur chic [*sic*] qui couvre, chez Larue ou chez Maxim's, la carcasse bien emplumée d'une poule de luxe? Le tribunal a compris. Il a condamné Mme Miler à payer à l'irascible Madeleine Vionnet 16.000 francs de dommages intérêts; Madame Boudreaux ne paiera que 12.000 francs. Chacune, en outre, versera dans les caisses de l'Etat 1000 francs d'amende."

78. Simon, *La haute couture*, 7, 14.

79. Ibid., 145.

80. Palfrey, *Intellectual Property Strategy*, 11; Stewart, *Dressing Modern Frenchwomen*, 132; Année 1930, November 29, 1929, 1, D1U10 0479, Prud'hommes, CPA.

81. Contract letter signed by Armand Trouyet and Muguette Buhler, Paris, May 18, 1925 (copy), 1, D1U10 0479, Année 1930, Prud'hommes, CPA: "Les créations de Madeleine Vionnet étant déposées et publiées conformément à la loi, il est interdit de les reproduire ou de s'en inspirer. Vous déclarez accepter de travailler pour le compte de la Société Madeleine Vionnet, et vous déclarez également savoir que toute copie, toute reproduction même modifiée de ses modèles entraîne pour son auteur les peines édictées par la loi."

82. Madeleine Vionnet to Muguette Buhler (copy), November 20, 1929, 1, D1U10 0479, Année 1930, Prud'hommes, CPA.

83. Madeleine Vionnet to Martiale Constantini (copy), November 20, 1929, 1, D1U10 0479, Année 1930, Prud'hommes, CPA.

84. Affaire 4636, February 14, 1930, 1, D1U10 0479, Année 1930, Prud'hommes, CPA.

85. Vionnet to Buhler, November 20, 1929.

86. Ibid.: "l'introduction d'un fonctionnaire de la police dans ma maison."

87. Stewart, *Dressing Modern Frenchwomen*, 131–132; Simon, *La haute couture*, 17–24.

88. Affaire 4636, February 14, 1930, 1; Affaire 1717, March 7, 1930, Marguerite Héricourt contre Fanny Simmonds (Maison Simone Voinot), 1, D1U10 0479, Année 1930, Prud'hommes, CPA; Madeleine Vionnet & Compagnie, Acte sous seing privé du 15 juin 1919, July 5, 1922, 2, D31U3 002083, CPA; Affaire 4077, July 31, 1931, Société Mag Helly Couture contre Mlle Sollet Lucie, première, 1, D1U10 0483, Année 1931, Prud'hommes, CPA; Affaire 3145, July 24, 1931, 3, D1U10 0483, Année 1931, Prud'hommes, CPA; Mag Bertrand contre Augusta Bernard: "Me Ullmo rappelle au Conseil le secret qui s'attache aux modèles."

89. Omnès, *Ouvrières parisiennes*, 34, 42; Miller, *Bon Marché*, 215–230.

90. Bertram J. Perkins, "Rumors Outstrip Repeated Denials" and "Couturiers' Terms Balk US Capital," *Women's Wear Daily*, April 11, 1929, p. 5.

91. Jean-Claude Daumas, *Les territoires de la laine: Histoire de l'industrie lainière en France au XIXe siècle* (Lille: Presses Universitaires du Septentrion, 2004), 232–238; Coudurier, Fructus,

Descher advertisement, *L'Officiel,* February 1921, p. 30; Diederichs-Soieries advertisement, *L'Officiel,* May 1922, inside front cover; Olré fabrics advertisement, *L'Officiel,* August 1923, p. 12.

92. Jeanne Lanvin advertisement, *L'Officiel,* August 1923, p. 8; Daumas, *Les territoires de la laine,* 306–310; Perkins, "Couturiers' Terms"; Philippe Montégut, "Boué Soeurs: The First Haute-Couture Establishment in America," *Dress* 15 (1989): 83; Madeleine Vionnet & Cie, acte sous seing privé, April 4, 1923, D31U3 002170, CPA.

93. Troy, *Couture Culture,* 232–244; Palfrey, *Intellectual Property Strategy,* 1–7.

94. *Archives commerciales de la France,* August 28, 1897, 1085; July 15, 1899, 887; April 11, 1903, 454; and July 27, 1904, 1035.

95. Françoise Tétart-Vittu, "The Origins of Haute Couture," in *Paris Haute Couture,* ed. Olivier Saillard and Anne Zazzo (Paris: Flammarion, 2012), 20; Milbank, *Couture: The Great Designers,* 70; "Tribunaux: Un procès parisien à New-York," *Le Temps,* December 31, 1915, p. 4; Lourdes M. Font, "International Couture: The Opportunities and Challenges of Expansion, 1880–1920," *Business History* 54, no. 1 (2012): 39.

96. Montégut, "Boué Soeurs," 83.

97. "Tribunaux: Un procès parisien à New-York," 4; Font, "International Couture."

98. Simon, *La haute couture,* 128.

99. "Revue de la Presse: La douane américaine et les exportateurs français," *La Soierie de Lyon,* June 1, 1926, p. 450: "Le but poursuivi ne peut être que la copie de nos modèles et la connaissance du secret de nos affaires, afin de créer, aux Etats-Unis, une industrie concurrente de la nôtre; par la décomposition des prix, les Américains espèrent pénétrer nos secrets de fabrication et s'approprier nos méthodes."

100. *Le 18e au goût du jour, guide de l'exposition* (Paris: Musée Galliéra, 2011), 14.

101. Madeleine Vionnet & Cie, livres de ventes, UCAD.

102. "Vionnet Brings Action against Butterick Co.," *Women's Wear Daily,* January 30, 1922, p. 1.

103. Twelfth Criminal Court of the Seine, 1921, CPA: "qu'aucun document ne permet de supposer que des commerçants américains concurrents s'approvisionnent des modèles Vionnet chez la dame Boudreau [sic]."

104. "Charles and Ray Sue Vionnet for $100,000," *Women's Wear Daily,* March 14, 1924, p. 3; "Charles and Ray Show Extensive Vionnet Collection," *Women's Wear Daily,* October 11, 1923, p. 23.

105. "Echos," *Le Rappel,* March 19, 1924, p. 2; "Vionnet Sails for New York January 26," *Women's Wear Daily,* January 17, 1924, p. 1; Troy, *Couture Culture,* 330–331.

106. "Vionnet Sails for New York," 1.

107. *Women's Wear Daily,* February 19, 1924, n.p.; "Vionnet, Pioneer of Paris Designers, Comes Preaching Happiness in Dress," *New York Times,* February 24, 1924, n.p.

108. Société Madeleine Vionnet, Livre des ventes, 1923–1924, UCAD.

109. Kirke, *Madeleine Vionnet,* 132; "Vionnet Opens Her Own Retail Concern Here," *Women's Wear Daily,* February 19, 1924, p. 1; Maison Vionnet, Collaborateurs: correspondance, presse, Madeleine Vionnet boxes, Documentation Center, UCAD; Marie Lyons, "New York Opening of the House of Vionnet," *Harper's Bazaar,* April 1924, p. 8.

110. "Vionnet Sails for New York," 1.

111. O'Bryant, "Innovative Cut of Madeleine Vionnet," 82.

112. Kirke, *Madeleine Vionnet*, 132.

113. Vionnet chronology, Madeleine Vionnet file, Vertical files, Metropolitan Museum of Art, New York.

114. See "Proskauer Rose LLP," *National Law Review*, accessed September 12, 2013, http://www.natlawreview.com/organization/proskauer-rose-llp.

115. "Vionnet Opens Retail Concern," 1.

116. "Says Hickson's Have Vionnet Rights," *Women's Wear Daily*, February 20, 1924, p. 1.

117. "Vionnet Sails for New York," 1; "Vionnet Opens Retail Concern," 1.

118. "Charles and Ray Sue Vionnet," 3.

119. Kirke, *Madeleine Vionnet*, 132–133; "Vionnet Models Shown Here Reveal Modern Treatment," *Women's Wear Daily*, March 10, 1925, p. 2; "Vionnet Models Outstanding Feature in Private Showing of Paris Originals," *Women's Wear Daily*, November 10, 1924, p. 2.

120. Société Madeleine Vionnet, accounting books, UCAD; Carine Claude, "Les livres de vente de la maison Vionnet," documentation for the exhibition *Madeleine Vionnet* (The Hague: Gemeentemuseum, 1999).

121. Golbin, *Madeleine Vionnet, puriste*, 34–35; Evans, *Mechanical Smile*, 146; "Vionnet Starts Wholesale Reproduction of Own Models," *Women's Wear Daily*, October 7, 1926, p. 1.

122. Lamoreaux and Rosenthal, "Legal Regime and Contractual Flexibility"; D31U3 002083, July 5, 1922, and D31U3 002170, March 15, 1923, CPA; Champsaur, "Vionnet and the *Galeries Lafayette*," 48–66; Béatrice Touchelay, "La diffusion et l'application des normes comptables standardisées en France des années 1920 aux années 1960: L'utopie de la transparence?," in *Fraude, contrefaçon et contrebande de l'Antiquité à nos jours*, ed. Gérard Béaur, Hubert Bonin, and Claire Lemercier (Geneva: Droz, 2006), 389.

123. Daumas, *Les territoires de la laine*, 309–310.

3. Dressing for Crisis

1.   Louise Bonney and Thérèse Bonney, *A Shopping Guide to Paris* (New York: McBride, 1929), v; Lisa Schlausker Kolosek, *Therese Bonney and Paris Moderne* (New York: Thames and Hudson, 2002); Betty Kirke, *Madeleine Vionnet* (San Francisco: Chronicle Books, 2012), 26; Germaine Deschamps, "La Crise dans les Industries du vêtement et de la mode à Paris pendant la période de 1930 à 1937" (PhD diss., Librairie technique et économique, Paris, 1937), 39; Philippe Simon, *La haute couture: Monographie d'une industrie de luxe* (Paris: Presses Universitaires de France, 1931), 94–96; Claude A. Rouzaud, *Un problème d'intérêt national: Les industries du luxe* (Strasbourg: Librairie du recueil Sirey, 1946), 139; Committee meeting minutes, May 30, 1933, 6, CSCPA; Booton Herndon, *Bergdorf's on the Plaza: The Story of Bergdorf Goodman and a Half-Century of American Fashion* (New York: Knopf, 1956); Penelope Rowlands, *A Dash of Daring: Carmel Snow and Her Life in Fashion, Art, and Letters* (London: Atria Books, 2005).

2.   Interview of Lucien Schloss, *L'Officiel*, July 1928, p. 1; Simon, *La haute couture*, 80, 85; Caroline Evans, *The Mechanical Smile: Modernism and the First Fashion Shows in France and in America, 1900–1929* (New Haven, CT: Yale University Press, 2013); "Budgets Cost of a Buyer's Trip," *Women's Wear Daily*, May 19, 1931, p. 6; Simon, *La haute couture*, 72; Josephine Baker in an Agnès hat, *L'Officiel*, August 1926, p. 27; Charles Glass, *Americans in Paris: Life and Death under Nazi Occupation, 1940–1944* (London: Harper, 2009); Petrine Archer-Straw, *Negrophilia: Avant-Garde Paris and Black Culture in the 1920s* (London: Thames & Hudson, 2000), 73–79; Tyler Stovall, *Paris Noir: African Americans in the City of Light* (Boston: Houghton Mifflin, 1996), 112–118; *L'Officiel*, July 1935, p. 30. Conversion of dollar values was done with the EH.net measuring worth tool, using the consumer price index (CPI).

3.   Andrew Goodman, interview about the Uptown Retail Guild, [anonymous and undated] transcript, 3, x–20, Gladys Marcus Library, Special Collections, FIT; "Copies of French Models Emphasized in This Week's Retail Dress Offerings," *Women's Wear Daily*, March 17, 1929, p. 8. Conversion of dollar values was done with the EH.net measuring worth tool, using the CPI.

4.   Deschamps, "La Crise," 65; Roy B. Helfgott, "Women's and Children's Apparel," in *Made in New York: Case Studies in Metropolitan Manufacturing*, ed. Max Hall (Cambridge, MA: Harvard University Press, 1959), 19–134; Helen Everett Meiklejohn, *Dresses: Impact of Fashion on a Business* (New York: McGraw-Hill, 1938); Morris De Camp Crawford, *The Ways of Fashion* (New York: G. P. Putnam's Sons, 1941).

5.   *L'Officiel*, March 1927, p. 14; Alma L. Kenney, "Carnegie, Hattie," in *Notable American Women: The Modern Period; A Biographical Dictionary*, ed. Barbara Sicherman and Carol Hurd Green (Cambridge, MA: Belknap Press of Harvard University Press, 1980), 135–136; Paul M. Gregory, "An Economic Interpretation of Women's Fashions," *Southern Economic Journal* 14, no. 2 (October 1947): 149–150; Crawford, *Ways of Fashion*, 234–235. Conversion of dollar values was done with the EH.net measuring worth tool, using the CPI.

6.   Guillaume Garnier, *Paris-couture, années 30* (Paris: Musée de la Mode et du Costume, 1987), 124; *Lilly Daché, Glamour at the Drop of a Hat*, exhibition catalog (New York: Fashion Institute of Technology Museum, 2007); Stephanie Amerian, "Fashioning and Selling the American Look: Dorothy Shaver and Modern Art," *Investigaciones de Historia Economica— Economic History Research* 12, no. 2 (2006): 100–108; Valerie Wingfield, *The Fashion Group International, Records c. 1930–1997* (New York: New York Public Library, 1997), 11; Meeting, New York, January 26, 1928, folders 11 and 12, box 73, FG, NYPL; Wingfield, *Fashion Group*, 4–5.

7.   Meetings, New York, April 7, 1931, folder 1, box 72, FG, NYPL; April 20, 1939, folder 5, box 73, 5, FG, NYPL; January 20, 1932, folder 6, box 72, FG, NYPL; September 27, 1939, folder 6, box 73, FG, NYPL; November 9, 1931, folder 4, box 72, FG, NYPL; Kathleen Howard, [ca. 1931–1932], folder 5, box 72, FG, NYPL; Fashion Forecast Conferences, September 6 and 7, folder 10, box 72, FG, NYPL; Fashion Group Bulletin, box 144, FG, NYPL.

8.   *Tableau général du commerce et de la navigation: Commerce de la France avec ses colonies et les puissances étrangères* (Paris: Direction Générale des Douanes, 1920–1939), Institut

National de la Statistique et des Etudes Economiques; "French Export of Wearing Apparel to U.S. Declines," *Women's Wear Daily,* March 8, 1929, p. 1; Deschamps, "La Crise."

9. Simon, *La haute couture,* 119–121, 128–129.

10. Geoffrey G. Jones, *The Evolution of Multinational Business: An Introduction* (New York: Routledge, 1996), 9, 27; Paul Bairoch, *Victoires et déboires: Histoire économique et sociale du XVIe siècle à nos jours,* vol. 3 (Paris: Gallimard, 1997), 76–78; Simon, *La haute couture,* 122–126, 141; Yves-Georges Prade, "Il faut organiser la défense de la production française," *L'Officiel,* March 1932, p. 9; Rouzaud, *Un problème,* 135.

11. "Paris Speculates on Future Policy of Allied Purchasing," *Women's Wear Daily,* March 29, 1929, p. 2; "Allied Purchasing Co. to Operate on Smaller Scale," *Women's Wear Daily,* December 26, 1929, p. 6; "Allied Purchasing Personnel in Paris Get New Posts," *Women's Wear Daily,* December 6, 1929, p. 5; Bertram J. Perkins, "Commissionaires Fed Up with Non-buying Buyers," *Women's Wear Daily,* May 19, 1931, p. 6; Bertram J. Perkins, "Complexion of Couture Undergoes Periodic Change," *Women's Wear Daily,* June 27, 1933, p. 4; Bertram J. Perkins, "Export Producers Passing Out," *Women's Wear Daily,* October 13, 1933, p. 7; Rouzaud, *Un problème,* 139; Prade, "Il faut organiser," 9; Bertram J. Perkins, "Paris Going 'Cut Rate' to Maintain Tourist Trade," *Women's Wear Daily,* September 25, 1933, p. 4; Douglas A. Irwin, "The French Gold Sink and the Great Deflation," in *Cato Papers on Public Policy,* vol. 2 (Washington, DC: Cato Institute, 2012), 13.

12. Bertram J. Perkins, "Paris Not Reflecting Country's Trade Troubles," *Women's Wear Daily,* September 29, 1933, p. 8; "They Can Use More Tourists Here," *Women's Wear Daily,* July 18, 1933, p. 4; Deschamps, "La Crise," 39; "Budgets Cost of a Buyer's Trip," p. 6.

13. *Le 18e au goût du jour, guide de l'exposition* (Paris: Musée Galliéra, 2011), 14; "August-abernard Reorganization Being Planned," *Women's Wear Daily,* October 4, 1934, p. 1; "August-abernard to Close Couture Firm," *Women's Wear Daily,* October 5, 1934, p. 28; Deschamps, "La Crise," 75–77; Bertram J. Perkins, "House May Close and Reopen on Smaller Scale," *Women's Wear Daily,* October 10, 1934, p. 5; Numéro du greffe (registration number) 50211, Jugement déclaratif du 24 août 1934, Aine Montaillé société anonyme au capital de 850,000 francs, 1, Place Vendôme, cloture pour insuffisance d'actifs, D10U3117, CPA.

14. Unsigned document, June 9, 1942, Paris, F12 10503, FNA.

15. Questionnaire relatif à la classification Couture création, January 1952–1954, F12 10504, 10505, FNA; Garnier, *Paris-couture,* 98; Bertram J. Perkins, "Robert Piguet to Show First Collection Soon," *Women's Wear Daily,* September 29, 1933, p. 8.

16. "Speaker: Miss Lilian Fisher, Paris Fashion Representative of Bonwit-Teller," Luncheon Meeting Minutes, June 29, 1932, 16, folder 7, box 72, FG, NYPL; Garnier, *Paris-couture,* 122; "The Dressmakers of France," *Fortune,* August 1932, p. 76; *Vogue* (US ed.), January 1, 1931, p. 45; John Bayley Swinney, *Merchandising of Fashions* (New York: Ronald Press, [1942]), 40–41; Gilbert Millstein, "Mainbocher Stands for a Fitting," *New York Times,* March 25, 1956, p. 42; Claudia B. Kidwell and Margaret C. Christman, *Suiting Everyone: The Democratization of Clothing in America* (Washington, DC: Smithsonian Institution, 1974), 193.

17. Evans, *Mechanical Smile;* Simon, *La haute couture,* 137; Bertram J. Perkins, "Couturiers' Terms Balk US Capital," *Women's Wear Daily,* April 11, 1929, p. 5; Bergdorf Archive, Andrew Goodman file, x-20, 51, 13–14, Gladys Marcus Library, Special Collections, FIT; Herndon, *Bergdorf's on the Plaza.*

18. Bertram J. Perkins, "Says Couture Background Helps in Couture Business," *Women's Wear Daily,* June 26, 1930, p. 5; Sonya Mooney and Sarah Scaturro, *Modern Master: Lucien Lelong, Couturier 1918–1948,* exhibition catalog (New York: Fashion Institute of Technology Museum, 2006), 8; "Patou, Inc., May Open in 2 Months," *Women's Wear Daily,* May 19, 1930, p. 6; Bertram J. Perkins, "Glimpses of Paris," *Women's Wear Daily,* April 12, 1939, p. 4.

19. *L'Officiel,* September 1937, p. 77.

20. Société anonyme Lucien Lelong, statuts, Paris, 1925, 1–32, H1137, Lucien Lelong, ANMT; Dartey, "Lucien Lelong. L'art de la robe. The art of the dress," *La Renaissance de l'Art Français et des Industries de Luxe,* January 1927, Lucien Lelong File, UCAD; Donald L. Pratt, "Meet M. Lucien Lelong, French without Frills," *Women's Wear Daily,* September 8, 1937, p. 7; Bertram J. Perkins, "Glimpses of Paris," *Women's Wear Daily,* February 15, 1939, p. 4; Swinney, *Merchandising,* 41; "Dressmakers of France," 72, 76; Mooney and Scaturro, *Modern Master;* Didier Grumbach, *Histoires de la mode* (Paris: Editions du Regard, 1993), 168.

21. "M. Lelong's Visit to the United States," *L'Officiel,* November 1925, p. 15.

22. *L'Officiel,* November 1926, p. 17.

23. Maggy Rouff, *L'Amérique au microscope* (Paris: Edition des Portiques, 1933), 22; Garnier, *Paris-couture,* 252–253; Philippe Roger, *L'ennemi américain: Généalogie de l'anti-américanisme français* (Paris: Seuil, 2002); Victoria de Grazia, *Irresistible Empire: America's Advance through 20th-Century Europe* (Cambridge, MA: Belknap Press of Harvard University Press, 2005).

24. *L'Officiel,* August 1935, p. 18; "La mort de Jean Patou," *L'Officiel,* April 1936, p. 33; *L'Officiel,* September 1937, p. 54.

25. Committee meeting minutes, June 20, 1928, 1, CSCPA; Lucien Lelong, Inc., v. Lenel, Inc., et al., 181 F.2d 3 (5th Cir. 1950), http://law.justia.com/cases/federal/appellate-courts/F2/181/3/173642/; "Lucien Lelong, Inc., Leases N.Y. Office," *Women's Wear Daily,* July 24, 1939, p. 1; "Chez Péhel," *L'Officiel,* February 1928, p. 52; Bertram J. Perkins, "Glimpses of Paris: Pierre Lelong to Visit U.S. Accounts Next Month," *Women's Wear Daily,* February 18, 1929, p. 4.

26. Earle Ludgin to Edward L. Bernays, September 28, 1931, box 1: 220 Edward Louis Bernays Papers, Library of Congress, Washington, DC; "For release, Radio talk given by M. Lelong on the nationwide chain of the Columbia Broadcasting System," October 12, 1931, 4, Scrapbook I 697, Edward L. Bernays Papers, Library of Congress; Luncheon Meeting Minutes of the Fashion Group for M. Lucien Lelong, Sherry's, 300 Park Avenue, October 22, 1931, folder 72, section 3, 1, FG, NYPL; "Paris Goes in Form and Colour," *Vogue* (US ed.), April 1, 1931, p. 44; I. Magnin & Co advertisement, *Vogue* (US ed.), October 15, 1934, p. 9; Sketches, 1934, 1935, box 32, 3, Davidow Archive, FIT; Jacqueline Demornex, *Lucien Lelong* (New York: Thames & Hudson, 2008), 23–24, 29, 50, 59.

27. Simone de Beauvoir, *The Second Sex* (New York: Vintage Books, 1949), 534; "Word Expected Soon of First Lelong Reproductions," *Women's Wear Daily*, September 18, 1934, p. 4; Bertram J. Perkins, "Details of Lelong Venture Interests Wholesale Market," *Women's Wear Daily*, September 25, 1934, p. 4; *Vogue* (US ed.), December 15, 1934, p. 59; "Lelong Opens *Departement d'Edition*," *Women's Wear Daily*, October 9, 1934, p. 1; Bertram J. Perkins, "Expect about 100 Models in First Collection," *Women's Wear Daily*, September 25, 1934, p. 4; "Lelong *Robes d'Edition* Endorse Capes for Sports," *Women's Wear Daily*, October 9, 1935, p. 9.

28. Elizabeth Hawes, *Fashion Is Spinach* (New York: Random House, 1938); Elizabeth Hawes Papers, x-149, Gladys Marcus Library, FIT; "Pour que la femme moderne puisse s'habiller aux conditions de prix de notre époque Lucien Lelong a créé la robe édition," *La robe et l'époque par Lucien Lelong*, Robes d'Edition advertising brochure, 1935, Lucien Lelong file, UCAD; *Vogue* (US ed.), December 15, 1934, p. 59; *La robe et l'époque par Lucien Lelong*, Robes d'Edition advertising brochure, 1935, Lucien Lelong file, UCAD; Perkins, "Expect about 100 Models," p. 4.

29. "La robe française et la lingerie à la main," *L'Officiel*, September 1926, p. 1.

30. Florence Brachet Champsaur, "'Créer c'est avoir vu le premier': Les Galeries Lafayette et la mode (1893–1969)" (PhD diss., EHESS, Paris, 2018); Jacques Lanzmann and Pierre Ripert, *Weil: Cent ans de prêt-à-porter* (Paris: Editions P.A.U., 1992), 4; Bonney and Bonney, *Shopping Guide*; "The Dressmakers of the US," *Fortune*, December 1933, p. 37.

31. Advertisement, *L'Officiel*, June 1922, p. 26; "L'installation moderne des Etablissements Cain et Rheims," *L'Officiel*, August 1927, p. 102.

32. "Paris Store Explains Dress Orders Here," *Women's Wear Daily*, May 25, 1931, p. 3.

33. "La tunique Radiah," *L'Officiel*, August 1922, p. 39; *L'Officiel*, October 1922, p. 20; "Paris Wholesalers Sponsor Higher Waistlines in Fall Collections," *Women's Wear Daily*, June 24, 1929, p. 6.

34. Dépôt Toutmain, CPA; *L'Officiel*, August 1926, p. 1; "La robe française," 1; *L'Officiel*, March 1927, p. xii; "War Economies Help Paris Retaildom to Adjust Itself to Period of Lower Value," *Women's Wear Daily*, October 11, 1939, p. 2.

35. "French House under American Management Favors Gored Handlings and Incrustations," *Women's Wear Daily*, October 29, 1929, p. 16; *Women's Wear Daily*, March 15, 1940, p. 25.

36. "Paris Makers Expect Bigger US Business," *Women's Wear Daily*, October 24, 1929, p. 7; Garnier, *Paris-couture*, 248; Grumbach, *Histoires de la mode*, 103; *L'Officiel*, September 1935, p. 29.

37. Alain Chatriot, "La construction récente des groupes de luxe français: Mythes, discours et pratiques," *Entreprises et Histoire* 1, no. 46 (2007): 143–156; Garnier, *Paris-couture*, 98; "Aubert, Klein Agree on Need for Anti-style Piracy Laws," *Women's Wear Daily*, November 12, 1929, p. 6; H660, Dœuillet file, ANMT; U159bis, 1927, Haute Couture Parisienne file, ANMT; Bertram J. Perkins, "French Apparel Factors Greatly Interested in Proposed Aubert Visit to United States," *Women's Wear Daily*, September 23, 1929, p. 1; Hubert Bonin, *Les métiers financiers des banques (1919–1935): Les banques françaises de l'entre-deux-guerres* (Paris: Plages, 2000), 378–379; Nancy Troy, *Couture Culture: A Study in Modern Art and Fashion* (Cambridge, MA: MIT Press, 2003), 321.

38. "Aubert Disposes of Agnes Store Lease," *Women's Wear Daily*, December 26, 1929, p. 6; Bertram J. Perkins, "Fewer Couture Firms Likely by End of Year," *Women's Wear Daily*, October 10, 1934, p. 5; "Doeuillet-Doucet Accounts Approved," *Women's Wear Daily*, June 5, 1929, p. 4; "Doeuillet Doucet Reports 1929 Loss," *Women's Wear Daily*, June 26, 1930, p. 1.

39. "Agnès Shareholders' Meeting on Proposed Merger Is Postponed," *Women's Wear Daily*, June 16, 1930, p. 1; Bertram J. Perkins, "Agnès-Drecoll Balance Shows 556,686 Rf. Net," *Women's Wear Daily*, June 29, 1931, p. 6; Jacques Makowsky, *Histoire de l'industrie et du commerce en France* (Paris: Editions d'Art et d'Histoire, 1926), 117; January 22, 1932, and February 12, 1932, File Mirande, Conseil des Prud'hommes, 1932, 1, D1U10 485, CPA.

40. Interview of Paul Poiret, *L'Officiel*, August 1921, pp. 11, 13; Bertram J. Perkins, "Glimpses of Paris: Maison Paul Poiret Explains Dispute with Paul Poiret," *Women's Wear Daily*, April 25, 1929, p. 2; Bertram J. Perkins, "Glimpses of Paris," *Women's Wear Daily*, April 25, 1929, p. 14; Makowsky, *Histoire de l'industrie*, 118; Troy, *Couture Culture*, 54–57; Palmer White, *Poiret le magnifique: Le destin d'un grand couturier* (Paris: Payot, 1986).

41. "Poiret May Open Shop in West and Here," *Women's Wear Daily*, February 15, 1929, pp. 2, 15; Bertram J. Perkins, "Glimpses of Paris: Paul Poiret's Return to Paris Revives Trouble," *Women's Wear Daily*, March 18, 1929, p. 8; Bertram J. Perkins, "Correspondents Spy Good Poiret Story," *Women's Wear Daily*, May 24, 1929, p. 4; "Font Designer—Lucian Bernhard," Linotype, accessed April 23, 2011, http://www.linotype.com/688/lucianbernhard.html; Bertram J. Perkins, "Glimpses of Paris: Paul Poiret Disclosed as Contempora Vice-President," *Women's Wear Daily*, May 29, 1929, p. 4.

42. Art et Couture file, 1987 003 0689, ANMT; Jugement déclaratif du 22 février 1935, Art et Couture, clôture pour insuffisance d'actif, March 30, 1935, D10U3 0121, CPA.

43. Bertram J. Perkins, "Paul Poiret Again Does the Unusual" and "Settles Down in Creative Setting," *Women's Wear Daily*, May 22, 1931, p. 9.

44. Garnier, *Paris-couture*, 98.

45. "Rentner Dies," *Women's Wear Daily*, July 8, 1958, p. 19, Resseguie Collection, BL, HBS; Meiklejohn, *Dresses*, 304.

46. "Business Notes," *New York Times*, June 17, 1939, p. 32; "Summing It Up in Brief—Here Is Our Credo on Skirt Widths for the Coming Fall . . . ," *Tobé Report*, June 2, 1938, p. 2D; *Tobé Report*, June 22, 1938, p. 32, FIT; Committee meeting minutes (committee meeting enlarged to the Chamber), April 2, 1940, 2, CSCPA; "Varied Versions of Flare on Dressmaker Coats Characteristic of Elsie Cobin Imports," *Women's Wear Daily*, February 26, 1929, p. 26.

47. "Tobe Outlines Fashion Program in St. Louis Department Store," *Women's Wear Daily*, October 21, 1929, p. 16; "Tobe Forum to Interpret New Apparel Styles," *Women's Wear Daily*, August 28, 1939, p. 1; "2d Tobe Style Forum at Ritz March 25 to 27," *Women's Wear Daily*, November 19, 1929, p. 2; "New Incorporations," *New York Times*, May 21, 1930, p. 51; "Corporate Changes," *New York Times*, January 31, 1931, p. 34; "Mannish Styles Coming," *New York Times*, January 12, 1933, p. 32; "Coordination Retail Topic," *New York Times*, June 2, 1929, p. N18; "Dry Goods Men See Need for Big Drive," *New York Times*, June 20, 1930, p. 44; "Herbert H. Davis," *New York Times*, March 13, 1934, p. 24.

48. "New Home of Tobe Officially Opened," *Women's Wear Daily,* May 1, 1934, p. 2; "Tobé," *Fortune,* June 1934, p. 44; "Many World Events Influencing Styles," *New York Times,* March 1, 1936, p. F9; "Business Notes," *New York Times,* September 26, 1934, p. 30; "Tobe Works with Pathé on Picture," *Women's Wear Daily,* June 19, 1934, p. 31.

49. "Sports Dresses Popular," *New York Times,* August 11, 1935, p. F10; "Designers Called Mass Dress Need," *New York Times,* December 20, 1949, p. 48.

50. "Style and Trade to Be Forecast at Seminar," *Women's Wear Daily,* June 19, 1930, pp. 1, 23; "Mannish Styles Coming"; advertisement, *Women's Wear Daily,* August 1, 1929, p. 7; "Winter Sports Wear Faces Good Outlook," *New York Times,* October 30, 1932, p. F8.

51. "Fashion Forecasting Success, Says Parrish," *Women's Wear Daily,* August 6, 1929, p. 5; "Trimmings Revived at Millinery Association," *New York Times,* February 4, 1931, p. 27; advertisement, *Women's Wear Daily,* June 6, 1929, p. 7; Sylvan Gotshal, *The Pirates Will Get You: A Story of the Fight for Design Protection* (New York: Columbia University Press, 1945), 13.

52. Earl Dash, "Rentner in Stormy Career Steered True to Fashion," *Women's Wear Daily,* July 8, 1958, p. 19, Resseguie Collection, BL, HBS.

53. Ibid.; Jessica Daves, *Ready-Made Miracle: The American Story of Fashion for the Millions* (New York: Putnam, 1967), 61–62; Gotshal, *Pirates Will Get You,* 22; "Interview of Selma Frankel, daughter of Maurice Rentner," interview by Mildred Finger, New York, August 31, 1982, 22, Memoirs of Maurice Rentner from Varying Perspectives, Oral History Project of the Fashion Industries, FIT.

54. Gotshal, *Pirates Will Get You,* 10; Geoffrey Jones and David Kiron, "Cisco Goes to China: Routing an Emerging Market" (Harvard Business School Case no 805020, June 2012).

55. Gotshal, *Pirates Will Get You,* 30.

56. Ibid., 31–32.

57. Daves, *Ready-Made Miracle,* 10, 15; Gotshal, *Pirates Will Get You,* 37.

58. Gotshal, *Pirates Will Get You,* 38.

59. Ibid., 40–41; Sara Beth Marcketti, "Design Piracy in the United States' Women's Ready-to-Wear Apparel Industry: 1910–1941" (PhD dissertation, Iowa State University, 2005), 112–115.

60. Simon, *La haute couture,* 166.

61. Deschamps, "La Crise," 65; "Vogue's Eye View of the Mode," *Vogue* (US ed.), December 1, 1932, p. 41; "Dressmakers of the US," 37–38; Claudia B. Kidwell and Margaret Christman, *Suiting Everyone: The Democratization of Clothing in America* (Washington, DC: Smithsonian, 1974), 193.

62. Goodman, interview about Uptown Retail Guild, 1–2; "Dressmakers of the US," 38; Marcketti, "Design Piracy," 53, 81; Sara Beth Marcketti and Jean L. Parsons, *Knock It Off: A History of Design Piracy in the US Women's Ready-to-Wear Apparel Industry* (Lubbock: Texas Tech University Press, 2016), 98–144.

63. "Dressmakers of the US," 142; Marcketti, "Design Piracy," 130.

64. Advertisement for the Fashion Originators' Guild of America, *Women's Wear Daily,* June 26, 1933, pp. 10–11; advertisement, "Members of the Fashion Originators Guild of America

Announce Their Opening Dates," *Women's Wear Daily,* June 28, 1933, p. 3; "Fashion Week Announced," *New York Times,* December 7, 1956, p. 42.

65. "Garment Leaders Draft Code Today," *New York Times,* July 5, 1933, p. 10; "Fashion Guild on 5-Day Week," *New York Times,* August 23, 1933, p. 26.

66. "Mrs. Roosevelt and Mrs. Dall to Get First NRA Coat Labels," *Women's Wear Daily,* October 4, 1933, p. 1; Marcketti, "Design Piracy," 145–146.

67. "Rentner to Be Honored," *New York Times,* November 20, 1933, p. 17; "Retailers See NRA as a Lasting Boon," *New York Times,* November 22, 1933, p. 5.

68. "Fashion Guild Plans Protection Campaign," *Women's Wear Daily,* May 22, 1934, p. 8; Marcketti, "Design Piracy," 133–135.

69. "Dressmakers of the US," 142; "Piguet Divulges Names of Firms to Which Early Model Shipments Went," *Women's Wear Daily,* September 1, 1936, p. 1.

70. "FOGA et al., Sue Lucille Baldwin Here," *Women's Wear Daily,* October 14, 1936, p. 35.

71. Goodman, interview about Uptown Retail Guild, 1–2; Marcketti, "Design Piracy," 137.

72. "Business World," *New York Times,* June 14, 1933, p. 26; "Two Guilds in Accord," *New York Times,* March 4, 1936, p. 30.

73. "Question Dress Guild Plans," *New York Times,* January 21, 1933, p. 29; Marcketti, "Design Piracy," 130.

74. "Peace Move Made in Guild Dispute," *New York Times,* March 3, 1936, p. 30; "Retailers Attack Dress Style Plan," *New York Times,* December 21, 1935, p. 30; Marcketti, *Design Piracy,* 119–120, 131–138.

75. "Retailers Attack," 30.

76. Lunch Meeting Minutes, New York Fashion Group, September 11 and 26, 1933, folder 25, box 75, FG, NYPL.

77. "First Fall Fashion Group Meeting Honors Mrs. Chase and Reports on Fashion Futures," *Women's Wear Daily,* October 1, 1935, p. 2; "Proper Sales' Timing Urged by Hirschmann," *New York Times,* June 25, 1937, p. 40; Ruth Kerr, Treasurer, January 26, 1938, Biltmore Hotel, New York, 3, Speeches and transcripts 1938 January–April, box 73, FG, NYPL.

78. Elihu Katz and Paul Lazarsfeld, *Personal Influence: The Part Played by People in the Flow of Mass Communications* (New York: Free Press, 1955).

79. *L'Officiel,* September 15, 1923, p. 6; and same issue, advertisement for "Etablissements Robert, confectionneur," p. 41.

80. "Mlle. Chanel to Come Here Again Oct. 1," *Women's Wear Daily,* July 16, 1931, p. 4.

81. "Mlle. Chanel to Come," p. 4.

82. "Plans Chanel Bags, Scarfs to Match Gloves," *Women's Wear Daily,* July 5, 1929, pp. 1, 23; Bertram J. Perkins, "Glimpses of Paris: Glove Mfrs. Seeking Couturier's Special Cachet," *Women's Wear Daily,* May 29, 1929, p. 4; advertisement for Chanel gloves by Chanut, *L'Officiel,* October 1932, p. 4.

83. "It's Paris It's New York," advertisement, *Women's Wear Daily,* July 19, 1929, p. 15; "Chanel Style Raincoats Uses Corduroy," *Women's Wear Daily,* May 31, 1933, p. 20; "Mfr. Presents Chanel's

New Scarf Made in Oval Shape," *Women's Wear Daily,* January 11, 1929, p. 27; "Les bijoux Chanel," *L'Officiel,* December 1932, p. 28.

84. Advertisement for dresses in "Chanel Cloth" for the brand Rose Amado, Madison Ave., New York, *Vogue* (US ed.), March 15, 1932, p. 26; *Bulletin,* January 1933, 3, box 144, FG, NYPL; *L'Officiel,* March 1933, p. 18; *L'Officiel,* February 1934, p. 62; *L'Officiel,* August 1933, pp. 18–19; *L'Officiel,* March 1933, p. 23.

85. René Bizet, *La mode* (Paris: F. Rieder & Cie, 1925), 21; Hawes, *Fashion Is Spinach,* 46; Chanel contre Laniel, Tribunal civil de la Seine, March 29, 1930, D1U6 002234, CPA.

86. Elizabeth Castaldo Lundén, "Oscar Night in Hollywood: Fashioning the Red Carpet from the Roosevelt Hotel to International Media" (PhD diss., University of Stockholm, 2018); Adrienne Munich, ed., *Fashion in Film* (Bloomington: Indiana University Press, 2011), 17–20; Nigel Cawthorne, *The New Look: The Dior Revolution* (New York: Wellfleet Press, 1996), 28; "Lelong Emphasized Internationalism of Design at Fashion Group Luncheon," *Women's Wear Daily,* September 29, 1937, p. 3; *L'Officiel,* December 1937, p. 22.

87. Bertram J. Perkins, "Glimpses of Paris," *Women's Wear Daily,* August 8, 1939, p. 11.

88. Paul Mazur, address, Hotel Roosevelt, New York, April 7, 1931, folder 11, box 72, 1, FG, NYPL.

89. "Lyolène in New York," *New York Times,* July 1, 1934, p. X6; "Dressmakers of France," 75; "Exclusive Lyolene Group Reported for Retailers," *Women's Wear Daily,* June 26, 1933, p. 20; "Stylists See Paris Shunning Fashions," *New York Times,* August 17, 1934, p. 17; Sté Lyolène Couture Sport Lingerie, 16 place Vendôme, August 31, 1934, Bankruptcy (faillites) files no 50288, D12 U^{3}268 (LINA-MAIS), CPA.

90. Questionnaire relatif à la classification couture-création, January 1952, 1, Maison Marcel Rochas, F12 10504, FNA; "Rochas, Renouvellement dans la Haute Couture," *International Textiles* 2, no. 24 (December 28, 1934): 12, Archives of Art and Design, London; Roger Nalys, "Lorsque Marcel Rochas requiert et plaide," *L'Officiel,* January 1935, p. 17.

91. Bertram J. Perkins, "Rochas Coming with Plan to Open NY Shop," *Women's Wear Daily,* October 2, 1936, p. 1; "Un jeune couturier français à New-York," *L'Officiel,* December 1937, p. 26; "Dressmaker Denies Smuggling," *New York Times,* January 18, 1938, p. 11; "Marcel Rochas à New-York," *L'Officiel,* December 1937, p. 20; "Navy Blue and White Simplicity for Marcel Rochas N.Y. Maison," *Women's Wear Daily,* September 29, 1937, p. 3.

92. "Marcel Rochas N.Y. Premiere Dramatizes Fabrics and Colors in Fashions of Distinction," *Women's Wear Daily,* September 30, 1937, p. 3; "Un jeune couturier français," 26.

93. "Un jeune couturier français," 26; "Smuggling Is Investigated," *New York Times,* December 28, 1937, p. 29; "Smuggling of Gowns Charged in US Trials," *New York Times,* June 2, 1938, p. 3; "Dress Smuggler Gets Year's Term," *New York Times,* June 11, 1938, p. 3.

94. "Smuggled Dresses Bring $6,200 Total," *New York Times,* September 23, 1938, p. 32; "Marcel Rochas Inc. Same Brings $7,990," *Women's Wear Daily,* September 23, 1938, p. 5; Questionnaire relatif à la classification couture-création, January 1952–1954, F12 10504, 10505, FNA.

95. "New York City 1937 Dress Output Put at $332,300,798," *Women's Wear Daily,* April 21, 1939, p. Z 25; "New York Rounds Up Fashions and Manufacture for Nation," *Women's Wear Daily,* September 19, 1939, p. 3.

96. Committee meeting minutes, May 7, 1930, 1–3, 6, and July 4, 1930, 2, both CSCPA.

97. Committee meeting minutes, October 1, 1931, 10, and May 7, 1930, 11, 20, both CSCPA.

98. Committee meeting minutes, September 13, 1921, 1, CSCPA; Débats parlementaires, *Journal officiel de la République française,* April 1, 1926, p. 174; "France," Informations sociales, Bureau international du travail, August 6, 1923, p. 18; "Le marché du travail," *Revue d'économie politique* 1 (1924): 382–383.

99. Nancy L. Green, *Ready-to-Wear and Ready-to-Work: A Century of Industry and Immigrants in Paris and New York* (Durham, NC: Duke University Press, 1997), 89; Michel Offerlé, "Patrons et patronat en France au XXème siècle," *Vingtième siècle: Revue d'histoire* 114, no. 2 (2012): 90; "Le lock-out de la couture: Tous les ateliers ont été fermés à midi," *La Presse,* April 23, 1923, p. 1; General Assembly meeting minutes, April 4 and 6, 1923, 1, Committee meetings file, CSCPA; "Chronique: Aux Syndicats professionnels de l'Abbaye," *La vie au patronage: Organe catholique des œuvres de jeunesse,* January 1928, 26; "La Commission mixte, deuxième degré de l'organisation professionnelle," *Confédération Française des Travailleurs Chrétiens,* monthly newsletter, January 1928, 487–489.

100. Committee meeting minutes, October 1, 1931, 8–12, 10, M. Dupouy, CSCPA.

101. Committee meeting minutes, January 22, 1932, 4; June 16, 1932, 2; October 1, 1931, 5–10; January 22, 1932, 4–7, all CSCPA; Deschamps, "La Crise," 99.

102. Salaire minimum hebdomadaire des travailleurs de la haute couture par catégorie adapté à l'index du coût de la vie, applicable à partir de la semaine du 30 janvier 1932, Committee meeting minutes, January 22, 1932, 4, CSCPA.

103. Deschamps, "La Crise," 44; Danièle Fraboulet, "L'Union des industries métallurgiques et minières: Organisations, stratégies et pratiques du patronat métallurgique, 1901–1940," *Vingtième siècle: Revue d'histoire* 114, no. 2 (2012): 117–135; Georges Lefranc, *Les organisations patronales en France du passé au présent* (Paris: Payot, 1976), 50–51; General Assembly meeting minutes, July 9, 1937, 5, CSCPA.

104. Fraboulet, "L'Union," 131; Green, *Ready-to-Wear,* 91–92; General Assembly meeting minutes, July 31, 1937, 1, CSCPA.

105. Florent Le Bot, "La naissance du Centre des Jeunes Patrons (1938–1944): Entre réaction et relève," *Vingtième siècle: Revue d'histoire* 114, no. 2 (2012): 99–100; General Assembly meeting minutes, July 9, 1937, 7.

106. Jean-Charles Asselain, "Une erreur de politique économique: La loi des quarante heures de 1936," *Revue économique* 25, no. 4 (1973): 672–705; Deschamps, "La Crise," 65; Garnier, *Paris-couture,* 197; Véronique Pouillard, "Managing Fashion Creativity: The History of the Chambre Syndicale de la Couture Parisienne during the Interwar Period," *Investigaciones de Historia Economica/Economic History Research* 5, no. 2 (2015): 76–89.

107. General Assembly meeting minutes, July 9, 1937, 5, 3; "Modification d'application des nouveaux décrets-lois concernant la durée du travail," Committee meeting minutes, November 18, 1938, CSCPA; General Assembly meeting minutes, July 31, 1937, 2, 51; "Convention collective de travail réglant les rapports entre employeurs de la couture et leurs ouvrières dans les départements de Seine et de Seine-et-Oise," *Journal officiel de la République française,* July 13, 1937, pp. 7932–7933; *Journal officiel de la République française,* August 10, 1938, p. 9548; General Assembly meeting minutes, March 15, 1939, 7–8, CSCPA; Bertram J. Perkins, "U.S. Buying in France at Standstill as Franc Devaluation Is Speeded," *Women's Wear Daily,* September 28, 1936, pp. 1, 4; Bertram J. Perkins, "Rush Orders from US Follow Devaluation Moves," *Women's Wear Daily,* October 1936, p. 1.

4. Fashion in World War II

1. "Aquitania Arrivals See Spring Trade Influenced by European Conditions," *Women's Wear Daily,* February 17, 1939, p. 1; Bertram J. Perkins, "Glimpses of Paris," *Women's Wear Daily,* April 26, 1939, p. 4; Bertram J. Perkins, "Glimpses of Paris," *Women's Wear Daily,* May 2, 1939, p. 4; Bertram J. Perkins, "Glimpses of Paris," *Women's Wear Daily,* May 17, 1939, p. 7.

2. Bertram J. Perkins, "Glimpses of Paris," *Women's Wear Daily,* April 17, 1939, p. 4; Bertram J. Perkins, "Glimpses of Paris," *Women's Wear Daily,* April 24, 1939, p. 4; Irene Guenther, *Nazi Chic: Fashioning Women in the Third Reich* (London: Berg, 2004), 144–147, 159, 167–204.

3. "Developments in Europe Spur N.Y. Drive to Aid Refugees," *Women's Wear Daily,* March 17, 1929, p. 31; Guenther, *Nazi Chic,* 159, 165.

4. Bertram J. Perkins, "Glimpses of Paris," *Women's Wear Daily,* April 24, 1939, p. 4; *Women's Wear Daily,* May 10, 1939, p. 1; Bertram J. Perkins, "Believed in Move to Curb Model Renters," *Women's Wear Daily,* February 13, 1939, p. 7; "Ship Arrivals Stress Paris Aids to Selling," *Women's Wear Daily,* August 11, 1939, pp. 1, 36Z; "Narrow Silhouette, Front View, Stressed in Models Import Group," *Women's Wear Daily,* August 23, 1939, pp. 3, 26.

5. "Style Leadership Called City's Due," *New York Times,* August 5, 1940, p. 15; Kaori O'Connor, "Anthropology, Archaeology, History and the Material Culture of Lycra," in *Writing Material Culture History,* ed. Anne Gerritsen and Giorgio Riello (London: Bloomsbury, 2015), 73–91.

6. "Members in Paris See FOGA Final Victor," *Women's Wear Daily,* February 12, 1939, p. 1.

7. *Women's Wear Daily,* April 6, 1939, p. 6.

8. *Women's Wear Daily,* May 16, 1939, p. 4; Bertram J. Perkins, "FOGA-Paris Plan to Check Delivery to Model Renters Interests Returning Buyers," *Women's Wear Daily,* May 3, 1939, p. 1; Bertram J. Perkins, "Trouyet, PAIS Piracy Defense Head, Resigns," *Women's Wear Daily,* May 26, 1939, p. 1.

9. Bertram J. Perkins, "Glimpses of Paris: Many Advantages Seen in Air Service," *Women's Wear Daily,* August 11, 1939, p. 36Z; Bertram J. Perkins, "Shipping Paris Models by Air This Weekend," *Women's Wear Daily,* August 3, 1939, p. 4.

10. J. W. Cohn, "Clipper Arrival from Paris Couture Openings Emphasize Fast Service," *Women's Wear Daily*, August 8, 1939, p. 1.

11. Bertram J. Perkins, "Glimpses of Paris: Many Advantages"; *Women's Wear Daily*, August 25, 1939, p. 1; "Believe War Would Only Slow Couture," *Women's Wear Daily*, August 28, 1939, p. 1; *Women's Wear Daily*, August 25, 1939, p. 1.

12. Kathleen Cannell, "Paris Couturiers, in United Front, Decide to Reopen Immediately," *New York Times*, October 9, 1939, p. 3; General Assembly meeting minutes, April 9, 1940, Lucien Lelong, 4–5, CSCPA.

13. General Assembly meeting minutes, October 6, 1939, Lucien Lelong, 1–2, 13, CSCPA; Bertram J. Perkins, "Couture Acts to Maintain French Style Leadership," *Women's Wear Daily*, September 5, 1939, p. 1; "Buyers Here Wary on Price Boosting," *New York Times*, September 9, 1939, p. 32; "FOGA Cables Encouragement to Haute Couture," *Women's Wear Daily*, September 8, 1939, pp. 1, 35.

14. Cannell, "Paris Couturiers, in United Front," 3; Kathleen Cannell, "Fashion Carries On Despite the Blackout," *New York Times*, November 26, 1939, p. 114; Bertram J. Perkins, "International Fund Is Proposed to Help Preserve French Couture," *Women's Wear Daily*, September 11, 1939, pp. 1, 19; Bertram J. Perkins, "Collective Paris Couture Showing in New York Suggested," *Women's Wear Daily*, September 18, 1939, pp. 1, 18; General Assembly meeting minutes, October 6, 1939, 3; The Fashion Group International, Wednesday afternoon, September 27, 1939, Biltmore Hotel, New York City, Edna Woolman Chase, 28–31, folder 6, box 73, FG, NYPL.

15. Alice K. Perkins, "A Fashion Editor Writes of War-Time Paris," *Women's Wear Daily*, September 22, 1939, p. 4; Nancy L. Green, *The Other Americans in Paris: Businessmen, Countesses, Wayward Youth, 1880–1941* (Chicago: University of Chicago Press, 2014).

16. General Assembly meeting minutes, October 6, 1939, 1, 4, 7, 11–13, and April 9, 1940, 9, both CSCPA; Cannell, "Paris Couturiers, in United Front," 3.

17. General Assembly meeting minutes, April 9, 1940, 13–14, CSCPA.

18. The Fashion Group Inc., Wednesday afternoon, September 27, 1939, Biltmore Hotel, New York City, Edna Woolman Chase speech transcript, 30, folder 6, box 73, FG, NYPL; *L'Officiel* 218–219, October 1939, p. 29; General Assembly meeting minutes, April 9, 1940, 13–14, CSCPA.

19. Bertram J. Perkins, "Couture Carries On as Plans Widen for Midseason Openings," *Women's Wear Daily*, October 10, 1939, p. 1; "Lelong Confirms Trend to Becoming Normalcy," *Women's Wear Daily*, November 2, 1939, p. 1; *L'Officiel* 220–221, Christmas 1939, pp. 38, 49.

20. Dominique Veillon, *La mode sous l'Occupation* (Paris: Payot, 1990); "Molyneux Reendorses Full Skirts in Ankle-Lengths," *Women's Wear Daily*, October 23, 1939, p. 1; Bertram J. Perkins, "Paris Cheerfulness Inspires American Colony," *Women's Wear Daily*, October 11, 1939, p. 7; Bertram J. Perkins, "Glimpses of Paris," *Women's Wear Daily*, October 10, 1939, p. 8; Cannell, "Fashion Carries On," 114.

21. Kathleen Cannell, "Normal Styles in Paris," *New York Times*, October 22, 1939, p. 64; Kathleen Cannell, "Molyneux," *New York Times*, October 29, 1939, p. D8; "*Silhouettes* Vary in New Paris Modes," *New York Times*, August 15, 1939, p. 16.

22. "War Economies Help Paris Retaildom to Adjust Itself to Period of Lower Volume," *Women's Wear Daily,* October 11, 1939, p. 2, p. 25.

23. Alice K. Perkins, "Fashion Editor Writes," p. 4; General Assembly meeting minutes, October 6, 1939, 13–16; Cannell, "Paris Couturiers, in United Front," 3.

24. Ateliers d'Equipement Militaire de la Couture Parisienne, 282.302B, D33U3 1362, CPA; Committee meeting minutes, October 6, 1939, 2–3; General Assembly meeting minutes, April 9, 1940, 3–4, and January 28, 1942, 36, both CSCPA.

25. Mad Carpentier, 282.252B, D33U3 1362, CPA; Marcelle Chaumont, 282.280B, D33U3 1362, CPA; Maison Charles Montaigne, 290.564B, D33U3 1386, CPA; Questionnaire relatif à la Classification Couture-Création, January 1952, Mad Carpentier, 1; Marcelle Chaumont, 1 AN F12 10504, FNA; *Women's Wear Daily,* April 26, 1939, p. 1; *L'Officiel* 217, September 1939, p. 24; Bertram J. Perkins, "Mme Vionnet to Form New Couture Firm," *Women's Wear Daily,* May 1, 1939, p. 28; "New Couture House Opening," *Women's Wear Daily,* December 22, 1939, p. 1; Bertram J. Perkins, "Marcelle Chaumont Is Name of New House," *Women's Wear Daily,* January 18, 1940, p. 4; Bertram J. Perkins, "To Bar Radio Photos from Paris Openings," *Women's Wear Daily,* January 22, 1940, p. 1.

26. Bertram J. Perkins, "Glimpses of Paris," *Women's Wear Daily,* January 18, 1940, p. 4; *Women's Wear Daily,* January 22, 1940, p. 5; General Assembly meeting minutes, April 9, 1939, 20–23, and October 6, 1940, 24.

27. Meeting of the Committee enlarged to the Chambre Syndicale de la Couture Parisienne, April 2, 1940, 4, General Assembly meeting minutes, April 9, 1940, Résolution n. 2 de l'Assemblée générale de la Chambre Syndicale de la Couture Parisienne, part 2; "France's New Decrees Seen Aid to Couture," *Women's Wear Daily,* March 1, 1940, p. 2; Bertram J. Perkins, "Lelong Heads French Government Unit to Promote De Luxe Industries," *Women's Wear Daily,* April 12, 1940, p. 1; Bertram J. Perkins, "Glimpses of Paris: Lelong, in Government Post, Expected to Bring Couture Closer to Outlets," *Women's Wear Daily,* April 30, 1940, p. 4; Kathleen Cannell, "Fate of Paris as Fashion Capital Rests in Hands of French Soldier," *New York Times,* January 21, 1940, p. 31.

28. "Manifestation parisienne à Amsterdam," *L'Officiel,* May 1940, p. 33; "Most Couture Showings to Begin April 17," *Women's Wear Daily,* April 3, 1940, p. 1; "Show of Fashions to Support Relief," *New York Times,* May 5, 1940, p. 58; "Important Artists to Design Tableaux for French Benefit Fashion Show," *Women's Wear Daily,* April 25, 1940, p. 1; "Gown Brings $700 at French Benefit," *New York Times,* May 10, 1940, p. 27.

29. The Fashion Group Inc., Biltmore Hotel, Madison Avenue, Wednesday afternoon, March 20, 1940, 4–5, 9, folder 8, box 73, FG, NYPL.

30. "Trousers Move Fast into First Line of War Fashions," *Women's Wear Daily,* September 29, 1939, p. 14; Alice K. Perkins, "Fashion Editor Writes," p. 4; "To USA Fashions," *Women's Wear Daily,* September 19, 1939, p. 2; "American Fashion Records," *Women's Wear Daily,* September 19, 1939, p. 3; "Investment in Americanism," *Women's Wear Daily,* September 26, 1940, p. 6.

31. Bertram J. Perkins, "No Canceling, US Importers Cable to Paris," *Women's Wear Daily*, May 15, 1940, pp. 1, 3; J. W. Cohn, "US Business Men Ponder Europe's Political Status," *Women's Wear Daily*, May 10, 1940, pp. 1, 35; "Paris Hopeful of 'Normal' War Status Shortly," *Women's Wear Daily*, May 21, 1940, p. 36; Bertram J. Perkins, "Paris Skips Holiday as Work on Exports Is Undiminished," *Women's Wear Daily*, May 13, 1940, p. 1; Bertram J. Perkins, "Glimpses of Paris," *Women's Wear Daily*, May 14, 1940, p. 8.

32. Bertram J. Perkins, "Glimpses of Paris," *Women's Wear Daily*, May 14, 1940, p. 8.

33. "Paris Couturiers Carry On in Unity," *New York Times*, May 25, 1940, p. 5; General Assembly meeting minutes, May 27, 1940, 1, CSCPA; Alice K. Perkins, "Paris Designers Busy Helping Refugees and Making Models," *Women's Wear Daily*, June 11, 1940, p. 1.

34. Bertram J. Perkins, "Will Couture Accept Nazi Domination?," *Women's Wear Daily*, June 19, 1940, p. 23; "France's Couture Seen Continuing," *New York Times*, June 27, 1940, p. 27; "US Designers Can Carry On Alone, Is View," *Women's Wear Daily*, June 19, 1940, p. 23; "Couture Fate in Conquered Land Awaited," *Women's Wear Daily*, June 24, 1940, pp. 1, 24.

35. "Direct Style Theft Question Posed by FOGA," *Women's Wear Daily*, June 5, 1940, p. 1; Morris D. C. Crawford, "Holds Laws, Courts Favor Pirate More Than Style Creator," *Women's Wear Daily*, July 11, 1939, p. 4.

36. Sara Beth Marcketti, "Design Piracy in the United States' Women's Ready-to-Wear Apparel Industry: 1910–1941" (PhD diss., Iowa State University, 2005), 136–143; "Retail Emotions Mixed on FOGA," *Women's Wear Daily*, July 30, 1940, p. 16; Sylvan Gotshal, *The Pirates Will Get You: A Story of the Fight for Design Protection* (New York: Columbia University Press, 1945), 17.

37. "New York," *New York Times*, September 8, 1940, p. 74; advertisement for New York fashion designers in Vogue, *New York Times*, September 5, 1940, p. 12; Kathleen McLaughlin, "America Searched for Style Motifs," *New York Times*, August 9, 1940, p. 13.

38. "All-American Modes Are Presented Here," *New York Times*, August 23, 1940, p. 11; "Ellerbe Wood Coordinated Collection Projects Spring and American Names," *Women's Wear Daily*, October 8, 1940, p. 3; "Ellerbe Wood's US Models Showing Stresses Individual Cuts," *Women's Wear Daily*, October 10, 1940, p. 3.

39. "Design American Way, Advises Dorothy Shaver," *Women's Wear Daily*, July 30, 1940, p. 31.

40. "World Fashion Hub New Council's Arm," *New York Times*, August 21, 1940, p. 34.

41. "Lanvin Partly Reopened, Says Diplomat in New York," *Women's Wear Daily*, August 19, 1940, p. 1.

42. "Better Houses Begin Official Fall Openings," *Women's Wear Daily*, July 1, 1940, p. 1.

43. Kathleen Cannell, "Paris Couturiers Look for Revival," *New York Times*, July 23, 1940, p. 16; "Some Couture Firms in Paris Map Fall Lines," *Women's Wear Daily*, August 5, 1940, p. 23.

44. Bertram J. Perkins, "Enthusiasm for Revival of Paris Creativeness Cools," *Women's Wear Daily*, July 8, 1940, pp. 1–2; Kathleen Cannell, "Paris Couturiers, Led by Lelong, Plan Method to Hold Industry," *New York Times*, August 25, 1940, p. 37; General Assembly meeting minutes,

August 6, 1940, 5, CSCPA; Statutory meeting minutes, April 9, 1940, 25–26, CSCPA; *L'Officiel*, February 1941, p. 40; *L'Officiel*, March 1941, p. 38.

45. General Assembly meeting minutes, August 6, 1940, 5, CSCPA.

46. Cannell, "Paris Couturiers, Led by Lelong," 37.

47. "New York," 74; "Resume of Paris Couture Showings Indicates Accent on Big Coats and Culottes," *Women's Wear Daily*, October 10, 1940, p. 4; Kathleen Cannell, "Paris Styles Draw German Officers," *New York Times*, October 26, 1940, p. 5; "Rosevienne Shows Street-Length Dinner Frocks of Black Velvet," *Women's Wear Daily*, September 23, 1940, p. 1.

48. Secrétariat général, Ministère des Finances, to the Secrétaire d'Etat à la Production industrielle, Direction des Textiles et des Cuirs, Paris, June 11, 1942, F12 10503, FNA; Nadine Gasc, "Haute Couture and Fashion 1939–1946," in *Théâtre de la Mode*, by Edmonde Charles-Roux (New York: Rizzoli / Metropolitan Museum of Art, 1991), 101; Yvonne Deslandres, *Mode des années 40* (Paris: Seuil, 1992), 83; Véronique Pouillard, *Hirsch & Cie: Bruxelles, 1869–1962* (Brussels: University of Brussels Press); Dirk Luyten, "L'épuration économique en Belgique," in *L'épuration économique en France à la Libération*, ed. Marc Bergère (Rennes: Presses Universitaires de Rennes, 2008), 210–211.

49. "Secours National: Entr'aide d'hiver du Maréchal," advertisement, *L'Officiel*, March 1941, n.p.; Colette, "Chronique de France: Paris," *L'Officiel*, March 1941, pp. 17–18; Kathleen Cannell, "Paris Papers Score Frivolity in Dress," *New York Times*, September 5, 1940, p. 27; Veillon, *La mode sous l'Occupation*.

50. Bertram J. Perkins, "Glimpses of Paris," *Women's Wear Daily*, May 15, 1940, p. 5; Bianchini-Férier advertisement, *L'Officiel*, April 1941, inside of front cover; "Documents," *L'Officiel*, April 1941, p. 9; *L'Officiel*, May 1941, pp. 5–6, 52; G. Lussy-Bessy, "Le roman de la lingerie," *L'Officiel*, May 1941, pp. 48–50; G. Lussy-Bessy, "Le travail-main revient à l'honneur," *L'Officiel*, June 1941, pp. 20–21.

51. General Assembly meeting minutes, September 17, 1940, 11, and January 28, 1942, 1, both CSCPA.

52. Veillon, *La mode sous l'Occupation*, 50; Philippe Verheyde, *Les mauvais comptes de Vichy: L'aryanisation des entreprises juives* (Paris: Perrin, 1999), 21–44; Jean-Pierre Azéma and Olivier Wieviorka, *Vichy, 1940–1944* (Paris: Perrin, 2004), 269–271.

53. Report: Rapport concernant la S.A. Chanel "Parfumeur" 135 av. de Neuilly, Neuilly sur Seine, Confiscation des profits illicites, Ordonnance du 18 Octobre 1944, dossier de citation no. IX 133, Nom: parfums Chanel S.A., Adresse: 135 Avenue de Neuilly à Neuilly sur Seine, Série 3314-IX/71/1 0008, CPA.

54. Sté des parfums Chanel, 215.042B, D33U3 1078, CPA; Chanel Couture, 93.879, D33U3 0031, CPA; Rapport concernant la S.A. Jean Patou, parfumeur, 11, Bd de la Madeleine, 5–6, Paris, Citation no. III/41, 3ème Comité de confiscation des profits illicites de la Seine, Versement 3314-III/71/1, 3ème Comité, 0004, CPA; Bertram J. Perkins, "Glimpses of Paris: No Gabrielle Chanel Showing This Season," *Women's Wear Daily*, January 11, 1940, p. 4; Bertram J. Perkins, "Glimpses of Paris," *Women's Wear Daily*, February 13, 1940, p. 10; Florence Brachet Champsaur, "'Créer

c'est avoir vu en premier': Les Galeries Lafayette et la mode (1893–1969)" (PhD diss., EHESS, Paris, 2018); Nancy L. Green, *Ready-to-Wear and Ready-to-Work: A Century of Industry and Immigrants in Paris and New York* (Durham, NC: Duke University Press, 1997), 95–100; Florent Le Bot, *La fabrique réactionnaire: Antisémitisme, spoliations et corporatisme dans le cuir (1930–1950)* (Paris: Presses de Science Po, 2007); Hal Vaughan, *Sleeping with the Enemy: Coco Chanel's Secret War* (New York: Knopf, 2011); Veillon, *La mode sous l'Occupation*, 167–170; "French Restrictions on Dyeing Industry Limit Colors and Clothes in Spring Showing," *New York Times*, March 5, 1945, p. 16.

55. Letter, Paris, June 9, 1942, F12 10503, FNA; Committee meeting minutes, September 26, 1942, 7; General Assembly meeting minutes, January 28, 1942, 33, Discourse of Lucien Lelong, March 23, 1945, 4, and March 18, 1948, 3–4, all CSCPA.

56. General Assembly meeting minutes, January 28, 1942, 6–9.

57. Ibid., 11, 26.

58. Ibid., 32, Lucien Lelong report.

59. Ibid.; Robert O. Paxton, *Vichy France: Old Guard and New Order* (New York: Columbia University Press, 2001), 220, 236.

60. Secrétariat général, Ministère des Finances, to the Secrétaire d'Etat à la Production industrielle, Direction des Textiles et des Cuirs, Paris, June 11, 1942.

61. Veillon, *La mode sous l'Occupation*, 152–153.

62. Comité d'organisation du vêtement, Groupe I, F12 files, FNA; Claude Rouzaud, *Les industries de luxe, un problème d'intérêt national* (Paris: Recueil Sirey, 1946), 203.

63. General Assembly meeting minutes, January 28, 1942; Rouzaud, *Les industries*, 47, 203–204.

64. Didier Grumbach, *Histoires de la mode*, 2nd ed. (Paris: Editions du Regard, 2008), 434.

65. Compte-rendu de la commission de classement et de contrôle couture-création du 11 Octobre 1943, 2, F12 10503, FNA.

66. Pouillard, *Hirsch & Cie*, 80–81; "Desire to Keep Up the Spirit of France Is Motivating France," *Women's Wear Daily*, July 14, 1943, p. 14; Julie Summers, *Fashion on the Ration: Style in the Second World War* (London: Profile Books, 2015), 168; Lou Taylor and Marie McLoughlin, eds., *Paris Fashion and World War II: Global Diffusion and Paris Control* (London: Bloomsbury, 2020).

67. "Manifestation parisienne à Barcelone," *L'Officiel*, January 1942, p. 31; "Madame Lyolène to Fly Saturday on Clipper," *Women's Wear Daily*, December 6, 1939, p. 1; "Hattie Carnegie Imports Keep Young, Dashing Styles Types Alive," *Women's Wear Daily*, March 8, 1940, p. 4; "Madame Lyolene American Jeune Fille Collection," *Women's Wear Daily*, March 5, 1940, p. 1; "New Carnegie *Jeune Fille* Department Blooms with Lyolene Originals," *Women's Wear Daily*, March 5, 1940, p. 1; "U.S. Urged as World Fashion Hub; Experts Say It Can Replace Paris," *New York Times*, July 12, 1940, p. 17; "Lyolène Urges End of Talk on Substitution," *Women's Wear Daily*, October 2, 1940, p. 18.

68. "Main Bocher Back, Winces at Corset," *New York Times*, October 15, 1939, p. 22; Virginia Pope, "Mainbocher Shows His Fall Fashions," *New York Times*, September 10, 1941, p. 18;

"Mainbocher to Start Apparel Business Here," *Women's Wear Daily,* September 18, 1940, p. 1; Gilbert Millstein, "Mainbocher Stands for a Fitting," *New York Times,* March 25, 1956, p. 38; "Main Bocher Shifts Here," *New York Times,* September 20, 1940, p. 20.

69. Virginia Pope, "Mainbocher Opens First Salon Here," *New York Times,* November 1, 1940, p. 31; Virginia Pope, "The Fashion Capital Moves across Seas," *New York Times,* August 18, 1940, p. 92; "Mainbocher-Warner Collaboration Forges New Link between Foundation and Fashion," *Women's Wear Daily,* January 17, 1940, p. 1; Pope, "Mainbocher Shows," 18; Millstein, "Mainbocher Stands," 42.

70. "Mainbocher Adds Waves to Clients," *New York Times,* August 15, 1942, p. 7.

71. Kathleen McLaughlin, "New York Seeks Crown of Fashion,", *New York Times,* August 4, 1940, p. 31; Alice K. Perkins, "Tempo of Paris Fashion Designers Essential to World of Creation," *Women's Wear Daily,* July 1, 1940, p. 3.

72. Pope, "Fashion Capital Moves," 92; Alice K. Perkins, "Designers Say Test of Creative Work Is Its Individuality," *Women's Wear Daily,* August 5, 1940, p. 3; Kathleen McLaughlin, "Fashion Industry Looks for Leader," *New York Times,* August 7, 1940, p. 17; Alfred D. Chandler, *The Visible Hand: The Managerial Revolution in American Business* (Cambridge, MA: Belknap Press of Harvard University Press, 1977), 71.

73. "Holds US Fashion Industry Must Organize to Achieve Greatness," *Women's Wear Daily,* September 24, 1940, pp. 2, 27.

74. Paul Cromwell, "Study Is Ordered on Fashion Area," *New York Times,* December 5, 1955, p. 33; "A World Fashion Center," *New York Times,* December 10, 1955, p. 20.

75. Veillon, *La mode sous l'Occupation;* Summers, *Fashion on the Ration;* Fabienne Falluel and Marie-Laure Gutton, *Elégance et système D: Paris 1940–1944, accessoires de mode sous l'Occupation* (Paris: Paris Musées, 2009); Grumbach, *Histoires de la mode,* 49.

76. General Assembly meeting minutes, January 28, 1942, 40; Philippe Verheyde, "Guerres et profits en longue durée, une approche politique et morale de l'économie," in Bergère, *L'épuration économique,* 20–21.

77. Dossiers no. 41–42 C4, IIIème Comité; Rapport Concernant la S.A. Jean Patou, parfumeur, 1–4, 11–21; Raymond Barbas to the 3ème Comité, Paris, March 27, 1945; Raymond Barbas to Lieutenant-Colonel Jacques de Sieyès, Paris, June 29, 1945; Confiscation des profits illicites, avis de décision du 21 décembre 1945 concernant la Société Jean Patou, 1–2; Citation no. III/41, 3ème Comité de confiscation des profits illicites de la Seine, Versement 3314-III/71/1, 3ème Comité, 0004, CPA.

78. Extrait du procès-verbal de la séance du 9e Comité du 23 octobre 1947. Citation no. 133.—Société des Parfums CHANEL S.A.; Paris, Ministère des Finances, Confiscation des profits illicites, Avis de Décision, 1–2; Confiscation des profits illicites, Ordonnance du 18 Octobre 1944, dossier de citation no. IX 133, Nom: parfums Chanel S.A., Adresse: 135 Avenue de Neuilly à Neuilly sur Seine, Série 3314-IX/71/1 0008, CPA.

79. "Madame Jeanne Lanvin vient d'être décorée de la Légion d'Honneur," *L'Officiel,* March 1926, p. 14; "Jean Labusquière," *L'Officiel,* December 1941, p. 37.

80. "Lanvin Partly Reopened," p. 1.

81. Valerie Steele, ed., *The Berg Companion to Fashion* (Oxford: Berg, 2010), 468.

82. Comité de Confiscation des Profits Illicites, IIIe Comité de Confiscation des Profits Illicites de la Seine, Rapport concernant la S. A. "Jeanne Lanvin" Haute Couture, 15, rue du Faubourg Saint-Honoré, M. Faure Inspecteur Principal, Paris, 3314-III, Cit. III/393, CPA.

83. Comité de Confiscation des Profits Illicites, IIIe Comité de Confiscation des Profits Illicites de la Seine, Rapport concernant la société anonyme "Lanvin-Parfums," Inspecteur principal M. Faure, Paris, July 1, 1949, 1, CPA.

84. Comité de Confiscation des Profits Illicites, IIIe Comité, Rapport concernant la S. A. "Jeanne Lanvin" Haute Couture.

85. Comité de Confiscation des Profits Illicites, IIIe Comité, Rapport concernant la société anonyme "Lanvin-Parfums," 1; Veillon, *La mode sous l'Occupation;* Falluel and Gutton, *Elégance et système D;* INSEE franc converter: https://www.insee.fr/fr/information/2417794.

86. Figures are from the INSEE franc converter, https://www.insee.fr/fr/information/2417794.

87. Comité de Confiscation des Profits Illicites, IIIe Comité, Rapport concernant la société anonyme "Lanvin-Parfums," 7–8, 10.

88. Sources of the table: Perotin/3314/71/1/3 27. IIIème Comité. 393, Jeanne Lanvin S.A. Inventory sheets, CPA; INSEE franc converter: https://www.insee.fr/fr/information/2417794.

89. Alfred D. Chandler, *Scale and Scope: The Dynamics of Industrial Capitalism* (Cambridge, MA: Belknap Press of Harvard University Press, 1994), 59–61.

90. Comité de Confiscation des Profits Illicites, IIIe Comité de Confiscation des Profits Illicites de la Seine, Rapport concernant Jeanne LANVIN, décédée, Inspecteur principal M. Faure, Paris, June 30, 1949, 2–4, CPA.

91. Décision du 22 juin 1950 concernant la Société Anonyme "Jeanne LANVIN," 15, rue du Fbg St-Honoré à Paris (8e), Comité de Confiscation des Profits Illicites, IIIe Comité de Confiscation des Profits Illicites de la Seine, CPA; IIIème Comité de confiscation des profits illicites, Perotin/3314/71/1/3/27, numéro 393, Jeanne Lanvin SA. Décision du 22 juin 1950 concernant la Société Anonyme "Jeanne Lanvin"—15, rue du Faubourg Saint-Honoré à Paris (8e), CPA.

92. Enquête préalable Société Haute Couture Maggy Rouff, Comité de la Seine, December 9, 1945; Lucien Faure, Inspecteur, Rapport concernant la SA Maggy Rouff, 136 av. des Champs-Elysées Paris (8e), November 5, 1949, Comité de Confiscation des Profits Illicites, IIIe Comite de Confiscation des Profits Illicites de la Seine, 3314 -/71/1/3, CPA.

93. Note sur une forme de "Résistance" des Etablissements Cazaux par Henri Darmat, gérant, March 11, 1945; Rapport, Inspecteur Sutra, Paris, June 26, 1946; Decision, Paris, January 21, 1948, Société Pierre Cazaux & Cie, 17–19 Cité Voltaire, Paris, 5ème comité de confiscation des profits illicites, 3314/71/1/5 9, CPA.

94. General Assembly meeting minutes, January 28, 1944, 2, CSCPA; Fabrice Grenard and Kenneth J. Mouré, *"Une justice difficile:* Confisquer les profits illicites du marché noir à la Libération," in Bergère, *L'épuration économique*, 53–58.

95. General Assembly meeting minutes, January 28, 1944, 2.

96. Ibid.

97. Ibid., 3.

98. Ibid.

99. Ibid., 4.

100. Ibid.

101. Rouzaud, *Les industries*, 204; Bertram J. Perkins, "Couture's Four-Year Skirmish with the Nazis," *Women's Wear Daily*, November 30, 1944, p. 6.

5. Global Haute Couture

1. Jean Fourastié, *Les Trente Glorieuses ou la révolution invisible* (Paris: Fayard, 1979).

2. *Dior by Dior: The Autobiography of Christian Dior* (1957; London: Victoria and Albert Museum, 2007), 5–7; Tomoko Okawa, "Licensing Practices at Maison Dior," in *Producing Fashion: Commerce, Culture, and Consumers*, ed. Regina Lee Blaszczyk (Philadelphia: University of Pennsylvania Press, 2008), 182; Alexandra Palmer, *Dior: A New Look, a New Enterprise (1947–57)* (London: Victoria and Albert Museum, 2009); Farid Chenoune, *Christian Dior* (Paris: Assouline, 2007); Jean-Claude Daumas, "Marcel Boussac, 1889–1980," in *Dictionnaire historique des patrons français*, ed. Jean Claude Daumas (Paris: Flammarion, 2010), 121; Nigel Cawthorne, *The New Look: The Dior Revolution* (London: Hyman, 1996), 128–131.

3. Okawa, "Licensing Practices," 88; Marie-France Pochna, *Christian Dior* (Paris: Flammarion, 2004), 125, 151–152; *Dior by Dior*, 17; General Assembly meeting minutes, March 22, 1949, prologue, 1, CSCPA; Ingrid Brenninkmeyer, "The Diffusion of Fashion," in *Fashion Marketing: An Anthology of Viewpoints and Perspectives*, ed. Gordon Wills and David Midgley (London: Allen and Unwin, 1973), 270; Catherine Omnès, *Ouvrières parisiennes: Marché du travail et trajectoires professionnelles au 20ᵉ siècle* (Paris: Editions de l'EHESS, 1997), 34, 42.

4. Richard Kuisel, *Capitalism and the State in Modern France: Renovation and Economic Management in the Twentieth Century* (Cambridge: Cambridge University Press, 1981), 223; Penelope Rowlands, *A Dash of Daring: Carmel Snow and Her Life in Fashion, Art, and Letters* (New York: Atria Books, 2005), 364–365; "Ankle-Length Suit Displayed in France," *New York Times*, October 30, 1947, p. 29; Valérie Guillaume, *Jacques Fath* (Paris: Adam Biro, 1993), 176; Cawthorne, *New Look*, 13; Roy B. Helfgott, "Women's and Children's Apparel," in *Made in New York: Case Studies in Metropolitan Manufacturing*, ed. Max Hall (Cambridge, MA: Harvard University Press, 1959), 57; Bernard Roshco, *The Rag Race: How New York and Paris Run the Breakneck Business of Dressing American Women* (New York: Funk and Wagnalls, 1963), 127–128.

5. Adelheid Rasche, "Christian Dior in Germany," in *Christian Dior in Germany, 1947 to 1957*, ed. Adelheid Rasche and Christina Thomson (Stuttgart: Arnoldsche, 2007), 35; "Queen Elizabeth Brings 2,258 Here," *New York Times*, September 2, 1947, p. 26.

6. Christian Dior, interviewed by Elie Rabourdin and Alice Chavanne, *Je suis couturier* (Paris: Editions du Conquistador, 1951), 26–44; Guillaume Garnier, *40 années de création, Pierre*

Balmain (Paris: Musée de la Mode et du Costume, 1985); Lourdes Font, "Dior before Dior," *West 86th: A Journal of Decorative Arts, Design History, and Material Culture* 18, no. 1 (2011): 26–49.

7. Dior, *Je suis couturier*, 77.

8. "Dior Says Textiles Give Him Ideas," *New York Times*, February 5, 1955, p. 24; "Christian Dior Creates His Models" and "The Setting-Up of a Collection," in *Christian Dior*, booklet, English ed., n.p., all in Dior S.A. Archive (hereafter cited as DSAA).

9. Dior, *Je suis couturier*, 98–99.

10. "Dior to Celebrate 10th Birthday," *Women's Wear Daily*, January 2, 1957, p. 3.

11. As shown by the three books of sales of the House of Vionnet, Centre de Documentation, UCAD.

12. Files Préparation des collections, 1947–49, DSAA.

13. Okawa, "Licensing Practices," 85; Jean-Louis Paucelle, "Henri Fayol, 1841–1925," in Daumas, *Dictionnaire historique*, 279–281; John C. Wood and Michael C. Wood, eds., *Henri Fayol: Critical Evaluations in Business and Management*, vol. 1 (London: Routledge, 2002), 88–89; Pochna, *Christian Dior*, 259; Georges Lefranc, *Les organisations patronales en France du passé au présent* (Paris: Payot, 1976), 134, 152; Roshco, *Rag Race*, 158.

14. Lourdes Font ("Dior before Dior") has examined Dior's stylistic continuities.

15. Balance sheets, Documents "Société Christian Dior," 1987003 0251, CIC Archive, ANMT.

16. Ibid.; "Représentation aux Assemblées Générales" and "Mandataires," 1987003/0162, no. 61, CIC Archive, ANMT.

17. Didier Grumbach, *Histoires de la mode*, 2nd ed. (Paris: Edition du Regard, 2008), 49; Kuisel, *Capitalism and the State*, 219; Claire Wilcox, "Dior's Golden Age: The Renaissance of Couture," in *The Golden Age of Couture: Paris–London, 1947–1957*, ed. Claire Wilcox (London: Victoria and Albert Museum, 2007), 49.

18. Statutory General Assembly meeting minutes, April 27, 1955, 3, CSCPA; Rapport d'activités de l'année 1954, 14, 18, CSCPA; Joseph Schumpeter, *Capitalism, Socialism and Democracy* (New York: Harper and Brothers, 1942).

19. Béatrice Touchelay, "La comptabilité et l'expertise à l'origine d'un empire industriel: Marcel Boussac et la contribution extraordinaire sur les bénéfices de guerre, 1916–1928," *Journée d'histoire de la gestion et du management, Roubaix*, no. 12 (2007): 5; Joseph Schumpeter, "Capitalism in the Postwar World," reprinted in *Essays of J. A. Schumpeter*, ed. R. Clemence (Cambridge, MA: Addison-Wesley, 1989), 185; Committee meeting minutes, September 28, 1950, 13, and January 12, 1951, 3, CSCPA; Rapport d'activité de la Chambre Syndicale de la Couture Parisienne pour l'année 1952, 9–10, CSCPA; Kuisel, *Capitalism and the State;* Véronique Pouillard, "Keeping Designs and Brands Authentic: The Resurgence of the Post-War French Fashion Business under the Challenge of US Mass Production," *European Review of History* 20, no. 5 (2013): 818–819; Matthias Kipping, "Les relations gouvernement-monde des affaires dans la France de l'après-guerre: Adaptations et adaptabilités d'un système original," *Histoire, économie, société* 20, no. 4 (2001): 577, 579, 582–584.

20. Direction des industries diverses et des textiles, sous-direction des textiles, note, Paris, November 12, 1952, 2, F12 10425, FNA; Committee meeting minutes, March 8, 1945, 10, CSCPA.

21. R. Catin, Union des Industries Textiles, letter, Paris, November 10, 1952, F12, 10425, FNA; Direction des industries diverses et des textiles, 1n1, 2–3, F12 10425, FNA.

22. Direction des industries diverses et des textiles, 1n1, 1, 3–4, F12 10425, FNA. The Commission d'Aide à la création couture comprised members affiliated with the Union of the Textile Industries, the Syndicats des Négociants en Tissus Spéciaux à la Couture, and the Chambre Syndicale de la Couture Parisienne, one government commissioner appointed by the minister of industry and commerce, and one controller of the state appointed by the state secretary of economic affairs.

23. "Paris: Profit and Piracy in Fashions," *New York Times*, August 28, 1957, p. 24; Roshco, *Rag Race*, 130. Conversion uses the standards of living measure of EH.net, 2014.

24. Raymond Barbas to the State Secretary of Economic Affairs, Paris, November 7, 1952, F12 10425, FNA; Grumbach, *Histoire de la mode*, 76.

25. For an early case, see Florence Brachet Champsaur, "Les Galeries Lafayette et le financement de la couture pendant l'entre-deux-guerres: le cas Jean Patou," *Entreprises et Histoire* 3, no. 64 (2011): 183–185.

26. Classification Couture-Création, F12 10425, FNA.

27. General Assembly meeting minutes, May 3, 1960, and Activity Report for the Year 1959, 13, both at CSCPA; Rapport d'activités de l'année 1955, n.p., CSCPA; Guillaume, *Jacques Fath*, 72; Caroline Rennolds Milbank, *Couture: The Great Designers* (New York: Stewart, Tabori & Chang, 1985), 244; Geoffrey G. Jones, *Beauty Imagined: A History of the Global Beauty Industry* (Oxford: Oxford University Press, 2010), 209, 245; Statutory General Assembly meeting minutes, March 26, 1957, 3, CSCPA; Dilys Blum, *Elsa Schiaparelli* (Philadelphia and Paris: Philadelphia Museum of Art and Musée de la Mode et du Textile, 2003), 254–255; "Fashion Piracy Charges Recall Long-Pending Suit," *New York Times*, August 29, 1959, box 4, Resseguie Collection, BL, HBS; Philippe Simon, *La haute couture: Monographie d'une industrie de luxe* (Paris: Presses Universitaires de France, 1931), 7.

28. "$1 Million Dream Pact," *Women's Wear Daily*, January 2, 1957, p. 8.

29. Les accords Paris-Province, January 6, 1950, 4 pp., DSAA; Correspondence from the Chambre Syndicale de la Couture parisienne, Bulletin 1, July 5, 1950, 7, File Préparation des collections, 1950, Chambre Syndicale de la Couture parisienne, DSAA; Rapports d'activité, 1954–1961, CSCPA, data compiled by the author.

30. Committee meeting minutes, December 13, 1948, 4, CSCPA: "Politique de répression prudente et d'action éducative et préventive."

31. "*Inspiration* Held No Excuse for Fashion Piracy in Paris," *Women's Wear Daily*, April 17, 1957, p. 1; Anne-Laure Catinat, "Les premières avocates du barreau de Paris," *Mil neuf cent. Revue d'histoire intellectuelle (Cahiers Georges Sorel)* 16 (1998): 43–56; Chambre Syndicale de la Couture parisienne, Bulletin 1, 10; Dior, *Je suis couturier*, 86–88; "Dépôt des modèles," ii, iii, File préparation des collections, 1950, Chambre Syndicale de la Couture parisienne, DSAA.

32. Committee meeting minutes, December 13, 1948, 4, CSCPA; General Assembly meeting minutes, March 15, 1948, 1–2, CSCPA.

33. "Dior Rents on 5th Avenue," *New York Times*, August 21, 1948, p. 23; Roshco, *Rag Race*, 122.

34. *Christian Dior*, booklet, English ed. (Paris, 1953), n.p., DSAA; "Christian Dior Will Design Clothes Here; Wholesale Salon to Be Opened in October," *New York Times*, August 2, 1948, p. 18; Grumbach, *Histoires de la mode*, 74; Virginia Pope, "Dior, at Opening, *Copies Himself,*" *New York Times*, November 9, 1948, p. 32.

35. Office des Changes to the CIC, February 4, 1947, 1987003/0618, CIC archives, ANMT.

36. "Sociétés américaines," 1987003/0618, CIC archives, ANMT.

37. Ray Lynch, "Obituary: George Engel-Kron Fled Russia," *Sun Sentinel*, February 4, 1990, accessed October 1, 2020, https://www.sun-sentinel.com/news/fl-xpm-1990-02-04 -9001220812-story.html; Dorothy L. Wallis, "The Dior Story: Fashion Business Moves into International Field," *Women's Wear Daily*, July 13, 1953, p. 4; Dominique Veillon, "Le Théâtre de la Mode ou le renouveau de la Couture Création à la Libération," *Vingtième Siècle, Revue d'Histoire* 28 (1990): 118–120; Dominique Veillon, *La mode sous l'Occupation* (Paris: Payot, 1990), 232–233; "Le Théâtre de la Mode à New York," *L'Officiel*, June 1946, pp. 84–85.

38. Michael Porter, *The Competitive Advantage of Nations* (New York: Free Press, 1990); April Dougal Gasbarre, updated by M. L. Cohen, "Christian Dior S.A.," in *International Directory of Company Histories*, Encyclopedia.com, accessed April 10, 2014, http://www.encyclopedia .com/topic/Christian_Dior_S.A.aspx.

39. Alexandra Palmer, "Inside Paris Haute Couture," in *The Golden Age of Couture: Paris–London, 1947–1957*, ed. Claire Wilcox (London: Victoria and Albert Museum, 2007), 63–80.

40. Ellen Engel to Jacques Rouët, New York, July 9, 1948, 1, file "Préparation des collections—1948," DSAA.

41. Committee meeting minutes, October 27, 1931, 2, CSCPA; Engel to Rouët, July 9, 1948, 2.

42. "Notre technique n'a pratiquement pas varié depuis des siècles. . . . Cela ne changera pas et si nous devions un jour renoncer à travailler à la main, une certaine notion de qualité, qui n'a rien d'équivalent au monde, viendrait à disparaitre avec nous." "L'influence de Christian Dior sur la mode aujourd'hui," Conférence de Boston, 1958, 2–3, DSAA. Translated by the author.

43. Engel to Rouët, July 9, 1948, 3.

44. Helen Everett Meiklejohn, *Dresses: Impact of Fashion on a Business* (New York: McGraw-Hill, 1938), 313–315; "Dior Showroom on 5th Ave.," *New York Times*, August 17, 1948, p. 17.

45. "Business Notes," *New York Times*, September 13, 1948, p. 29; "Coppola Joins Dior New York," *New York Times*, August 20, 1952, p. 33; Wallis, "Dior Story," 4; Roshco, *Rag Race*, 34.

46. "Confectionneurs," 1949, 6 pp., File Préparation des collections, DSAA.

47. "Statistiques des ventes enregistrées au 31 mars 1950, vendeuses," April 4, 1950, Service commercial, Collection Printemps 1950, File Préparation des collections, 1950, DSAA.

48. "Confectionneurs," 5.

49. Guillaume, *Jacques Fath;* Milbank, *Couture*, 264–266.

50. Palmer, *Dior;* Véronique Pouillard, "The Milton Case (1955–1962): Defending the Intellectual Property Rights of Haute Couture in the United States," *Journal of Design History* 30, no. 4 (2017): 356–370.

51. "Magasins," 2, File Préparation des collections, 1949, DSAA.

52. "No Dress under $69.95 Will Bear Name of Dior," *New York Times,* July 30, 1948, p. 25; Elizabeth Halstead, "Copies of Imports Will Go on Markets within Three Weeks," *New York Times,* September 2, 1955, p. 10.

53. Nan Robertson, "Piracy Runs Rampant over New Paris Styles," *New York Times,* August 26, 1958, p. 33; Halstead, "Copies of Imports," 10; Booton Herndon, *Bergdorf's on the Plaza: The Story of Bergdorf Goodman and a Half-Century of American Fashion* (New York: Knopf, 1956), 226.

54. Engel to Rouët, July 9, 1948, 2; Helfgott, "Women's and Children's Apparel," 22, 60; "Liste alphabétique des manufacturiers et détaillants américains," August 25, 1949, 6 pp., Service commercial, File Préparation des collections, 1949, DSAA.

55. "Garb for Beach Wear and Holiday Clothes for All Occasions Exhibited by Dior in Paris," *New York Times,* February 28, 1948, p. 13; Historique CDNY, Brief History, 1, DSAA; Okawa, "Licensing Practices," 102–106; Grumbach, *Histoires de la mode,* 113; Rasche, "Christian Dior in Germany," 35.

56. Enregistrement de la marque internationale Christian Dior, January 28, 1948, no. 134476, Institut National de la Propriété Industrielle.

57. The first US patents were registered in 1948. Heftler-Louiche bottle, USD158380S, registered December 10, 1948, published May 2, 1950.

58. The scent, however, was not protected under any intellectual property rights scheme.

59. Carma Gorman, "Why Post-War American Businesses Embraced Corporate Identity Design" (paper presented at Interrogating Intellectual Property Rights in Fashion and Design conference, University of Oslo, June 12, 2015); Carma Gorman, "The Role of Trademark Law in the History of US Visual Identity Design, c. 1860–1960", *Journal of Design History* 30, no. 4 (2017), 371–388; Samantha L. Etherington, "Fashion Runways Are No Longer the Public Domain: Applying the Common Law Right of Publicity to Haute Couture Fashion Design," *Hastings Communications and Entertainment Law Journal* 23, no. 43 (2001): 51–55; John Palfrey, *Intellectual Property Strategy* (Cambridge, MA: MIT Press, 2012), 42–44.

60. Haute couture balance sheets (1987003 0251) and perfume balance sheets (1987003 0252), Boussac CIC archives, ANMT.

61. Grumbach, *Histoires de la mode,* 113; Palmer, *Dior,* 88; "Contracts under Licenses. In England; In Australia" and "Contracts under Licenses. In Mexico. In Cuba. In Chile," in *Christian Dior,* work booklet, English ed., n.p., DSAA; Sydney Gruson, "Pay and Costs High in Caracas' Boom," *New York Times,* December 19, 1953, p. 7; "Venezuela Interests the Economic World," *New York Times,* January 5, 1955, p. 70; "Christian Dior—Venezuela," in *Christian Dior,* booklet, English ed. (Paris, 1953), n.p., DSAA; South American concern box, DSAA.

62. French Office des Changes to the CIC, January 13, 1959, 1987003 0252, Boussac CIC archives, ANMT.

63. Olivier Bomsel, *L'économie immatérielle: Industries et marchés d'expériences* (Paris: Gallimard, 2010), 157.

64. "L'influence de Christian Dior," 1.

65. Ibid., 2; Roshco, *Rag Race*, 122; Palmer, *Dior*, 96.

66. Chambre Syndicale de la Couture parisienne, Bulletin 1, 1, 10, 2.

67. "Saunier, Claire, Ancien sénateur élu(e) par l'Assemblée nationale," Sénat, accessed September 12, 2015, http://www.senat.fr/senateur-4eme-republique/saunier_claire0554r4.html.

68. Rapport d'activités de l'année 1952, 18–19, CSCPA; Chambre Syndicale de la Couture parisienne, Bulletin 1, 14; Grumbach, *Histoires de la mode*, 102; Rapport d'activités de l'année 1953, 11, CSCPA.

69. Rapport d'activités de l'année 1952, 16, CSCPA.

70. Ibid., 19; Rapport d'activités de l'année 1953, 11; Rapport d'activités de l'année 1954, 29, CSCPA; Rapport d'activités de l'année 1955, 2, CSCPA; Elisabetta Merlo and Francesca Polese, "Turning Fashion into Business: The Emergence of Milan as an International Fashion Hub," *Business History Review* 80, no. 3 (2006): 415–447.

71. "Fashion Piracy Charges."

72. "Frenchmen Plan Style Piracy Suit," *New York Times*, October 26, 1955, p. 48; Roshco, *Rag Race*, 162; Committee meeting minutes, January 31, 1949, 1–2, CSCPA; Grumbach, *Histoires de la mode*, 100; Robertson, "Piracy Runs Rampant," 33.

73. Rapport d'activité de l'année 1956, "Presse" document, n.p., CSCPA; "Frenchmen Plan."

74. Frederic L. Milton, sketch collection, 1940–1958, History, note, accessed June 7, 2015, https://atom-sparc.fitnyc.edu/frederic-l-milton-sketches-1942-1956.

75. "Fashion Piracy Charges"; "Court Sharply Critical of Style Piracy: Refuses to Dismiss Suit by Couturiers," *Women's Wear Daily*, July 30, 1956, p. 21, Design Copyright folder, box 4, Resseguie Collection, BL, HBS.

76. "Frenchmen Plan," 48; Leo Gottlieb, *Cleary, Gottlieb, Steen and Hamilton: The First Thirty Years* (New York: Donnelley, 1983), 62–65; "Court Sharply Critical," 21; "International Style Piracy Net Is Charged," *Women's Wear Daily*, January 28, 1960, p. 33, Design Copyright folder, box 4, Resseguie Collection, BL, HBS; "Jacob H. Gilbert," Biographical Directory of the United States Congress, accessed June 7, 2015, https://bioguideretro.congress.gov/Home/MemberDetails?memIndex=G000175; Joseph B. Treaster, "Jacob H. Gilbert, 60, an Ex-Representative and Bronx Legislator," obituary, *New York Times*, March 1, 1981, p. 1036.

77. Pierre Vernus, "Contrôler et définir la fraude dans la soierie lyonnaise (au XIXᵉ siècle et au début du XXᵉ siècle)," in *Fraude, contrefaçon et contrebande de l'Antiquité à nos jours*, ed. Gérard Béaur, Hubert Bonin, and Claire Lemercier (Genève: Droz, 2006), 491.

78. "Fashion Piracy Charges"; Roshco, *Rag Race*, 164.

79. Robertson, "Piracy Runs Rampant," 33.

80. "Fashion Piracy Charges."

81. "Frenchmen Plan," 48 (my italics).

82. "Court Sharply Critical," 21.

83. "Fashion Piracy Charges"; Rapport d'activité pour l'année 1956, 2, Presse, Affaire Milton, CSCPA.

84. Christian Dior et al. v. Frederick L. Milton et al., July 27, 1956, Special Term, New York County, Supreme Court of New York.

85. Ibid.

86. Ibid.; "Allocation de M. François Loos, Ministre Délégué à l'Industrie," 7èmes rencontres sénatoriales de l'entreprise, La contrefaçon. Risque ou menace pour l'entreprise, March 31, 2006, French Senate. https://www.senat.fr/colloques/colloque_contrefacon/colloque_contrefacon _mono.html#toc10, accessed October 21, 2020.

87. Accordingly, the motion to dismiss the complaint and for other relief was in all respects denied.

88. "Fashion Piracy Charges," 13; "L'influence de Christian Dior," 2–3; Palmer, *Dior*, 45; Robertson, "Piracy Runs Rampant," 33; Wilcox, *Golden Age*.

89. "Fashion Piracy Charges."

90. "Presse," n.p., Rapport d'activité de l'année 1956, CSCPA.

91. Rapport d'activité de l'année 1956, 12, CSCPA.

92. "Court Sharply Critical," 21.

93. "Détail des comptes débiteurs et des comptes créditeurs divers, au 31 décembre 1958," CSCPA. The firm still exists under the name Weil, Gotshal & Manges LLP.

94. Rapport d'activité de l'année 1956, 12, CSCPA.

95. "Points de droit," *L'Officiel*, December 1921, p. 19; "Loi numéro 57-298 du 11 mars 1957 sur la propriété littéraire et artistique," Legifrance, accessed November 20, 2015, http://www .legifrance.gouv.fr/affichTexte.do?cidTexte=JORFTEXT000000315384.

96. Rapport de la Chambre Syndicale de la Couture parisienne pour l'année 1957, "Propriété artistique," 11, CSCPA.

97. Robertson, "Piracy Runs Rampant," 33.

98. General Assembly meeting minutes, Rapport d'activités de la CSCPA, 1959, report on Propriété Artistique, 3, CSCPA.

99. Rapport d'activités de l'année 1959, 9, 11, CSCPA.

100. Rapport de la Chambre Syndicale de la Couture parisienne pour l'année 1957, "Propriété artistique," 11, CSCPA.

101. Okawa, "Licensing Practices," 91–93.

102. Geoffrey G. Jones and Véronique Pouillard, "Christian Dior: A New Look for Haute Couture" (Case Study No. 809-159, Harvard Business School, June 2009).

103. "Future of Paris Fashion Is Called Bright by Heim," *New York Times*, September 19, 1958, p. 20.

104. Earl Dash, "Rentner in Stormy Career Steered True to Fashion," *Women's Wear Daily*, July 8, 1958, p. 19, Resseguie collection, BL HBS.

105. Jones and Pouillard, "Christian Dior," 1–2.

106. "Fashion Piracy Charges"; "Deux directeurs de maisons anglaises et suisses ont été entendus par la police," *Le Parisien*, February 11, 1960, file Contrefaçons, DB 588, Paris Police Archives.

107. "International Piracy Net Is Charged," *Women's Wear Daily*, January 28, 1960, p. 33. Adams Photoprint was removed from the case, as the charges against this enterprise were not substantiated.

108. "International Piracy Net," p. 33; "Dresses," *Desert Sun*, August 17, 1959, p. 1.

109. Grumbach, *Histoires de la mode*, 100; Pouillard, "Keeping Designs and Brands Authentic," 815–835; "Propriété artistique," April 22, 1963, 1, CSCPA.

110. "Propriété artistique," April 22, 1963, 1; Palfrey, *Intellectual Property Strategy*, 33.

111. Véronique Pouillard, "Design Piracy in the Fashion Industries of Paris and New York in the Interwar Years," *Business History Review* 85, no. 2 (2011): 319–344; "Style Designers' Views Differ on Piracy Bill," *Women's Wear Daily*, March 29, 1957, Design Copyright folder, box 4, Resseguie Collection, BL, HBS; Milbank, *Couture;* "Fashion Piracy Is Termed Natural Trade Phenomenon," *Women's Wear Daily*, April 9, 1957, Design Copyright folder, box 4, Resseguie Collection, BL, HBS.

112. "Suit Charging Style Piracy Asks $2 Million," *Women's Wear Daily*, November 16, 1955, box 4, Resseguie Collection, BL, HBS.

113. Paul Duguid, "French Connections: The Propagation of Trademarks in the Nineteenth Century," *Enterprise and Society* 10, no. 1 (2009): 3–37.

114. "Effects of Dior Length Seen Six Months Away," *Women's Wear Daily*, August 13, 1953, p. 41.

115. Geoffrey G. Jones, *Multinationals and Global Capitalism from the Nineteenth to the Twenty-First Century* (Oxford: Oxford University Press, 2005), 17, 28–38; Mira Wilkins, *The Emergence of Multinational Enterprise: American Business Abroad from the Colonial Era to 1914* (Cambridge, MA: Harvard University Press, 1970), 75–79; Mira Wilkins, "The History of the Multinational Enterprise," in *The Oxford Handbook of International Business*, 2nd ed., ed. Alan M. Rugman (Oxford: Oxford University Press, 2009), 3, 4, 10.

116. Lourdes M. Font, "International Couture: The Opportunities and Challenges of Expansion, 1880–1920," *Business History* 54, no. 1 (2012): 30–47; Harold James, *The End of Globalization: Lessons from the Great Depression* (Cambridge, MA: Harvard University Press, 2001); Betty Kirke, *Madeleine Vionnet* (San Francisco: Chronicle Books, 2012), 130–133; Philippe Montégut, "Boué Sœurs: The First Haute Couture Establishment in America," *Dress* 15, no. 1 (1989): 79–86; Jones, *Beauty Imagined*, 166, 204–207, 311.

117. Garnier, *40 années de création*.

118. David Landes, "French Entrepreneurship and Industrial Growth in the Nineteenth Century," *Journal of Economic History* 9, no. 1 (1949): 45–61.

119. Barry Eichengreen, *The European Economy since 1945: Coordinated Capitalism and Beyond* (Princeton, NJ: Princeton University Press, 2008), 5, 6, 59; Kuisel, *Capitalism and the State*, 223–231.

120. Claude A. Rouzaud, *Un problème d'intérêt national: Les industries du luxe* (Strasbourg: Librairie du recueil Sirey, 1946), 219–220.

121. Patrick Fridenson, "France: The Relatively Slow Development of Big Business in the Twentieth Century," in *Big Business and the Wealth of Nations*, ed. Alfred D. Chandler Jr., Franco Amatori, and Takashi Hikino (Cambridge: Cambridge University Press, 1997), 207–245; Kenneth Mouré, "Vus d'Amérique," in Daumas, *Dictionnaire historique*, 1279–1284.

6. One World of Fashion

1. "French Stylists Here to Study US Methods," *Women's Wear Daily*, April 28, 1948, p. 20; Régis Boulat, *Jean Fourastié, un expert en productivité: La modernisation de la France (années trente–années cinquante)* (Besançon: Presses Universitaires de Franche-Comté, 2008); Gérard Bossuat, "L'aide américaine à la France après la Seconde Guerre mondiale," *Vingtième siècle: Revue d'Histoire* 9 (1986): 17–35; Paula Cristofalo, "Les missions de productivité dans les années 1950: Une tentative pour importer en France une fonction d'expertise syndicale," *Travail et emploi* 116 (October–December 2008): 69–81; Richard Kuisel, *Seducing the French: The Dilemma of Americanization* (Berkeley: University of California Press, 1997); Dominique Veillon, *La mode sous l'Occupation* (Paris: Payot, 1990), 232.

2. Notes de voyage de la mission aux U.S.A. de la délégation du vêtement féminin, supplément à la revue *L'Industrie du vêtement féminin*, November–December 1952 (Paris: Fédération de l'Industrie du Vêtement Féminin, 1954), 8–9, AJ 81.71, FNA.

3. Notes de voyage de la mission, 66; "French Team to Study US Apparel Trade," *Women's Wear Daily*, November 6, 1952, p. 2.

4. Notes de voyage de la mission, 15–25.

5. Ibid., 28–30, 71–75; Daniel E. Bender and Richard A. Greenwald, eds., *Sweatshop USA: The American Sweatshop in Historical and Global Perspective* (London: Routledge, 2003).

6. Notes de voyage de la mission, 66–67; Greg Whitmore, "Observer Archive: My Clothes and I, Simone de Beauvoir, 20 March 1960," *Guardian*, March 17, 2019, p. 3.

7. *Les Relations entre les Industries et la Presse de Mode aux Etats-Unis*, mission d'études, mai 1955, supplément à la revue *L'Industrie du vêtement féminin* (Paris, May 1956), AJ 81.64, AN; Rebecca Arnold, *The American Look: Fashion, Sportswear and the Image of Women in 1930s and 1940s New York* (London: I.B. Tauris, 2009), 99–101.

8. Andrew Goodman, speech, November 30, 1954, p. 7, Fashion Group speeches and transcripts, folder 12, box 76, FG, NYPL; *Les Industries et la Presse de Mode*, 25.

9. *Les Industries et la Presse de Mode*, 18–20; Georg Simmel, "Fashion," *American Journal of Sociology* 62, no. 6 (1957): 541–558.

10. Pap N'Diaye, *Du nylon et des bombes: Du Pont de Nemours, le marché et l'État américain (1900–1970)* (Paris: Belin, 2001); Regina L. Blaszczyk, "Styling Synthetics: DuPont's Marketing of Fabrics and Fashions in Postwar America," *Business History Review* 80, no. 3 (2006): 485–528.

11.   Marion Gough, *Unraveling the New Fabrics for Fashion and Function,* ca. 1945, folder 5, box 74, Fashion Group speeches and transcripts, FG, NYPL; Carmel Snow talk, Fashion Group Inc., luncheon meeting, Hotel Biltmore, New York, April 18, 1945, p. 19, folder 6, box 74, FG, NYPL; Veillon, *La mode sous l'Occupation;* Fabienne Falluel and Marie-Laure Gutton, *Elégance et système D: Paris 1940–1944, accessoires de mode sous l'Occupation* (Paris: Paris Musées, 2009).

12.   *Les Industries et la Presse de Mode,* 20–23; Goodman, speech, 3; Pierre Cayez, *Rhône-Poulenc, 1895–1975: Contribution à l'étude d'un groupe industriel* (Paris: Armand Colin / Masson, 1988), 189–219; Farid Chenoune, "Jalons pour une histoire culturelle de la mode: Une chronologie: 1952–1973," *Bulletin de l'Institut d'Histoire du Temps Présent* 76 (November 2000): 16; Valérie Jacquet and Gilles Lizanet, "La mémoire de la Rhodiaceta: Histoire d'une recherche," *Le monde alpin et rhodanien: Revue régionale d'ethnologie* 19, nos. 2/3 (1991): 114–116; Sophie Bramel and Claude Fauque, *Le génie du pli permanent: 100 ans de modernité textile* (Paris: Institut Français de la Mode, 2000); Débora Krichke Leitao, "La mode au Brésil dans les années 1960: Nationalisme brésilien et capitaux francais," in *La mode des sixties: L'entrée dans la modernité,* ed. Dominique Veillon and Michelle Ruffat (Paris: Autrement, 2007), 76–88; Regina L. Blaszczyk, "Synthetics for the Shah: DuPont and the Challenges to Multinationals in 1970s Iran," *Enterprise & Society* 9, no. 4 (2008): 670–723.

13.   Joseph C. Furnas, *How America Lives* (New York: Henry Holt, 1945), 241–243.

14.   Regina Lee Blaszczyk, *The Color Revolution* (Cambridge, MA: MIT Press), 77–83; Thierry Maillet, "Histoire de la médiation entre textile et mode en France: Des échantillonneurs aux bureaux de style (1825–1975)" (PhD diss., Ecole des Hautes Etudes en Sciences Sociales, 2013); Regina L. Blaszczyk, "The Rise of Color Forecasting in the United States and Great Britain," in *The Fashion Forecasters: A Hidden History of Color and Trend Prediction,* ed. Regina Lee Blaszczyk and Ben Wubs (London: Bloomsbury, 2018), 53–58.

15.   Milton P. Brown and Malcolm P. McNair, foreword to *Tobé Lectures in Retail Distribution* (Boston: Harvard Business School, 1959), v; Véronique Pouillard and Karen J. Trivette, "Tobé Coller Davis: A Career in Fashion Forecasting in America," in Blaszczyk and Wubs, *Fashion Forecasters,* 79–81.

16.   Comité de Coordination des Industries de la Mode, appendix to *Les Industries et la Presse de Mode,* 18–20.

17.   Ibid.

18.   Farid Chenoune, "Chronologie. Jalons pour une histoire culturelle de la mode: 1952–1973," in Veillon and Ruffat, *La mode des sixties,* 252; Gilles Fouchard, *La mode* (Paris: Editions du Cavalier Bleu, 2005), 25; Alexis Romano, "*Elle* and the Development of *Stylisme* in the 1960s Paris," *Costume* 46, no. 1 (2012): 75–91.

19.   Virginia Pope, "Paris Couturiers in New Venture," *New York Times,* August 9, 1950, p. 32; W. Granger Blair, "Paris Aims to Improve Fashion Tie," *New York Times,* April 4, 1958, p. 14.

20.   Nancy L. Green, *Ready-to-Wear and Ready-to-Work: A Century of Industry and Immigrants in Paris and New York* (Durham, NC: Duke University Press, 1997); Philip Scranton, *Endless*

Novelty: Specialty Production and American Industrialization, 1865–1925 (Princeton, NJ: Princeton University Press, 1997); G. Fowler, "Preparation of a Line: 4 Months from Paris Trip to Next Week's Openings," *Women's Wear Daily*, May 27, 1953, p. 1; Ira Rentner, interview, 1982, pp. 92–95, Memoirs of Maurice Rentner Collection, Oral History Collections, FIT; Véronique Pouillard, "Design Piracy in the Fashion Industries of Paris and New York in the Interwar Years," *Business History Review* 85, no. 2 (2011): 319–344.

21. "Lelong Arrives Here to Renew Couture Ties," *Women's Wear Daily*, May 17, 1945, pp. 1–2; "Room of US Styles, says Lucien Lelong," *Women's Wear Daily*, June 1, 1945, p. 1; "Lelong, Inc. Buys Chicago Building," *Women's Wear Daily*, January 10, 1947, p. 21; Bertram J. Perkins, "Illness Forces to Close Couture House: Advised to Retire for Year," *Women's Wear Daily*, July 21, 1948, pp. 1, 48; "Coty Purchases Controlling Share of Lelong Firm," *Women's Wear Daily*, July 8, 1953, pp. 1, 13; "Future of Paris Fashions Is Called Bright by Heim," *New York Times*, September 19, 1958, p. 20; Lucien Lelong & Cie, Registre de Commerce 68.693, D33U3 0144, CPA; General Assembly meeting minutes, April 16, 1959, p. 1, CSCPA.

22. Couture subventions files, F12 10505, FNA.

23. Balenciaga, RC 274.232B, D33U3 1340, Archives de Paris; Bettina Ballard, *In My Fashion* (Paris: Séguier, 2016), 176–181; Nathalie Beau de Loménie, *Biarritz & la mode: La haute couture et la mode sur la Côte basque—de 1854 à nos jours* (Paris: Atlantica, 2015), 81–87, 230; Lesley Ellis Miller, *Balenciaga: Shaping Fashion* (London: Victoria & Albert Museum Publications, 2007), 60, 70, 92.

24. Carrie Donovan, "French Styles en Route; Dior's Skirt Split Critics," *New York Times*, August 26, 1959, p. 32; "Future of Paris Fashions"; Regina L. Blaszczyk and Véronique Pouillard, "Fashion as Enterprise," in *European Fashion: The Creation of a Global Industry*, ed. Regina Lee Blaszczyk and Véronique Pouillard (Manchester: Manchester University Press, 2018), 1–3; Solange Montagné-Villette, "La mode de la centralité à l'acentralité," in Veillon and Ruffat, *La mode des sixties*, 21.

25. "World-Wide Styles Seen in Near Future," *New York Times*, December 6, 1946, p. 30; *Pierre Balmain, 40 années de création* (Paris: Musée Galliera, 1985), 45–46; "Balmain's Styles Show No Age Bar," *New York Times*, March 11, 1950, p. 55; "Balmain Plans American Line," *New York Times*, December 6, 1951, p. 55; Bess Furman, "Paris Dressmaker Decries Trade Lag," *New York Times*, October 23, 1952, p. 37.

26. Jacques Fath & Cie, RC 272.092B, D33U3 1267, CPA; Note to the press, November 25, 1948, Box USA 2, DSAA; "Halpert Tells of Fath Deal," *Women's Wear Daily*, November 3, 1948, p. 48; Didier Grumbach, *Histoires de la mode*, 2nd ed. (1993; Paris: Editions du Regard, 2008), 135–136; Veillon, *La mode sous l'Occupation*.

27. "Drawstrings at Cape Hem," *Women's Wear Daily*, August 12, 1957, p. 4; "Tellin, Newest Paris Couturier, Also Youngest," *Women's Wear Daily*, August 23, 1957, p. 2; "Tellin's Spencer Jacket Suit with Overcoat," *Women's Wear Daily*, August 1, 1958, p. 5.

28. Richard Kuisel, *Capitalism and the State in Modern France: Renovation and Economic Management in the Twentieth Century* (Cambridge: Cambridge University Press, 1981), 215, 248–

250; Véronique Pouillard, "Keeping Designs and Brands Authentic: The Resurgence of Post-War French Fashion Business under the Challenge of US Mass Production," *European Review of History* 20, no. 5 (2013): 815–835; Ministry of Economy, application files, Jacques Heim, Madeleine de Rauch, F12 10505, FNA; Committee meeting minutes, October 25, 1955, 8, CSCPA; Jacques Heim application file, F12 10505, FNA.

29. "Dior to Celebrate 10th Birthday," *Women's Wear Daily*, January 2, 1957, p. 13; Alexandra Palmer, *Dior: A New Look, a New Enterprise (1947–1957)* (London: Victoria and Albert Museum, 2009); Joseph Schumpeter, "Capitalism in the Postwar World," in *Essays of J.A. Schumpeter*, ed. Richard V. Clemence (Cambridge, MA: Addison-Wesley, 1989), 185.

30. Rapports d'activité, figures from the years 1952–1961, CSCPA; Gabrielle Chanel, RC 93.879, D33U3 0031, CPA; Société des Parfums Chanel, RC 215.042B, D33U3 1078, CPA; Hal Vaughan, *Sleeping with the Enemy: Coco Chanel's Secret War* (New York: Vintage, 2011).

31. *Fall Fashions—Born in Paris—Bred in America*, June 1957, pp. 2–3, folder 3, box 77, Fashion Group speeches and transcripts, FG, NYPL; "Chanel Look, Top to Toe, Favorite in Minneapolis," *Women's Wear Daily*, April 25, 1957, p. 4; "The Neiman Marcus Award: Chanel Sole Recipient in 1957," *Women's Wear Daily*, August 19, 1957, p. 5.

32. "Concern over Model Gown Ruling," *Daily Mail*, February 1933, p. 33; "Mode: Made in Great Britain?," *The Ambassador*, December 1, 1934, p. 6.

33. Sonnet Stanfill, "Anonymous Tastemakers: The Role of American Buyers in Establishing an Italian Fashion Industry, 1950–55," in Blaszczyk and Pouillard, *European Fashion*, 146–169; Chiara Fagella, "'Not So Simple': Reassessing 1951, G.B. Giorgini and the Launch of Italian Fashion" (PhD diss., University of Stockholm, 2019), 264.

34. Marie-Laure Djelic and Antti Ainamo, "The Coevolution of New Organizational Forms in the Fashion Industry: A Historical and Comparative Study of France, Italy, and the United States," *Organization Science* 10, no. 5 (1999): 622–637; Elisabetta Merlo and Francesca Polese, "Turning Fashion into Business: The Emergence of Milan as an International Fashion Hub," *Business History Review* 80, no. 3 (2006): 415–447; Carlo Marco Belfanti, "Renaissance and *Made in Italy*: Marketing Italian Fashion through History (1949–1952)," *Journal of Modern Italian Studies* 201, no. 1 (2014): 53–66; Elisabetta Merlo and Marco Perugini, "Making Italian Fashion Global: Brand Building and Management at Gruppo Finaziaro Tessile (1950s–1990s)," *Business History*, published online June 1, 2017, https://www.tandfonline.com/doi/abs/10.1080/00076791.2017.1329299; Lisa Rofel and Sylvia J. Yanagisako, with Simona Segre Reinach, *Fabricating Transnational Capitalism: A Collaborative Ethnography of Italian-Chinese Global Fashion* (Durham, NC: Duke University Press, 2019); Dana Thomas, *Deluxe: How Luxury Lost Its Luster* (London: Penguin, 2007); Ingrid Giertz-Mårtenson, "H&M: Documenting the Story of One of the World's Largest Fashion Retailers," *Business History* 54, no. 1 (2012): 108–115; Ingrid Giertz-Mårtenson, "H&M: How Swedish Entrepreneurial and Social Values Created Fashion for Everyone," in Blaszczyk and Pouillard, *European Fashion*, 202–208.

35. Michael E. Porter, *The Competitive Advantage of Nations* (New York: Free Press, 1990), 308–331, 421–453; Pierre-Yves Donzé, *Les patrons horlogers de La Chaux-de-Fonds (1840–1920):*

Dynamique sociale d'une élite industrielle (Neuchâtel: Alphil, 2007); Daniel Lefranc, "The Metamorphosis of *Contrefaçon* in French Copyright Law," in *Copyright and Piracy: An Interdisciplinary Critique*, ed. Lionel Bently, Jane Davis, and Jane C. Ginsburg (Cambridge: Cambridge University Press, 2010), 55–79; Susan Scafidi, *Who Owns Culture? Appropriation and Authenticity in American Law* (New Brunswick, NJ: Rutgers University Press, 2005); Mary Lynn Stewart, "Copying and Copyrighting Haute Couture: Democratizing Fashion," *French Historical Studies* 28, no. 1 (2005): 103–130; Gérard Bossuat, *Faire l'Europe sans défaire la France, 60 ans de politique d'unité européenne des gouvernements et des présidents de la République française (1943–2003)* (Brussels: PIE Peter Lang, 2006); Alan Milward, *The European Rescue of the Nation State* (London: Routledge, 2000); Valérie Marchal, "Brevets, marques, dessins et modèles: Evolution des protections de propriété industrielle au XIXe siècle en France," *Documents pour l'histoire des techniques* 17 (2009): 8; Gabriel Galvez-Behar, *La République des inventeurs: Propriété et organisation de l'innovation en France (1791–1922)* (Rennes: Presses Universitaires de Rennes, 2008), 210; Hermine Valabrègue, "La propriété artistique en matière de modes" (PhD diss., Librairie générale de Droit et de Jurisprudence, 1935); Marie-Christine Piatti, "Le droit de la mode" (unpublished paper, Fashion History Seminar, Institut d'Histoire du Temps Présent, Paris, April 28, 2006), 3–7; "La propriété artistique. Les dessins et modèles. S.P.A.D.E.M., activité internationale (1958–1959)," p. 1, Sodema file, DSAA.

36. Grumbach, *Histoires de la mode*, 74; General Assembly meeting minutes, Rapport d'activités de la Chambre Syndicale de la Couture Parisienne (1959), Propriété Artistique, n.p., folios 3 and 4, CSCPA; Emmanuelle Fauchart and Eric von Hippel, "Norms-Based Intellectual Property Systems: The Case of French Chefs," *Organization Science* 19, no. 2 (2008): 187–201; Bernard Roshco, *The Rag Race: How New York and Paris Run the Breakneck Business of Dressing American Women* (New York: Funk & Wagnalls, 1963), 154.

37. "Conseils à nos adhérents," 1964, Sodema file, DSAA; Yves Saint-Gall, "Aspects actuels de la notion de marque et ses rapports avec la réglementation de la concurrence, plus spécialement dans le cadre de la Communauté Economique Européenne" (paper presented at Université de Liège, December 21, 1962); Republic of France, Conseil supérieur de la propriété littéraire et artistique website, accessed November 29, 2019, https://www.culture.gouv.fr/Sites-thematiques /Propriete-litteraire-et-artistique/Conseil-superieur-de-la-propriete-litteraire-et-artistique.

38. General Assembly meeting minutes, Rapport d'activités de la Chambre Syndicale de la Couture Parisienne (1959), folios 3 and 4, CSCPA; Luca Lanzalaco, "Business Interest Associations," in *The Oxford Handbook of Business History*, ed. Geoffrey Jones and Jonathan Zeitlin (Oxford: Oxford University Press, 2007), 294; Michel Offerlé, "L'action collective patronale en France, 19e–20e siècles: Organisations, répertoires et engagements," *Vingtième siècle: Revue d'histoire* 114 (2012): 83–97; Ministère de l'Industrie, Comité National d'Etudes sur le Rapprochement des Législations de Propriété Industrielle des Pays membres de la Communauté Economique Européenne, Groupe "Dessins et Modèles," February 1, 1962, DSAA.

39. "Questionnaire relatif à la protection des dessins et des modèles," February 1, 1962, 4 pp., Sodema file, DSAA; "Conseils à nos adhérents," 1.

40. General Assembly meeting minutes, Rapport d'activités de la Chambre Syndicale de la Couture Parisienne (1959), May 3, 1960, CSCPA; "Future of Paris Fashions."

41. Report on Propaganda (January–December 1958), 1, CSCPA; Philippe Montégut, "Boué Sœurs: The First Haute Couture Establishment in America," *Dress* 15, no. 1 (1989): 79–86; Veillon, *La mode sous l'Occupation;* "Couture Unit to Open Bureau in New York," *New York Times,* December 6, 1957, p. 35.

42. "French Designers Study US Tastes," *New York Times,* June 10, 1958, p. 37; Blair, "Paris Aims to Improve"; Report on Propaganda (January–December 1958), 2, CSCPA.

43. "Couture Appoints NY Office Head," *Women's Wear Daily,* May 6, 1958, p. 49; "Couture Hires Gottlieb Firm," *Women's Wear Daily,* June 25, 1958, p. 1; "Heim Here Gives Details of Paris Package Trip," *Women's Wear Daily,* September 22, 1958, p. 1.

44. Report on Propaganda (January–December 1958), 2–5, CSCPA; Accounting sheet, 1958; Statutory General Assembly meeting minutes, May 3, 1960, 4, CSCPA.

45. A. D. Galloway, "Ready-to-Wear Trade Due for Gain in France," *Women's Wear Daily,* January 2, 1957, p. 14; Report from Jean Manusardi, General Assembly meeting minutes, May 8, 1962, 15, CSCPA; Statutory General Assembly meeting minutes, May 8, 1962, 10, CSCPA.

46. Statutory General Assembly meeting minutes, May 8, 1962, appendix, 3–5.

47. Activity report for 1959, 5; General Assembly meeting minutes, May 8, 1962, 3.

48. Statutory General Assembly meeting minutes, May 8, 1962; Jacques Heim, conclusions, 1–4.

49. Maison Mad Carpentier, RC 282.252B, D33 U3 1363, CPA; Maison Marcelle Chaumont, RC 282.280B, D33 U3 1362, CPA; Société Marcel Rochas, RC 260.585B, D33U3 1127, CPA; Houses of Worth and Paquin Ltd., Catalog, Reference AAD/1982/1, AAD/1990/4, Archives of Art and Design, London; Société Carven, RC 272.272B, D33U3 1269, CPA; "Official— Balenciaga Will Close His House," *Women's Wear Daily,* May 23, 1968, p. 10; Marcel Rouff, "Une industrie motrice: La haute couture parisienne et son évolution," *Annales: Economies, Sociétés, Civilisations* 1, no. 2 (1946): 116–117; Valerie Steele, *Paris Fashion: A Cultural History* (New York: Bloomsbury, 1998); Schumpeter, "Capitalism in the Postwar World," 185; Porter, *Competitive Advantage of Nations,* 540; Christian Barrère and Walter Santagata, *La Mode: Une économie de la créativité et du patrimoine, à l'heure du marché* (Paris: Ministère de la Culture, 2005), 53–77.

50. *Encyclopedia Universalis France Online,* s.v. "Arnodin Maïmé (1916–2003)," accessed May 15, 2020, https://www.universalis.fr/encyclopedie/maime-arnodin/; Françoise Vincent-Ricard, interview by the author, Paris, April 16, 2006; "Eye-Juniors," *Women's Wear Daily,* October 13, 1964, p. 10; Françoise Vincent-Ricard, "Le rôle des bureaux de style," in Veillon and Ruffat, *La mode des sixties,* 164–171; Regina Lee Blaszczyk and Ben Wubs, "Beyond the Crystal Ball: The Rationale behind Color and Trend Forecasting," in Blaczszyk and Wubs, *Fashion Forecasters,* 11–20; Florence Brachet-Champsaur, "Créer c'est avoir vu le premier: Les Galeries Lafayette et la mode (1893–1969)" (PhD diss., Ecole des Hautes Etudes en Sciences Sociales, Paris, 2018); Sophie Chapdelaine de Montvalon, *Le beau pour tous* (Paris: L'Iconoclaste, 2009); Gilles Lipovetsky, *L'empire de l'éphémère: La mode et son destin dans les sociétés modernes* (Paris: Gallimard, 1987),

91; Maillet, "Histoire de la médiation"; Solange Montagné-Villette, *Le Sentier: Un espace ambigu* (Paris: Masson, 1990), 18; The Fashion Group: Paris Memberships 1975–1989, box 127, folders 10–13, FG, NYPL.

51. Beryl Williams, *Fashion Is Our Business* (Philadelphia: Lippincott, 1945), 156–170, 184–195.

52. Vincent-Ricard, interview.

53. Marnie Fogg, *Boutique: A '60s Cultural Phenomenon* (London: Mitchell Beazley, 2003), 20–26; Caroline Evans, "Postwar Poses: 1955–1975," in *The London Look: Fashion from Street to Catwalk*, ed. Christopher Breward, Edwina Ehrman, and Caroline Evans (London: Museum of London; New Haven, CT: Yale University Press, 2004), 118–128.

54. Montagné-Villette, *Le Sentier*, 19, 22; Véronique Pouillard, "Fashion and Youth," in *Restless Youth: Growing Up in Europe, 1945 to Now*, ed. Christine Dupont and Kieran Burns (Brussels: European Parliament, 2019), 113–123.

55. Mary Burdell, "How We Look," May 6, 1948, pp. 1–3, folder 1, box 75, Fashion Group speeches and transcripts, FG, NYPL.

56. Daniel Miller and Sophie Woodward, eds., *Global Denim* (London: Berg, 2010); Rika Fujioka and Ben Wubs, "Competitiveness of the Japanese Denim and Jeans Industry: The Cases of Kaihara and Japan Blue, 1970–2015," in Blaszczyk and Pouillard, *European Fashion*, 223–243; Pascale Gorguet-Ballesteros, *Histoires du jeans de 1750 à 1994* (Paris: Paris Musées, 1994); Pierre Bourdieu, *La Distinction: Critique sociale du jugement* (Paris: Les éditions de Minuit, 1979).

57. "Our History," Fashion Institute of Technology, accessed March 2, 2016, http://www.fitnyc.edu/about/history.php.

58. Virginia Pope, "One World of Fashion," *New York Times*, September 7, 1952, p. SMA52; Ballard, *In My Fashion*, 406–407.

59. Julia Faye Smith, *Something to Prove: A Biography of Ann Lowe, America's Forgotten Designer* (Washington, DC: Julia Faye Dockery Smith, 2016), 78–91.

60. These figures are in constant francs of 1952. Vincent Dubé-Sénécal, "La mode française: Vecteur d'influence aux Etats-Unis de l'après-guerre à l'orée des années 1960" (PhD diss., Université de Montréal, 2018), 195.

61. "Fashion Week Announced," *New York Times*, December 7, 1956, p. 42; Roshco, *Rag Race*, 135; Green, *Ready-to-Wear*.

62. "Limited-Scale Copyrights Set in Textiles," *Women's Wear Daily*, December 7, 1954, pp. 1, 56, box 4, Resseguie Collection, BL, HBS; Peter Zill, "New Textile Poser: What Is 'Work of Art'?," *Women's Wear Daily*, December 8, 1954, p. 1.

63. Al Perkins, "Test Case Held Needed on Copyright," *Retailing Daily*, December 17, 1954, p. 11, box 4, Resseguie Collection, BL, HBS.

64. "Stores Urged to Act against Style Piracy: FOGA Supports Views of Marcus," *Women's Wear Daily*, p. 4, June 28, 1955, box 4, Resseguie Collection, BL, HBS; Samantha L. Etherington, "Fashion Runways Are No Longer the Public Domain: Applying the Common Law Right of Publicity to Haute Couture Fashion Design," *Hastings Communications and Entertainment Law*

Journal 23, no. 43 (2001): 51–55; Stanley Marcus, *Minding the Store: A Memoir* (Denton: University of North Texas Press, 1974), 297–321.

65.   Gabriel M. Goldstein and Elizabeth E. Greenberg, eds., *A Perfect Fit: The Garment Industry and American Jewry (1860–1960)* (Lubbock: Texas Tech University Press; New York: Yeshiva University Museum, 2012); Stephanie M. Amerian, "Fashioning and Selling the American Look: Dorothy Shaver and Modern Art," *Investigaciones de Historia Economica* 12, no. 1 (2016): 100–108; Jessica Daves, *Ready-Made Miracle: The American Story of Fashion for the Millions* (New York: G. P. Putnam's Sons, 1967), 10–15; Caroline Rennolds Milbank, *New York Fashion: The Evolution of American Style* (New York: Harry N. Abrams, 1989), 172.

66.   "*The Look* in Clothes Sets the Style, says Bonnie Cashin," *Women's Wear Daily,* December 14, 1944, p. 3; "The Meaning of Fashion Today Discussed at the Fashion Group," *Women's Wear Daily,* June 19, 1953, p. 7; Bonnie Cashin speech, June 18, 1953, folder 7, box 76, Fashion Group speeches and transcripts, FG NYPL; Stephanie Lake, *Bonnie Cashin: Chic Is Where You Find It* (New York: Rizzoli, 2016), 32, 131–132.

67.   Bettina Berch, *Radical by Design: The Life and Style of Elizabeth Hawes, Fashion Designer, Union Organizer, Best-Selling Author* (New York: E. P. Dutton, 1988), 97–104, 192–193; Nancy Nolf and Kohle Yohannan, *Claire McCardell: Redefining Modernism* (New York: Harry N. Abrams, 1998); Sandra Stansbery Buckland, "Promoting American Designers, 1940–1944: Building Our Own House," in *Twentieth-Century American Fashion,* ed. Linda Welters and Patricia A. Cunningham (New York: Berg, 2005), 105–107; Arnold, *American Look,* 153–158, 203–206.

68.   Margaret De Mille, "Fall Important Show 1962," Commodore Hotel, New York, September 14, 1962, pp. 1–2, folder 10, box 77, FG, NYPL; Bernardine Taub, "Designer Builds a Junior Business Success on the Chemise Dress," *Women's Wear Daily,* August 22, 1957, p. 2; Patricia A. Cunningham, "Dressing for Success: The Re-suiting of Corporate America in the 1970s," in Welters and Cunningham, *Twentieth-Century American Fashion,* 201–207.

69.   Yuniya Kawamura, *Fashion-ology: An Introduction to Fashion Studies* (London: Berg, 2004).

70.   Kristin Bateman, "Versailles 1973: How One Show Changed American Fashion History," *Harper's Bazaar,* July 2, 2015; Jacob Bernstein, "*Battle of Versailles* Relives 1973 Win for American Fashion," *New York Times,* March 4, 2016, p. ST9; Daniela Morera, ed., *Stephen Burrows: When Fashion Danced* (New York: Skira Rizzoli in association with the Museum of the City of New York, 2013); Robin Givhan, *The Battle of Versailles: The Night American Fashion Stumbled into the Spotlight and Made History* (New York: Flatiron Books, 2013), 5–6, 205–207.

7. End of the Century

1.   Ruth La Ferla, "Imitate That Zipper," *New York Times,* September 2, 2009, , p. E1; Kaori O'Connor, "The Body and the Brand: How Lycra Shaped America," in *Producing Fashion: Commerce, Culture and Consumers,* ed. Regina L. Blaszczyk (Philadelphia: University of Pennsylvania

Press, 2007), 207–227; Eugene Kanazawa-Choi, "The Rise of Uniqlo: Leading Paradigm Change in Fashion Business and Distribution in Japan," *Entreprises et histoire* 3, no. 64 (2011): 85–101; Pei-Yuh Huang, Shigeru Kobayashi, and Kazuhito Isomura, "How UNIQLO Evolves Its Value Proposition and Brand Image: Imitation, Trial and Error and Innovation," *Strategic Direction* 30, no. 7 (2014): 42–45; David Edgerton, *The Shock of the Old: Technology in Global History since 1900* (London: Profile Books, 2007).

2.   Alexander Engel, "Colouring Markets: The Industrial Transformation of the Dyestuff Business Revisited," *Business History* 54, no. 1 (2012): 10–29; P. J. Federico, "The Invention and Introduction of the Zipper," *Journal of the Patent Office Society* 28, no. 12 (1946): 855–875; Andrew Godley, "Selling the Sewing Machine around the World: Singer's International Marketing Strategies, 1850–1920," *Enterprise and Society* 7, no. 2 (2006): 266–314; Gordon J. Pearson, "Innovation in a Mature Industry: A Case Study of Warp Knitting in the UK," *Technovation* 9, no. 8 (1989): 657–679.

3.   Roland Barthes, *Système de la mode* (Paris: Seuil, 1967), 330–338; Teri Agins, *The End of Fashion: How Marketing Changed the Clothing Business Forever* (London: William Morrow, 2000); Susan Strasser, *Waste and Want: A Social History of Trash* (New York: Holt, 1999), 188–189; "Faster, Cheaper Fashion," *Economist*, September 5, 2015, https://www.economist.com/business/2015/09/05/faster-cheaper-fashion.

4.   Michèle Ruffat and Dominique Veillon, eds., *La mode des sixties: L'entrée dans la modernité* (Paris: Autrement, 2007); Mary Quant, *Quant by Quant: The Autobiography of Mary Quant* (London: V&A Publications, 2012), 36; Marnie Fogg, *Boutique: A '60s Cultural Phenomenon* (London: Mitchell Beazley, 2003), 79, 136; Sabine Chrétien-Ichikawa, "La réémergence de la mode en Chine et le rôle du Japon" (PhD diss., EHESS, Paris, 2012); Kazunori Takada and Grace Huang, "Uniqlo Thinks Faster Fashion Can Help It Beat Zara," *Bloomberg*, March 16, 2017, https://www.bloomberg.com/news/articles/2017-03-16/uniqlo-turns-speed-demon-to-take-on-zara-for-global-sales-crown; Alfred D. Chandler, *Scale and Scope: The Dynamics of Industrial Capitalism* (Cambridge, MA: Harvard University Press, 1994), 59–61; Jeffrey R. Bernstein, "Toyoda Automatic Looms and Toyota Automobiles," in *Creating Modern Capitalism: How Entrepreneurs, Companies, and Countries Triumphed in Three Industrial Revolutions*, ed. Thomas K. McCraw (Cambridge, MA: Harvard University Press, 1995), 422, 426; Josefina Figueras, *Moda Española: Una historia de sueños y realidades* (Madrid: Ediciones Internacionales Universitarias, 2003), 32; Xabier R. Blanco and Jesus Salgado, *Armancio Ortega, de cero a Zara* (Madrid: La Esfera de los Libros, 2011), 76.

5.   Andrew McAfee, Vincent Dessain, and Anders Sjöman, "Zara: IT for Fast Fashion" (Case Study No. 9-604-081, Harvard Business School, September 6, 2007).

6.   Jennifer Le Zotte, *From Goodwill to Grunge: A History of Secondhand Styles and Alternative Economies* (Chapel Hill: University of North Carolina Press, 2017), 158–162; Véronique Pouillard, "The Rise of Fashion Forecasting and Fashion PR, 1920–1940: The History of Tobé and Bernays," in *Globalizing Beauty: Consumerism and Body Aesthetics in the Twentieth Century*, ed. Hartmut Berghoff and Thomas Kuehne (New York: Palgrave, 2013), 151–169; William R.

Leach, *Land of Desire: Merchants, Power, and the Rise of a New American Culture* (New York: Vintage, 1994), 311–313; Brian Hilton, Chong Ju Choi, and Stephen Chen, "The Ethics of Counterfeiting in the Fashion Industry: Quality, Credence and Profit Issues," *Journal of Business Ethics* 55, no. 4 (2004): 350; Diana Crane, *Fashion and Its Social Agendas: Class, Gender and Identity in Clothing* (Chicago: University of Chicago Press, 2000), 196–198; Jessica Daves, *Ready-Made Miracle: The American Story of Fashion for the Millions* (New York: Putnam, 1967); Claudia B. Kidwell and Margaret Christman, *Suiting Everyone: The Democratization of Clothing in America* (Washington, DC: Smithsonian, 1974).

7. Crane, *Fashion and Its Social Agendas,* 161.

8. Yann Truong, Rod McColl, and Philipp J. Kitchen, "New Brand Positioning and the Emergence of *Masstige* Brands," *Journal of Brand Management* 16, nos. 5/6 (2009): 375–382; Justin Paul, "Masstige Marketing Redefined and Mapped: Introducing a Pyramid Model and MMS Measure," *Marketing Intelligence and Planning* 33, no. 5 (2015): 691–706.

9. Véronique Pouillard, "Design Piracy in the Fashion Industries of Paris and New York in the Interwar Years," *Business History Review* 85, no. 2 (2011): 319–344; Kathryn K. Sklar, "The Consumers' White Label Campaign of the National Consumers' League, 1898–1918," in *Getting and Spending: European and American Consumer Societies in the Twentieth Century,* ed. Susan Strasser, Charles McGovern, and Matthias Judt (Cambridge: Cambridge University Press, 1998), 17–35; Marie-Emmanuelle Chessel, "Women and the Ethics of Consumption in France at the Turn of the Twentieth Century," in *The Making of the Consumer: Knowledge, Power and Identity in the Modern World,* ed. Frank Trentmann (Oxford: Berg, 2006), 81–98; Nancy L. Green, *Ready-to-Wear and Ready-to-Work: A Century of Industry and Immigrants in Paris and New York* (Durham, NC: Duke University Press, 1997).

10. Pietra Rivoli, *The Travels of a T-shirt in the Global Economy: An Economist Examines the Markets, Power, and Politics of World Trade* (New York: Wiley, 2005).

11. Helen E. Meiklejohn, "Section VI, Dresses—the Impact of Fashion on a Business," in *Price and Price Policies,* ed. Walton Hamilton (New York: McGraw-Hill, 1938), 313–315.

12. Thierry Charlier, "Un exemple de coopération entre les pouvoirs publics et le secteur privé: Le programme quinquennal de restructuration de l'industrie belge du textile et de la confection en août 1980" (MA thesis, Université Libre de Bruxelles, 1985), 15–16.

13. Paul Stroobant, "La protection de la dentelle à la main," *Im-ex: La grande revue belge pour le développement & l'expansion des industries du vêtement, de la mode et accessoires* (October 1926): 8–9; Lawrence B. Glickman, "'Make Lisle the Style': The Politics of Fashion in the Japanese Silk Boycott, 1937–1940," *Journal of Social History* 38, no. 3 (2005): 573–608; Regina Lee Blaszczyk and Véronique Pouillard, "Fashion as Enterprise," in *European Fashion: The Creation of a Global Industry,* ed. Regina Lee Blaszczyk and Véronique Pouillard (Manchester: Manchester University Press, 2018), 24–25; "Une Conférence technique tripartite du textile aux Etats-Unis," *Textilis* 9, no. 4 (April 1, 1937): 63; Charlier, "Un exemple de coopération," 5–7, 12; Liesbeth Sluiter, *Clean Clothes: A Global Movement to End Sweatshops* (London: Pluto Press, 2009).

14.   Christopher A. Bayly, "The Origins of Swadeshi (Home Industry): Cloth and Indian Society, 1700–1930," in *The Social Life of Things: Commodities in Cultural Perspectives,* ed. Arjun Appadurai (New York: Cambridge University Press, 2008), 285–321; Glickman, "'Make Lisle the Style,'" 586; Geoffrey G. Jones, Kerry Herman, and P. K. Kothandaraman, "Jamnalal Bajaj, Mahatma Gandhi, and the Struggle for Indian Independence" (Case Study No. 807028, Harvard Business School, 2006 [rev. 2015]), 1–21; Tereza Kuldova, *Luxury Indian Fashion: A Social Critique* (London: Bloomsbury, 2016), 11.

15.   An Moons, "To Be (In) or Not to Be (In): The Constituting Processes and Impact Indicators of the Flemish Designer Fashion Industry Undressed," in *Modus Operandi: State of Affairs in Current Research on Belgian Fashion,* ed. Nele Bernheim (Antwerp: Mode Museum, 2008), 69–81.

16.   Véronique Pouillard, "Production and Manufacture," in *The End of Fashion,* ed. Adam Geczy and Vicki Karaminas (London: Bloomsbury, 2018), 141–154; Sluiter, *Clean Clothes,* 20, 48–49; Joseph E. Stiglitz, *Globalization and Its Discontents* (New York: W. W. Norton, 2002); Jason Burke, "Bangladesh Factory Collapse Leaves Trail of Shattered Lives," *Guardian,* June 6, 2013, https://www.theguardian.com/world/2013/jun/06/bangladesh-factory-building-collapse -community; Noemi Sinkovics, Samia Ferdous Hoque, and Rudolf R. Sinkovics, "Rana Plaza Collapse Aftermath: Are CSR Compliance and Auditing Pressures Effective?," *Accounting, Auditing and Accountability Journal* 29, no. 4 (2016): 624–625; Enrico D'Ambrogio, European Parliamentary Research Service, "Workers' Conditions in the Textile and Clothing Sector: Just an Asian Affair? Issues at Stake after the Rana Plaza Tragedy," briefing, European Parliament, August 2014, http://www.europarl.europa.eu/EPRS/140841REV1-Workers-conditions-in-the-textile-and -clothing-sector-just-an-Asian-affair-FINAL.pdf; Ian M. Taplin, "Who Is to Blame? A Reexamination of Fast Fashion after the 2013 Factory Disaster in Bangladesh," *Critical Perspectives on International Business* 10, nos. 1/2 (2014): 77–79.

17.   Sinkovics, Hoque, and Sinkovics, "Rana Plaza Collapse Aftermath," 624; Adam Davidson, "Economic Recovery, Made in Bangladesh?," *New York Times,* May 14, 2013, p. MM16; Robert Kloosterman, Joanne van der Leun, and Jan Rath, "Across the Border: Immigrants' Economic Opportunities, Social Capital, and Informal Business Activities," *Journal of Ethnic and Migration Studies* 24, no. 2 (1998): 249–268; Green, *Ready-to-Wear;* Daniel E. Bender and Richard A. Greenwald, eds., *Sweatshop USA: The American Sweatshop in Historical and Global Perspective* (London: Routledge, 2003); Stiglitz, *Globalization and Its Discontents;* Sluiter, *Clean Clothes.*

18.   Sluiter, *Clean Clothes,* 12, 71; Taplin, "Who Is to Blame?," 76; Sankar Sen and C. B. Battacharya, "Does Doing Good Always Lead to Doing Better? Consumer Reactions to Corporate Social Responsibility," *Journal of Marketing Research* 38, no. 2 (2001): 240.

19.   Peter Lund-Thomsen and Adam Lindgreen, "Corporate Social Responsibility in Global Value Chains: Where Are We Now and Where Are We Going?," *Journal of Business Ethics* 123, no. 1 (2014): 13; Knut-Erik Mikalsen, "Nordea-sjef: Dette ville en skjorte kostet om fabrikkarbeiderne i Bangladesh skulle fått en levelig lønn," *Aftenposten,* June 2, 2017, http://www.aftenposten .no/okonomi/Nordea-sjef-Dette-ville-en-skjorte-kostet-om-fabrikkarbeiderne-i-Bangladesh -skulle-fatt-en-levelig-lonn-622467b.html.

20. Le Zotte, *Goodwill to Grunge*, 239–243; Thomas R. Eisenmann and Laura Winig, "Rent the Runway" (Case Study No. 812-077, Harvard Business School, November 2011 [rev. December 2012]); Albert O. Hirschman, *Exit, Voice, and Loyalty: Responses to Decline in Firms, Organizations, and States* (Cambridge, MA: Harvard University Press, 1972); Paul M. Barrett and Dorothée Baumann-Pauly, *Made in Ethiopia: Challenges in the Garment Industry's New Frontier* (New York: NYU Stern Center for Business and Human Rights, 2019).

21. Taplin, "Who Is to Blame?," 78; Rina Rafael, "Is This Sewing Robot the Future of Fashion?," *Fast Company*, January 24, 2017, https://www.fastcompany.com/3067149/is-this-sewing-robot-the-future-of-fashion; Godley, "Selling the Sewing Machine"; Tansy Hoskins, "Robot Factories Could Threaten Jobs of Millions of Garment Workers," *Guardian*, July 16, 2016, https://www.theguardian.com/sustainable-business/2016/jul/16/robot-factories-threaten-jobs-millions-garment-workers-south-east-asia-women.

22. World Trade Organization (WTO), *World Trade Organization Reports: Top Ten Exporters of Clothing* (Geneva: WTO, 2017); Frédéric Godart and Charles Galunic, "Explaining the Popularity of Cultural Elements: Networks, Culture, and the Structural Embeddedness of High Fashion Trends," *Organization Science* 30, no. 1 (2019): 151–168; Frédéric Godart, "Culture, Structure, and the Market Interface: Exploring the Networks of Stylistic Elements and Houses in Fashion," *Poetics* 68 (June 2018): 72–88; Rivoli, *Travels of a T-shirt*, 160–170.

23. Van Dyk Lewis and Keith A. Fraley, "Patrick Kelly: Fashion's Great Black Hope," *Fashion, Style and Popular Culture* 2, no. 3 (2015): 333–350; Dilys Blum, *Patrick Kelly: Runway of Love* (Philadelphia: Philadelphia Museum of Art, 2014); Elizabeth Way, "Immigration and the Making of Fashion in Paris and New York" (Paris Capital of Fashion Symposium, Fashion Institute of Technology, New York, October 18, 2019); Elizabeth Wilson, *Adorned in Dreams: Fashion and Modernity* (London and New York: I.B. Tauris, 2003), 196–201; Lourdes Font, "Un rêve devenu réalité: Les créateurs américains à Paris," in *Fashion Mix: Mode d'ici, créateurs d'ailleurs*, ed. Olivier Saillard (Paris: Flammarion, 2014), 151–153.

24. Historique Christian Dior New York (hereafter cited as CDNY) file, "Brief History," DSAA; Olivier Bomsel, *L'économie immatérielle: Industries et marchés d'expériences* (Paris: Gallimard, 2010); Jean-Noël Kapferer and Vincent Bastien, *The Luxury Strategy: Break the Rules of Marketing to Build Luxury Brands* (London: Kogan Page, 2009).

25. Florence Müller, *Yves Saint Laurent* (Paris: La Martinière, 2010), 38–40; Laurence Benaïm, *Le pantalon, une histoire en marche* (Paris: Editions de l'Amateur, 1999), 130–131; Christine Bard, *Les Garçonnes: Modes et fantasmes des années folles* (Paris: Flammarion, 1998); Elodie Nowinski, "Yves Saint Laurent et l'exotisme dans les années 1960. De l'exception insolente à la naissance du métissage dans la haute couture," in *La mode des sixties: L'entrée dans la modernité*, ed. Dominique Veillon and Michelle Ruffat (Paris: Autrement, 2007), 141–154.

26. John Rockwell, ed., *The Times of the Sixties: The Culture, Politics, and Personalities That Shaped the Decade* (New York: New York Times Publications, 1968); Florence Müller and Farid Chenoune, *Yves Saint Laurent* (Paris: La Martinière, 2010), 40, 54, 226–232.

27. Tomoko Okawa, "Licensing Practices at Maison Dior," in *Producing Fashion: Commerce, Culture, and Consumers,* ed. Regina Lee Blaszczyk (Philadelphia: University of Pennsylvania Press, 2008), 93–95, 99.

28. Memo on Dior licenses (1987), 1, CDNY, DSAA.

29. Republic of France, Senate, report of proceedings, September 18, 2007, http://www.senat.fr/seances/s200709/s20070918/s20070918001.html; Geoffrey G. Jones and Véronique Pouillard, "Christian Dior: A New Look for Haute Couture" (Case Study No. 809-159, Harvard Business School, 2009 [rev. 2017]); Okawa, "Licensing Practices," 82–107; Alexandra Palmer, *Dior: A New Look, a New Enterprise (1947–57)* (London: Victoria and Albert Museum, 2009); Marie-France Pochna, *Christian Dior* (Paris: Flammarion, 2004); Michael E. Porter, *The Competitive Advantage of Nations* (New York: Free Press, 1990), 35–40.

30. Jones and Pouillard, "Christian Dior: A New Look"; Pierre-Yves Donzé, *Les patrons horlogers de La Chaux-de-Fonds (1840–1920): Dynamique sociale d'une élite industrielle* (Neuchâtel: Alphil, 2007), 2009.

31. Historique Christian Dior New York, "Brief History"; Memo on Dior licenses (1987), 1; "Legal," 1, CDNY, DSAA; John G. Palfrey, *Intellectual Property Strategy* (Cambridge, MA: MIT Press, 2012), 33.

32. "Legal," 1, CDNY, DSAA.

33. Couture-Création files by couturier, F12 10505, FNA; Portfolio of haute couture labels, *Vogue,* February 1950; Standard licensee contract with name of licensee left in blank, 1–2, CDNY, DSAA.

34. Christian Dior USA box, Historique file, "Brief History" (undated note from the mid-1980s), CDNY, DSAA.

35. Ibid., 4; Okawa, "Licensing Practices"; Nicolas Stotskopf, "Frères Willot," in *Dictionnaire historique des patrons français,* ed. Jean-Claude Daumas (Paris: Flammarion, 2010), 723–725.

36. Jean-Claude Daumas, "Bernard Arnault," in Daumas, *Dictionnaire historique des patrons français,* 32; Eugene Di Maria, "Bergé, Others Join Bidermann in Agache-Willot Takeover Bid," *Women's Wear Daily,* December 17, 1984, p. 11.

37. Booton Herndon, *Bergdorf's on the Plaza: The Story of Bergdorf Goodman and a Half-Century of American Fashion* (New York: Alfred A. Knopf, 1956), 226; Caroline Rennolds Milbank, *New York Fashion: The Evolution of American Style* (New York: Harry N. Abrams, 1989), 238–247, 250.

38. Véronique Pouillard, "Christian Dior–New York: French Fashion in the US Luxury Market," in *Global Luxury: Organization Change and Emerging Markets in the Luxury Industry since the 1970s,* ed. Pierre-Yves Donzé and Rika Fujioka (New York: Palgrave, 2018), 111–131; "Brief History" (undated note from the mid-1980s), Christian Dior USA box, Historique file, CDNY, DSAA; "Arnault: Recharging Dior," *Women's Wear Daily,* February 7, 1986, pp. 4–5; Okawa, "Licensing Practices," 95–96, 104; Pierre-Yves Donzé and Véronique Pouillard, "Luxury," in *The Routledge Companion to the Makers of Global Business,* ed. Teresa da Silva Lopes, Christina Lubinski, and Heidi Tworek (London: Routledge, 2019), 111–131.

39. Summary of Christian Dior licensees (men's), 1987, 1, 2, CDNY, DSAA; Eugene Di Maria, "Dior, Nearing 40, Has Big Plans in Works," *Women's Wear Daily*, October 28, 1986, p. 11; Nivedita Bhattacharjee, "PVH United Calvin Klein Lines in \$2.8 Billion Deal," *Reuters Business News*, October 31, 2012; Lewis and Fraley, "Patrick Kelly."

40. Summary of Christian Dior licensees, 1, 2; Dominique Morlotti to Bernard Arnault, n.d., p. 1, Design Information, Menswear division, dossiers from CD Paris, CDNY, DSAA.

41. Summary of Christian Dior licensees (women's), 1987, 5, CDNY, DSAA; Eugene Di Maria, "Dior's Net Slips 8.9% in '85," *Women's Wear Daily*, June 27, 1986, p. 2; Daumas, "Bernard Arnault," 33.

42. Pouillard, "Christian Dior–New York," 123.

43. Summary of Christian Dior licensees (accessories), 1987, 2, CDNY, DSAA.

44. Ibid., 3.

45. Okawa, "Licensing Practices," 93.

46. Di Maria, "Dior, Nearing 40," 11.

47. Morris De Camp Crawford, *The Ways of Fashion* (New York: G. P. Putnam's Sons, 1941), 190; Eugene Di Maria, "Agache to Go to Real Estate Firm," *Women's Wear Daily*, December 18, 1984, p. 8; "Arnault Will Become Dior Chairman Today," *Women's Wear Daily*, March 20, 1985, p. 13; "Arnault: Recharging Dior"; Geoffrey Deeny and Kevin Doyle, "Bernard Arnault: Dream Merchant," *Women's Wear Daily*, April 16, 1990, pp. 4–5; Daumas, "Bernard Arnault," 30–32; Jean-Claude Daumas, "Marcel Boussac, 1889–1980," in *Dictionnaire historique des patrons français*, ed. Jean-Claude Daumas (Paris: Flammarion, 2010), 120–122; Okawa, "Licensing Practices," 94–99; Stotskopf, "Frères Willot," 723–725.

48. Summary of Christian Dior licensees (men's), 1987, 4, CDNY, DSAA; Pouillard, "Christian Dior–New York," 111–131; Donzé, *Les patrons horlogers*.

49. "Advertising," one-page document, CDNY, DSAA.

50. Ibid.; Marie-Claude Sicard, *La métamorphose des marques: Le roc, l'étoile et le nuage* (Paris: Eyrolles, 1998).

51. "Public Relations," 1–2, CDNY, DSAA.

52. Historique Christian Dior-New York, Real estate folder, CDNY, DSAA; Milbank, *New York Fashion*, 268.

53. Vincent Bastien and Jean-Noel Kapferer, *Luxe oblige* (Paris: Eyrolles, 2012), 414–415.

54. Dana Thomas, *Deluxe: How Luxury Lost Its Lustre* (London: Penguin, 2007), chap. 6; Keith Hayward and Majid Yar, "The *Chav* Phenomenon: Consumption, Media, and the Construction of a New Underclass," *Crime, Media, Culture* 2, no. 1 (2006): 9–28; Okawa, "Licensing Practices," 97–99, 106; Pierre-Yves Donzé and Rika Fujioka, "European Luxury Big Business and Emerging Asian Markets, 1960–2010," *Business History* 57, no. 6 (2015): 822–840; Jean-Noël Kapferer, "Abundant Rarity: The Key to Luxury Growth," *Business Horizons* 55 (2012): 453–462; Ben Dummet and Suzanne Kapner, "Tiffany Receives \$14.5 Billion Takeover Offer from LVMH," *Wall Street Journal*, October 28, 2019, https://www.wsj.com/articles/lvmh-makes-all-cash-takeover-bid-for-tiffany-at-roughly-120-a-share-11572190804.

55. Daumas, "Bernard Arnault," 34.

56. Donzé and Fujioka, "European Luxury Big Business"; Lisa Rofel and Sylvia Yanagisako, with Simona Segre Reinach, *Fabricating Transnational Capitalism: A Collaborative Ethnography of Italian–Chinese Global Fashion* (Durham, NC: Duke University Press, 2019).

57. Roy Y. J. Chua and Robert G. Eccles, "Managing Creativity at Shanghai Tang" (Case Study No. 410-018, Harvard Business School, 2009); Chrétien-Ichikawa, "La réémergence de la mode en Chine et le rôle du Japon"; Rofel and Yanagisako, *Fabricating Transnational Capitalism*.

58. Uché Okonkwo, "The Luxury Brand Strategy Challenge," *Journal of Brand Management* 16, nos. 5/6 (2009): 287–289; Deloitte, *Global Powers of Luxury Goods 2019: Bridging the Gap between the Old and the New* (London: Deloitte, 2019), 3; Pierre-Yves Donzé and Ben Wubs, "LVMH: Storytelling and Organizing Creativity in Luxury and Fashion," in Blaszczyk and Pouillard, *European Fashion*, 63–85; Jones and Pouillard, "Christian Dior: A New Look."

59. *Azzedine Alaïa*, catalogue d'exposition (Paris: Paris Musées–Palais Galliéra, 2013); Caroline Rousseau, "Dans l'antre d'Azzedine Alaïa," *M Magazine Le Monde*, September 28, 2019, pp. 61–67.

60. Emilie Gandon, "Vent d'Est sur la mode parisienne," in Saillard, *Fashion Mix*, 42; Pierre-Yves Donzé and Véronique Pouillard, "The Luxury Business," in Lopes, Lubinski, and Tworek, *Routledge Companion to the Makers of Global Business*, 433.

61. Deloitte, *Global Powers of Luxury Goods 2015: Engaging the Future Luxury Consumer*, Deloitte Touche Tohmatsu Ltd., 2015, https://www2.deloitte.com/content/dam/Deloitte/ch /Documents/consumer-business/ch-en-cb-global-powers-of-luxury-goods-2015.pdf; Donzé and Pouillard, "Luxury Business," 432; Raphaëlle Bacqué, *Kaiser Karl* (Paris: Albin Michel, 2019).

62. Christopher Breward, "Shock of the Frock," *Guardian*, October 18, 2003, https://www .theguardian.com/artanddesign/2003/oct/18/art.museums; Delphine Dion and Gerald Mazzalovo, "Reviving Sleeping Beauty Brands by Rearticulating Brand Heritage," *Journal of Business Research* 69, no. 12 (2016): 5894–5900; Johanna Zanon, "The 'Sleeping Beauties' of Haute Couture: Jean Patou, Elsa Schiaparelli, Madeleine Vionnet" (PhD diss., University of Oslo, 2017); Sara Skillen, "Dior without Dior: Tradition and Succession in a Paris Couture House" (PhD diss., University of Stockholm, 2019).

63. Claudia d'Arpizio, Federica Levato, Daniele Zito, and Joëlle de Montgolfier, *Luxury Goods Worldwide Market Study: A Time to Act; How Luxury Brands Can Rebuild to Win* (Milan: Bain Consultancy, 2015), 2, 9–11.

Conclusion

1. Imran Amed, Achim Berg, Leonie Brantberg, Saskia Hedrich, Johnattan Leon, and Robb Young, *The State of Fashion 2017* (London: McKinsey, 2016).

Acknowledgments

I have enjoyed discussing various aspects of this book over the years with numerous colleagues and friends: Carlo Marco Belfanti, Anne-Jorunn Berg, Sundeep Bisla, Géraldine Blanche, Regina Lee Blaszczyk, Christopher Breward, Kristine Bruland, Florence Champsaur, Sophie Chapdelaine de Monvalon, Eugene Kanazawa Choi, Sabine Chrétien-Ichikawa, Victoria de Grazia, Pierre-Yves Donzé, Waleria Dorogova, Anne-Françoise Drion, Vincent Dubé-Sénécal, Christine A. Dupont, Caroline Evans, Kjetil Fallan, Patrick Fridenson, Robert Marc Friedman, Rika Fujioka, Andrew Godley, Nancy L. Green, Andreas Hellenes, Pierre-André Hirsch, Helge Høibraaten, Alice Janssens, Serge Jaumain, Mukti Khaire, Tereza Kuldova, Ginette Kurgan-van Hentenrijk, Sophie Kurkdjian, Malcolm Langford, Eirinn Larsen, Mariangela Lavanga, Grace Lees-Maffei, Thierry Maillet, Nicole Lesseux, Einar Lie, Andrea Lluch, Jakob Maliks, Stephen Mihm, Jose Antonio Miranda, Minja Mitrovic, Klaus Nathaus, Kim Oosterlinck, Alexandra Palmer, Marco Pecorari, Kari-Anne Pedersen, Stéphanie Pezard, Kim Priemel, Daniel Raff, Joanne Roberts, Michèle Ruffat, Emanuela Scarpellini, Valerie Steele, Noëlle Streeton, Lou Taylor, Stina Teilmann-Lock, Barbara Townley, Karen Trivette, Ben Wubs, Johanna Zanon, and Steve Zdatny. The late Erling Sandmo encouraged me to use microhistory in Chapter 2.

At the Harvard Business School, Geoffrey Jones and Walter Friedman offered invaluable encouragement, support, and advice for developing my research into a book.

At various stages of this research, I have benefited from funding from several institutions, to which I offer my warmest thanks: the Fonds de la Recherche Scientifique de Belgique, the Belgian-American Educational Foundation in the form of a Hoover Fellowship, the Harvard Business School in the form of a Harvard-Newcomen Fellowship, the Senter for Tverrfaglig Kjønnsforskning at the University of Oslo, and

UiO: Norden. The final stages of research and writing received funding from the European Research Council under the European Union's Horizon 2020 research and innovation programme, ERC Consolidator Grant 818523 for my project Creative IPR: The history of intellectual property rights in the creative industries.*

At the Press, James Brandt, Kathi Drummy, Thomas LeBien, Mihaela Pacurar, Joseph Pomp, Sharmila Sen, and Stephanie Vyce were of great help in the final stages of the publication process. I thank the anonymous referees for their extremely valuable comments.

My thanks go to Nils Nadeau for copyediting, and to Alison Jacques, who copyedited the final manuscript with great skill and insight. Sherry Gerstein worked on the last details with great care. I owe a special word of thanks to Julianne Rustad, who helped prepare the artwork for the book. Many thanks to the bookshop Librairie Diktats, which has generously granted permissions of use for some images.

Without the libraries and repositories that make archives accessible, the research for this book would not have been possible. My gratitude goes to the archivists and librarians at the Archives du Monde du Travail in Roubaix, the Archives Nationales de France, the Archives of the City of Paris, the Centre de Documentation de l'Union Centrale des Arts Décoratifs, the Chambre Syndicale de la Couture Parisienne, the Archives of the Maison Dior, the library at the Musée du Costume de la Ville de Paris at the Palais Galliéra, the British National Archives in Kew, the Archives and Special Collections at the Fashion Institute of Technology in New York, the Special Collections and Archives at the New York Public Library, and the Special Collections at the Library of Congress in Washington, DC.

My thanks go to the librarians and staff at Butler Library at Columbia University, the New York Public Library, Widener Library at Harvard University, Baker Library at the Harvard Business School, the Royal Library Albert I in Brussels, the libraries at the University of Oslo, the British Library, and the National Library of France.

The warmest thanks go to my family, and especially my parents and parents-in-law, who have helped me make time for writing with small children: Dagmar Førland, who spent countless Sundays keeping the children busy, the late Leif Maliks, Patrick Pouillard, Violette Pouillard, Sylvestre Pouillard, and my mother, Marguerite Vermandere, who taught me how to sew. Reidar Maliks, who is also the best writer I know, read numerous drafts and helped me improve my writing skills. Reidar, Amélie, and Louise, you inspire me every day. This book is dedicated to the three of you.

Index

Note: Figures are identified by *f* following the page number. End notes are identified by n and the note number following the page number.